Riding Full Circle

Riding Full Circle

What the World Taught Me About Motorcycles, Risk,
and Someone I Barely Knew

TWO YEARS. 40 COUNTRIES. 58,000 MILES.

Heather Lea

Sidekick Press
Bellingham, Washington

Publisher's Note: This memoir represents the author's recollection of her past. These true stories are faithfully composed based on memory, photographs, diary entries, and other supporting documents. Some names, places, and other identifying details have been changed to protect the privacy of those represented. Conversations between individuals are meant to reflect the essence, meaning, and spirit of the events described.

Published 2025
Printed in the United States of America

ISBN: 978-1-958808-48-1
LCCN: 2025918562

Sidekick Press
2950 Newmarket Street, Suite 101–329
Bellingham, Washington 98226
sidekickpress.com

Riding Full Circle: What the World Taught Me About Motorcycles, Risk, and Someone I Barely Knew
Cover design by HL Creatives
Cover image by Dave Sears

Author's Note: This journey took us over 700 days to complete. As much as I'd love to include each exceptional moment along the way, I've had to consolidate and even leave out some of the countries we traveled through. This is not because I didn't enjoy a partic-ular place or the experience I had there—it's simply to get to some of the finer points of what this journey brought me overall. In writing this book, I relied heavily on my trip journal. I looked up facts whenever I could and spoke with some of the people who appear in these pages. In some cases, I've adjusted details to protect people's privacy and changed names. Nothing in this book is invented—there are no composite characters or imagined events.

 Placing color images in this book was cost-prohibitive, so my solution is to bring you our travel photos digitally. To see color images for each country, scan the QR code or visit Photos under Riding Full Circle on my website, heatherleawriter.com.

To Dave, for having this wonderfully crazy idea—
and to my family for gifting me with the
spirit of adventure.

Contents

Foreword

Some people travel to escape reality, to leave troubles behind and start—or even live—a new life elsewhere. This wasn't the case for me. I lived in a beautiful part of the world and already had a life rich with adventure. I'm one of the lucky ones, born free into a first-world country.

Still, I've always held a curiosity about other countries. What does a street taco taste like in Baja? Is Siberia cold in the summer? Are the Galapagos Islands as pristine as everyone says?

When Dave and I set out to ride our BMW GS motorcycles around the world from 2015 to 2017, all I hoped for was that doing so would enhance my already good life. I knew we'd have the best and worst of times and, since we were also newly dating, learn the best and worst about each other. Traveling, after all, doesn't mean you're exempt from life's ups and downs—or your partner's annoying personality traits. If anything, you are challenged beyond the scope of what you can imagine during the planning stages.

Countless calories in red wine and dark chocolate were consumed to bring you this story. My life is as busy as anyone's. I wrote in snatches of time on rainy Sundays, long flights, when I couldn't sleep, or even when I could but felt the need to open my laptop. And of course, when I purposely sat down in my home office and gave it everything I had for hours at a time. Finalizing this book became especially difficult in the last year before publishing, when I accepted a demanding full-time job that often exceeded forty hours a week. Suddenly, I had far less free time and cursed myself for not finishing the book sooner.

Riding Full Circle has been years in the making, and often that was frustrating—not just for me but for my family and friends who got tired of hearing me say, "I have to get this book done!" But the distance between the first day of the trip and the last word I typed in this manuscript gave me time to be more objective. It allowed this trip of a lifetime to settle so I could pull out only the best nuggets from my experiences.

My hope is that the stories within shine sunbeams into what is sometimes cast as a shady world. The strangers we met in every country along the way are really the star characters here; without putting full trust into people we didn't know, we wouldn't have gotten far.

Riding Full Circle is the true narrative of a newly dating couple with a spur-of-the-moment idea to ride motorcycles around the world—with the challenges, hardships, and all the good parts, too. If you're after a raw-emotions read; an ambitious tale of strength and perseverance; a love story between a man, a woman, and the road; or an exciting armchair adventure, I hope you'll join me on this journey covering over 58,000 miles through forty countries.

Heather Lea
HeatherLeaWriter.com

 Placing color images in this book was cost-prohibitive, so my solution is to bring you our travel photos digitally. To see color images for each country, scan the QR code or visit Photos under Riding Full Circle on my website, heatherleawriter.com.

YEARONE

ROUTE MAP

What the hell are we doing?

The still-smoldering remains of late-summer fires make dramatic back-drops and smoky lunch stops in Idaho's backcountry. Dave points out a cluster of burned trees on a ridge and says they remind him of quills on a porcupine's back. Where blazes haven't burned nature black, vibrant fall foliage colors the landscape like fire itself.

We've been on the road for over a week, camping in the forest, by rivers, or in free statewide campgrounds. There are few pestering bugs so late in the year, and we wake to frost on the seats of our motorcycles after a clear night. Sometimes we meet other campers, and they ask about our bikes and where we're going. Dave and I are only too proud to tell them we're riding around the world. We're totally winning at life.

After a breakfast of instant oatmeal and hot chocolate, we pack up the tent and strap all our gear down onto the bikes.

I follow Dave down the dirt track we came up last night, then onto the logging road. The morning sun lights up the dust disturbed by his rear tire.

We come to a junction, and Dave turns left. After crossing a bridge over the St. Joe's River, we're back on the Idaho Backcountry Discovery Route. As soon as we hit the double track made for all-terrain vehicles, Dave's off like a flash. He's the only person I know who speeds up when he sees a dirt road, whether he's in a 4×4 truck or on two wheels.

I ride carefully. Ahead on the trail I see two boulders as large as wood-stoves that I'll need to squeeze through, but I'm concerned about my hard-case panniers fixed onto luggage racks on both sides of my bike. *Am I too wide to fit between them?*

Just when I think I'm past the rocks, an abrupt impact slams into my body and my motorcycle starts veering out of control. I take in the Ponderosa pines above me, the river to my right, and the ditch on my left.

Look where you want to go. Half a second later, I'm stuck under my bike, where it has come to rest in a pine-cone-scattered gully.

I hold still, waiting for pain. Feeling nothing sharp or tingly, I pull my left leg out from where it's wedged between the dirt and the bike's frame. I stand, relieved there's still no pain, and stare at my fallen steed. The handlebars are askew, and one pannier is still attached to the luggage rack—which, along with my tall boots and knee armor, helped keep the 500-pound bike from crushing my leg.

Looking around for the other pannier, I find it ahead on the trail, sheared off its bolts and motionless after skidding a few meters along the dirt.

My brain elbows through the last few minutes of memory. I was off-center and hit one of the boulders with the hard aluminum pannier on my right side. The collision was so jarring, it sent me into the ditch.

Sound comes flooding back to my ears once the white noise of alarm has quieted. I hear the river and listen for Dave. No sign of my boyfriend. Even his dust has settled on the track ahead, which follows a curved line of deciduous trees dropping golden leaves to the ground. If the stars were aligned any different, I'd be face down in the St. Joe's River right now. Luckily, I'd swerved left instead of right, toward the ditch, not the drop-off.

A gulping cry-laugh bursts from my mouth.

Shit!

When Dave suggested we ride our motorcycles around the world, one of my self-generated fears was crashing. Now, less than two weeks into a two-year adventure, I've done just that.

Finding my point-and-shoot camera in the tank bag strapped between my handlebars, I walk up the trail for a different perspective of the accident scene. In twenty-plus years as a freelance writer, I know a good story is nothing without photos. Snapping off a couple shots, I return to zip the camera back into my bag. It's then that a searing pain shoots into my wrist at the base of my right thumb. Adrenaline—nature's morphine—is clearing out, and boiling blood rushes up and down my arm. Dizzy and frantic, I sit, cradling my hand.

Please don't be broken, please don't be broken.

It's September 25, 2015—my forty-first birthday.

The beginning

Dave and I had been dating twenty-seven days when he asked me a question that would leave skid marks at that fork in the road.

"Do you want to ride motorcycles to Patagonia?"

I said *yes* before he finished the last syllable, but there was one problem: Dave didn't have a motorcycle.

When we met in the spring of 2014, I had a 250cc Kawasaki Super Sherpa. I'd learned to ride the previous fall as a gift to myself for my fortieth birthday, having wanted a motorcycle since I was twelve when my dad took me out on his Honda Gold Wing one afternoon before he sold it. The feeling of flying along with other vehicles but being *outside*—instead of confined by a seatbelt in the back seat with the family dog—was my first taste of complete and utter freedom. My mom, having worked in emergency rooms for a career, was not thrilled about me getting a motorcycle, but at forty, I was starting to have thoughts, like, *if not now, when?*

The only two-wheelers Dave had were bicycles. Within a week of asking me to travel with him, he had enrolled in a motorcycle course, got his endorsement, bought a used BMW F800GS—not a beginner bike—and rode through Seattle rush hour to his house in Bellingham, Washington. In Canada, I'd trained for six Saturdays and Sundays, but Dave had a license in one weekend.

Soon, our route to Patagonia expanded to include other countries.

"We'd have to fly home from Patagonia anyway," Dave said, staring at a world map tacked onto the wall facing his bed, "so why not just fly to another continent and keep going?"

Everything was happening fast. A month ago, I didn't even know David Scott Sears existed. Now, I was planning to travel around the world with him. It reminded me of a meme I'd once read: *You know that tingly little feeling you get when you like someone? That's common sense leaving your body.*

The proposed world route would start in Revelstoke, British Columbia, where I used to live and where my parents still lived, and take us south to Ushuaia, Argentina, then northeast to Buenos Aires to catch a flight over to Africa. We'd ride south to north on that continent, enter and cross Europe, then travel west to east in Russia, dipping down into Kazakhstan and Mongolia. Last, we'd hit Alaska and the Yukon, then head back to Revelstoke. Two years felt like all the time in the world. I couldn't wait to get started.

Except we'd both just learned how to ride. And we barely knew each other. Adventures like this were the sort of thing you planned with someone who had your back and had demonstrated that to you time and again.

Dave and I had no such history together—but I hoped we had a future.

Turn left at the Texaco

"How did you meet him?" a friend asked one day.

"I ordered him online," I joked, not elaborating.

I wasn't ready to tell people I'd been using a dating app for two years, on and off. On when loneliness slapped me like a cold, wet towel across the face. Off when I got tired of the creep factor. If a fortune teller predicted to my younger self that I'd meet someone like Dave online— handsome, adventurous, smart, employed—I'd have left the room. *Gross.* Weren't those dating websites for people who looked like final-round *Jeopardy* players? The internet was the *last* place I wanted to find a soul mate. I was hoping for something more like a chance meeting in a backcountry ski lodge or at a mountain town potluck.

In the late nineties, I was in my early twenties. I never worried about finding a partner and laughed along with my young, good-looking friends who made fun of the yet-to-take-off business of digitized dating. My thirties were more confusing; I owned a house and a nice truck and had founded an arts and culture magazine. But what I wanted long-term was still in question: kids, travel, career? All of the above? At the "right" age for having children, every relationship I got into involved agonizing over whether the guy wanted kids too and when was it too early to have that discussion because my ovaries would soon turn from grapes to raisins and *oh my god the pressure.*

Forty was just around the corner when I decided/realized having kids wasn't for me. Societal norms are dumb and outdated—especially for women, who, if still single and childless by a certain age, are regarded as something that went wrong in human evolution. Instead, I gifted myself motorcycle lessons.

The cards I'd been dealt in life had always landed face up for adventure. I've had many wonderful opportunities that seemed risky but I couldn't turn down—like riding a bicycle from Paris to Istanbul when I had rarely pedaled two wheels farther than the grocery store. Or climbing Peru's highest mountain with no high-altitude experience, or backpacking solo through Africa and South America with nothing to guide me but ignorance and wonder. I didn't want my youth squandered by working too much. Also, I considered "youth" to be well into my thirties.

Born in Calgary, Alberta, with a love for the mountains instilled by my parents, I moved westward the minute I graduated from high school. Trying out various mountain towns, like Banff and Canmore, I eventually found home in endearing Revelstoke, where I bought a house and started my arts and culture magazine, *Reved Quarterly*. But after eleven years, small-town life started to feel suffocating. I moved to Vancouver, BC, reinventing myself as a city girl, much to the surprise of my family and friends, who thought I'd be a dirtbag hippie forever. This was the first time in over a decade when I had to make new friends. In Revelstoke, I attended dinner parties, feeling comfortable in a room full of skiers and climbers. In Vancouver, however, I walked by groups of glitzy, well-dressed folks drinking on outdoor patios and felt shy and intimidated. How do you make friends in a city of over a million people?

A year into my new Vancouver life, I was happy but still single. Reconsidering my own judgments, I created an online dating profile in search of someone outdoorsy. I gave it a solid chance, but dating this way wasn't natural to me, and I had a lot of awkward encounters. I decided to delete my profile for good. Signing in one evening, I saw the usual "you have matches!" message at the top. Below, thumbnail images showed six photos of men, most of them shirtless selfies in front of grubby bathroom mirrors. Except one. A dark-haired guy standing in front of Denali—the highest mountain in North America—caught my eye. *Maybe just one more try.* I sent him a message. A phone call followed, and a ski date soon after that. We met in person for the first time at a Texaco near Mount Baker in

Washington state, and it turned into paradise after that. (Literally. It's now called Paradise Market.)

Dave was living in Bellingham—a beautiful coastal city in the Pacific Northwest just an hour from Vancouver, across the border. I'd visited Bellingham several times with friends for weekend getaways and now I was dating someone who lived in this "City of Subdued Excitement," as it's nicknamed.

Before meeting Dave, I would have put riding a motorcycle around the world in the same category as winning the lottery.

But even in a lottery, someone always wins.

 Placing color images in this book was cost-prohibitive, so my solution is to bring you our travel photos digitally. To see color images for each country, scan the QR code or visit Photos under Riding Full Circle on my website, heatherleawriter.com.

All in

It's been a year of long-distance dating, crossing the Peace Arch border between Vancouver and Bellingham most weekends. Door to door, we can be at each other's place in an hour.

Much of our time together is spent talking about or planning our trip. We've already decided to leave in the fall of 2016, which gives us another year and a half to check things off, like save money, take an off-road motorcycle course, learn Spanish, get an international driving license—and the thousand other items that get put on a world travel to-do list.

Designing a trip logo and travel website, I nickname us "Riding Full Circle" online, since the route plan is to leave from one point—Revelstoke—and return to the same place when the trip is complete. The title is metaphorical, as well; I've always liked the idea of circles having no beginning or end. Circles are also a symbol of blessing, which can't hurt.

My experience running a magazine funded solely by advertising gives me the thought to write emails and cold-call sales reps working in the motorcycle industry. As a newly dating couple planning to sell everything and travel around the world on motorcycles, our ambitious undertaking captures the interest of several companies who either heavily discount our gear or give it to us at no cost. This includes riding suits, bike parts, communication headsets, and lightweight camping gear—all amounting to several thousand dollars in savings.

One significant sponsor is InReach, now owned by Garmin. They send us two GPS tracking and SOS devices equipped with full subscriptions. When the tracking is turned on it will trace us traveling along our route, dropping a "pin" every five minutes. Those with the password to our online InReach account will be able to see where we are anywhere in the world. It can also be used to send text messages and alert emergency personnel, if needed. Our moms especially appreciate this addition to our gear.

I list each sponsor on our website, no matter the donation, and before I know it, we have over two dozen businesses on the page and are gaining followers interested in reading the blog as we travel. It's all very exciting and makes it hard to wait so long to leave.

Through his work as a carpenter, Dave has amassed a few hundred thousand airmiles and is willing to donate them—another huge cost savings. We'll be flying over water at least five times.

Dave works days for his carpentry business and nights modifying our motorcycles. We'll be putting them through their paces over the next two years, and both bikes need aftermarket modifications, like crash bars and skid plates, to protect the outsides and undersides of the bikes.

Having long suffered from lower back pain, I splurge and have a custom leather seat made. I've upgraded from the Super Sherpa to a used BMW G650GS. Because I weigh at least fifty pounds less than the typical male riders these types of bikes are marketed for, I keep the stock suspension in the rear but add upgraded forks up front. Dave buys a top-notch system from Touratech. He also upgrades to a BMW F800GSA—the "adventure" model, with a larger gas tank, higher clearance, and better overall performance.

Budgeting for twenty-four months without regular paychecks is tough, given all the uncertainty. After speaking with other long-term travelers, we decide one hundred dollars a day, or fifty dollars per person, is sufficient; we won't be staying in luxury hotels, but it isn't a shoestring budget, either.

Excluding side trips and flights, we want a combined savings of $73,000—an astronomical amount in my mind. Aside from my hope to sell stories and photos to magazines while on the road, neither of us will have income while traveling. Doing the math, that number works out to roughly $18,000 each per year. It's easy to spend that kind of money on material stuff at home. World travel buys a lifetime of memories.

This trip has become my life. I find it hard to concentrate on anything else.

If not now, when?

One rainy spring day driving down Interstate 5 near Bellingham, Dave says, "What do you think about moving our departure date ahead a year?"

"Are you serious?" I look at him. "So, this September?" An exciting prospect, but leave in six months instead of eighteen? I still need to get so much done, including sell my business. As for savings, I'd sold my house in Revelstoke just before meeting Dave, and the profit was scheduled for a retirement plan. *Maybe that can wait.*

"You know what? Yeah, let's do it."

Over the next few months, Dave and I work on reducing the contents of our separate lives to fit into a ten-foot-by-thirteen-foot room at his dad's house forty-five minutes south of Bellingham. We have multiple yard sales, selling everything from pots and pans to mountain bikes and camping gear.

Dave sells his truck and, after much deliberation, puts his house on the market. He considers renting it out but doesn't think he'll be able to fully immerse himself in our trip if he's a landlord, worrying about the home he spent years remodeling to his tastes. It's a hard decision for him.

I give up my apartment in Vancouver and begin the process of selling *Reved.* Letting go of my business is also a tough decision. After traveling, what will I do for money? But, like Dave, I don't want anything distracting me on the road. I'm at the point when, after a decade in the print and publishing industry, I'm ready for a change.

One of Canada's largest newspaper producers hears I'm selling my magazine and expresses an interest. Revelstoke is on its way to becoming an iconic four-season resort destination. To my dismay, after months of negotiations, that falls through. I'm just starting to think I'll have to let the magazine go, when one of my staff writers approaches me with an offer a few days before Dave and I are about to leave. I'm elated and agree on the spot.

Saying goodbye to my ten-year-old pride and joy is both heartbreaking and liberating. I'm grateful *Reved* will continue, and the sale adds a decent financial boost to my travel funds. But I created something from nothing, and I'm damn proud of it. I don't have the energy to start from scratch again, and I hope I'm making the right decision.

Fear & freedom

When friends and family hear we're riding motorcycles around the world, we get mixed reactions.

"Aren't you afraid of getting robbed or killed by one of those overloaded chicken buses?" Or: "An adventure of a lifetime! You two are really doing it right."

Some people think we're crazy to liquidate our lives since we'll have to acquire everything again. I don't feel we're being reckless; we're committing ourselves to the road ahead. Any distractions requiring problem-solving or extra worry must go.

The sale of my business and Dave's house—big-ticket items that plump up our bank accounts—are finalized mere days before we leave, causing much anxiety and stress. Together, Dave and I focus on the trip's forward trajectory. Alone, I question everything.

I'm not flippant about big life choices, but I am a Libra. We come out of the package whimsically agreeing to stuff, then worrying with an obsession few understand about whether we made the right decision. The bigger the commitment, the more sleepless nights we will pass in the dark, eyes wide open. When Libras are adventurous, they are also fearful—the scales must be balanced.

As our departure date gets closer, what I'm about to take on with someone I barely know keeps me up at night.

Everything that can make the world both beautiful and terrible could happen on a trip like this. What if I don't have what it takes? What if we can't stand each other and break up? Maybe I should back out while I still can.

Dave and I have spent only weekends together over the past year and a half. We're still in the honeymoon stage, even though there already have been a few intense arguments, which I've explained away as pre-travel jitters.

"How will we find enough water in the Namib Desert?" I implore Dave.

"Or stay warm in Siberia?"

"We'll figure something out," he replies, searching Netflix for one of Ewan McGregor and Charley Boorman's *Long Way* series about their moto adventures around the world. "Don't worry."

He always says that.

"What if I'm not strong enough to control five hundred pounds of motorcycle in the sand or mud? Six hundred if you add my gear. Shit, over seven hundred if I add me!"

I'm disconcerted by Dave's nonchalance. I want him to validate my anxiety.

"Just twist that throttle," he says, tipping back a beer. "Remember, speed is your friend."

I sigh.

"But you won't see me wipe out because you're always so far ahead."

That summer, we'd done a multiday trip to test our gear in the Chilcotins, a mountain range of British Columbian beauty Dave called his happy place and where I cried more than I had in years. The roads were technical and difficult thanks to heavy erosion. I fell off my bike multiple times and had to wait longer than was comfortable before Dave circled back to help me lift it. We discovered an upsetting discrepancy between our riding styles. Dave was impatient waiting for me to catch up, and I felt pushed past my limits. Pushed and helpless. Although I learned to ride before Dave, he had natural confidence with speed. I, on the other hand, was ever-cognizant of becoming an example of the Dunning-Kruger effect—overestimating my competence and ending up hurt or dead.

My excitement about traveling for two years competes with doubt and terror. *What if one of us gets into an accident or contracts some awful disease? What if we get kidnapped and held for ransom?* I worry about how our BMWs will stand out and that we may appear wealthy. I stress about the challenges and opportunities for failure, like actually making it around the world while nurturing a budding relationship. I think some of my friends are placing bets on how long it'll take me to throw in the towel; I have a tendency for making U-turns at any bump in the road of relationships and technically have never had a long-term boyfriend before Dave. My time with men usually topped out in the "few months" range.

Pre-trip days are spent glassy-eyed, wavering between glee and trying to douse the acid reflux creeping into my throat after every meal. Compartmentalizing is my tonic. That and beer. I focus on one thing to get done or rationalize, then move on to the next. There's always something to shoehorn into a tiny corner of my brain.

At a dinner party one August evening, a friend of Dave's approaches me with a comment that starts me second-guessing everything again.

"He's so...*particular.*" She's taking care with her words, and I think of the time he came to stay with me in Vancouver and brought his own pillow. "I'm surprised Dave wants to do something like this."

The comment disturbs me; I'm already doubting my commitment and am now overthinking Dave's lack of travel experience and blasé approach to my concerns. Over the past twenty years, I've been to twenty-seven countries. Dave has barely traveled outside Canada and the US. His interest in adventure is obvious; he loves riding a motorcycle and is a natural at it, and he's been to France and Argentina for climbing and skiing expeditions—all of which speaks of strength and stamina in the outdoors. But Dave doesn't like surprises or things out of his control. If something doesn't run smoothly, he takes the reins and tries to steer it. If that doesn't work, he's agitated. How will these traits play out in parts of the world where things are not likely to go as we expect?

Not that I'm without flaws. Along with my second-guessing habit, I also have an overactive imagination. This comes in handy as a writer but can be self-sabotaging as well. I won't be able to hide these less-appealing personality traits from Dave for long. *What if he leaves me on the side of the road somewhere?*

Despite uncertainties, I don't back out. At least not yet. I'm used to risk being the precursor to reward. Like kayaking down raging rivers or climbing mountains, I'm in it to reach the exhilarating finish line, even through the absurdity of it all.

Everything will get easier once we get on the road. We'll be having the time of our lives.

Ride like a girl

I pop a champagne cork off my parent's deck, watching it land on the lawn between our motorcycles. Friends and family cheer into the warm mid-September evening. I read aloud a poem from my sister, Vanessa, who lives in Nova Scotia:

> "And the time has come indeed,
> this trip you want and need.
> You'll be in my heart each day,
> as you and your love make your way.
> Know I love you and am so proud.
> When stormy I will pray to lift your cloud.
> When sunny, bask in the sun.
> And above all, have so much fun."

I tear up reading her words and then a card from my parents:

"Live large, dear heart! Love, Dad." And from my mom: "Our love travels with you."

Alcohol helps put out the flare of fear, and for the rest of the evening, I concentrate on enjoying the celebrations.

Departure morning is chaotic. Trying to fit everything I'll need for two years onto my bike is overwhelming. I can't comprehend why, after spending weeks whittling down my gear to the bare necessities, there is still too much.

Dave comes over to help me scrap items, his bike perfectly packed like this isn't his first time organizing a trip around the world.

"I need a damn trailer!" I cry. "What about this?" I fling a heated jacket I can plug into my bike across the lawn. "Where the hell is that supposed to go?"

My parents stay inside, out of the way. I yearn to spend our last few moments together relaxing, but Dave and I have an interview with CBC Radio soon and will set off right afterward.

"Hey," Dave cups my crumpling face and says softly, "breathe." He points to a pannier on the right side of my bike. "What's in this one?"

"Rain jacket, clothes, sun hat, quilted liners for inside my riding pants, mosquito netting…"

"Okay, all things you'll need. What about in this duffle bag?"

"Sleeping bag, sleeping mat, that small folding camp chair…"

"Hmm," Dave scratches his bearded chin. "I can take the first aid kit and your spare tire tube. Do you still have room for your laptop and the folding saw?"

"I think so." I wipe my wet nose on my sleeve like a child.

How am I going to maneuver this hulking beast of a motorcycle over anything that isn't straight, flat, and smooth? And what if something jumps in front of me on the highway and I have to swerve?

"Where are my deer whistles?" I screech, looking for the tiny, over-priced gadgets that are supposed to alert wildlife on the road.

While Dave crams my bags down with his fist so I can insert more "absolute necessities," I busy myself fitting good luck charms to my bike. Vanessa has given me a white ceramic Buddha on a chain, which I wind around the middle of my handlebars. Dad hands me a gremlin bell—a traditional gift from one rider to another. An engraved message inside reads: *Never ride faster than your angels can fly.* I tuck a long-stemmed rose into my tank bag from a flower bunch Mom bought me earlier that week. It won't last long, but I love the vibrant red against so much black, and I will know she's thinking of me.

Dave says the business of attaching stuff to my bike is ridiculous.

"You're going to look like one of those South American buses with Jesus posters tacked to the windows and trinkets glued to every surface."

I ignore him and stick a metal dragonfly from my Nana to the front fender.

Then, the moment I've both anticipated and dreaded arrives. After our CBC interview, during which I felt like a total impostor faking confidence, we hug my parents goodbye.

Dad puts a commanding hand on my boyfriend's shoulder.

"Take care of each other," he says, looking straight into Dave's eyes.

I walk over to Mom again.

"One more hug," I say, swallowing around a lump in my throat.

What will it be like not to wrap my arms around her for so long? To not see the twinkle in Dad's eyes when he smiles? What about the wacked sense of humor my sister and I share? Would Dave understand jokes about homemade corduroys or laugh over the excessive, unrelated emojis in the text messages she and I send each other?

We don't prolong our exodus; drawing it out would only make leaving harder.

I breathe out a long exhale and start the engine on my world travel buddy for the next two years. Merv and Barb, friends and neighbors to my parents, wave us off. Dad runs to the end of the block with his camera to film our bikes riding past. I'm so unaccustomed to my overloaded burden that I can't make the tight turn out of the driveway and with a wide, sweeping arch, ride over Barb's garden.

The Black Stallion's first buck

A motorcycle engine buzzes nearby. I don't want Dave seeing the accident before he sees me, so I stand in front of it all.

"Are you okay?" he shouts, coming to a stop beside me.

If I've broken something, the trip is over for me.

Maybe it's just a deep bone bruise or a pulled muscle.

"My arm hurts, but I'm okay."

Dave removes his helmet and slides off his seat, eyes wide.

"What happened?" He puts a hand on my back and guides me to sit, checking movement in my arm.

"It was so stupid…" I tell him that I clipped the boulder and lost control.

As a novice rider, I'm mentally ill prepared for navigating anything but smooth pavement with a fully loaded motorcycle—even one meant for going off-road. The aluminum panniers strapped to the sides for carrying my gear make me almost as wide as a small car. My G650GS measures forty inches in the back with luggage—far less svelte than most motorcycles.

"Don't worry," Dave says. "I'm just glad you're all right."

He walks over to my bike. It looks like a downed, heaving horse with dirt settled on its flanks. *Black Stallion. That's your nickname now.* The moniker seems apt for a steed that's just bucked off its rider.

Pressing his ass into the seat sideways, Dave lifts with one hand on the bars and the other on the luggage rack. Flicking the side stand down, he clicks the clutch into neutral and starts the engine. The Black Stallion fires up.

"Your bike seems fine. Let me take care of it." He picks up the orphaned pannier. "I think I have something to strap this back on. Are you good to walk down the trail half a mile? The road into Avery starts there. I'll ferry the bikes down."

I nod, feeling more depressed by the minute. Some birthday. I can already hear the comments from some of our more judgmental, mostly-male followers: *Of course you crashed on that big bike. It's too heavy for a girl!*

Ten minutes later, my feet hit pavement. I shuffle under a bridge to the river and sink my aching arm into the icy cold while Dave rides one bike ahead, then hikes back to get the other one. I wonder what he's thinking. Is he doubting my abilities? Can I blame him if he is?

I can't even ride this easy trail without an accident...

Once both bikes are on the main road, Dave helps me get back into my seat.

"Can you shift into first?" he asks. When I grip the handlebars, a stabbing pain shoots from the base of my right thumb, near the wrist.

"No."

Dave clicks me into neutral and I coast the remaining mile downhill into Avery, Idaho, holding on with my left hand.

A fish and tackle supplier owned by a sixty-something man called "Sheffy" comes to my rescue. When Dave tells him I crashed and we might need a hospital for X-rays, Sheffy tosses over the keys to his van.

"She'll be more comfortable in a vehicle than on the back of your bike, son," he says. "Come on, roll them motorcycles into this here garage." He waves over to a large building beside the store. "I'll lock 'em inside."

We stare at him.

"It's all right," he winks. "I've got your bikes as collateral if you steal my van."

Encased in self-loathing for ruining things so soon into the journey, I force healing thoughts on the drive to Saint Maries, fifty miles west of Avery.

It's probably nothing, just bruises. Those can hurt. Maybe a day off tomorrow...

A good break

"On the plus side, it's what's considered a good fracture."

Dr. Luther shows us an X-ray of my right hand. Below the thumb, where the wrist bends at the scaphoid, is a hairline crack. When I crashed, the handlebars jerked with enough force for an extensor tendon to pluck the top corner of bone from my radius, like a strummed guitar string. It's a "good fracture" because the bone shard repositioned itself back into place, and no surgery is needed.

The three of us stand in the emergency room. I can't look at Dave.

"You'll probably heal okay in about ten days," I hear the doctor say.

"This," I scoff at my wrist, "has to work in a day or two *at most*. I just sold everything to ride around the world and literally left only two weeks ago!" And then, as though it's up for negotiating, I ask, "Can you build the cast so it fits around my throttle?"

Dr. Luther chuckles until he realizes I'm serious.

"Oh, I won't be casting this. You're better off with just a splint."

After settling the bill and collecting receipts for my travel insurance, we walk out to the parking lot. My right arm is in a sling and a black splint is wrapped snug around my thumb, wrist, and forearm. Dave uses his cell to call Sheffy, explaining we'll be returning late. It's 8 p.m. and we still need dinner. Sheffy tells Dave to keep the van overnight and suggests a hotel, saying it's better than camping on his lawn. The chivalry from the old-time Idahoan lifts my spirits.

"I can't believe how trusting Sheffy is," Dave says. "For all he knows, we're on our way to Mexico right now."

"I'd rather take our bikes to Mexico than a minivan," I mope.

At a nearby golf course, we find a nice restaurant and order double margaritas, hoping to salvage what's left of my birthday. If we can't get to Mexico yet, we can at least bring Mexico to us.

"I can't believe this happened," I lament, "and on my birthday."

Our plan was to ride through Idaho, Utah, and Arizona to the border using a series of secondary roads called Backcountry Discovery Routes, or BDRs. These dirt-focused byways have been developed and mapped out in twelve states and take riders and other off-pavement enthusiasts through rural America, highlighting some of the history and best public lands the country has to offer. Riding a BDR is a rite of passage for any rider with a dual-sport bike—like the ones Dave and I have—because of the degree of difficulty. High mountain passes, hot dry deserts, and everything in between are found along these remote side roads and trails mixed with dirt, rocks, mud, and sand—all of which we expect to encounter. Up until a few hours ago, I was ready to tackle a BDR.

Our dual-sport bikes—also referred to as "ADV" or "adventure" motorcycles—switch easily between paved roads and all the places we want to go in between that are unmaintained or less than smooth. Even without including the rough-and-tumble BDRs, our world route would take us through Africa and Russia, where main throughways could be gravel or sand, and filled with potholes. I'm grateful for our ADV bikes and their capabilities, even if I'd already exceeded my own.

That morning, before jumping onto the Idaho Backcountry Discovery Route, Dave picked up some groceries in Coeur d'Alene. Usually that's my job, but he wanted to surprise me by making dinner that night. We were hoping to get to the Blue Cabin before dark. Literally a cabin painted blue, it sits in the woods off a northern section of the BDR and was built and maintained by hunters. Riders and other BDR users are allowed to use the cabin anytime.

"What did you buy earlier for dinner, anyway?" I ask Dave, glad I haven't yet taken any pain meds and can sip my tequila Slurpee with birthday-girl zeal.

"Lamb steaks, asparagus, and your favorite: black forest cake."

I blink back tears and finally lock eyes with him.

"I'm so sor—"

"Hey," Dave says, grabbing my hand—the one that isn't broken. "It could have been much worse. You'll heal soon and we'll get back out there, okay? Ten days isn't so bad. It might be nice to have a rest after all the stress before we left."

Dave's right. I'm not hurt that badly. Except my ego; failure is what hurts the most.

The unexpected upside

We sit on the motel bed watching TV.

"What's our plan?" I ask.

"I don't know."

Dave's less optimistic than the night before.

One option is to stay in Saint Maries. Everyone is so nice. Our server from the restaurant last night even offered her backyard for setting up our tent—free accommodation versus seventy dollars a night for a lackluster motel advertising its name noncommittally on a loose, flapping banner over the front door.

Another option is to rent a U-Haul and heal up while driving south, but that would be expensive.

The thought of going home doesn't cross my mind. "Home" is on two wheels now.

After another camp stove breakfast of oatmeal and hot chocolate, Dave drives to Avery to return Sheffy's van and pick up his bike. We've arranged to leave mine there for now.

Calling my parents, I tell them the bad news. I want to keep this setback a secret, but they're going to wonder why we're holed up in one place for so long.

Mom and Dad are relieved my crash wasn't worse. I detect concern that I've already had an accident so early into the trip. After the phone call, I update our blog, typing awkwardly as a lefty. I debate explaining my predicament, fearing judgment and opinions about my lack of riding skills and my heavy bike.

I think my BMW G650GS is perfect; it carries gear without any performance hiccups, feels solid at highway speeds, and transitions smoothly off-road. I just need more time to get used to it.

Posting about a nonserious accident can't hurt, I decide; traveling isn't always rainbows and unicorns. A few hours later, I get an email from a man who's about to save our asses.

We met Neil three days earlier at a gas station in Samuels, Idaho. Tall and barrel-chested, he approached us as we sat by our bikes eating ice cream.

"Now where you folks going with all this stuff?" he drawled, with a sideways smile making his blond mustache twitch.

I took in his cowboy boots, dark leather vest, and bolo tie while he stared down at us, shadowing the sun.

"Well, we're hoping to ride around the world," I answered with a laugh, almost like I didn't believe it when said out loud.

Neil braced himself theatrically against a parked car and placed a giant palm over his heart.

"Kids, that's just wonderful. Name's Neil." He reached down to shake our hands.

Looking to be in his early seventies, Neil told us he used to travel long distances on motorcycles, getting into "fun trouble" with his riding partner, Uncle Buck.

"Do you have a website?" I handed him one of the business cards I'd made for passing around. "Riding Full Circle," he read aloud. "Well, Heather, Dave, this is just wonderful. I'm going to follow along. You kids take care, now!"

Nursing my wrist at the motel, I read Neil's message, again in awe of the Idahoan kindness and generosity.

"Hi Heather, sorry about the break. Do you and Dave need a place to rest up for a week or two? If so, let me know and I will work on some logistics to get you and your machines to Sandpoint."

I reply we are more than grateful to take him up on the offer.

Dave calls me from Avery to check in.

"Guess what?" I tell him about Neil's email.

"Wow, that's great! Sheffy says it's fine to leave your bike here as long as needed. Anything else you want me to grab?"

When Dave gets back, we check out and ride two-up to Sandpoint, not wanting to bother Neil with a 200-mile round trip. I've only been a passenger on Dave's bike once, when we practiced at his mom's place on the Sunshine Coast in BC. I'm able to find a comfortable position folding my arms loosely around Dave's stomach. Every now and again, I squeeze hard, reminding him to slow down in the corners. Every now and again he yells back that I'm fidgeting too much. I have no idea how couples travel on one motorcycle.

When we arrive at the twenty-acre ranch, Neil and his wife, Linda, show us the cozy, two-story guest cabin we'll be staying in. A hot tub bubbles on the deck. Inside, the lower level holds a woodstove and full kitchen. Upstairs, the bedroom loft has a king-size bed with heated blankets. The fall nights are already getting cool, I've noticed.

Windows look out over a pond stocked with trout, where Neil tells us he taught his grandkids to fish. Wild turkeys gobble around the lawn, and I spot deer passing through dappled light in the aspen trees. Linda has three horses, one of which is currently licking bugs off Dave's windscreen. We have sheets, towels, dishes, a TV—everything I've left behind but am already missing.

"I thought this was your house when we pulled up," I say, mouth gaped open.

"Nope, down there is our home." Neil points down the hill to a large log home.

Linda opens the cabin's fridge and cupboards, stocked with groceries.

"We'll be offended if you don't eat all of it," she smiles. Pretty and slender, she looks to be at least ten years younger than Neil. Her white-blonde hair is in a high ponytail, and she has a youthful energy. I like her immediately.

"Are you a drinkin' man, Dave?" Neil claps a hand on my boyfriend's shoulder and almost makes him wince. Opening a cupboard beside the sink, Neil reveals a variety of unopened liquor.

Pushing past them, I reach for a bottle of gin. "I'm certainly a drinkin' man, Neil."

"Well now," our host's deep laugh fills the cabin, "we'll all get along just fine now, won't we?"

Dave and I spend two weeks at the ranch. Our time there is like an all-inclusive resort vacation. Neil and Linda take us out on their boat and treat us to delicious meals at home or in restaurants. They scold us whenever we try to pay, telling us to save our money for traveling. I want to make up for their hospitality by cooking dinners, but they keep piling on the generosity, even trusting us with a completely refurbished three-on-the-tree 1985 Chevrolet custom half-ton and a 2002 Thunderbird convertible for getting around. I feel like we're family.

One afternoon, the four of us drive back to Avery in Neil's truck to retrieve the Stallion, then on to Saint Maries where I have a checkup X-ray. Dr. Luther says my wrist is showing signs of mending but will need another three to four weeks because of damage to the soft tissue.

"I thought he said I'd heal in ten days," I complain to Dave.

"I heard him say that too."

Earlier, I tried sitting on my bike and twisting the throttle, but a jolt of pain had me off the seat in a hurry. I knew broken bones didn't heal in ten days but somehow believed mine would. The doctor said it was a "good" break, after all, and I was crushed to hear we'd be delayed even longer. Much longer, little did I know.

On the return drive to the ranch, with my steed strapped down in the back, Neil offers to take us all the way back to Revelstoke. I don't want that for many reasons—not least of which is shame. Everyone knows everyone's business in small towns; that was one reason I moved away in the first place. Returning to Canada is the only practical solution, however. I don't want to take advantage of Neil and Linda, and going anywhere else means spending trip savings without any actual forward momentum. Plus, I have health care in BC.

We store our bikes in Neil's garage and a few days later, he and Linda take us six hours north. Our return coincides with Canadian Thanksgiving and my parents are happy to have us—along with our new friends—for this celebratory time of year.

Who knows when I'll see my motorcycle again, but when Neil and Linda leave the next morning, I'm happy we'll be seeing them again when I retrieve it.

Shift happens

Only three weeks have passed since our going-away party. We weren't supposed to be back for at least two years. Dave and I run into people who know about our trip, and telling the story repeatedly takes its toll. I don't want to leave the house and am edgy, like a cat being stroked backward. Dave and I bicker, and the mental stress stalls my physical healing.

Additional X-rays show the bone continues to mend, but I still have sharp pain bending my wrist—the result of the over-stretched tendon. I see a physiotherapist, who tells me these types of injuries take even longer to heal than bones.

Mom and Dad left Revelstoke soon after Thanksgiving for a vacation on Vancouver Island, so Dave and I have their place to ourselves. Dave leaves the house one day to go for a walk after we've argued to the point of yelling. I have a change of heart, knowing this isn't fun for him.

"Nothing's stopping you from continuing on without me," I say to Dave later.

"What are you saying?" His dark-brown eyes melted my heart when I first saw him, and they tug at me now. Dave's mom, Cathy, once told me a funny story about how she warned teachers never to look young Dave in the eye when they were trying to reprimand him. I laughed then, but I'm not laughing now; it kills me to send Dave away on *our* adventure.

Knowing it might be months until I can ride again makes me feel guilty. It's kind of Dave to stick by my side, but there's no need for him to be stuck with the same jail sentence.

"You're able bodied," I say. "You should just keep going."

"But...you *will* meet up with me again when you're better, right?" Those eyes—imploring, expectant...

"Of course."

Is that true? Will I want to get back on a motorcycle again?

I drive Dave to the US border, where his dad, Rick, picks him up, and they continue to Neil and Linda's. Dave's plan is to ride south along the BDRs, like we had planned. Rick, heading to Arizona for the winter, has a covered trailer with room for my bike and gear. This means I need to get to Phoenix at some point, and I enjoy having something to look forward to although I'm sad I won't see our friends at this time.

With Dave gone, my guilt dissipates. I give myself the freedom to heal. But I'm bored, so I book a flight to Nova Scotia and stay with Vanessa for three weeks. Nobody makes me laugh like my sister does, and our shared humor helps snap me out of my malaise.

By the end of November, I'm in Phoenix. My wrist still won't bend all the way, but I miss everything—my bike, my boyfriend, our trip…most of all, I've missed having a sense of purpose. Goals propel me forward in life, forcing me to zero in on the big picture, not the little things in my way like ego and phobias.

When Dave picks me up at the airport, we're as giddy as when we were first dating. The two-hour drive west to Quartzite—where Rick lives during the winter in an RV park—is filled with positive chatter. Dave is so excited to see me, it seems ridiculous I ever doubted his commitment to me and our trip.

"I've been scouting places around Dad's to take the bikes," he says, "to test your wrist."

Anxiety socks me in the gut, but I ignore it. I'm here for a do-over.

Quarters are tight in Rick's fifth-wheel trailer with three of us. I look forward to evenings when neighboring RV park occupants host happy hour. Starting at 4:30 p.m., snowbirds and retirees come from all corners of the park, dragging lawn chairs and drinks in plastic cups. Dave and I feel like movie stars when word gets out that we're attempting to ride our motorcycles around the world. No one expresses concern or reservation; these folks know life is short. "Do it while you can," they say.

Several times a day, I bend my wrist this way and that, testing new positions and keeping it from seizing up. Despite any enthusiasm to get back in the saddle, I'm shit scared of another buck-off when the day finally comes to start up the Black Stallion. Dave and I follow Rick on his ATV out into the desert. Every sandy corner has me clenching my butt cheeks so hard I think they might get swallowed up into my back. But I'm also elated. Everything works. The suspension on my bike absorbs the bumps better than I thought, and my wrist barely feels a thing. Nobody can stop me now.

Not even me.

Placing color images in this book was cost-prohibitive, so my solution is to bring you our travel photos digitally. To see color images for each country, scan the QR code or visit Photos under Riding Full Circle on my website, heatherleawriter.com.

So long, order

Mexico

We cross into Mexico from California at the Tecate border. Patrol officers wave Dave and I through two open yellow gates. With no lineup, we roll from one world into another within seconds.

"So...was that the border?" I ask Dave via a new Bluetooth intercom fixed to my helmet that will help us communicate to each other while riding.

Mexico is our first foreign country, but no one stops us to ask for documents. We assumed Tecate would be more chill than Tijuana, but this is suspiciously easy.

"I guess so...?" Dave's attempting to snake through large, round speedbump discs painted yellow and implanted into the pavement like hard plastic breasts.

Coming from America, a place of relative order, downtown Tecate is sensory overload. We move along with local cars, trucks, motorcycles, and bicycles, dodging pedestrians and stray dogs. Red lights and stop signs are mere suggestions. Any sort of traffic obedience disrupts the flow and will prompt a cacophony of horn-honking. I'm unsure where to position my bike on the road. Nothing defines its center or lane width, just a wide slab of broken up concrete littered with garbage and potholes. I follow Dave, who follows everyone else.

We exit the craziness and rise out of the city on a vast, sweeping highway where local driving behaviors only get more confusing. In a corner, I tilt my bike right and watch an oncoming car cross into my lane, impatient to get around a semitruck. The car ahead of us moves over to let the other vehicle pass, avoiding a head-on collision. Nobody else seems to think this is shocking, but Dave and I shake our middle fingers, like we'd do at home.

As we become more streetwise for Mexico, we notice patterns: Slower cars drive on the shoulder, letting others by, and oncoming traffic of equal or larger size passes on blind corners or double solid lines, assuming lesser drivers will move out of the way.

We occasionally notice piles of twigs or cut bushes laid on the road. This, we discover, is to signal an accident or broken-down vehicle ahead.

To stay with traffic and avoid getting hit, Dave and I must fast learn this lawless and puzzling way of the road.

Our first night in Mexico is spent camping along a dead-end rural street.

"I'm not sure we should just set up here," Dave says, looking around. "What if it's someone's property?"

The air smells like raked dirt—an earthy scent that grows stronger as the sky gets darker. We haven't passed a single car since a turnoff ten miles back. The surroundings are harmless and peaceful, especially when I look around at the farmhouses, gardens, goats, and chickens.

I watch Dave, amused. He doesn't often take on the role of "worrier."

"Babe," I say, "we have to get used to camping or we're going to spend all our savings in the first few months."

"I know. It's just…everything we've heard about Mexico…"

Dave's fearful about tourist beheadings and kidnappings, but that happens more in bigger, touristy cities nowhere near here. The Mexico portrayed in the media scares me, as well, but I'm too excited for any negativity. Our trip is happening again in real life, not just something I'm pining for. We've left our countries and comfort zones behind and don't know the language. Rudimentary tasks—like finding food and accommodation—will become daily challenges. This thrills me; we're spending our first night in a foreign place, and I already feel a new world welcoming us.

I agree to be inconspicuous. The bikes are parked behind a small nearby hill, and we put up the tent behind some head-high bushes. Nobody will see us if they don't know we're there. We go to bed before it gets dark enough to need lights around camp. Feeling secure and hidden in our tent, I turn on my headlamp to read a book.

"Turn your light off," Dave hisses when we hear a vehicle coming up the gravel road. I cover the light with my book, and we lay still listening for signs of the car slowing, but it keeps driving.

In the dark, it's easy to think the worst. I understand Dave's nervousness, even if it seems out of character. So much of our foreign "education" comes from myopic newscasts and online videos, when really it should come from reading National Geographic and watching travel shows.

That said, bad things happen—just like at home—and vigilance is key. I fall into a deep sleep with my foldable knife within arm's reach.

We begin to melt into the peninsula's quiet rhythm, which rises and falls like the sea we travel alongside. Baja—separated in part from the country's mainland like a thumb from a hand—is safe, statistically. Crime is a fraction of what it is on the mainland, and even the food can be counted on. We eat at brightly painted roadside taco stands, consuming several tacos at a time. The huts are disheveled looking, but there is nothing fresher than a Mexican taco made on the spot with juicy and diced radish, onion, and tomatoes, along with savory meats and a tart lime wedge. We top everything off with burning salsa that makes our eyes water and our mouths catch fire. The sauce turns our intestines inside out and we have frequent bathroom stops, but the food isn't the problem; our stomachs just need to get used to a new microbiome—one that can boil bile.

The Trans-peninsular Highway, or Federal Highway 1, starts in Tijuana and travels for 1,063 miles south, ending in Cabo San Lucas. The road is uncrowded and wide open, with considerable distances between villages, towns, and cities. This vastness allows for uninterrupted scenery. Despite the brownscape of dry foothills to the east and the unending desert floor spread before us, the arid beauty is plentiful. With cacti reaching several feet high, coastlines of perilous cliffs, and washouts to watch out for, riding the Trans-peninsular is anything but boring.

On Christmas Eve we camp along the Pacific Ocean with no one in sight but three wild donkeys (burros) watching Dave set up the tent while I rehydrate dried chili in a pot. Although I miss my family, it's hard to beat the calming sound of waves and a perfect sunset bowing off to the west.

Sand traps of self-doubt

In San Felipe, a small town along the Gulf of California, 120 miles south of the US border, we meet two other riders. Brenda, forty-something with ginger hair and pretty brown eyes, is from Washington state. Ruppert— tall with dark hair and a British accent—lives in Vancouver, BC. We laugh at the coincidence that they both live where Dave and I just left.

Brenda and Ruppert invite us to ride with them into Coco's Corner— a remote desert homestead infamous among the ADV crowd. I'm excited to travel with another female rider. So far, I've only seen or been around males in the dual-sport world. Men helped me pick out my riding attire. Men sold me modifications for my bike. Men commented on my blog posts. I didn't know any other women who rode ADV bikes like mine. This always made me question my decision. On the other hand, it feels empowering.

The couple are riding on lightweight dirt bikes and—with only three weeks for their holiday—have impressively small bags strapped on the back. Our bikes are like minivans in comparison.

We follow Brenda and Ruppert out of San Felipe to the highway. For several miles, the road is paved, with plenty of yellow speed bump discs like the ones we encountered at the border. Dave takes to calling them *tortugas de muerte*, or "death turtles." They cause our front tires to deflect in different directions while the rear slips down the sides, throwing us off balance. After a lunch stop, we turn onto a gravel road leading twenty miles to Coco's Corner.

Coco is a Mexican man who might have gone unnoticed in life if not for the Baja 1000—a desert motorsport race held every year that coursed past his clay-built house. He sells surprisingly cold beer from his baking desert abode and enjoys drawing the unsuspecting visitor's eye to a disturbing cluster of women's underwear hanging from his ceiling—donations from past travelers, who sometimes bring an extra pair to add to the collection or offer them up on the spot for legacy's sake.

Coco has diabetes, and both legs have been amputated below the knee. He gets around by wheelchair or by pulling himself along the sandy concrete floor. We each buy two beers from him to enjoy later in camp. Coco demands we all sign one of the guest books and points to a stack of thick tomes filled with thousands of foreign signatures and writings in different languages. While Ruppert signs our names, Coco eyes up Brenda and me, perhaps hoping for a contribution to his panty ceiling.

I doubt Coco is aware of his own legendary status. Although there are several published articles mentioning Coco's Corner and the man himself, he lives a humble, quiet existence without digital distractions. Riding in earlier that day, we encountered paving crews on the road pouring hot tarmac over the gravel, inching ever closer to Coco's home. Will he see more visitors because it's easier to get here? Or will a paved road past his house make Coco's Corner less of a novelty?

The four of us point our bikes toward a spot named White Rock, where Coco mentioned good camping. After a half hour, we turn off the gravel road onto sand. I come to a skidding halt. In the wide-open desert world ahead, a faint track stands out indicating somewhat of a road. It ripples and swells with raised, sand-covered "whoops" (mounds and dips), like motionless ocean waves. My riding partners fade into a mirage, unstopping. Ruppert and Brenda catch air off the whoops with their lighter machines and expertise. Dave's rear tire lashes snake-like while he works to get his 500-pound load under control in the loose ground. Our bikes are far too heavy for this type of riding, but no one hears my complaints. My stomach sinks. Dave just took off, assuming I'd follow. He's not about to pander to my reluctance. When I get up the nerve to twist the throttle, all I can think about is falling off and breaking another bone.

Beating back fear with some good old deprecating self-talk—like, *come on, don't be such a lame ass*, and, *I'm not dead until I say so!*—I move forward, feeling the rear tire sink before it catches and lurches me ahead. *Too fast, too fast!* My legs shoot out and I dab my toes to the ground, dragging a line of terror in the sand for several meters before finding my balance and sticking my boots back onto the foot pegs.

I stand quickly. In technical terrain, it's easier to retain your balance by standing and using your legs to absorb hits as the bike moves beneath you. Another important technique I have yet to master is keeping my speed up while riding in sand, mud, and dirt. Just as a water-skier needs the boat at high throttle to stay afloat, riders use speed to keep from getting bogged down in anything that's not hard packed.

The logic makes sense but goes against my survival instinct. I want to go slower in case I fall over, but that isn't fast enough for buoyancy. I twist the throttle more, and then a little more, gaining momentum and staying upright. Brenda floats through the desert, skipping off the bumps like a moto-queen. *Maybe I'll be that good someday.* Once or twice, someone waits for me, but I zip past in case I can't get going again.

Just before our camp for the night, we enter a dry wash filled with deep sand. As feared, I wipe out, stuffing my right fist into the ground. Yelping in pain, I lie there holding my arm. Dave comes rushing over. *Not again! Please god not again.* I walk the last few hundred meters into camp and Dave brings my bike in. Ruppert whips out a tequila bottle and a tensor bandage, wrapping my wrist.

"Good as new?" he asks.

Flexing my hand, I'm relieved to feel the pain has subsided. Nothing's broken, just a sore landing.

Dave hugs me and says, "You're my hero." He doesn't often verbalize compliments or feelings, so when he does, they're impactful.

While we sip tequila around a crackling campfire, Brenda asks me when I learned to ride. She's surprised to hear I've just recovered from a broken bone.

"Are you serious? And now you're back on the same bike? That's bad-ass!"

I fall asleep that night feeling loved and brave.

If the Baja peninsula is a thumb and the rest of Mexico the other fingers, then the Sea of Cortez is the space in between. On a boat tour with Brenda and Ruppert in Loreto, a national marine reserve on the Sea of Cortez, we float past blue-footed boobies and a gang of cantankerous seals needing buckets of mouthwash. The captain pulls ashore on an island where the water is crystal blue. Wading in, I'm unpleasantly surprised that the tropical-looking water feels much cooler than the 66°F averaged for that time of year.

"Better than forty degrees, like the ocean is year-round in Vancouver," I say.

Brenda and I hike and snorkel while the guys fish in deeper waters. They catch a dorado we later eat after finding a restaurant that will cook and serve the fish for a five-dollar fee. The chef turns the dorado into *ceviche*, a citrus marinade that "cooks" raw seafood to perfection.

"How have I never had this before!" I declare *ceviche* my new favorite meal.

After a few tequila shots for dessert—hard to turn down in Mexico—we shuffle through the streets, dropping Ruppert and Brenda at their hotel. Dave and I walk back to our campsite near the city center. The dark, unpopulated dirt roads are anything but threatening, and we enjoy the quiet fifteen-minute stroll to the campground. My heart goes out to the stray dogs sniffing through garbage piles and gutters for food scraps.

Ever since riding in the sand with Brenda and Ruppert, Dave and I are desperate to lighten our loads. I strike up a conversation with a Canadian guy camped beside us, who it turns out is heading north in his van. He asks if there's anything we want him to bring back.

First to go are our folding camp chairs. Although they're compact, at twelve inches long, they weigh about five pounds each. Most places we've camped have a log or rock to sit on, or even an actual picnic table. It's time to downsize on such luxuries. I put my chair in the pile along with a bottle of Tylenol, a bag of cotton balls, some electrolyte drink mixes, a foam neck brace and other items from the first aid kit, a roll of duct tape, a small ball used to massage knots out of body parts, and a bottle of sunscreen.

Dave adds two empty dry bags, his own camp chair, a battery-powered light, and some clothing items. It looks ridiculous now that I see it all in a pile. What did we think we needed this stuff for? Most of it could be bought anywhere in the world. I layer everything into a large box and guess it weighs about thirty pounds.

I feel like we're seasoned travelers now, getting rid of so much bulk and weight. We are traveling by motorcycle, after all, not by bus.

The On-road Baja 2000

Riding into La Paz a day before New Year's Eve, we find the hostel where Brenda and Ruppert are staying. Since entering Mexico, we've been camping most nights, and a real bed sounds extraordinary. When we arrive, the street outside is busy and loud, and there isn't anywhere to leave our bikes. We haven't considered this dilemma yet—until now, they've always stayed close by the tent, within eyesight.

Isaac, the hostel owner, says we can bring them inside. Laying a wood plank over the curb, I watch Dave swing a wide turn in the street while Isaac blocks traffic. No one honks. Everyone stares. Dave lines up his front wheel and bounces over the plank and in through the hostel's doorway. The lobby is narrow and lined with an odd collection of figurines in glass shelves. Dave slides my bike carefully through the entryway, his feet grazing the ground for balance. He parks in a cluttered courtyard next to a freaky taxidermized monkey sitting in a Model T Ford. It's an odd and intriguing place to call home for a few nights.

After some tequila shots with Isaac—a customary welcome for all travelers—we chitchat with him while waiting for Brenda and Ruppert to come back from downtown.

Feeling conversational by the second shot of tequila—a distilled beverage made from the blue agave plant endemic to this part of Mexico—I talk with Isaac about our route plan.

"We're going to take the ferry to Mazatlán then ride south into Central and South America."

"Do you have your FMM card?" Isaac asks.

We shake our heads.

"You would have gotten one on entry into Mexico."

My brain flashes back to when Dave and I questioned the ease of the border crossing in Tecate over a week ago.

"Where can we get one?"

"It has to be from a port of entry," Isaac sighs, telling us this is common. Travelers end up in La Paz wanting to get over to the mainland but don't have the *Forma Migratoria Múltiple* card. "You don't need it in Baja, but mainland Mexico requires the FMM. The ferry does not let you on without one."

If what Isaac says is true, we need to backtrack to Tecate nine hundred miles. That's like driving from Vancouver, BC, to Swift Current, Saskatchewan, or from Seattle, Washington, to Jackson, Wyoming.

Leaving us to stew in traveler-mishap misery, Isaac helps another guest. Dave's eyebrows are knit together. Even tequila can't help us now.

"What about the airport?" I suggest. "Maybe we can talk nice to a customs agent and get the permit?"

"Good idea. Let's do that first thing tomorrow."

We find a customs agent who speaks English, but he gives a firm shake of his head. No FMMs are forthcoming from the airport. Taking pity, he calls a friend in Los Cabos, who agrees to get us two permits but it's going to cost us $200. Dave and I aren't about to ride over two hours to pay some random guy for something we don't even know is legit or not.

We're going back to Tecate.

Dave and I half-heartedly ring in 2016 on a bar patio with Brenda, Ruppert, and some other riders they've befriended. Our minds are on the FMM dilemma, not partying, so we return to the hostel well before midnight. In our room, Dave thinks of another option.

"What about renting a car? It would save wear and tear on our tires."

Tires—or more specifically the tread—make a massive difference in how a bike performs on the road and off. We almost exclusively use 50/50 tires, with raised tread knobs that help grip loose surfaces. The rubber pattern combination works best on all road surfaces and means we can hop off a highway onto a dirt trail at will. But 50/50s wear down much faster on pavement. Saving 2,000 miles would prolong their longevity.

With Isaac's help—and a lot of running around on New Year's Day—we find a rental car, paying just twenty dollars for four days, with unlimited mileage. No question this is the best choice.

On the road, the advantages are reinforced. We play music, eat snacks, turn on the air conditioning—everything we can't do riding motorcycles. Plus, we can drive well into the night, which we never do on the bikes—especially in Mexico, where potholes can swallow a bus.

We stop once for seven hours to camp on a beach, joking that, after more than nine hundred miles one way, we're racing in the On-road Baja 2000, sponsored by Fiat.

Reaching Tecate twenty-six hours after leaving La Paz, we find the immigration office—a not-obvious white shack lacking signs of any kind, except a gold plaque by the door. Inside, a friendly officer sits behind a desk and passes Dave the FMM paperwork to fill out. The permits cost half what the border agent's friend wanted—and are legal.

"I wonder if we miss things traveling by motorcycle, or if we actually experience more," I say from the passenger seat on our way back, stuffing my face with yet another *carne asada* taco.

"I think it's both. Sometimes we miss out because we need to pay more attention than drivers. That said, our senses are enhanced. Like if we were on bikes right now, we'd smell that dead cow."

I look to where Dave points. Half a dozen vultures are posed on the poor dead animal's swollen belly.

"Actually, I want to get a shot of that." Dave pulls over and reaches for his camera.

"We are *not* putting that on our website!" I call after him.

Tequila with a side of dead things

We say goodbye to Brenda and Ruppert in La Paz—the furthest south they'll go before turning around for home. After exchanging emails and promising to visit when we return next year, Dave and I wait to board the ferry for Mazatlán, FMM cards in hand.

As two of the last people to buy tickets, we can't get a cabin for the 200-mile overnight crossing, so after parking on deck and working with the crew to make sure our bikes are strapped down good and tight, we carry our sleeping bags into the lounge area.

The ferry is not luxurious, but it is uncrowded, and I'm able to stretch out over three seats when people head to their berths for the night.

What should have been a twelve-hour crossing, however, takes twenty-four. The captain announces halfway through that one engine is down. A

Mexican man sitting nearby rolls his eyes and says, "Eez de same bullshit ee always say."

Apparently, the boat has been floating at half-pace for years.

I spend my time lost at sea writing blog posts and editing photos. The ferry doesn't have Wi-Fi, so I prepare everything in Word and Photoshop to upload later. Dave reads and watches movies playing on a roll-down screen at the front of the atrium. In between, he gets us food and drinks from a terrible cafeteria.

At sunset, I visit the upper deck and watch the Sea of Cortez, dead flat and glimmering in the orange light. The warm sea breeze on my face and bare skin feels sumptuous.

It's late when we dock in Mazatlán, and we're warned by concerned ferry-goers that arriving in the dark is dangerous. Dave and I take our chances and follow the GPS to a hotel, getting there safe and sound. The owner allows us to bring our bikes into a courtyard, and I hope this kind of security can be counted on for most of our travels.

After a good night's sleep, Dave and I are ready to hop back on the road by early morning. Resorts aren't our thing. But first, we need breakfast.

My flip-flops kick up sand that tickles the backs of my calves as we walk along the beach to a restaurant. It's barely 8 a.m., but tourists are already suntanning around pools under skyscraper hotels.

At a thatched-roof beach café, a middle-aged man dressed formally in a white shirt and black pants brings a menu to our table. I order an omelet and fresh-squeezed *jugo de naranja*, then sit back to enjoy the orange juice in the breeze. Even this early, temps are in the high 80s. I dread getting back into my "ski suit"—a nickname for our riding gear.

Made from Kevlar, a non-abrasive material, with plastic armor at the elbows, back, knees, and hips, the suits are nearly bulletproof but are sweltering in anything over 70°F. We'd promised each other (and our moms) we'd ride ATGATT (All the Gear, All the Time). Odds are high that in over 700 days of riding, we'll hit the deck at some point. As I've already proven, a thick jacket and riding pants keep us protected.

We also wear sturdy plastic waterproof boots with buckles up our shins—another sweat-festering piece of gear, but it's better than losing a foot.

Deciding which helmets to wear was a challenging decision. A full-face style covers the entire head, jaw, and eyes when the visor is down and is considered safer than a modular helmet. The latter is nice in that the lower half of the helmet pivots up to reveal the face. I liked this attribute for showing our smiles when in less touristy places, but in the end we both settled for the ADV-style full-face helmet. Mine came with drop-down sunshades that made me look like a geriatric cop but kept me from fidgeting with sunglasses while riding. Plus, I could flip those sweet blockers up or down on the fly using a tab on the side of my helmet.

The server returns with our food and produces a bottle of clear liquid with a dead scorpion swirling at the bottom.

"Tequila?"

We shake our heads. *Gracias, pero no gracias.* Thinking perhaps we've declined because of the scorpion, the man returns with more bottles filled with different dead things.

"*Señor*, you no like scorpion? Try—" he grabs one of the bottles—"Try dis one instead." A coral snake corpse spins in the yellowish liquid. "I make myself. I sell here!" He puffs out his chest, stretching the embroidery on his white *guayabera* shirt. His nametag reads *José*. "But for you, amigo? *Gratis.* Free!"

I sit back, fold my arms, and look at Dave with an *I dare you* grin. José takes my boyfriend's hesitation as permission and wastes no time filling a shot glass with snake-booze. Dave shrugs. "It'll probably kill any viruses I'm carrying from that ferry ride anyway." Tossing it back, he says, "Huh…that actually wasn't bad."

Creature-infused tequila is said to have medicinal value for ailments like arthritis and even cancer. The snake in the bottle was gutted before being doused in Mexico's signature liquor, then sat for several months before serving, we're told.

"*Por favor…*" I gesture to my glass, which gets filled to the brim. José waits, hands clasped behind his back. I think the drink will taste like how the dead frogs in formaldehyde smelled in biology class, but it just tastes like…tequila.

"*Muy bien!*" I smile.

Our booze hustler grins with pride.

During the crossing to Mazatlán, Dave had tallied our mileage. Two years felt like ample leeway for mishaps like the longer ferry ride and the Tecate marathon, but we are having trouble planning around seasons. If we want to make it to our southernmost objective—Ushuaia, Argentina—we need to be there by the end of March. Otherwise, it'll be winter. The Southern Hemisphere is just coming into summer now in January. We still have

Mexico and Central and South America to get through—10,000 miles between us and the end of the Americas.

I'm getting increasingly nervous about the winds in Patagonia, which I've heard can gust up to and over 100 miles an hour. I've also heard stories of riders getting swept off their bikes, crashing into ditches and other vehicles, and I've seen a YouTube video of a semitruck getting pushed over on the highway from wind.

We start to leave Mazatlán's city limits, but an enticing display of road-side strawberries for sale further delays our progress south. Eating is becoming one of our favorite pastimes. Dave's voracious appetite for anything new or delicious-looking is fun to witness, and I follow him over to the fruit stand. Putting aside thoughts of exhaust fumes landing on the berries from the heavy traffic, I give in to my body's craving for vitamins and nutrients.

We order a dozen orbs each, dipping the fat, sweet berries into freshly whipped cream. My eyes roll back in my head and Dave almost passes out in food-induced ecstasy.

"These are so much better than anything we get at home," he says.

Mexico's toll roads—*autopistas*—are smooth and much faster than the *libre*, or free, roads and have plenty of rest stops with decent bathrooms and even food vendors, like this one. The downside is the tolls are frequent—like every fifty miles—and expensive. Also, two motorcycles are charged as two vehicles. So far, we'd spent twenty dollars in 200 miles, and we planned to use toll roads for several days to get past some of the riskier places along the coast, like Acapulco.

Toll roads are boring, much like freeways and interstates back home, and I miss the *libre* roads we preferred, which are far more scenic, but very slow.

La Ventosa

In Puerto Escondido, Dave and I are walking back from a beach swim when we spot a couple standing beside an ADV motorcycle loaded with gear. Taking any opportunity to talk to fellow adventure riders, we introduce ourselves. Omar and Luciana are from Villahermosa, a few hours to the southeast. They ask where we're going next.

"Guatemala," Dave says.

"Come and stay with us before you leave our beautiful country," Omar suggests.

The next morning, we follow them out of town, already roasting in the heat. An hour later, I'm sweating buckets, despite having soaked my T-shirt with water before leaving. When Omar pulls into a rest stop, I'm overjoyed to see fresh, cold coconuts for sale. Omar orders four from a young woman selling the large husks for a dollar each. I watch her slash off the tops with a machete, insert straws, then go back to breastfeeding a toddler.

We sit at a shaded picnic table, drinking down to the meat before anyone utters a word. Then Omar says, "A warning. We will be passing along the Gulf of Mexico. Some days it's very windy."

The route to Villahermosa travels through La Ventosa—the windiest region in Mexico. Some even argue the world. I don't have to wait for Patagonia to live out my fear of wind.

"*Vámonos,*" Omar waves. We dutifully go back to our bikes.

The wind turbines in the distance are a clue that shit's about to get real. The toll booth agent does a double take seeing a girl among men on big bikes and warns me about the heavy winds ahead. *"Vientos muy fuertes más adelante!"*

Gales racing through the gulf hit the Pacific and slam into anything in the way; today, it's our three motorcycles. It doesn't take long to notice the change. Sand is swirling across the desert floor, covering the blue-sky horizon like low-lying fog. I strain my ears, hoping to meditate on the rhythmic clickety-clack of each granule. *What would they sound like if I could focus on that instead of my fear? Crickets scurrying across a hard surface? Someone typing softly on a keyboard?* It's impossible to hear anything over the wind's roar, punching me from the side and changing direction on a whim. I stress-grip my handlebars, fighting with every muscle to stay upright. A strand of hair whips around inside my helmet visor, itching, but I don't want to lift a finger in case it's the difference between balance and getting pushed over.

Right then, I think I will die on this Mexican highway—not from something I was warned about, like tourist beheadings or a tequila overdose, but because Dave and I accepted an invitation from strangers. *We should have stayed with the plan for Guatemala. "A little windy ahead."* Come on!

I'm alarmed to see my elbow hovering mere inches off the pavement. Ahead, Dave's leaning at a 45-degree angle to the wind. Luciana clings to her husband like a backpack. I want to film it all because no one will believe how crazy it really is—but that would mean lifting my hand to start my helmet camera and there's that whole *death by smearing body parts across the road* thing.

Omar's parting words after our innocent coconut water stop just a few miles ago advised us to ride as fast as possible. "Otherwise, the wind will overtake you!"

A lightning-fast glance to my dash tells me I'm going seventy-seven miles an hour. I don't want to be going this fast. I back off on the throttle, but then things get far worse. I almost go down. *Shit!* I have no idea what's preventing me from crashing. Certainly not knowledge and skill; my riding resume totals a few months at most to this point.

How will it feel when I fall off? A low-side crash means I'll be closer to the ground. A high-sider will fling me into the air and is usually what kills motorcyclists when they get off course.

My hands have no more strength left to hang on, and my neck feels like it's about to snap. Then, a Pemex gas station appears. Omar turns on his signal.

I scream happiness into my helmet and pull in behind Dave, Omar, and Luciana. The vicious gale is so suddenly cut by the station's walls, I almost fall over from the lack of it. Sliding from my seat, I reach for some nearby steps and sit to catch my breath. My legs are pins and needles. A painful knot sits between my shoulders. I regret sending my massage ball home.

If I'm this scared in Mexico, what will Patagonia do to me? Soon, I'll have to leave the safe shelter of the gas station and get back out there. *No, I can't do it!* I literally contemplate living here at the Pemex forever, or at least until the wind goes away.

Dave puts a hand on my shoulder.

"I'm so sorry!" Omar runs over. "I didn't know you were so new to the motorcycle."

I wave off his concerns, telling him it's not like I can avoid wind forever.

"Excuse me." Omar leaves to answer his ringing cell.

"Do you want anything?" Dave asks. "A drink or a snack?"

"No!" I snap, then, "Sorry, I'm just so nervous to get back on my bike." A metal road sign flaps in the gale and the *clang, clang, clang* jars my nerves.

"I have great news!" Omar says, coming back to where I'm still heaving on the steps.

"When is this over?" I demand.

"That was my friend riding ahead of us." Omar ignores me.

"What time of year does this wind stop?" I plead. "I'll wait."

"He says there is less wind if we cut up into the mountains."

"Where's the turnoff?" I'm already putting on my helmet.

"Back there." Omar points to a road half a mile back. "The trees will cut the wind. *Muy bien!*"

"Can we go?" I'm impatient now that there will soon be an end to this madness.

Omar links his arm to Luciana's.

"¡Vámonos!"

Rolling back into the wind is nerve-racking. But after a wobbly U-turn, it's only a few minutes until I'm swallowed up in a protective forest that blocks the wind considerably. My shoulders are no longer glued to my ears. I can feel the buzz of adrenaline still vibrating through my body. I think of the mantra in the gremlin bell my dad gave me almost four months ago: *Never ride faster than your angels can fly.*

Looks like my angels can fly at least seventy-seven miles an hour.

Four days later, Dave and I are packing our bags to leave Villahermosa. While I'm saddling up my bike, Omar notices my good luck charms and points out that Dave doesn't have any. He hands my boyfriend a laminated wallet-sized card with a painting of Jesus. We're not religious and I think Dave's going to politely accept, then forget about it later or even throw it out. But he seems touched by the gesture. It makes me happy to see his gratitude, and I wonder if the generosity we've experienced from others so far is helping us open up to the world.

Failure to connect

Guatemala

The heat—mid-90s and humid—is unbearable. Dave's rash is worse. He has a skin condition called *tinea versicolor*—a chronic, sweat-induced fungal infection that takes over his body in palm-sized, itchy red patches. He's had the issue for years. A doctor recommended lathering up with dandruff shampoo in the shower and covering himself in tea tree oil, but that doesn't help when you're on the road and can't bathe daily.

I'm sympathetic and help rub the oil on his back, where the rash is the worst. Watching him rake his fingernails over his lower legs makes me want to tie his hands behind his back, but the relief scratching gives him isn't something I want to deny him, and it doesn't seem to make it worse anyway. Just heat, and especially humidity.

I get headaches almost every day now and don't know if they're from overexertion, dehydration, or vibration from my single-cylinder bike. I keep a hydration bladder inside one of my panniers, with a tube straw hanging out the side for easy access. It holds almost a gallon of water, and I top it up often, consuming up to two gallons or more a day. This seems insane, but I'm perpetually thirsty. Even Dave—not much of a water drinker—consumes far more than usual. No matter how cold the water is at first, it's tea-warm within the hour. Thinking my headaches are from a lack of electrolytes, I buy Gatorade when I can. That doesn't work either, and I don't like all the sugar.

We sleep restlessly in new beds or locations almost every night. Sometimes a place to lay our heads comes as a welcome relief. Other nights are a fitful fight with too many or too few covers. Pillows either squish flat like pancakes or are so bulbous we wake with kinks in our necks. Even after so many days in our tent, I still don't have my sleeping bag, mat, and inflatable pillow dialed in and usually end up sliding sideways into Dave.

Our love life is hit and miss, reserved for hotel rooms with showers and air conditioning. Otherwise, we can't stand being so close to each other.

"Don't touch me! You're making me too hot."

"Oh my god, can't you do something about your BO?"

Traveling in all our safety gear doesn't help. Not an inch of skin can breathe, and we ride festering in perspiration. By the end of the day, Dave and I can wring out our socks and produce a tablespoon of sweat. Whenever we find a water source—roadside rivers, gas station hoses, public bathroom sinks—we remove our shirts and wet them, then groan in ecstasy when the cooled fabric hits the smalls of our backs. The relief is temporary, however, and as soon as we start riding again, the airflow dries us in minutes. But the moisture helps, even if just psychologically.

Dave's rash and the unrelenting heat make him short-tempered.

"Why are you stopping there?" he asks over the intercom.

"I'm taking a photo."

We're on a high road overlooking a village, and I'm trying to zoom in for a shot of a girl hanging clothes on a laundry line.

"We don't have time." Dave keeps riding. "BMW closes in an hour."

Our bikes are due for some maintenance, and we need to be in Guatemala City before the dealership closes at 4 p.m.

I swear, snap a quick shot knowing it's probably out of focus, then click into gear to hurry after Dave.

With less than two months to get through twelve countries before winter in Ushuaia, Dave has been picking up the pace. The world's passing me by; I can't even photograph it, let alone slow down and enjoy the experience. We'd agreed not to let a schedule stress us out, but my broken wrist cost us three months—three months we need to make up somehow.

Closing in on Guatemala City—home to almost three million people—urban traffic swallows us like we're sticks thrown into a river's current. I have an eye on Dave ahead, but a dozen cars surround us, and I lose sight of his bike. I next see him taking an off-ramp connecting to another busy road. I'm two lanes over and can't make the turn without killing myself, so I watch him split away, the road unzipping between us. Our headsets are supposed to have a one-mile range, but sometimes we can't even connect them riding side by side. I try to get hold of him now. Through the crackle, all I hear is Dave saying, "Shit."

"I'll pull off after this overpass ahead and stay there until you can re-route back to me," I say. More static.

Finding a safe place to stop, I pull out my InReach. "Waiting on right from where u last saw me," I type. The message will include coordinates to my location. Since Dave has the GPS mounted onto his handlebars, he can type them in and follow the route on the three-by-five-inch screen.

Removing my helmet, I put on a hat to shield the sun. This road is quieter, and a few cars slow.

"¿Está bien?"

I reply yes, all is good, thank you.

Concern doesn't cross my mind. I look forward to mishaps here and there; they give me a chance to think for myself. All I've been doing for months is acting like Dave's tail. I miss autonomy. *What would I do now as a solo rider?* I consider the thought. First, I'd have a map or GPS, or I'd ask a local for directions.

When Dave proposed the idea of this trip, I'd never heard of anyone who'd ridden a motorcycle around the world. What did that even mean? Surely, you can't actually ride around the entire globe. I knew no female riders except my mom, who rode "pillion" on the back of my dad's bikes. Doing some research, I soon learned that many women have broken records on motorcycles, starting in the early twentieth century.

Della Crewe was thirty when she hit the road with her dog in a Harley Davidson sidecar. She rode through the United States, Caribbean Islands, and Central America in 1914. Two years later, the Van Buren sisters couldn't even vote, but they became the first women to ride across America. Anne-France Duatheville is credited for being the first solo female to ride around the world in 1973, covering 12,500 miles through three continents on a Kawasaki 125. In 1982, Elspeth Beard did a global tour, returning in 1984 as the first British woman to have done so. Steph Jeavons is known as the first woman to have ridden her motorcycle on all seven continents, starting in 2014 and covering fifty-four countries. Fellow writer/rider and founder of the Adventure Travel Film Festival, Lois Pryce has written popular books about riding alone in places like Iran and Africa. And although she isn't on the scene yet while I'm stranded on a road in Guatemala, Itchy Boots/Noraly Schoenmaker will soon become a YouTube star for her solo journeys around the world.

These stories and people intrigue and empower me; *if they can do it, why not me?* Those traveling with significant others also inspire me. I like knowing I have allies out there doing what I'm attempting to do, maybe even arguing just as much with their partners.

I savor the thought of riding alone, stopping wherever and whenever I want without having to ask. Many of my world travels before meeting Dave were solo. I'm used to being independent and blazing my own trail. During our trip prep, I even suggested to Dave that we do our own thing for a week here and there, to keep things interesting. But logistics make that harder than anticipated. If one of us has the tent, the other is forced to stay in hotels. Dave also carries all the tools. Embarrassingly, I have no clue how to service my bike.

Food is my department and specialty; I like control over what I eat, when possible. There are other ways Dave and I combine to form a team. My Spanish is limited, but knowing some of the language is an asset, especially when looking for accommodation, restaurants, or help. I'm aware of our somewhat-sexist roles, but skills allocation is necessary to get the job done.

Solo travel has advantages, but I don't want to be without Dave on this trip. I hope he feels the same. The point isn't to go find myself and prove I can survive in the world; I've been doing that for forty years. The time has come to make room for someone in my life.

Twenty minutes pass. I check the screen on my InReach again—nothing. I'm contemplating my next move when I hear a *beep, beep*. Dave rolls by and stops on the shoulder, waiting for me to get my helmet on. With a thumbs up, we ride back onto the freeway. I click the intercom.

"What happened?"

"I radioed you to say 'get in the right lane' but it wouldn't connect. Sorry, I thought you'd have enough time to see me and get over. I hate these things," he says, referring to the new headsets. "They never work when we need them."

"Well, at least the InReach came in handy."

"How so?"

"I used it to send you a message with my coordinates," I say, confused. "Didn't you use that to find me?"

"No."

"Then how did you know?"

"I turned around and came back to where I last saw you."

"But that's why we *have* these things. To message each other if we get separated."

"Huh…" Dave replies. "Well, it all worked out."

I click back to the music playing in my helmet speakers, pissed off even though everything "worked out." Dave's cavalier attitude irks me. I notice he doesn't even mention my quick thinking; some people might have totally freaked out in that situation.

Pressing the intercom button again, I say, "Why aren't you more concerned about keeping me in sight, so this kind of thing doesn't happen?"

"Heather," Dave huffs, "it's much easier for you to watch me. I'm in front. You need to stay closer behind me." I can tell that's been brewing for a while.

"You ride too fast. I'm not going to risk my life just to keep up. Are you trying to lose me?"

"Of course I'm not trying to lose you."

"Well, it feels like it some days. You're always speeding ahead, and I hate riding fast."

"I'm not even speeding. I'm going with the flow of traffic."

"You are speeding!"

"When you stop yelling, we can have a conversa—FAILURE TO CONNECT."

I want to rip the headset off the side of my helmet and run over it multiple times. Instead, I play Tool as high as the volume will go, which isn't very satisfying since the wind noise, along with my earplugs, blocks most of the music.

We find our exit into the downtown core of Guatemala City, which looks like any urban sprawler with shops, traffic, tall office buildings, and millions of people. Dave weaves in and out of traffic. I stay close behind. It's easier in places where traffic lights and stop signs give me the chance to catch up.

One lovely thing about traveling is losing sense of time. Sadly, that sometimes works against us. It's Monday—the day motorcycle dealerships almost everywhere in the world are closed.

Volcano sunrises

"I think we should relax on the schedule to Ushuaia and fit in some off-bike side trips," I suggest the next evening, keeping my tone even. "It's just as important to take care of our bodies as our bikes. We need days off. Why are we doing this trip if we blast past everything just to stop an extra hundred miles down the road? Or in the case of yesterday, rush all day to a place that's not even open?"

We're sitting in a guest house on the outskirts of Guatemala City. The owner's teenage son brings us a savory chicken-and-rice soup and sets it down on the round table. Dave picks up a napkin to smooth it over a drip running down the side of his bowl. He takes time to respond, which normally makes me anxious. I've never spent so much time with someone who doesn't keep the flow of conversation going. Arguments have started just because I say something, and Dave doesn't reply right away. But I'm learning more and more about my boyfriend each day. His silence often means he's thinking about what I've said. In the past, I've gotten confused and frustrated, wanting answers, feedback, something to let me know he's heard me. Deliberation is something I'm starting to accept and appreciate about Dave, however. When he does communicate, he takes care with his words, as though each one costs something and he wants to spend wisely. He rarely spouts out something just to make someone—or himself—feel better. I, on the other hand, have lost count of how many times I've verbalized something without thinking or calming down first, which results in escalated tension or backpedaling.

After a spoonful of soup, Dave says, "Okay, let's find a nicer place to hang out than the city and take a few days off after we get the bikes serviced tomorrow."

Relieved to see he understands this is my trip too, I spend the rest of the evening online looking for things to see and do nearby.

Antigua—an attractive, small city with Spanish colonial architecture and smoldering volcanoes—isn't far from the city, but it's a whole other world. The perfect place for some off-bike memories.

On a cobblestone street, we're stopped and checking the GPS for a hostel address, fending off dirty-faced, barefoot kids, yelling, "Gringo, give me money! Gringa, I want candy!" Although traveling can sometimes make you feel poor—in that you have only a few items and may not shower for days or weeks at a time—you're constantly reminded how rich you really are, especially when viewed through the eyes of children. Still, I don't have a lot of patience for these demanding kids in my face, even though I know it's all they know. They're rude and mean, reaching out to pinch me when I ignore them.

The rugrats retreat into the street after I give them a firm reprimand. While Dave goes back to checking the GPS, another overland motorcyclist pulls up beside us on a Triumph dual-sport loaded with gear. Ismail is on a solo trip riding through Central America and is also looking for a place to sleep. We invite him to join us in the search.

Born in Turkey, Ismail has been living in Canada for over a decade—most recently in Vancouver, BC. He left the city in November and is taking seven months to travel through Central America. I like Ismail's easygoing nature and know Dave and I can learn from his more relaxed itinerary.

"I'm a software developer," he tells us over a beer in a sunny courtyard once we're settled for the night. "I've always been envious of people doing long-distance motorcycle trips and asked myself, why can't I do this, too?"

Finding another long-distance rider is exciting and therapeutic. After more than a month on the road, Dave and I need someone to talk to besides each other. Ismail wants to stay in Antigua for a few days, so the three of us decide to do an overnight hike up the 13,000-foot Volcan Acatenangoc. After we borrow some backpacks from the hostel owner, it's suggested we find a guided group because of banditos on the mountain. This seems unnecessary to me and is likely a make-work project for locals, but we hire one anyway.

Ismail, Dave, and I meet our trekking group the next day. Our guide, Ramon, has a hard time wrangling us together. He resorts to a tyrannical approach, which doesn't work well for those of us who go to the mountains for peace. We're herded along during the seven-hour hike, with orders to stay together and not stop for long.

When we get into high camp at 11,500 feet, before we can even put up our tents and rub our sore feet, Ramon orders us to find firewood for that night's meal. I look around at the sparse forest, already raped and pillaged from past campers. I'm saddened to see branches sawed or cracked off healthy, green trees. Ramon lies down with his pack as a pillow while we go scavenging, walking half a mile back down the trail to find anything burnable. When we return with just a few scraps, Ramon isn't impressed. He pulls a collection of ramen noodle soup packages from his bag—the kind that already come in Styrofoam cups.

"*That's* for dinner?" Dave whispers. My meat-loving man is crushed. We're tired and hungry and had been told dinner was provided. We should've known when there was only one guide carrying a small backpack.

I'm glad for the extra granola bars stashed in my pack and hand one to Ismail, who's taking the whole ordeal in stride, as are most of the others. Dave and I seem to be the only ones exasperated.

After an uncomfortable night of growling stomachs, nine out of twelve of us rise at 4 a.m. for the summit. Everyone else is sick from the altitude and lack of food. They have no spare energy. Dave and I climb the steep scree path in the dark with Ismail. There's nothing to talk about that early, so we're silent, focused on our feet. Ramon has given up on keeping the group together, and we're all scattered along the treeless, zigzagging slope.

Near the summit, long-suppressed endorphins fill my body with glee. I love arriving at the top of a mountain. My whole self is centered around achievements like this. I think of how I will write of this experience on our blog and tie it into our round-the-world trip by using mountains as a metaphor—something about rocky slopes at times, a push to succeed, anger, exhaustion, a lack of resources—all to reach a head-in-the-clouds dream in the end.

Dave and I sit by a big rock and cuddle each other warm. The view from the top of Acatenango is backlit by the dawn of a vibrant sunrise, and a black volcano across the valley sticks up through the fog covering Antigua. Ismail takes summit photos of us. We return the favor. Everyone ignores Ramon's demand to turn and begin the long trek down to the trailhead. "Just a few more minutes, for god's sake," I hear someone say.

We watch Volcan de Fuego's 12,000-foot peak smoking like the tip of a triangular cigar. I glow in harmony and forgive everything: Dave's hurried riding pace, my inability to keep up—even Ramon's desensitized ignorance. I have so much to look forward to during the next two years. I want to slow it all down, yet I can't wait to turn the next corner.

I can fix that!

Central America—comprising Guatemala, Belize, El Salvador, Honduras, Nicaragua, Costa Rica, and Panama—is notorious for border-crossing sketchiness. Exorbitant bribe requests, long waits, detainment, and even kidnappings have travelers and tourists nail-biting their way through this part of the world. Capitalizing on confusion and fear, locals see a work opportunity and become "fixers."

Fixers solve problems, arrange logistics and, in some situations, carry out illicit assignments for others. They seek the out of place, the nervous, the apprehensive—and pounce. Theirs is a competitive occupation. Being the fastest fixer to approach a bumbling foreigner is the only way to make money in the game. And it is a game.

Whenever Dave and I approach border crossings, fixers run at us from all sides, dozens at a time. They're aggressive and loud, each attempting to stand out from the other. The more successful ones know a little English.

"*Señorita!* I can save you much time!"

"*Señor!* There is no bank here. You must now exchange your money with me. Best rate!"

They jog alongside us, shouting to be heard above each other, and threaten that our immigration won't go well unless we hire them. They don't touch us—an oddly polite formality in an otherwise harassing experience. Dave and I ignore them for the most part. Not all are untrustworthy, and fixers can be useful. However, we have several countries to travel through over the next two years, and it's in our best interest to be self-sufficient.

Although I think he might not like our faster pace, Ismail continues to travel with us from Antigua. He says he likes riding with others because he doesn't have to worry about leaving his bike unattended at border crossings. If I rode alone, I'd pay a fixer to watch over my things.

Una más

El Salvador/Honduras

Two days after leaving Guatemala, Dave, Ismail, and I are at the border between El Salvador and Honduras. I wish we could give these Central American countries more time, but the sweltering heat keeps us running southward.

So far, crossing any border in Central America takes two to four hours. Dave and I have a system: Because I speak some Spanish, he stays with the bikes and I deal with logistics. We always try to cross in the morning so we have all day if something goes awry. It's key to have plenty of water and snacks, as well.

Dave's settled in under the shade of a balsa tree with an ice-cold Fanta he bought from a woman selling drinks from a cooler. Ismail and I go inside the *aduana* (customs) building on the El Salvadorian side. The only consistent thing about border crossings in Central America is how different they are: a smattering of buildings without signs or directions; a good deal of time figuring out which one needs what paperwork; and never, never, enough photocopies of our documents, no matter how well we prepare.

It's my turn, and I walk up to the custom agent's window for exit stamps out of the country in both passports. Afterward, I stride with purpose to keep the fixers away—even though I have no idea where I'm going—and find something that resembles a vehicle import office. Here, our temporary permits for the bikes are canceled. The permits are obtained on entry to each country as proof we aren't importing the bikes to sell. They need to be stamped out, just like us, and involve photocopies of passports, licenses, bike registration, and titles. I've already run out of copies, so I hoof across the street to a small shack beside an archaic copier plugged into an extension cord. Ten copies cost me ten dollars, but now I have extras.

Ismail finds us back at the bikes. Together, the three of us ride the few miles between El Salvador and Honduras through "no-man's land." This is something new to me; at home, you cross one border and are immediately in the next country. But since leaving Mexico, we've encountered large gaps between countries. It's confusing. What if we have an accident or mechanical issue? We're no longer admissible in the country we've just exited. Yet the new country hasn't received us yet. Whose land is it?

At *aduana* on the Honduras side, I pay six dollars for some suspicious "admin" fee. The cashier takes my American ten-dollar bill, disappears around a corner, then returns with a five. Holding it up, she says, *"Una más."*

Oh, you clever little thing. But I'm not the sleepy tourist you're hoping for. I gave her a ten, not a five, and I remind her of that. She quickly gives in and hands me my change without making eye contact.

Before crossings, I try to find updated information on travel blogs or government sites stating what things like travel visas and other border fees should cost. I want to have enough cash and avoid scams. I read a recent post on a trustworthy website saying the fee to import a vehicle into Honduras is thirty dollars and can be paid at a nearby bank.

Overnight, the cost has magically increased to forty dollars.

"Is this a scam?" I ask the customs agent flat out. Behind me, Ismail laugh-coughs.

The officer pretends to shuffle paperwork, assuring me the cost has always been forty dollars.

The convenient bank is inconveniently closed, according to the agent, who likely has a money exchanger friend waiting outside.

"Can you show me a receipt from another foreign vehicle please?"

"No receipts."

I look at his dark mustache. The more I dig my heels in, the angrier the furry mouth decoration becomes, twitching like an electrocuted caterpillar. Ismail and I walk back to the bikes without paying. The three of us try to come up with a plan. Pooling our money, we have enough for just two out of three bikes. Cash is always a problem; we don't want too much because borders aren't the best places to exchange money, usually giving crap rates. Yet if we don't have enough, we end up in a situation like this.

The closest operating bank is back in El Salvador. Dave offers to go, but that will mean re-immigrating and re-importing his bike, then undoing it all again on his way out. That already took two hours in one direction the first time. If one of us immigrates into Honduras, we need to do the same thing to get the money back to the two who stay behind. Also, there's no way to know how far the next bank is on the Honduras side. No one wants to give us any info, especially not the fixers, who are hoping to profit from our compromised position.

With growing impatience, Dave says he'll enter Honduras, find a bank, then try to pass us the money through the gate.

"Ummm, no," I say, my mind already flashing to images of guns pointed at my boyfriend's head. "What we need is a Good Samaritan."

I've been watching a lone, brown-haired male wearing a large backpack. He's waiting in line. Fixers circle him like flies on meat.

I walk over to him. "Hi, do you speak English?"

He hesitates before answering. "Yes."

"Great, I'm wondering if you can help us? We're thirty dollars short to cross into Honduras. By any chance would you have enough cash on you to get yourself and one of us through the border? We will repay you." It's a long shot, but I'm hoping to cash in on some good karma.

The young man watches me intently. "Sorry, can you please repeat?"

I detect an accent but also notice something else; his speech is monotone and without enunciation. The man is hearing-impaired. I smile and repeat my question, slower and more to the point.

"I'm Heather, by the way." I stick out my hand.

"I'm Jan—deaf adventurer!" he says with a happy grin. "I can help, yes."

While Jan discreetly checks his wallet, I learn he's from Czechia. After graduating from university, he decided that working eleven months a year in exchange for one month of freedom wasn't for him. Jan has been hitchhiking around Central America and has no plans of stopping his travels any time soon.

"You will pay me back sometime?" Jan gives me the money. In Central America, a savvy traveler could live for a week or more off thirty dollars.

"I promise I will repay you in the next town where there is a bank. How will I find you?"

"Please email it to me." He hands me a business card with his information. I give him our card, as well.

"You can harass us on social media if I don't pay you." I laugh.

With a wave, Jan is on his way through a different lineup. Paying the angry customs officer our forty dollars each—from which I imagine him peeling off three extra tens for himself—we're at last admitted into Honduras.

Before we can continue, our motorcycles are fumigated—another common thing we're finding as we move south. A woman—unprotected from the fumes and wearing just sandals and shorts—douses our bikes in a fine spray. I hope the chemicals won't find their way into the food in my pannier or destroy anything that isn't metal, like seats and baggage.

When we find accommodation that night, I get online to send Jan his money. In the end, I send him cash in the mail due to foreign bank account issues. I email him with an update, hoping it doesn't seem like a cop-out. Six weeks later, he informs me that his mom picked up his mail, that he got the money and is still happily hitchhiking around Central America.

Dave and I are never sure whether that border crossing counted as paying a bribe. Buying someone off is an easy way out of a jam or harassment, but it also escalates corruption. We agreed to follow the same principals we used with fixers and avoid using anything as a crutch. That includes not falling for bribe payments.

The roads may be lawless, but the cops aren't

Nicaragua

Something else we're newly on the lookout for are fake road fines handed out by shady policemen. We're flagged down by cops almost daily now. Mostly they accuse us of speeding and want money. The first two times we stop, but when they can't prove our speed through a radar gun or otherwise, we keep going. These officers are perhaps new recruits with the shittier jobs—a stakeout behind trees or other obstacles without expensive luxuries like patrol vehicles or radios. In time, Dave and I learn we can ignore them by waving, smiling, and feigning ignorance. No one ever chases us.

Leaving Granada, Nicaragua, one afternoon, we say goodbye to Ismail. He'll continue east, and we're heading south. We miss our friendly traveling companion, but that's the nature of our trip: hellos and goodbyes.

Riding up a hill on the main highway, I admire Ometepe Island to my left and its twin volcanoes jutting from Lake Nicaragua. Bringing my eyes back to the road, I see Dave's brake lights as he slows for an overloaded garbage truck farting out thick, black fumes. Until then, I was breathing in the sweet smell of pink trumpet trees lining the highway on both sides. Now, I choke on toxic diesel fumes and rotting meat.

As we've done many times before when coming up on a slow or stinky vehicle, we pass. More than two months into our travels, Dave and I are road wizened to the local ways. Rule number one: It's not against the rules if you can get away with it. Drivers pass anywhere they dare. They speed or drive as slowly as they want. Kids on bicycles hold onto the back of trucks going uphill, and some even drive cars underage. It's so far removed from the order of home, we start to appreciate the freedom.

Feeling lawless, Dave and I pass the crawling garbage truck on a double solid line. Before we're even back in our lane, a policeman comes out from behind a tree and waves us down. This time, we're definitely in the wrong and pull over. The officer struts over to Dave, his chest expanding inside his tidy, beige uniform. He spits out something in Spanish.

"No entiendo," Dave says and points behind him to where I'm trying to balance my heavy load on one toe. The frustrated officer walks over to me. With full-face helmets and riding gear covering every inch, Dave and I look like two men. I ride with my medium-long hair in a braid down my back, and it's not easy to detect my gender until up close. I take joy in watching the officer's reaction when I remove my helmet. Women are mostly just passengers on motorcycles in this part of the world, and the bikes are much smaller 125cc engines compared to my 650.

The self-important cop tucks away his surprise while asking for my ID.

Before leaving home, we made copies of our licenses and had them laminated. A common scam is for corrupt officials to ask for documents then not give them back until a bribe is paid. We keep the copies in our jacket pockets and the originals hidden so we can leave the disposables behind and ride away if needed.

Handing over my laminated copy, I wonder if the first thing the cop will do is check the gender category, just to be sure. Some days, I want to do the same, feeling anything but female while muscling my bike around like an ape and wearing the same grimy riding suit day after day.

I'm dismayed when Dave gives the other officer his real license. Mine is from British Columbia, and Dave's is from Washington state. The two IDs don't look the same and risk tipping off the officer. Although we've committed a road violation, I'm sure we'll still be viewed as large fish to reel in for extra cash. Our only escape is to let the officer keep the cards and ride away, but now Dave's real ID is in his hands.

He's going to keep our licenses, he tells me, until one of us returns to Granada to pay the traffic fine at a bank. I mention it's illegal to ride without a license, so can we please have them back.

"I think we should just do as they say, Heather," Dave's voice is a warning inside my helmet.

The paper fine in my hand looks official, though I don't see an amount. I offer to ride back into the city while Dave stays behind so we can keep an eye on our IDs. Before I leave, I ask how long the cop will be there.

"Una hora más."

I have one hour to ride fifteen miles back into Granada, find a bank, stand in line, fumble my way through Spanish, then ride back out. I briefly worry whether Dave will still be there on my return or whether he'll get dragged to another stakeout location I won't know how to find. I zip the tickets into my tank bag and ride off, shaking my head. *So, it's illegal to cross a double solid line but okay to ride without a license.* I check my speedometer. How ironic it would be if I get pulled over for going too fast. I guess I could pull out my international driver's license, which I have yet to use.

I find a bank and present the tickets to the teller, who writes down the amount and hands it to me: 1,215 Nicaraguan *córdobas*, or thirty-six dollars. At home, the infraction would have cost four times that. I ask for a receipt and ride back to Dave in well under an hour. He's sitting under a tree, keeping out of the sun as usual—my melting adventure partner.

Sloths & monkeys

Costa Rica

Costa Rica is out of place in most of Central America, as though pulled from somewhere prettier, like Spain or Portugal, and dropped into this sketchier part of the world for added class and sophistication.

After riding through the humidity and smoldering garbage piles of El Salvador and Honduras, CR is like stepping out of a meat locker into a greenhouse—the whole country smells like flowers. The humidity is still intense, but the sweat on my face and body feels more like the cleansing mist from a spa. In the northern regions of Central America, our towels still had dark spots on them after showering—residue from riding behind vehicles spewing exhaust. Not in CR, where things are more regulated. Here, we drink from the taps, just like at home, and I don't have to wet my toothbrush with bottled water or keep my mouth closed in the shower.

"Mmmmm…" Murmuring like a drunk, I stick my nose in every bud and blossom popping from the thriving foliage. "This one smells like cotton candy," I call over to Dave, "but not in a synthetic way. I think it's frangipani."

"Who's Frangi, and what about her panties?" Dave rocks in a hammock, one arm behind his head.

That night's campground is a sanctuary. A family lives on the premises in a modest house with a manicured lawn. In the front yard, an open, yurt-shaped building, outdoor kitchen with tables, chairs, and even a barbecue, are all for campers to use. The roof provides shelter from the sun and from the torrential afternoon downpours common in the tropics. Colorful hammocks hang from posts, and the surroundings infuse me with much-needed calm.

A little girl of maybe six comes out of the house wearing a pink-and-purple sundress with spaghetti straps. Her dark hair is piled on the top of her head, and loose strands stick to the back of her neck. She already has the pose and style of a Latin American beauty. Offering me a shy smile, she sits on the step and throws chunks of bread onto the lawn. I wait, curious what will come out to eat. Soon, a cluster of orange baby monkeys—small like kittens and with tails already a foot long—bubble out of the shrubbery and skip over to her. They sit on their haunches and eat the white bread with their hands. Or are they paws? I've always enjoyed the human-like movements of monkeys.

When evening comes, the rainforest takes things up a notch, chirping, trilling, and tweeting with insects and animals I wish I could see. The monkeys become more rambunctious, racing around the campground and squawking like overexcited kids before bedtime. Dave and I swing in the hammocks, lacking the energy to start dinner.

Everywhere we stay in Costa Rica is a lesson in biodiversity. Our accommodation, although paid for, feels like we're camping in the wild. Together with the monkeys, we sleep alongside iguanas and sloths. The trees are filled with lyrical birds and creatures singing us into sleep—and then awake the next day. I'm surprised we haven't seen many snakes, spiders, or other insects since entering Mexico and Central America. Especially since we camp so much. But we find nothing when we shake out our riding boots every morning.

Panama City is just a few hundred miles away when we stop for lunch at a modest Costa Rican restaurant with *ceviche* on the menu. Tall fans stand in four corners of the patio, providing a breeze, but it's warm. We order my new favorite meal with shrimp and homemade tortilla chips. Dave grabs some wafer-thin paper towels to wipe the sweat off his brow.

"Why are napkins in the developing world like tissue paper? I need to use like forty of them."

He's removed his riding boots and jacket and has every zipper open for airflow through his gear. I take off my boots, as well. My socks are soaked. I have no idea if they're wet from sweat or an hour ago when I dumped half a gallon of water over my head. Probably both.

I watch Dave scratch his lower legs until they bleed.

"Maybe we should reconsider riding through Africa," I say, thinking of what his rash might look like after four months in a place that could be even hotter than here.

"Yeah, maybe." Dave peels up his shirt to mop his face. Futile. "I can't wait until we get farther south."

Parts of Patagonia are at a higher altitude and will give some reprieve from the heat, but we're still thousands of miles away. It's now the first week of February. Although we want to be in Argentina within the next six weeks to beat the Southern Hemisphere's winter, we still have Colombia, Ecuador, Peru, Bolivia, and Chile. We haven't even crossed into South America yet.

Our conversation shifts to a more immediate issue—getting our bikes across the Darién Gap. The "Gap" connects North and South America, but that's a loose adjective for this roadless bisection of the Pan-American Highway. Thick jungle, dangerous fauna, political violence, and drug runners make up the lawless wilderness spanning over sixty miles between Panama and Colombia. Few dare to cross, but some have—even by motorcycle.

That's not quite the adventure Dave and I are after. We look into taking the *Stahlratte*—a sailboat that allows passengers and can fit a handful of motorcycles on board. But February is not ideal for sailing, and the *Stahlratte* is moored elsewhere in calmer waters.

We think about organizing a container ship with other travelers who have vehicles. These folks can usually be found on social media and travel websites. But without our bikes and most of our gear for the weeklong sailing, costs will add up in hotels and cab fares while we wait.

The only option left is to fly.

Goodbye, Central America

Panama

A fast eighteen days after crossing into Central America, we're at its end in blustery, bustling Panama City. The acrid smells are back. Combusted diesel fumes cake our white helmets gray while plastic burns in roadside garbage fires, along with food scraps and whatever else humans have discarded. Either there's no garbage pickup in place, or the filth exceeds the sanitation resources, forcing people to set everything ablaze or live in it.

Panama City does have a first-world feel, however, with classy skyscrapers and plenty of high-end restaurants.

After crossing over the gusty Bridge of the Americas spanning the Pacific entrance of the Panama Canal, we find a hotel with underground parking. We shower and hail a cab to the airport, hoping to find an airline that will transport our motorcycles to Bogotá, Colombia, as soon as possible—our hotel is expensive, and so is eating out. The mission pays off when we locate a cargo office willing to load the bikes on a flight leaving the next day. Back at the hotel, we collect any gear we don't want to carry onto our flight and ride to the hangar's address.

Dave rolls each bike onto a wooden pallet with help from the cargo crew, who then lash everything down with thick ratchet straps. As a test, we shove the bikes from either side. They don't budge an inch. One crew member starts up a forklift and scoops Dave's bike to position it for loading the next day. I hold my breath, expecting to hear a *crack* when the pallet gives way, but everything stays intact. Watching the Stallion, I feel more confident.

The concept of motorcycles on airplanes seems inconceivable to me, but a medium cargo aircraft can carry up to forty tons, so the extra thousand pounds of two bikes is nothing. The whole process is exciting and nerve-racking. It's the first time since leaving the US that we'll be without our bikes, which have been our home, transportation, and travel companions. But I'm relieved the logistics for getting to South America are over.

That relief is short-lived, however, when we can't pay the $2,000 invoice with a credit card and have less than twenty-four hours to come up with the cash.

Before leaving home, Dave and I arranged for maximum foreign ATM withdrawals at our banks, but we didn't realize other countries would have much lower daily withdrawal limits. In Panama City, the most we can take out per day per card is $300. Since we both have a debit and credit card, we're able to amass $600 each, but that's not two grand. After some negotiating, the shipping company agrees we can pay the remainder when we land in Bogotá, since they have offices in both Panama and Colombia. I don't know if we'll find a bank on landing, but with travel, it's one day—or problem—at a time.

Just get lost

Colombia

Above the city of Bogotá, on a dark, quiet road that was supposed to be a well-lit street in the La Candelaria district, Garmin says, "You have arrived at your destination."

Either I gave Dave the wrong coordinates for our Airbnb, or the GPS is lost and making shit up. We're most certainly not at our destination. I dismount and look around. A man nearby makes his presence known by lighting a cigarette, which blends with the city lights in the distance. He's a security guard standing at the bottom of a steep cobblestone driveway. I lift my hand and he waves. Forcing a smile on my tired face, I leave Dave agonizing over technology and approach the man.

"¡Hola! ¿Tienes un teléfono?" If he has a cell phone with data, we might be able to access the message from our Airbnb host. Since we've just landed and gotten the bikes through customs, Dave hasn't yet bought a SIM card for his phone.

"No, pero arriba…" The man points up the driveway, telling me there's a restaurant above. The street is dark and dismal; what could possibly be up there? I tell Dave I'm going to look for help then clomp up the almost-vertical driveway in my boots. I think of how this would look at home, my boyfriend letting me walk up a dark driveway to…what? But I have a feeling it's all safe, and something is pulling me. I trust my gut.

Sweat is running down my sides when I get to the top and discover a new world. The three-story restaurant is designed in a modern wood-and-thatch combination. Soft amber lights make the place glow like a campfire. Inside through the floor-to-ceiling windows, I see the hairstyled heads of diners all the way down to their expensive shoes. Valets park and retrieve cars for Bogotá's elite eaters while I walk across the large lot to see the view. Before, the city just looked like burning cigarettes. Now, I see diamonds dropped in a phosphorescent sea. I'm spellbound and out of place in my riding pants and sweat-soaked T-shirt. How the hell does anyone find this place? Only those in the know must come here, yet we'd stumbled upon it by accident; something so out of context from the street below and far from any trendy areas in the city where such a restaurant might seem more suited.

A sign beside the double front doors reads TRAMONTI. The sexy, Italian-sounding name piques my curiosity, and I roll the word off my tongue, holding the door open for a young couple leaving. She is dark haired and wearing a red dress that wraps attractively around her small waist. Her stilettos would be problematic on the driveway I just hiked up. The man, also dark haired, has on a suit the color of brushed nickel. When he breezes by, I catch the scent of lemongrass and cloves. The beautiful people pass me without a glance. I have a strong urge to be sitting at one of the dimly lit tables, dressed like that couple—minus the heels—and gazing into Dave's eyes.

Inside the front door, a young woman greets me with a smile. She's behind a host stand and asks if I want a table for one. I laugh and gesture to my clothes, but she shrugs as if to say, "So you're a little dirty…who cares?" I inquire about Wi-Fi. *"Estamos perdidos,"* I say, telling her we're lost.

"Momento." Holding up a red-lacquered nail, she dashes off. Her shoes—also heels—make a pleasant tapping sound as she walks upstairs to the dining area. How do women tolerate standing jobs in footwear like that?

I admire the room. A coat check in a corner of the lobby is styled like a wealthy person's living room, with leather chairs and huge windows overlooking the view. I want to sit down, but there's probably chain oil on my pants, or something worse.

"¡Hola, señorita!"

A handsome older man comes over to me, dressed in a sharp gray suit and shiny black shoes. Is everybody just gorgeous in Colombia? He extends his hand to me with a toothpaste-commercial smile.

"Please, my name is Antonio. I am the manager. You are lost?" He looks concerned.

"Yes, thank you," I smile back, hoping there are no bugs in my teeth. "Would it be possible to access Google Maps? I have this address…" Antonio brings the paper over to the computer near the host.

"Where are you from?"

"Canada." I tell him I'm on a motorcycle, trusting that will explain my attire.

"And you are alone?"

Oh my god. Dave! How long have I been up here acting like Alice in Wonderland? I've been taken to another world; a world where I almost forgot I had a Dave.

"I should probably go get my boyfriend," I laugh.

Loping down the driveway, I find a solemn-looking Dave standing by our bikes.

"You have to see this place," I pant, not giving him a chance to ask why I took so long. "Come on."

We reposition our bikes for the steep driveway and get off the pitch-black road. I stand on my foot pegs to keep balanced going up to the parking lot. At the top, I can see Dave's also surprised the restaurant exists off the unassuming side street.

Antonio and the hostess are working to find our destination, which we learn is clear across the city. Antonio calls the Airbnb host, Santiago, and after a short conversation, announces Santiago is sending over a taxi.

"But we have our motorcycles," I remind him.

"No, no, you follow the taxi!" Antonio says. "He will take you right there."

Following lead vehicles instead of just giving directions is common in the lower Americas. One day, while lost in Guadalajara, Mexico, we asked a couple for directions and they told us to follow them in their car, ensuring we got where we needed to go. People are proud of their countries and want us to have the best experience possible.

Antonio waves a hand in the air. "Please, sit, sit!" He gestures to the expensive-looking chairs.

"Oh, our pants are pretty dirty," I say.

"No problem. Please sit. Wait! What would you like to drink?"

"Just water would be great, thank you," Dave says.

"No, but that's boring!" Antonio quips, erasing months of my hard work in getting my boyfriend to hydrate more. "How about a gin and tonic—a light one, yes? The taxi will take an hour or longer."

Antonio leaves, not waiting for an answer, and Dave and I sink into the chairs.

"It's like sitting on lightly roasted marshmallows," I sigh, thinking of the turn of events. Four hours ago, we were still in Panama City about to board an airplane. Now, we're drinking G&Ts in leather chairs overlooking Bogotá. We should get lost more often.

"Please forgive me," Antonio says, "I must attend to a matter in the kitchen. However, I do hope you are in Bogotá long enough to come for dinner some night?"

I almost spit out my G&T. This place would easily blow our budget of one hundred dollars a day. And what would I wear, anyway?

When the cab arrives, we follow it into the city. Tailing someone who knows where they're going is nice for me, but even better for Dave, who doesn't need to consult the GPS at every fork in the road.

The La Candelaria district is a cultural hotspot. Colonial-era buildings have been turned into stores selling sophisticated art, and the homes are chic with neoclassical design. Santiago is waiting outside his three-story walk-up on a narrow stone-paved street. I'm disappointed to hear loud music and see a large group of people laughing and drinking inside his house. It's almost midnight. I'm overtired and desperate for a bed. Santiago hands over some bills to pay the taxi driver, thanking him. Dave and I also thank the driver and Santiago. There is a lot of *gracias*-ing going on.

Larger cities are often challenging for secure overnight bike storage. Hotels usually have parking lots behind gates or underground, but those are the more expensive options. We're never okay with leaving our bikes on the street—not so much because they might get stolen, but because the open nature of motorcycles makes them inviting to touch and sit on. We don't want someone to get hurt or find our bikes fallen over the next morning.

With no street parking and room for only one bike in Santiago's hallway, he asks a security guard at the end of the street if I can park the Stallion beside his cubicle overnight. The guard agrees. Again, I'm nervous leaving it out of my sight—even with an armed guard—but my bike is older and less flashy than Dave's. Still, the farther it takes me, the more valuable it becomes.

Dave covers Santiago's front steps with a wide piece of wood, making a ramp, then pushes his bike inside. Squeezing by people, we mutter *"Perdón, excusa..."* when we bump into them with our bags. On the third floor, Santiago leads us to our room, which I'm happy to hear cuts the noise from the party. We talk to our host about his plans for the large apartment, currently in various stages of remodel. This twenty-something college kid with a good head on his shoulders—and maybe a wealthy family—is turning the first floor into a bar/restaurant. The rest of the house will be partitioned off as an Airbnb and a place for him to live. Santiago invites us downstairs to party, but we're feeling every one of our forty-plus years and say goodnight.

I fall asleep right away, even though we're on sheets that have rested a few bodies between launderings. By this point in the trip, unwashed bedding rarely deters us, and we aren't very clean ourselves anyway. Hopefully there's room in Santiago's budget for a future housekeeper.

Dave surprises me the following day by saying we're going back to *Tramonti* for dinner.

"Are you serious? But why?"

"Because it's Valentine's Day."

Dave isn't big on celebrating such occasions, or even remembering them, so I'm touched by his consideration. I've totally forgotten today is February 14, which is unlike me. I love any excuse to dress up and go out for a nice dinner. The problem is the only glam I can pull from my panniers is a pink, purple, and gray scarf, which I drape loosely over one of two T-shirts I've packed. Since we're riding two-up on Dave's bike, my sundress is out of the question. Bare flesh and motorcycles don't mix in my world.

The dining room is just as enticing as I imagined and exudes warmth and class. Our table is covered in rose petals. I recall telling friends when I was single that flowers and other cheesy romantic gestures weren't for me. But falling in love has softened me, and I like all that "corny" stuff now. The old me was just putting on a facade, acting tough. I'm not sure now why I felt I needed to do that.

Antonio is excited to see us again and brings over a bottle of Colombian red wine. When we mention the rose petals are a nice touch for Valentine's Day, he tells us that Colombians call it *Dia del Amor y la Amistad*, or Day of Love and Friendship.

"For people to show appreciation for their friends, too," he says. "Not all here tonight are lovers."

I adore my friends and the idea of an official day of friendship. But that night in Colombia, I'm happy to just look into my boyfriend's eyes and toast our accomplishments together.

As we make our way south toward Ecuador, the mountainous Colombian roads switch between dirt and pavement for no apparent reason, eventually taking us to 11,000 feet, where cacti grow and where temps are desert hot at 102°F.

The following day, the topography changes, and we sweep the bikes around corners that are corkscrew tight, as if we're doing U-turns at every bend. Jungle-like rock walls covered in dripping plants cool me as I pass by. Camping that night, I watch clouds race between tree-topped peaks. That evening, I cook dinner in my down jacket when the temperature drops and pours buckets of rain I hope will stop by morning.

Placing color images in this book was cost-prohibitive, so my solution is to bring you our travel photos digitally. To see color images for each country, scan the QR code or visit Photos under Riding Full Circle on my website, heatherleawriter.com.

A tank bag full of pudding

Ecuador

At last, the Andes appear, along with sweet-smelling, high-altitude air—a pleasing contrast to the stinking, sweltering days of Central America. At over 5,500 miles long, the Andes start in Venezuela and curve like vertebrae down the Pacific coast to the southern tip of Chile.

We're hoping to camp near Vulcan Cotopaxi, Ecuador's second highest peak at 19,347 feet. Our steeds sniff out a dirt road and up we go, passing through small rural communities where men dress in dark blue ponchos, knickers, and felt hats. The traditional theme for women is a dark blue skirt worn with a white, embroidered blouse. Colorful shawls and jewelry wrap up the ensemble.

Before climbing higher into the mountains, we need groceries. I've learned how to find food supplies in small towns and villages—no easy task since most of the stores don't have signs. A small, white building ahead has its doors open to the street, and when I ride closer, I see canned goods on shelves inside. Dave stays with the bikes, and a handful of kids soon gather around him. They cover up giggles with brown hands when Dave takes off his full-face helmet and waves. They probably think we look funny, like we're dressed for space.

Inside the two-hundred-square-foot *tienda*, an elderly man stocks shelves behind an ancient cash register. An older lady I assume is his wife grins a wide, gap-toothed smile when I come through the door. Foreigners often overlook these mom-and-pop stores, which usually have the best food around. More and more modern grocery stores are popping up and extending outside the city limits. Corporations know visitors want convenience and the refrigerated perishables we're used to. I prefer finding a genuine home-cooked meal when possible, and we don't often regret the choice.

The old woman pours something thick into a cup, then hands it to me to try. *Morocho* is a popular comfort beverage in the Andes made from cracked corn, milk, cinnamon, sugar, and raisins.

"Gracias." I drink the delicious, sweet pudding and look around the small space for items that will travel well over rough roads. I smell something else that gets my mouth watering and hope for fresh, hot *empanadas*. Dave and I love the savory, doughy turnovers packed with meat, onion, and spices. Even if we don't know the exact protein used, it's likely far less jacked up with hormones and antibiotics than meat at home.

I ask the nice lady if she sells *empanadas*. She nods and disappears through a curtain behind the cash register. Dave comes in to partake in the culinary delights of the village kitchen. When the *señora* returns, she hands me a plastic bag that holds something heavy. Heat soaks into my hands, and I peek inside to find the pudding drink in a to-go tub shaped like a yogurt container. Not *empanadas*. She may speak *Quechua*—the Indigenous language of the highlands—and didn't understand my Spanish. *Oh well.*

Although delicious, *morocho* isn't the salty, hearty meal I'm craving for dinner. And where to store the precious, precarious container while I bounce along a mountain road to Cotopaxi? Not wanting to insult her, I accept the bagged drink, then buy some pasta, red sauce, cheese, crackers, and Chips Ahoy! cookies. How American-made brands make it somewhere like here, I have no idea.

At the counter, the old woman places a small baggie down beside my items, looking at me with a question.

"No, gracias," I say, turning down the coca leaves. I tried the plant twenty years ago, when I was in Peru for a climbing expedition. Chewing coca leaves is said to enhance physical performance, curb your appetite, and ward off altitude sickness. The plant is also used in the making of cocaine. In its natural form, coca leaves provide a harmless stimulant, much like drinking coffee. I didn't notice any difference when I chewed the leaves, though many high-altitude climbers swear by the practice. I doubt Dave wants to try the leaves, since it's like chewing dehydrated kale.

I want to ask the old couple how often foreigners come into their store, but I don't know any words in *Quechua*. How much richer our experiences would be if we could speak all languages.

I try to find a place for the *morocho*, which will be perfect for tomorrow's breakfast. By now, Dave and I have our luggage system figured out. Although his bags are generally heavier than mine, he has the advantage of unchanging contents and is always organized, whereas my panniers need to be rearranged as we buy and consume groceries. I'm often loaded down with canned and dried goods, wine—even meat, if it isn't too hot outside. It's hard getting used to how my bike handles with the constant weight flux, and I'm always forgetting where I put things. The fussing around annoys us both, but there isn't much I can do about it.

The only option for the pudding is inside my tank bag, which has firm sides. Removing my camera and a few granola bars, I position the warm tub inside. For several miles, I avoid bumps—not an easy task on Andean roads.

An ideal camping spot appears in a large depression off-road, where we're hidden but can also enjoy the view. Dave and I have a rule to stay inconspicuous when possible, whether or not we think the area is safe.

Our backdrop is the snow-covered cone of Cotopaxi poking high into a cerulean sky. I spend an hour taking photos of our bikes at different angles, like they're supermodels—which to me, they are. With fuel-injected engines, our rides perform well even at altitude. A few days ago, we'd put the "high" in highway, reaching a personal record riding to 13,851 feet without a single sputter from the engines. Our bodies, on the other hand, feel the lack of oxygen. Any exertion beyond sitting leaves me out of breath. We also reached another less enjoyable trip record earlier in the week, riding in wind chill temperatures down to 39°F. I tried to recall the miserable heat of just a few weeks back, but the mind game did little to warm me up.

The *morocho* container is unscathed. After pulling out dinner supplies, I grab the water filter and wander to a nearby stream, where the late afternoon sun warms my shoulders. A surge of happiness hits me. What an incredible place to spend the night. I want to stay longer and wish we had time to climb the volcano.

We're behind Cotopaxi and will soon lose the sun, even though it's only 4:30 p.m. Peru was the first foreign country I traveled to when I was in my early twenties. I remember being confused that it got dark around 6 p.m., due to the sun setting faster at the equator and slower near the poles. Maybe I'd been taught that in school, but I was not the best student at times. We'd recently crossed the equator when we left Quito to come to Cotopaxi National Park.

My mood immediately lifts when we find places like this; camping deepens the true intent of our trip. Dave seems content here, as well. We use an app called iOverlander that helps travelers find camping, hotels, restaurants, and other amenities, all over the world. Wild camping is something we hope to do often on this trip—not only because it's no cost, but for a more genuine experience. Finding something discreet, level, accessible, and not on private land, however, has so far been harder than we thought.

Before crawling into the tent, I photograph some llamas roaming the *altiplano* in front of Cotopaxi. I love these slower days and ache for them when it seems we're just clocking miles from one destination to the next.

Flippers, flamingoes & the mother of all sunburns

After a week of quiet, scenic riding, pulling into horn-honking Guayaquil is an assault on the senses, and I'm yearning for an off-bike adventure somewhere quieter. We've been clipping along for several weeks now, and I'm hoping to sway Dave toward a trip into the Galapagos Islands.

Through my cousin, Kari, we already have a connection in the city. While volunteering with the Civil Defense during El Niño in the '90s, Kari stayed with an Ecuadorian host family. She became lifelong friends with their daughter, Lula. Lucky for us, Lula and her six-year-old daughter, Flavia, have room in her apartment, and she extends an invitation.

Showered and lying in the comfortable guest bed, I broach the idea to Dave about the Galapagos.

"We're as close as we'll ever be. When will we have another chance like this?"

I expect resistance due to our timeframe for Ushuaia, but Dave agrees to go. We have a safe, free place to store the bikes, and the stars are aligned. Island-hopping isn't something Dave seeks out, and I appreciate him yielding to the expensive side trip.

Our flights don't leave for a few days, so we have some time to explore Guayaquil with Lula and her welcoming family. An afternoon is spent at her sister's tucking into an incredible meat feast, barbecued in an elaborate outdoor kitchen. To his dismay, Dave misses out because of a stomach bug.

Three days later, Lula drops us off at the airport, where we board a flight for Santa Cruz, the main Galapagos Island from which most boat tours start.

The Galapagos are a series of volcanic islands crossing the equator, famous for gorgeous, clear waters and a striking number of endemic species, including penguins, flamingoes, land iguanas, blue-footed boo-bies, and flightless cormorants.

I'm excited for the detour. When I traveled to South America in my twenties, I couldn't afford the Galapagos. Heck, it was hard to afford now, twenty years later, at $1,000 each for five days on the islands. But from what I'd heard, it would be worth the cost.

"Use your flippers!" I yell over my laughter. "Swim!"

Dave is thrashing about in the water, trying to stay afloat. He's just taken on a large gulp of the ocean through his snorkel and is coughing up saltwater through the breathing tube, like a whale spraying from its blowhole.

I've never seen Dave so anxious. That I find it funny—at least in this case—means I'll surely burn in hell. The tour boat has just dropped us offshore from Santa Fe Island and is a mere ten feet away, with the guide keeping a watchful eye on Dave, ready for a rescue.

Until now, Dave has exuded nothing but utter confidence in almost everything I've seen him do—especially in outdoor sports. I'm surprised snorkeling is the one thing that shatters that self-assurance. He grew up in BC on Quadra Island but has never been much of a water guy.

I reel in my giggles and help him get back to the boat, where he stays, arms crossed, for the rest of the day.

It's the first time snorkeling for us both. I love it. Nothing feels more peaceful and relaxing than floating in the warm, bath-like sea, using my underwater camera to capture the yellow tailed surgeonfish, rainbow basslet, and Galapagos clingfish. A few feet below, a giant tortoise breast-strokes inches above white, swirling sand. Our guide tells us the turtle is over 100 years old. How has life changed for this centenarian? Does she notice a difference in the ocean's temperature? More garbage drifting through her home?

I don't want to leave, but our boat is heading back to Santa Cruz.

To save money, Dave and I stay on the main island each night. After filling ourselves with prawn *ceviche*, we wander the busy, tourist-filled streets looking for last-minute budget trips to nearby islands. Though for the first three days we have had several excellent tours and guides who are informative and respectful of the fragile ecosystem, the cheaper excursions catch up to us on our fourth day.

We start out jettisoning across the open water from Santa Cruz over to Isla Isabella. The boat holds twenty people and is at capacity, with wooden planks bolted bench-style to the floor. Each time we crest a wave and crash down the other side, I fear the contents of my digesting breakfast are about to make an appearance. The seas are rough, and providing comfort is not in the captain's job description. Dave and I are the only white people on the boat, and it's clear we will not be catered to. We paid for an English-speaking tour, but our guide speaks only Spanish. For whatever reason, the rest of the participants seem unfriendly toward us, too.

Landing on Isla Isabella, I cringe when the guide tramples over some native succulents while walking backward and talking. When she laughs along with another tourist who—by accident—crushes a turtle egg, which the mother is frantically trying to protect, I'm heartbroken and disgusted. I try not to let this one experience taint the whole Galapagos holiday, but my mood is waning. Dave is so uncomfortable in the hundred-degree heat, he spends most of the time looking for shade.

The day rewards us, however, with non-human interactions. On an island covered in lava rock and inhabited only by sea life, we find flamingos, sea turtles, white tip sharks, penguins, dolphins, manta rays, and many iguanas. Trailing behind to photograph some blue-footed boobies, Dave and I notice the boat filling up. No one has told us we're leaving, and we almost get left behind. By the time we get to the boat, all the good seats are taken, so we sit backward. For the next two hours, I throw up over the side of the boat while Dave rubs my back, nauseous himself.

The main island is far busier and more catered toward tourists than I imagined the Galapagos to be. In hindsight, taking a multiday cruise is probably the way to go, since they drift further out to sea. What would become of this sanctified place, defined by Charles Darwin as "bleak"? Its ecosystem is certainly better off without people ogling everything and stepping everywhere. As a world traveler, I cherish these idyllic, foreign places where I'm really out there experiencing something exotic. But I also feel responsible. I'm a contributor to the problem, exposing such places on social media, swept up in the ease of instant gratification and real-time validation.

I've acquired the worst sunburn of my life in the Galapagos after falling asleep face down on a boat. Dave takes a photo of me naked in our room after I've covered myself head to toe in aloe vera. I look like I'm wearing a white bikini after painting the rest of my body red. It's hard to sleep, and I consider lying all night in the cold bathtub.

High hopes, low clearance

Flying back to Guayaquil, we stay one more night with Lula and Flavia, then set the GPS for Cuenca. My riding suit feels like it's lined with black-berry vines when I slid my blistering, flaking arms inside my jacket.

Outside Guayaquil's city limits, we gain elevation quickly, topping out at 13,648 feet. Rain hammers us and temps drop to the mid-forties. This reprieve from the heat should be welcome, but it's a shock to my system. Just that morning, I was dripping in sweat as we left the humid city. Now, I stop to pull on rain gear and turn on the heated grips on my handlebars, feeling the warmth seep into my fingertips.

Using the little wiper affixed to the index finger on my left glove, I clear raindrops from my visor every two seconds. The rain tapers off as we come across a 500-foot-long mudslide, where a tractor is shoveling loads of wet, black dirt and rocks off the edge. I watch everything slosh down the hill and smack into the trees below. When the driver waves for us to pass, Dave goes first. He slips and slides in the deeper bits, and I think he must've installed invisible training wheels on his bike to stay up-right in that mess. I can count the number of times he's fallen off his bike on one hand, whereas I've wiped out too many times to remember.

I'm starting to notice more flaws with my Stallion. Low clearance, for one; the G650GS drags its belly in deep mud or sand, throwing me off balance. The custom seat I thought would cushion my spine is as wide as a horse's back and makes it tough to get my feet down.

Despite these criticisms, I remain loyal to the Stallion. Dave, however, is growing to loathe it. He thinks my bike is too short, and not agile or quick enough. I remind him I bought the bike for my 135-pound, five-foot-six frame, not his at 165 and five-ten. Tension builds on the days we ride more difficult terrain. I dread asking him to ride my bike over or through obstacles, like creek crossings, rocky trails or, as is the case today, landslides.

But I'm feeling good this afternoon—emboldened, actually. Instead of stopping at the mudslide and waiting for Dave to take my bike through, I twist the throttle and shoot forward. *If alone, what would I do? I sure as hell wouldn't turn around and go home.*

At the other end of the mudslide, Dave is walking back to help me, navigating the slide by hopping from rock to boulder, trying to keep his boots from sinking in. His face fills with surprise when he sees me going for it. I stay focused on my line and pin it, but when I hit a muck-covered rut, the Stallion slides out from under me, and I land with a splash. The day before, I'd hand-washed my riding suit in the shower.

"Are you okay?" Dave calls out.

I'm laughing because I can't get purchase to upright myself.

The tractor driver is already climbing out of his seat. Seeing my heavy bike on its side is probably alarming to him, but for us, picking up fallen bikes—especially mine—is routine. I wave to the driver that everything's okay.

"Well, hey, good for you for trying." Dave grins when he comes over. He squeezes my muddy shoulder then wipes his now-filthy glove onto his pants. "Your bike just really likes to lie down. It's so lazy."

His optimism is encouraging and not what I expected. Maybe travel is bringing out the best in us.

My bike makes a suction noise when we lift it, as do my riding boots when I follow Dave through the remainder of the slide. When I catch up, our bikes are waiting side by side—dripping, dirty dogs hoping for a stick tossed into the next adventure.

Campfire cocaine &
an accidental pig slaughter

Peru

Travelers are prone to unintended ignorance. We bring our wants and needs on tour and pay to be satisfied and comfortable in foreign lands. Money goes into the local economy, and everybody's happy. But not everyone wants tourism interrupting their quiet lives.

Northern Peru feels like such a place. Relatively untouched and unknown, there are almost no overlanders, backpackers, or foreigners here compared to the more populated and popular southern regions of the country, like Lima, Cusco, and Arequipa. The very thing businesses aim to promote in those areas is what it seems northern Peru is hoping to avoid: commercialization, hordes of strangers, and the exploitation of hallowed spaces.

The lack of signage for travelers is somewhat endearing. I wouldn't want to travel like this for several months, but it adds some intrigue to the day when one needs to use detective skills for rudimentary, basic needs, like fueling our bikes and bodies. Restaurants are obscure, like gas stations and grocery stores, and take some sleuthing. When we do come across something, it's *arroz con pollo, pollo y papas fritas, pollo con más pollo*. We've been consuming a ton of starch along with these omnipresent chicken dishes. When we eat meals on the road, there are almost no veggies but always two combinations of carbs, like mashed potatoes and fries or rice. They're the best potatoes around, and it's safe to say they're non-GMO, but the excessive carb loading is too much for my liking. I crave the salads I make at home.

We find a room in San Ignacio. The price is right in the run-down border town. For twenty *soles* (six dollars), we get a narrow, sagging bed, a cold-water shower, and a toilet without a seat. The no-seat thing is also universal worldwide, as if hotel and hostel owners subscribe to websites with titles like *The Rim* is *a Seat and Other Money-saving Tips.*

In the morning, a drunk is hanging around outside the hotel with a rabid-looking rottweiler. When we ride off, the canine chases after Dave, snapping at his heels. Something about the sound of our engines seems to set dogs off, and they often run after us, which is my least favorite part about riding a motorcycle. I never know if one is crazy enough to lunge at me or dash in front of my bike.

Dave kicks at the rottweiler, but that just makes it crazier. I follow with no small amount of hesitation. *What happens when it gives up chasing Dave and sees me?* In a halfhearted attempt to distract the dog—or maybe because he's angry at Dave for kicking his best friend—the drunk tosses a beer bottle at Dave's retreating back. Glass shatters into tiny amber triangles on the potholed road in front of me. I swerve to avoid a puncture and am happy when the light ahead turns green so I can keep moving and leave the chaos behind.

Northern Peru is like a woman uncomfortable with her own beauty, doing everything to avoid unwanted attention by dressing down, hoping to convince admirers she's unattractive. *Nothing to see here, move along.* There's no hiding her splendor, however. Here, we experience some of the most exciting roads I've ever seen. Villages set in narrow valleys for river access and temperate gardening and farming mean a steep, winding ascent to get up and over mountain ranges. Curvier than a slinky coil, the roads keep our handlebars at a constant tilt through cloud forests and the Amazon watershed. Dave's in heaven and is moved enough to write a post for our blog titled "The Roads of Peru":

The further we have traveled into Peru, the better the riding has become, with the exception of the Pan-American coming into Lima. Heather may not agree with some of this; I seem to enjoy mud, landslides, and creek beds a bit more. I think we would both agree, though, that the paved mountain roads have been the best of the trip. Some of the switchbacks are so close together it feels like a slalom course. The amount of relief in this landscape is incomprehensible by North American standards. Relief on average seem to range from 2,500 to 3,500 meters, or 8,200 to 11,400 feet. Also, there is rarely a guardrail, and if you screw up the first turn, you're going to the bottom some 2,500-plus meters below to meet the raging, swollen river. Most of these roads are also single lane, with virtually no pullouts to navigate around oncoming traffic—which may be a tour bus or transport truck. And even when the road seems to be smooth and fast, you'll likely round a corner to find mud, potholes, livestock, and a handful of brick-sized rocks in your lane. It's perfect!

The country's rainy season causes waterfalls to slide like rolls of white silk down the mossy rock walls. Rivers run chocolate-milk brown, carrying tree trunks and other debris ripped from the edge by the current. As a former whitewater rafting guide and kayaker, I try to scout lines where, if I happened to be a Class Six paddler—or crazy—I'd point my boat downstream and let the water carry me away.

Our highs become less high when we ride through northern Peru's smaller villages and towns, looking for food and accommodation.

"Is it my imagination, or are people not happy to see us?" Dave says over the intercom.

We look like astronauts in all our gear, so we lift our helmet visors to show our eyes and smiles, riding in first gear to avoid stirring up dust. Our approachable gestures are not appreciated—no waves, no smiles. I dodge a rock thrown from a sneering teenager, and the dogs seem extra pissed off at our bikes here. Back home, I imagined we might find a small village on our travels and stay long enough to weave a flower basket or help build a school. Most days in these places, however, I just want to keep going.

One afternoon, leaving what can only be described as an unfinished village, where structures stand just a few feet high and abandoned mid-build, we meet another adventure rider. Joe is a US lawyer, riding a Kawasaki KLR650. He's standoffish at first but wants to join us once he learns we're all going in the same direction.

An hour later, we come across two other riders stopped on the side of the road. CJ and John are also on a two-year world tour, riding Yamaha WR250 dirt bikes. Like several ADV riders we've met on our travels, they also live in Vancouver, BC, but John is originally from Australia. With five of us now together, camping is safer, and we start looking for places away from the less-than-desirable Peruvian towns.

As we ride higher into the *altiplano*, it begins to pour. After some searching, we see a clearing surrounded by fragrant eucalyptus trees. A handful of modest homesteads with ancient rock fences are scattered in the hills above us. Everyone but me rips up a choppy embankment into the clearing, rear wheels spinning in the steep, unstable soil. The obstacle is only a few feet high, but I can't get the nerve to ride it. I sit astride my bike with mounting embarrassment, waiting for Dave to come back. I wonder if the guys are judging me. *She wants to ride around the world, and she can't even get up that tiny mound of dirt?*

Dave returns and stares first at me, then at the Stallion, then back at me. I shrug. He sighs and reaches for my bike, steading it so I can get off since I'm stopped at a weird angle.

Dave has a hard time gauging the progress in my riding. He'll say, "But you rode something much harder than this yesterday!" and I'll cling to excuses, like my wrist/back/leg/brain hurts or I haven't eaten enough cookies for breakfast. Sometimes, as with the mudslide, he's glad I try. Other times he wonders *why* I try if I'm just going to stop midway. Now, I've chickened out halfway, forcing him to roll my bike backward and get more of a run at it.

My lack of actual balls often has Dave working overtime, expending valuable energy, while I try to explain my vacillation between bravery and fear. What can I say? Somedays, it's the flick of a switch between worrier and warrior.

I walk the few hundred feet to where the others are parked, feeling out of place with four men who can ride anything in their path. When Joe pulls out a bottle of rum, however, we all find common ground. Without bothering to dig out cups, we drink straight from the bottle—something I'd regret later, when discussions about hookers and blow come up. *Does alcohol kill herpes?*

Five of us stand in the rain, passing the bottle around. No one makes a move to change out of wet riding clothes or set up tents. The night grows dark, with only pinpoints of soft light from the hillside homesteads in the distance. Water collects on the collar of my riding jacket and drips down my back, making it all the way to my boots and pooling around my feet. Despite the discomfort, I'm warming to the idea of being around other riders again. Our last riding companion was Ismail over a month and 3,000 miles ago.

Hunger and a chill in the air prompt us to set off with headlamps to collect firewood. There's plenty of evening left and not much else to do but drink around a fire. When the rain eases up, a dense fog weaves through the forest and out into the clearing. I'm unstable on my feet, feeling a dizzying rum glow more than I might have at a lower elevation.

Contributions to the wood pile are sufficient and, after pouring a little fuel over the wet bundle, we have a half-decent flare going in minutes. The burning eucalyptus smells like roasting cumin seeds, and my stomach grumbles. While Dave sets up the tent, I root around in my panniers for a meager dinner. We didn't plan on camping and have few edible reserves.

Soon we're laughing at each other's travel stories. Stirring a pot of rice and beans, I recount a story from a week earlier in Vilcabamba, Ecuador— a sleepy, picturesque town known for its retreat-like atmosphere. Dave and I had gone horseback riding, and I wanted to top off the day with a massage. When I pulled a purple curtain aside and called *hola* into a house with a sign out front, a petite Ecuadorian woman welcomed me in. She pointed to a massage bed with a questioning look.

"Sí, quiero un masaje, por favor," I nodded.

At first, everything was as per normal massage protocol, until I was instructed to turn onto my back. The woman rearranged a blanket over my lower half only, leaving my breasts exposed. I decided not to care. She massaged my neck, down to my shoulders and then—*hold up!* My entire chest was included in the kneading.

CJ tipped the rum to his lips, but it came out through his nose when I finished my story with: "And that was the time I got felt up by an old Ecuadorian lady in Vilcabamba."

It's great to be camping again, especially with the safety-in-numbers advantage. When a baggie of cocaine is produced, however, there's a needle-off-the-record moment. In our somewhat-short dating history, Dave and I haven't yet been in a situation together where hard drugs are on offer. Drug use is a deal breaker for me. I hold my breath when the baggie settles in front of Dave, then exhale a quiet sigh of relief when he passes it on.

CJ and John tell us about a points system they have for accidentally hitting things on their bikes. So far, they've each racked up a few for killing rodents and birds. Joe stays quiet.

I've only ridden into a smattering of small birds in Mexico, which made me sad at the time.

"Do flies count?" Dave jokes.

"So, you get no points," CJ declares, pointing at Dave, "and Heather, you get maybe one point for hitting some small birds."

"What? No point per bird?"

"Sorry, bud."

My eyes are having a hard time staying open, so I go to the tent to lie down. Inside the sleeping bag, my bare skin is damp and sticky against the fabric. Listening to the fireside chatter, I drift off, hearing Dave laugh until he chokes.

By morning, I have a splitting headache and Dave is still hacking. He refuses my cure of oil of oregano and its antioxidant properties because it's too bitter, and we have no liquid chaser. With barely any water, too much rum, and not enough food the night before, I'm unmotivated to start the day.

Dave gets out of the tent, and the fresh forest air wafts to my nose, encouraging me to leave my warm cocoon. I do a double take when I see John's face as he attempts to stoke the smoldering fire back to life. Veins pop out of his flushed forehead and neck, and his eyes are bloodshot. This thirty-something man looks like he's seconds away from cardiac arrest. *Is this just from drinking last night? Altitude sickness?*

CJ slashes around inside his tent, mouthing off the world in what we will come to discover over the next few weeks is true CJ style.

"Rough night, boys?" I smirk.

"*Pffft!*" CJ spits.

Unbeknownst to us, the other three stayed up after Dave came to bed around midnight. They were getting ready to call it a night when a short Peruvian man came out from the shadows. Who knew how long he was there watching us.

"He hovers around for a bit—" CJ emerges from his tent in bare feet, riding pants, and a soggy T-shirt "—and we're thinking we'll just ignore him. But he comes over to the fire and wants to talk, so we try and communicate to be polite." CJ's cropped, brown hair is matted down in directionless tufts. "Next thing we know, he's inviting us to his casa."

John points to a modest hut on a hill. "We didn't want to go, but he was kind of insistent."

"So," CJ continues, balancing on one leg to stick his opposing foot into a sandal caked in mud. "We go inside this little dude's house or shack or whatever, and there's an old TV and VCR playing porn and a used condom on the floor."

"*Whaaaaat?*" I laugh.

"Yeah. We chewed coca leaves with the guy and his weird little friends until about 2:30 in the morning, with porn in the background the whole time," CJ says. "I got sick of it and walked back to camp alone but got totally lost and stuck in mud up to my man tits."

John shakes his head. "Should've stayed with us, mate."

Dave and I are in hysterics, but I'm creeped out by our campsite and want to leave ASAP. I now picture the quaint little homesteads around us as dank dens filled with sex-crazed Peruvian men gnawing on bags of coca leaves while masturbating to porn.

The flu virus settles deep into Dave's lungs while we ride over a mountain pass in a cold, driving rain. He's too weak to stop and dig out his heated jacket—a gear godsend that can be worn under our riding jackets and plugged into an external twelve-volt outlet feeding the bike's battery.

In Santiago de Chuco, CJ and John store their smaller dirt bikes in the main-floor restaurant overnight. With bigger bikes, Joe, Dave, and I are taken to a woodshed up the street by the hotel owner's brother. Our bikes are locked out of sight, but it means an awkward walk with heavy bags and riding boots along cobblestone roads back to the hotel.

When I pay for the room, the guy working behind the desk tries to charge me forty *soles* (twelve dollars), even though a visible sign says double rooms are twenty *soles*. I point this out. Embarrassed, he accepts the lesser price, perhaps forgetting the sign was there or that travelers can read. A theme is developing, we're noticing, and it's hard not to feel bitter. Restaurants, hotels, even sidewalk food stalls often try to overcharge us. I tried buying a frozen fruit drink a few days ago, finding the plastic baggies wrapped around a straw intriguing. From a distance, I watched what the vendor charged a customer—a tactic I've learned during my solo travels in other countries. When it was my turn to pay, she quoted me double. It isn't that I can't afford a dollar instead of fifty cents; it's that I'm being taken advantage of.

Our room has a lumpy double bed with two inches of space between it and the wall. I can almost flush the toilet with a toe while lying in bed. Bored at only 5 p.m., I grab my book, leaving Dave to nap off his illness. In the lobby restaurant, consisting of a few sticky tables, some uncomfortable metal chairs, and John and CJ's dirt bikes, I order dinner. Dining in northern Peru is straightforward; you either eat what the restaurant has prepared, or you don't eat at all. There's no menu, you simply say *"almuerzo"* or *"cena, por favor,"* and you get whatever lunch or dinner is that day.

An unsmiling *señora* places a steaming bowl in front of me, turning her back to my *gracias*. Engrossed in my book, I slurp the flavorful chicken soup until my spoon hits something hard. Looking down, I see a chicken foot. My eyes fix on its clawed toes. Wrinkly, yellow skin and gray talons float in the opaque liquid. I fish out the appendage, place it on a stack of whisper-thin napkins, and continue eating, wondering if any snickering kitchen staff are watching. Or maybe the claw is a delicacy and they've given me the best part of the batch.

For weeks now, we've stayed in dirty, surly places. After a long day of riding, there's nothing better than entering a welcoming town, looking forward to trying local delicacies, and meeting happy people. But that's not always a given, and it's hard not to get depressed over the lack of friendliness. Usually, the scenery cheers us up between towns, but lately the weather is wet. Dark clouds hang down to our handlebars, and our gear never dries out.

Dave is still feeling rough the next morning, despite sleeping fourteen hours. I go in search of breakfast in the small central plaza and find a food stall selling takeout bowls of rice pudding with a dollop of berry jam on top and a warm tea-like drink, thick and sweetened with what tastes like molasses. Everything is delicious, even though the food vendor tries to overcharge me. I hope the meal will provide Dave some energy for another long day ahead.

CJ and John have already left, but Joe's bike is still in the woodshed when we leave.

Back on the road, I'm lost in thought, daydreaming about returning to the lush tropics of the Libertad region, with its tumbling roadside waterfalls and chirping-bird forests. Dave and I are cruising through a small village, chickens squawking and fluttering in our wake. I see no people, but livestock of all types roam the dusty street. Suddenly a flurry of activity bursts from the roadside. A family of hogs get spooked by the sound of our bikes. I dodge piggies like pylons in a road test, but one little guy charges headlong into my front wheel. The Stallion hops and dances before I reign it under control. The piglet is stuck under my skid plate, and, horribly, I drag it several feet. The human-like sounds of its pork family, squealing and grunting in heartache, fill my helmet, making me wince. Finally, the piglet is flung out from under my back tire. I can't bring myself to look back and see the outcome. Stopping to find its owner crosses my mind, but I keep going, guilty yet fearful of the wrath that might befall me for having, perhaps, killed someone's food source.

Until then, I had some amount of hope that if one of the stray dogs chasing us ever got in my way, I'd be able to absorb the hit with my heavy bike. Now I'm certain it would be a painful—perhaps deadly—experience.

That night, I dream of dogs darting out from between parked cars. I jolt and yank the sheets off Dave, who moans at me to stop being so restless.

Piss town, a story of survival

Our adventures through Peru's northern regions have been more than exciting thus far, what with the campfire cocaine and accidental pig slaughtering. When the Stallion overheats one day in *Cañon del Pato*, mishaps are beginning to feel like a daily norm.

Cañon del Pato, or Duck Canyon, is a remarkable dirt road forced through bedrock to allow passage by way of multiple tunnels. I stop counting the dark arches at forty-two but have heard there are more than fifty tunnels along the thirty-two-mile corridor from Caraz to Yuracmarca. Here, the Cordillera Blanca and Cordillera Negra mountain ranges come so close together at one point that only a fifty-foot bridge over the Rio Santa separates the two.

Late afternoon is setting in. We still have a long way to go when the warning light glows on my dash and coolant starts bubbling out all over my boots and pants. Dave looks for cracks, but nothing is obvious without taking the bike apart. I scout for somewhere to set up the tent if needed. We're almost out of food and water—bad news in the baking heat. I stare at Dave and the various tools and bike parts lying around him, then up at the afternoon sky. The pullout on the road is the only somewhat-level spot between a rock wall and the raging river. A few drivers stop along the quiet road asking what's wrong, but there's nothing anyone can do that we can't do ourselves.

I notice the passing vehicles have roof racks similar to those at home used to tie down bundles of camping gear. But these racks are sturdier. Made from thick steel and welded to the vehicle's frame, they extend over the windshield and hood. I come to the unnerving realization that the racks are there to protect the vehicle and its occupants from falling rocks.

"I don't think we want to hang out here too long," I tell Dave, pointing to the cliffs surrounding us.

"What do you want me to do? I'm working as fast as I can to find the issue." I'm about to retaliate, but Dave apologizes. He throws down a wrench and seethes, "I have no idea where the leak is coming from, and for fuck's sake, it's hot! Do we have any water left?"

A rumbling echoes through the canyon. I leap to my feet, expecting rockfall. Everything seems to be scaring me lately: loud noises, dogs darting out of nowhere—but it's just CJ and John on their loud bikes. We hadn't expected to meet up again for several days, having loose plans to reunite in Huaraz. I'm overjoyed to see them, hoping they can help us fix the bike—but also, perhaps, make the situation more fun.

In the gathering dusk, Dave puts my bike back together enough for me to limp it down the road to a flat area by the river, away from the crumbling rock walls.

"How is it you guys were behind us?" I ask CJ, using some of our dwindling water to boil pasta.

"We did a side trip that took longer than expected. The road was beat to hell."

Being stranded is less scary now with four of us. The traffic has all but stopped as darkness falls, but now and again, lights from an approaching vehicle scatter across the canyon walls, and people stare at us camping in plain sight.

I tell CJ and John I ran over a baby pig, for which I receive four points—high marks on the hitting-things scale.

Since CJ and John were planning on getting further up the road, we're caught in an unplanned overnight and only have half a gallon of water among the four of us. In the hot evening air, thirst creeps its dry claws up my throat. I keep the pasta water aside in case we get desperate. The Rio Santa is so full and close we have to raise our voices. But we can't get to it because of a dirt embankment precariously close to giving way. That's probably for the best; the iced-cappuccino color suggests we'd have a water-filtering fiasco.

"Any sign of Joe?" John asks.

"He caught up to us at a stream crossing a while ago," Dave says. "After that, he took off."

My slower pace is no match for three seasoned riders, and I wonder if I'm the reason we're all so spread out lately.

The sound of boulders rolling underwater and rocks crumbling off the river's edge lull me to sleep later that night. I dream I'm in a kayaking competition and win first place.

By 6 a.m., the tent is already baking. I'm soaked in sweat and thirsty enough to guzzle a gallon of water, but the communal jug has just a few cups left. I uncover the pot of pasta water but can't bring myself to drink its coagulated contents. Dave's already standing beside my bike with CJ and John. I hate being the damsel in distress, but I'm glad I'm not tackling the mechanical issue alone.

With the Stallion disemboweled, Dave removes the radiator. We need to use some of our precious water to wash away dirt in the fins. Once everything's clean and accessible, the problem becomes obvious; a pea-sized rock is wedged between the radiator and the frame. Vibration and bumpy roads have worn a hole, causing a coolant leak.

The hole is repaired with epoxy—a handy solution supplied by CJ, who slices off a piece for us to carry in our kit. Using the remaining water, we top up my rad, and I'm ready to roll again. CJ and John are soon way ahead. Dave and I ride slower, not wanting to push my bike's capabilities.

I'm so thirsty and dying to get somewhere that sells liquids in all forms, but within the half hour, the Stallion is overheating again.

Dave has just disappeared around a corner. Now I'm double-pissed. *Why didn't I insist on being in front?*

I stop and take off my helmet, soaked in sweat.

"For fuck's sake!"

The echo of my angry voice off the canyon walls is satisfying. Shutting off the engine, I wait for Dave, loathing my helplessness. If it's not fear or lack of riding experience holding me back, it's now my bike, as well.

Roasting on the exposed road, I crave water more than anything in life at that moment. Where is the next place to find some? Is it minutes or hours away?

When Dave comes back, his face does little to hide his full-on hatred for the Stallion, which he's now calling "Frankenbike" or the c-word. He theorizes my G650GS was built as a one-off, saying the BMW mechanics had a look in the parts room and assembled my bike out of odds and ends.

"Try to keep the RPMs low," Dave advises after the bike has cooled down.

Riding at twenty miles an hour in fourth gear instead of second keeps the warning light off, and we gain some ground. The tension in my neck and shoulders stays with me, though, and I brace myself for that amber light to reappear on my dash.

We're unwatered flowers drooping in our seats, our dehydration becoming a much bigger problem than the Stallion now. Not a single *pueblo* or even a shoddy roadside vendor selling drinks can be found for the next hundred miles. I pull over and lie on the ground when I get too dizzy to see straight. My head is pounding. I would suck a puddle next to a gas pump right now if I could.

Then, finally, we're saved late afternoon by some shack stores lining the roadside. Their ripped blue tarps flap in the hot wind. The acrid smell of human urine singes my nostrils. Another time, I'd ignore this filthy, desolate stop, but this day Piss Town is an oasis. I hurl myself toward a startled old lady whose wooden-crate counter holds bottles of pop and water. Behind her is a fridge filled with drinks. I have no idea how they get electricity in the canyon, and I don't care. Pointing to the half-gallon water bottles, I say, *"Cuatro, por favor."* The woman passes over four waters. I hold up two fingers and ask for the Gatorades, then add a bottle of Inca Kola—the toxic sugar load doesn't dissuade me from gulping it back, even though it's the same color as the concentrated pee I can smell boiling on the hot road.

A bag of fresh-looking oranges finishes the purchase, and I pay the *señora* three times what she'd charge a local. She needs the money more than we do, and she pretty much saved our lives.

Sitting in the shade of a vacant building, we drink as fast as our throats can swallow. The urine smell infuses into what I eat and drink, but I'm impervious. I feel the cold liquid sliding down my esophagus and swirling into my stomach. My energy returns.

Piss Town was truly a lifesaver; the next place for potable water turns out to be another 125 miles away in Huaraz.

An hour after our rehydration stop, I lose my rear brakes rounding a corner. I'm able to stay upright by gearing down and using the front brakes, but this causes another lengthy mechanical quest. Dave discovers the brakes are jammed due to dirt build-up from miles of dust. During the investigation, he also spies a broken bushing on the rear shock, which is why it feels like I'm riding a jackhammer over the rippling washboard filled with chunks of rocks and hard-packed mud ruts.

Dave's rarely at a loss for name calling when it comes to my bike, but now he's silent, taking the bike's malfunctioning personally. I coo and cajole words of kindness, as though my steed is a living thing I can nurture back to health. I hugely appreciate Dave's mechanical skills but am also taking something personally: Why is it always my bike and not his? We cover the same number of miles on the same brand of motorcycle, yet his bike never has a single hiccup.

Maybe I should put more effort into learning about motorcycle maintenance, but by the end of the day, we're both exhausted, and rudimentary needs come first. We ask a lot from our motorcycles and give them little in return. When something goes wrong, we curse them for not behaving. But I'm protective of the Stallion, and when Dave throws obscenities at it, I come to the bike's defense. Other people have ridden these motorcycles up and down the Americas and even around the world. Mine should be capable of doing the same.

Dave has everything back together, and I force more positive thoughts: Lima's just 300 miles away and has a BMW dealership. I just need some modifications and repairs. The Stallion is still round-the-world worthy.

The Stallion smokes again

The city of Huaraz sits at over 10,000 feet and is a mecca for climbers hoping to tackle mountaineering objectives in the Cordillera Blanca.

Dave and I stop in the village of Yungay so I can point out Peru's highest peak.

In the late '90s, my then-climbing partner, Ed, and I summited Huascarán—22,205 feet—in eight days. Most of that time was spent acclimatizing, allowing our bodies to rest and get used to the oxygen-depleted air, before going further up the mountain. Strong winds and clouds obscured the view from the summit that day, and we couldn't see a thing. That's the deal with mountaineering—you need to be happy with the journey, not just the prize.

That afternoon, Yungay is sunny and warm, and Huascarán's snow-capped peak is in full view—much different from two decades ago when I was feeling my way around its top in a total whiteout.

We decide to have lunch at a café in Yungay to enjoy the scene for longer.

In 1970, almost thirty years before Ed and I set foot on Huascarán's wind-blasted summit, a 7.8-magnitude earthquake hit the Peruvian coast, causing an avalanche to release from the mountain's northern wall. The slide turned into a monster's tongue of rock, snow, and ice ripping through the towns of Yungay and Ranrahirca at over 170 miles an hour. More than 20,000 people were killed, and Yungay was buried.

That earthquake is considered the largest disaster in Peru's history, and its resulting avalanche the world's deadliest.

It's hard to imagine the horror when I look up at the mountain today, with its white, snowy peak and blue-sky backdrop. I wonder if the people walking by on the sidewalk outside, or any of the patrons sitting and eating among us, lost somebody that day.

I'm cruising down a steep hill following the highway into Lima, a city of ten million people, when I smell something burning. Looking down, I'm horrified to see smoke billowing from between my feet. The evening rush hour scatters around me like a stepped-on ant colony when I pull over onto the shoulder. The rotor by my rear tire is glowing red, and my brake pads are filed down to nothing but metal shoes. *What happened?* Dave fixed my rear brakes in Huaraz, so why are they now completely gone?

Then I remember…he also had adjusted my brake pedal so it would be easier to use with my big riding boots. My foot, using muscle memory, had found its way back to the position it was used to. I'd been riding the brakes all day, and the hill I'd just burned down had finished them off.

For what it's worth, I flick on my hazard lights. Maintaining distance between me and everything else, I tail Dave to the *Miraflores* district—a trendy, well-to-do area popular for its variety of great food and seawall paths.

Lima is not a city for the faint of heart behind the wheel or handlebars. Drivers are erratic, and shoulder checks are not a thing. Hours later, Dave and I are still in traffic anarchy, having moved only a few miles. My bike's overheating again, its warning light extra bright now in the dark evening light. For fifteen minutes, we inch toward a traffic light changing from red to green to yellow without anyone moving much.

I need to shut off my engine and let it cool down. People watch as I bump my fat bike onto the sidewalk to get out of the way. Together, Dave and I sit, saying nothing, acting like everything's normal. I have a strong urge to pack it all in and get a flight home, or to somewhere less assaulting on the senses.

Once the Stallion has cooled, I start the engine and scout for a place to slot myself back into traffic. Nobody lets me in. Losing patience, I rev and thrust off the curb but forget about my rear brake issue and almost knock over a woman selling plantains. Grabbing a fistful of front brakes, I abruptly load the forks and fall over. Horns are honking at me. My body's on fire with embarrassment. I try to lift the Stallion, lying half-on, half-off the curb, but I'm not having one of those Wonder Woman days. Shaking with exhaustion and shame, I let Dave, and some men from the gathering crowd, help me.

By the time we get to our hostel in *Miraflores* that evening, we've spent five hours riding 250 miles from Huaraz to Lima, and another three hours going just ten miles within the city.

Dave and I ride to the BMW dealer the next day. I'm hopeful with my list of repairs—radiator, rear brakes, rear shock, and a few other tidbits—but leave with a bad feeling. The mechanic and sales rep don't speak English, and my sparse Spanish falls short in explaining what I need done. With little choice, I leave the Stallion there and we ride two-up to Touratech— a German service center catering to aftermarket parts for ADV and dual-sport bikes, with branches in several countries worldwide.

Our initial mission at Touratech is for Dave's suspension system, which needs some maintenance. When I learn they can do all the work on the Stallion and have most parts in stock—*and* speak English—I ask the receptionist to call BMW and cancel my work order.

We take the rest of the afternoon off and walk along the seawall, then try pisco sours—a citrusy-sweet traditional Peruvian cocktail involving frothy egg whites. The drink tastes like liquefied lemon meringue pie and goes down the gullet a little too easily.

I rescue the Stallion the next morning from BMW. On the way back to Touratech, I smell something burning again and my pants are covered in oil. The hot parts of my exhaust pipes are also smoking. *Oh my god, what now?!* Dave's ahead in a taxi I'm following. Squeezing between vehicles, I pull up beside the cab and motion for them to pull over, then shoulder-check across four lanes of traffic.

I immediately see the problem when I stop. The dipstick cap for checking the oil was left open and the liquid inside bubbled over. This mishap from the BMW mechanic, who'd opened things up before I could cancel the work order, almost destroyed my bike for good. Without oil lubricant, the engine would have seized.

The cab driver calls Touratech, and a truck and trailer pull up an hour later, adding a tow fee to my already large repair bill.

Four days pass in Lima before we're reunited with our bikes and are back on the road. The Stallion has new rear brakes, a rear wheel bearing, and a fresh oil change. The radiator is in the same state it was before. No one could find a replacement for a 2010 G650GS. BMW no longer made the part, and anything secondhand would be hard to find and take ages to ship. I could wait weeks, even months, and still come up emptyhanded. At least the epoxy patch job was redone and looks stout. With hope, it'll get me the distance.

Leaving Lima's madness behind in the late evening, we set the GPS to meet up again with John, Joe, CJ, and Angela, CJ's wife. Angela used her time off as a teacher to fly to Peru and ride on the back of CJ's dirt bike. It looks super uncomfortable but is the only way to fit in time together on CJ's two-year journey. I admire her trust and independence, doubting I'd be okay with my husband traveling around the world for that long without me.

CJ emailed GPS coordinates to where they'll be camping along the desert coastline near Paracas, over 100 miles south of Lima. In the black night, Dave and I bump off the highway onto a sandy track leading toward the ocean. My headlights splay across the ground and catch nothing in the form of trees or shrubs, just a vast expanse. I hear and smell seawater but can't see it. I look forward to morning, when the surprise of our surroundings is revealed.

Our friends are hard to spot in the dark until I see someone waving a flashlight. We ride up a sand dune that has my rear tire fishtailing, trying to maintain traction. At the top, tents rustle in the warm sea breeze. I shut off my engine and listen to the waves crashing below us. The moonless night exposes little aside from what's illuminated by our own headlamps. It's late. After some quick chitchat, Dave and I set up our tent, and everyone goes to bed.

The cry of seagulls wakes me at six the next morning. Dave's arm is slung over my hip. I stay on my side, not wanting to disturb him. I ache to see what's outside but use my other senses to draw the scene. After several days of Lima's pollution, the fresh, salty air tastes delicious. Sometimes it amazes me how good a deep, long breath can feel.

When Dave stirs, I get up and pull on some shorts. The view outside is dramatic. All the tents are perched atop an airy plateau dropping straight off to the Pacific Ocean several hundred feet below. Red-legged cormorants, Inca terns, and Peruvian pelicans flutter over the water, busy with morning rituals. After making a catch, they land on the sun-scorched sandstone buttresses that poke finger-like out of the ocean. The bluffs are covered in guano, like a dusting of snow that belies the promise of unbearable heat later in the day.

The Paracas Peninsula is a prehistoric geoglyph known for its beaches, home to pelicans, penguins, and sea lions. The most stunning sight for me this morning is the color of the ocean. I walk to the edge, mindful of how easily a chunk of sandstone could break off under my feet and send me to my death. The contrast of the desert-beige hues against the aquamarine water is peaceful yet powerful. Here—in nature's simplicity of just two basic colors in many shades, and a wide-open landscape without complication or busyness—I feel like I'm in one of those posters tacked to an office wall with a quote about relaxation.

We appreciate the extraordinary place we've called home for a night, but by 9 a.m. it's already ninety degrees. Dave and I must be acclimatized; a few months ago, we'd be dying in this heat. Perhaps it's the lack of humidity.

I could stay forever, but this isolated place has no water, food, fuel, or shelter. We need very little to travel around the world, but those basics are vital, so we pack up and swear while putting on our "ski suits" under the red-hot sun.

Sweat streams down my back. I roll the Stallion off the smooth-shouldered dune, knowing our tracks will soon be covered by the breeze, removing any trace of human interference. On the flat desert floor, I pick up speed to get some air flow. Dave flies past me, also eager to cool down. His rear tire flings out a dirt wake, or "rooster tail." Standing on his foot pegs, he looks over his shoulder at me. I know the grin under his full-face helmet while he nods up and down to music playing in his headset. Maybe he's listening to something like Pearl Jam. He loves changing the lyrics in songs, so that they're almost the same but not. In Pearl Jam's Better Man, he sings the chorus about finding a better man, to: "can't find the butter, man."

I'd fallen in love with Dave for many reasons—not least of which was for times like this, when he lets himself unwind and have fun. I stand on my pegs as well and chase him. In just one night, this place—with its ethereal landscape and lively birdlife—snuggled into our souls to lift our spirits. Such experiences are instrumental in filling our reserves with the energy needed to keep adventuring.

It's not a death wish

Dave and I mull over spending the time and money for another off-bike luxury. Our window for reaching Ushuaia by mid-April—only one month and still 4,000 miles away—is at stake, but I don't want to miss the Peruvian Incan ruins again. Just like the Galapagos, I couldn't afford a visit to Machu Picchu my first time in South America, and now I have another chance.

On a winding stretch of tarmac between Nazca and Cusco, we reach a new trip elevation record, riding to nearly 15,000 feet. The zippers on my jacket under my armpits and down my back are open, and I'm suddenly chilled as the warm air turns cool.

I had no idea paved roads existed so high and am continually impressed by how our bikes behave no differently at altitude than at sea level.

We plunge back into Peru's lush tropics. Beside me, a high, natural rock wall is covered in seeping ferns and other greenery that mist my face as I pass. My sister, a landscape specialist in Nova Scotia, would know what the plants are, having cared for living walls at a college where she's worked for over a decade. I feel a pang and miss her right now.

The road's so curvy there isn't a single moment I straighten my handlebars. Carving around the corners feels a little like skiing. I'm getting the hang of leaning left, right, left, right, shifting my butt to counterbalance my center of gravity.

Nearing a sharp right bend, I keep my focus on the car in front of me, following it through the turn. A semi passes on my left, blasting air up the sleeve of my jacket. *Shit, buddy, that was too close!* Big trucks often cut corners on tight mountain roads, and the driver had crossed over the center line, forcing both me and the car ahead onto the shoulder.

Dave's ahead, stopped on the roadside. I thinks he's waiting for me, but on closer inspection, I notice he's gripping his handlebars, head hung low like he's panting. I pull over, unnerved by the traffic whooshing past us. *Not a good place to stop. What is he doing?*

After a few frustrating jabs at my intercom button, it finally connects. "What's up?"

"That semi almost got me," Dave's voice cracks.

"What? How?"

"Didn't you see? He took up the whole road around that corner. All eighteen wheels were *in my shoulder lane!* I almost went off the edge."

I glance to my right to where the narrow roadway drops off to a valley below. No guardrails. A chill creeps up my neck into my hair. That's how fast everything can change.

"I'm sorry," I stammer. "I was concentrating on the corner, too. I didn't see what happened. I'm so glad you're okay."

I'm becoming increasingly aware of our mortality, which can take the fun out of riding. We've seen some crazy things on the road so far, especially in Peru, and have started saying things like, "We'll make it by such-and-such time—as long as nothing Peruvian happens."

Every second vehicle in South America is a bike or scooter. In a place where two-wheeled transportation is more common and more affordable than four wheels, motorcyclists have developed great agility at maneuvering around head-on traffic. But those bikes are smaller than ours and skinnier. In Peru, just like we discovered in Mexico, there's no right of way, just the *you move, I'm bigger* way. Perhaps when drivers see us on two wheels, they think we're locals. The trucker probably saw Dave and thought he'd simply move over. What the driver didn't realize is it's almost impossible to whip out of the way with a much larger, wider, and heavier bike, than a 125cc motorcycle.

Dave's ready to ride again after a few minutes. I continue with a sobering reminder. At our going-away party, a friend asked if one of us died on this trip, would it be worth it? "Of course not," I said, shocked she even asked. But it was a question I knew people had. Another word for *adventure* is *risk*, after all. And why do people take such risks, whether it be riding a motorcycle, climbing Mount Everest, or driving race cars? I didn't have a rational answer, except to say I wanted to feel breathless at the end of each day, knowing I'd spent my one valuable life on something that made my heart beat with passion and happiness. Somehow, the risk/reward ratio is worth it for me while traveling. I don't want to die, of course, but the reward of traveling the world makes it worth the danger.

That famous Incan ruin

An early morning fog obscures the fifteenth-century Inca citadel of Machu Picchu. Dave and I get off a bus that's taken us to the park entrance. So far, I can barely see my hand in front of my face as I stand in a whiteout, hoping we haven't come all this way just to see nothing.

Killing time before the sun burns off the fog surrounding the ruins, Dave and I do a steep, three-hour trek to the top of Machu Picchu Mountain—a perfect vantage point for the 33,000-hectare World Heritage Site. As the air warms, the clouds lose their density and pull apart, revealing the vegetation-covered tiers and stone structures of Machu Picchu below. Hundreds if not thousands of people spill through the ruins in all directions, like a flash flood. I don't want to join them, preferring my stealthy perch high on the mountain, but in the end, I, like them, am curious to see the ancient village that was cut into the side of a mountain at 7,970 feet so many eras ago.

Located up the Sacred Valley from Cusco, fifty miles away, the ruins were built using stones without mortar—just carefully selected rocks interlocked together. That the Incan architecture has lasted through the centuries is nothing less than astounding. For tourism, many of the buildings have been reconstructed so crumbling walls don't fall on people, but much of the original style and patina remains.

Weaving in and out of the stone structures, I understand why Machu Picchu (sadly) sees 1.5 million visitors a year. Having the grandeur to ourselves, instead of being two of many, would have been incredible but impossible. As happens the world over, places of significant beauty don't stay secret for long. Especially once such places are declared a UNESCO site (1983) and voted one of the New Seven Wonders of the World (2007).

Part of the allure of Machu Picchu is that much of the reason for its existence remains a mystery. Archaeologists, historians—even guides who regularly do tours in the area—know very little. Some speculate that Machu Picchu was created as an estate for Pachacuti, an Inca emperor from the fifteenth century who defended his homeland of Cusco during an invasion by the Chankas, the Incas' tribal enemies.

Ducking through a short doorway, I try to ignore the dozens of people around me and imagine what life was like for the 750 residents who lived here year-round back in the 1400s. I reach out to rub my hand lightly over a wall, feeling grit like fine sandpaper. Dust falls into the sunlight and settles onto the grass at my feet. Was this space once a living room? Kitchen?

To grow food, man-made terraces were constructed using impressive engineering into the steep tropical mountainsides, guaranteed to offer good soil and irrigation for farming. These areas are off limits to visitors and show signs of past landslides and mishaps due to gravity. What did people do with their days besides farm? Since much of the food grown in the terraces was just corn and potatoes, there had to be another source of nutrition. Did some of the sturdier folk hike up and down the valleys to collect meat and other vegetables? How long did that take?

Tourists normally take a train straight from Cusco up the Urubamba Valley. Had we the time, hiking in along the 26-mile Inca Trail would've been a fun option, allowing us to spend more time in the area.

We're just here for the day, but that brilliant green plateau, stone structures, and lush, pointy peaks in the background will always remain in my memory.

The affordable robbery

Scams—or what Dave has begun referring to as "traveler racism tax"— increase as we get deeper into central and southern Peru. We're always on alert for prices jacked up for tourists and illegal tactics at the expense of the unknowing.

Being constantly on the watch for ill intent is exhausting. I crave being able to let my guard down and relax. We said goodbye to CJ, John, and Joe in Cusco after a month of riding on and off together, and I miss the safety-in-numbers thing.

The upside to being in the more traveler-frequented areas of Peru is better accommodation and friendlier locals. I welcome the smiles and waves we missed in northern Peru. Here, the country brings back pleasant memories from when I first visited in my twenties. Street markets and central plazas are the place to be, filled with a lively energy and busyness only a South American gathering can bring. I admire the market stalls layered with fruits and veggies, full of color and matching the vivid traditional uniform worn by vendors.

Odd-looking meat cuts leave me guessing at their origin but also curious about what they're used for in recipes. Guinea pig is an expensive delicacy, usually fried whole. Although I want to try the meat, it costs forty dollars a plate in most restaurants, so I don't.

I see several different kinds of fish, some vibrant blue and yellow, and get too close to a bubbling cauldron, recoiling when an eyeball from some animal bobs to the surface. Baked howler monkeys lying in rows remind me of tiny, burned corpses, setting my stomach off for most of the afternoon.

Dodging a man on a bicycle pushing what looks to be 700 pounds of bananas through the market, Dave and I walk over to some kind *señoritas* selling handcrafted souvenirs. I wish I had room in my panniers to take some with me, but I'm also all about spending money on experiences rather than things these days.

Not everything at the market is food-based. We pass by voluptuous bottom halves of plastic mannequins in tight denim jeans, a young *chica* selling plastic bags with zippers, and someone shining shoes. Everywhere Latin music plays from distorted speakers and people use microphones or loudspeakers to hawk their wares. It's a crazy vibe and energy packed onto the streets, and it doesn't take long to get swept up in the excitement.

Riding toward Arequipa—a city of over one million people still 200 miles off in the distance—Dave and I pass through a cheerful village with front-yard gardens, clean streets, and happy, hospitable folks. We stop for groceries at a small food store, and I buy rice, olives, cheese, and cold drinks. The old lady behind the counter is sweet and follows me out. When I swing a leg over my motorcycle, she covers her face and peeks between her fingers, then claps. I adore bonding with people in their day-to-day lives; these simple connections and encounters make my day.

We want to camp well before Arequipa, but looking for a place to pitch our tent is getting more urgent as the afternoon darkens into evening. Navy blue and dark-purple clouds boil ahead on the horizon like steam off the Andean plateau. The storm is far away, but we have no idea where it's heading and how quickly. We discuss whether to ride through or put up the tent in the wide open *altiplano*. Considering we haven't seen anyone for miles—and that those we met were kind and helpful—we decide it's safe to stop and camp.

Dave bounces off-road to a flat area about a hundred feet below me. Steering my bike in his direction, I ride over the steep, clumpy surface, sure I'm going to dump my bike. I manage to get down to where he's already looking for a flat tent spot. At over 13,000 feet, we have spacious views of rolling highlands and the storm, which continues to keep us in suspense yet entertains with dramatic lightning stabs and low, rumbling thunder.

Once stopped, I pull out my yoga mat to help stretch the kinks in my back, neck, and shoulders.

Whenever we arrive somewhere for the night, I unpack everything, as though the contents of my bags are inanimate versions of me, restless and wanting out. To quote Virginia Woolf, "I like to have space to spread my mind out in." This psychological act helps the unknown become home to me.

While Dave unfurls the tent, I lay my stuff on the grass, using the opportunity to fold disheveled clothes and create some order inside my panniers. When the sun balances on the skyline before dropping off the face of the earth, I abandon housekeeping in favor of photography, pointing my lens toward the blood-orange light coating the landscape.

Behind me, a horn beeps from the road. Two men—the first people we've seen since leaving the last town—sit on a small motorcycle, staring at us. I wave, thinking they're just curious, but they honk again, longer and more insistent.

"What the hell?" Dave mutters.

One man yells and gestures with his hands, like he's asking, *What are you doing here?*

"Just ignore them," Dave says after I've offered another friendly wave. More honking.

"Let's walk up to the road," I say. "Maybe they can't tell I'm a woman."

My hair is tied back, and I'm wearing a hat. Men traveling together can sometimes appear more intimidating than a guy-girl combo. Still, I'm not about to go down without a fight, if needed, and something tells me to slip my folding knife into my pocket.

We intercept the men walking fast down the slope in our direction. I feel vulnerable with all my stuff lying out but relax somewhat when I see the men look like a grandson/grandpa duo. As they approach, however, the younger man keeps his hand inside his jacket, which is unnerving. I get a bad feeling; my little folding knife is no match if he has a gun. Somewhere under my fear, I wonder if weapons like that are as common in developing worlds as they are at home.

The men continue to yell even once we're all face-to-face.

"*¡Hola! Buenas noches, señor.*" I extend my hand to the younger man, hoping lots of smiling and calming tones might disarm their volatility. He ignores me and looks at Dave as if to say, *Why is she the one speaking?*

I glance at their clothes, grimy and threadbare. Both have displaced teeth and greasy hair. I can't smell alcohol, and they're not stumbling around, but their molten-red faces and protruding eyeballs tell me they're not just angry—these men are sprung like coils, high on something strong and lethal.

"*Somos touristas Canadienses,*" I say, placing a hand over my chest and pointing at Dave, hoping they think what most people know: that Canadians are awesome.

I explain we're tired travelers just wanting to camp for the night and will leave in the morning. I remark how beautiful Peru is, and—more to the point—how welcoming the locals have been.

The men are having none of it. *Shit, maybe they don't speak Spanish!*

"¡Vete inmediatamente!" the old man spits.

Okay, that's definitely Spanish for "get lost."

"Sí! No hay problema," I smile again, all teeth and quaking hope. My cheeks ache with tension. *"Nos vamos ahora."* I turn to Dave. "They said we have to leave. Right now."

Dave and I walk back to the bikes, but the men stay right behind us. I'm certain we're about to be robbed, or worse.

"I think we're in trouble here," I whisper to Dave. And why not? These guys probably have a weapon, there's no one around to witness, and we're two travelers with a bunch of nice stuff spread out like a yard sale.

I stand behind the Stallion, using it like a shield while Dave scoops up my fancy-looking laptop and quickly packs our things. *Should I pull my knife to scare them off?* I think. *No. Definitely, no.* I find some food and offer it to the men. They decline almost politely, which throws me off and makes me wonder if things are de-escalating.

"Muy bonita." I gesture to the view, then show the men some of the photos I've taken.

The old man reaches for my Nikon point-and-shoot. *Here we go.* I'm an idiot for taking out my camera. I expect him to pocket it and ask for my laptop next. Instead, he seems perplexed. I show him how to advance to the next photo, glad they're distracted. *Why didn't I park my bike for a quick escape?* I'd have to do a U-turn on the uneven ground to avoid a nearby stream. My stomach growls and churns into what I'm sure will soon become anxiety-induced diarrhea.

I ask if the men want a photo, but again they refuse my gesture.

The younger one barks, *"¡Dinero!"*

I ask why they want money, and the older one says it's because I've taken photos of their land.

"¿Cuánto quieres?" I inquire how much they want.

"¡Veinte soles!"

Twenty *soles* is about seven dollars—a laughably affordable robbery, if they don't demand anything else. I've already gotten my camera back.

I remove the money from my tank bag discreetly, since I have over fifty dollars in there, and try to hand ten *soles* to each man, but the younger one snaps the bills from me and commands me to give the old man more. *Oh, twenty soles* each. I want to argue. I want to tell these assholes that this is what makes people fear traveling outside of their own countries. Instead, I do what he says, telling myself to be grateful it's not worse. They seem content now but are still surly.

"*¡Váyase!*" they yell.

Yes, yes, we're leaving. It's not like we want to stay after all this anyway!

Dave has packed everything up during my negotiations. I turn around and see nothing but our bikes ready to bolt. He's even repositioned the Stallion so I have a straight shot to ride out. I get on and survey the view one last time—a beautiful place turned hostile. It makes me sad. I like to associate nature with peace and calm.

"*¡Adios!*" I wave, feeling absurd with the formality of saying goodbye. I half expect bullets to whizz past my helmet.

Dave blasts off, leaving a gash in the soft terrain. Bucking up the bumpy hillside behind him, my heart pounds as I watch the men jog back to their bike. They're not done with us yet. In my haste and nervousness, I lose balance and fall over on the uneven ground, rolling painfully down the hillside. I collect myself and run back up to my bike, but there's no way I can lift it at this angle. Tears of frustration and panic blur my vision as I look around for Dave.

Our harassers are beside him, revving their puny bike engine, still screaming for us to go away. I can only imagine the dismay Dave must feel seeing me upside down on the ground. He dismounts and runs down to help me, despite the yelling and honking. I'm close to hyperventilating in my riding gear and pray I don't pass out.

Dave rights my bike with superhuman adrenaline power and gets it up to the road. I trip-jog uphill, jump back onto my seat, and beg for bravery while twisting my throttle. I'm more than confident we'll outrun the men on their shitty 125cc but am shocked to see them pass me and catch Dave. Even with much faster bikes, we can't outride them. These guys have road familiarity—and maybe a cocaine buzz—in their favor.

My imagination goes into overdrive. *Maybe they're going to make Dave crash and kidnap me! Maybe they want to lure us to their village where they can get more guys to rob us properly.* I can't ride fast and furious like Dave, even with possible hostage takers in pursuit. *What if I'm the one to cause our demise?* If not for me, Dave can probably get away. Still, I'm going much faster than is comfortable on the sharp, gravelly corners, and part of me is proud of my performance.

I'm about to start fumbling in my tank bag for the InReach so I can hit the SOS button when the men slow at a junction and turn off, no longer interested in us. My shoulders drop in relief.

"What. The. *Fuuuuucck?!*" I scream, feeling a colossal headache forming in my skull.

For the next twenty miles, I check my mirrors every two seconds for anyone gaining on us, but we're alone in the dark. Forced to ride into the storm, we're soon soaked to the bone. Coming upon a roadside homestead, we stop to ask if we can camp in their yard, but the man shakes his head and points down the road. Are all people mean around here, or just scared?

At 9 p.m., we roll weary and freezing into a small town and find its only hotel. Safe, wet, dirty, and spent, we fall into bed. Dave holds me tight.

"I was working up the nerve to kick their bike when they got close enough," he says, which would have sent the men off a steep embankment.

"I considered pulling my knife," I say.

We never understood why the men were so agitated. I'm just relieved we didn't have to find out how far we'd go to protect each other and ourselves.

The deadliest road

Bolivia

Dave sits on the hotel bed in La Paz looking at Google Earth.

"We have to do the Death Road," he declares.

"No way. Sounds terrifying," I shake my head. "Why do they call it the Death Road anyway? I'm sure there's a reason. No way."

I picture a road cut into the side of a mountain where diesel-belching buses have the right of way no matter what. I picture coming around a narrow corner and meeting another vehicle and I'm the Courteous Canadian who gets too close to the crumbling edge. I picture the Stallion out of control on a muddy section heading straight off a cliff.

Dave pictures the road's beauty—and perhaps a 2013 episode of *Top Gear*—where we'll duck under waterfalls cascading off rock walls and descend over 10,000 feet from the Andes to the Amazon.

Since its construction in the '30s by Paraguayan Chaco War prisoners, the Death Road has famously killed thousands of people. Fog, landslides, and monsoon rains—combined with vertical drops of up to 2,000 feet, no guardrails, and sections so narrow only one driver can squeeze by—have caused many a vehicle, bus, and transport truck to slide off the edge. As such, Bolivia's Death Road is known as one of the world's most dangerous roads.

"Maybe you'll change your mind when I tell you that in 2007, the road was closed to buses and trucks," Dave says. "It only allows local traffic and tourists like us who want to ride up or down on two wheels."

Because of its catchy name and scenic location, *El Camino de la Muerte* has become a tourist attraction. There are even T-shirts with conversational wording like, "Ask me how I survived the Death Road!" Thousands of people mountain bike and motorcycle the road these days, with far fewer catastrophes. The new highway now spans a nearby mountain range and is the much safer alternative.

Dave's right; I'd regret not doing it.

Two days later, I'm at 14,000 feet on La Cumbre Pass, posing for a photo in front of a sign that says, DEATH ROAD. KEEP YOUR LEFT. Although South Americans drive on the right, by staying left, drivers can keep an eye on their cliff-side wheels and inch over to let other vehicles pass. With eroding edges, I can see why so many have plunged to their death.

From the top, we'll descend over 11,000 feet during the forty miles to the village of Coroico. To ride the attraction, we each pay twenty-five *bolivianos* (three and a half dollars). Bored young men working the cash register—a tin can on a rock—collect our money and hand us a map that looks like a child's drawing. We fill out a form with questions like: *what is your name; where do you live; where are you hoping to go next?* Apart from this one formality, there's no further instruction except a half-hearted wave in the direction of travel from one of the boys.

I soon understand how the *El Camino de la Muerte*—with its road-rivers cascading off the edge and water falling down cliffsides—would be terrifying with a steady stream of traffic—or during the rainy season. Throw in semitrucks and alcoholics, and yeah, I'd call it a death road. But thanks to the newer highway siphoning off most of the traffic, Dave and I coast along, enjoying every minute. We've been on far scarier roads over the past 10,000 miles anyway—mostly due to other drivers.

"Get me coming through the waterfall!" I hand Dave my camera and do a U-turn to ride through the wet sheet splashing off a rock wall.

At one of the few viewpoints, I pull over to photograph the road—a brown ribbon bordered by a sea of green and dropping out of sight around the mountain's shoulder—so narrow it could be mistaken for a hiking trail. Water drips down the cliff face beside me, covered in saturated tropical plants. I turn off my engine to hear the droplets slap the fatter leaves, unconcerned that anyone will come up behind me; we've only seen a handful of cyclists so far.

Walking to the edge, I glance down into the Amazonian gorge and try not to imagine how many skeletons are down there. On closer inspection, I see a rusting old bus chassis. I feel bad that we're having so much fun on the Death Road, where others' souls rest for eternity.

Dave stops on a corner and waits for a photo. His bike is parked close to the edge, nothing between it and 2,000 feet of air but a couple fern leaves sticking out from the cliff. It's a dramatic shot.

Later that night, Dave toasts me for agreeing to ride the Death Road. It's really not to be missed.

Street dogs & the Fuel Mafia

Never in our travels has the simple act of fueling up our bikes been a problem until Bolivia. Since 2016, gas has been subsidized by the government at fourteen *bolivianos* (two dollars) per gallon. The price has been known to double for anyone with out-of-country plates to cover the added hassle of filling out paperwork, which most gas station attendants can't be bothered with.

Both bikes are low on fuel. We've already been turned away at three other stations. Circling the sweltering, rotten-meat-smelling streets after leaving Coroico, we roll up to a fourth station, and I refuse to leave. A male attendant with oil-stained fingers taps away at a pocket calculator, then shows us what our gas will cost—more than double. He stares at our bikes and gear, uninterested in my argument about inflated tourist prices.

Exasperated, I pull out enough bolivianos to equal seventy dollars. If we were Bolivian, the amount would be less than thirty dollars, but we don't have much choice, and the Fuel Mafia knows it. I give the attendant the money, shaking my head when he folds the wad into his shirt pocket right before my eyes. No paperwork. No record of that cash transaction.

Dave fills our tanks. I try hard not to pet an adorable, disease-ridden dog who's wandered over. It's heartbreaking to see so many hounds trying to survive on the streets since Mexico. No one has the money, or care, to keep the animals from reproducing or have them as a family pet, and most have no homes and no one to love them. I give the poor pup some bread, which he scarfs down in one second flat.

I love dogs, but in the developing world they either break my heart or scare the shit out of me.

At our hostel in Lima, we met a guy recovering from a broken leg— and repairing his mangled bike—after he hit a dog that lunged at him while he was riding.

A low-hanging fog has settled into the mountains of southern Bolivia, and the view past my handlebars is an impenetrable gray. Ahead, Dave is ghostlike, and it takes me a few seconds to register two large German Shepherds in the ditch. They jump up and run barking after Dave, who's oblivious to the pursuit. When they don't catch him, the dogs turn and see a second option. They are smack in the middle of the road and force me to make a quick decision—swerve or brake.

I choose the former and veer rapid-fire fast into the oncoming lane, which I've scanned to make sure it's empty. One dog spins and snaps at my elbow, distracting me. I hear a horn seconds before I see the pickup, whose driver neglected to turn on his headlights in the haze. Twisting my handlebars sharply, I just manage to squeeze between the truck's bumper and the jumping dogs. The sound of the truck's tires squealing as he passes inches from my leg haunts me that night in my dreams.

These near misses fire cortisol through my body in an unhealthy overdose, and my sleep is affected with the aftershock of *what ifs*. I'm becoming increasingly short-tempered—a sure sign of stress overload. Is it all worth the risk, as my friend asked that day in Revelstoke?

Some nights, I lie awake wondering whether I can handle it all, but then a bright morning chases the dark thoughts away, and I hear that familiar voice in my head: *Just give it another day.*

A salt shaker's worth

I twist my throttle back as far as I dare and blast by Dave at eighty-eight miles an hour. Not about to allow me the glory of holding the trip's speed record, he passes me at 101 miles an hour with what I'm sure is a shit-eating grin.

Like Bonneville Salt Flats in Utah, Bolivia's Salar de Uyuni is a massive unobstructed salt pan resulting from a dried-up prehistoric lake. Also like Bonneville, speed records are set here.

During the rainy season from November to March, the largest salt flat in the world becomes the largest mirror in the world, reflecting the sky and anything on its surface in perfect replication. The photography can be stunning, with glassy sunsets and horizons with no beginning or end.

In April, however, the flats are mostly dried up. Crystalized hexagons bigger than dinner plates and arranged like jigsaw puzzle pieces span the dead-flat canvas with just two hues on its palette: white and blue, for salt and sky.

Salar's elevation fluctuates just three feet, on average, over its 6,575 square miles, making it safe(ish) to try for a personal speed record. Here, I don't worry about dogs or inattentive drivers, but my instinct for survival kicks in and I bring the Stallion back down to a reasonable gallop, unwilling to beat my own pace and certainly not Dave's.

Salar de Uyuni is made up of ten billion tons of salt, 25,000 of which are excavated and processed annually in the nearby village of Colchani. In the past, residents used the salt to barter for other goods, like maize, cocoa, and anything that can't grow in a salty plateau.

Nowadays, with transport infrastructure everywhere, the mineral is exported and sold.

I've never really considered where salt comes from, but who'd have guessed I'd be ripping across the source one day on a motorcycle? I dab my finger on the ground and lick. *Yep, salty.* I think about collecting some for added flair to our camp meals and doubt they'll miss a shaker's worth, but I'm guessing table salt requires some kind of processing first. I don't need to be sprinkling toxic elements like lithium over our pasta.

Salar de Uyuni's expanse makes it hard for the eye to judge what's near and what's far. Handing Dave my camera, I stand fifty feet behind the center of my bike and strike a yoga pose. In the photo, it looks like I'm just an inch tall standing on my bike's seat.

Dave's photo is a mini version of himself crouched at the rear wheel of his bike, looking to be pushing a giant motorcycle.

After playing around on the flats, our bikes are caked in corrosive salt, molded like hard-packed snow around our license plates and flung up under our seats. In the town of Uyuni, we ride to a car wash and try to rinse it all away. Months later, I still find the crusty brine in the nooks and crannies on my bike.

The hard way down

Chile/Argentina

Chile's Atacama region is home to the driest desert in the world—except during the *desierto florido*, a mass flower-blooming event that happens once every five to seven years after an early spring unleashes higher than normal rainfall.

In the Chilean spring of 2015, the Atacama saw the equivalent of years of rain in twelve hours—about one inch. The subsequent burst of plants and flowers popped up in stunning photos shared all over social media. Sadly, there's nothing left of this lush, colorful mosaic when Dave and I ride through months later, but the smoldering volcanoes, stick-legged flamingos, and bloodred boulder clusters scattered across the desert floor are awesome enough.

Along the Atacama's *Ruta 5* highway, Dave spots Nina. We first heard about this Wisconsinite through CJ and John back in Peru. After turning 70, Nina thought she needed a solo birthday mission and decided to ride from Cartagena, Colombia, to Ushuaia, Argentina—roughly 6,000 miles. She asked her husband to stay home.

Nina was popular on ADVRider, an adventure motorcycle website where motorcyclists tell travel stories, sell used gear, and chat from all over the world on a forum about everything ADV motorcycle related.

You're never too old to become a legend.

When Dave notices Nina's Honda CRF250L after we pass her rolling slowly down the road, we flag her down. She stops when Dave removes his helmet and says, "Nina?"

Confused, Nina cocks her head to the side.

"How do you know my name?"

"You're well-known in the online motorcycle travel world," I say.

"*Pffft!*" she hisses, waving a dismissive hand in the air. "I don't know why anyone would be interested in me."

Nina's running out of fuel and trying to keep her speed at a conservative forty-five miles an hour. At first, I thought she was just a slow rider and was about to pass with a wave to this stranger at the time, but Dave—who can pass a vehicle in the blink of an eye and tell you what kind of engine it has and whether the driver invested in aftermarket parts—recognized her bike right away.

Dave suggests the three of us ride together until Nina finds a place to fuel up. A few miles down the road, a gas station and restaurant appear. We invite Nina to lunch. Over grilled cheese-and-avocado sandwiches, I ask if she ever gets nervous or lonesome riding solo.

"Nope, and I speak fluent Spanish, so no problems there."

Does she ride off-road on her dirt bike?

"Not if I can help it!"

Does she camp or stay in hotels?

"At my age? Hotels! I don't sleep on the ground—oh *hell* no."

While I'm never lonely, since I have a travel companion, I admit to Nina that strong winds and stray dogs scare me on a motorcycle. I tell her I don't want to break my wrist—or anything else—again. These stories are divulged with a lighthearted, self-deprecating humor; an attempt to bond with another female rider. But Nina's having none of my sniveling.

"You sure worry a lot!" she informs me while Dave nods, ally-like, beside her. It's a gentle scolding, but her message is clear.

Somewhere along the line, I'd come to the erroneous conclusion that worrying about something means I had a better chance of controlling the outcome. I've tried to steer my life in certain directions, but sometimes that feels more like driving a 1970 Ford Torino with numb, powerless steering. If I want to enjoy the rest of my travels, I need to chill the hell out—no easy task when your head is on a swivel. There is magic in every day, and I've lost sight of that.

Our round-the-world trip is no holiday; it's proving tougher than either Dave or I could have imagined, and it isn't just me who could use a pep talk. Although Dave doesn't stress about the actual act of riding a motorcycle, his irritation for mishaps and snafus affects both of us and can bring out our worst.

Along with being a nervous rider, I've been thinking a lot about my future with him: Will I be able to handle two years together? Will he? Four months on the road already, and there are still so many questions.

But I was supposed to chill the hell out, wasn't I?

I would have enjoyed spending more than just a few hours sponging Nina's wisdom, but we never see her again after that day—she found a hotel, and Dave and I kept riding south along the Pan-American Highway.

A shadow by the lakeshore

In Chile, we discover a phenomenon: Gas attendants actually take our money and top up our tanks. Simple as that. No foreign-plate forms to fill out. No haggling over an invented price per gallon. What I like most about fueling up in Chile, however, are the attached cafés. Even when the bikes aren't that low on gas, we stop anyway for ice cream or hot chocolate, weather depending. Some days it takes forever to get anywhere because we spend an hour or two talking with locals, stocking up on food, or getting sucked into the free Wi-Fi vortex at the Shell or Copec.

Chile is a well-to-do country, for the most part, and grocery stores are spacious, modern, and stocked full of variety. I have fun shopping one afternoon and materialize from swishing automated doors with food items we haven't been able to buy fresh in months, like fruits, veggies, and meats.

"Where're we going to put all that?" Dave asks.

Setting the groceries down on the oil-splattered tarmac, I stuff everything into any available space. Carrots end up in my tank bag, and a box of cereal gets strapped over my duffle bag. I find room to fit the Chilean chocolate bars, fresh goat cheese, and even the raw red meat in my panniers. Dave packs the rest of my overzealous purchases into his panniers. To soften the blow of adding more bulky weight to his bike, I've bought bargaining treats: chocolate mousse and steak-flavored potato chips. When I present these pacifiers, Dave has serious snack gratitude.

Keeping perishables cold is an endless challenge. I carry an insulated soft-sided cooler, but a bag of ice takes up most of the space. I pour cubed ice into our water bladders, then put the rest in the cooler to keep the meat and yogurt cool. Sometimes we eat foods past their prime—the ice lasts a few hours at best, especially in the hotter areas—but so far, we've gotten away with only one day each with severe gastrointestinal issues. In Mexico, I had a battle with diarrhea that sent me to the bathroom sixteen times in one night. Dave had a bad case of constipation in Nicaragua from dehydration that left him writhing in pain on the floor of our hotel room. It's bound to happen; we're surprised it doesn't happen more.

Riding a motorcycle every day isn't the most comfortable thing in the world, and food is something fun to look forward to. I push for more rest stops so we can snack and hydrate to keep energy levels up. I'm constantly scanning my body for what it's telling me, like *get off and stretch your legs* or *have something to drink*. Dave can ride for hours nonstop. This becomes a regular source of contention. If we haven't had lunch yet and it's late in the day, Dave often votes to push on until we can stop for the night and have a sit-down meal. As a snacker, this doesn't work for me; I need food every few hours. It's reckless and unsustainable demanding so much from our bodies without replenishment.

Temps get cooler in the higher regions of Chile, and many days are downright cold. Although fresh mountain air is a pleasant change from the days when it felt like our faces were hovering over pots of boiling water, I'm now freezing on my bike in the approaching fall. Riding at seventy miles an hour with an air temperature of 30°F chills me to my weary bones.

Leaving a gas station café, where we've stopped to warm our hands around hot drinks, I waddle to my bike like a toddler overstuffed with layers, arms sticking out from my sides. It's all I can do to swing a thickly clad leg over my seat, and Dave takes much pleasure in calling me Nanook of the North. He doesn't like feeling constrained and has enough hair on his limbs that I'm sure adds at least an R1 insulation value. One of my nicknames for him is *Yeti*. But even Dave finally pulls out his warmer jacket and adds long underwear to his bare legs under his riding pants.

The heated grips on our handlebars are a godsend for icy fingertips. We always wear riding gloves, but they aren't insulated, like ski gloves. My battery-powered jacket is cranked on high, and under my riding pants, I wear both the quilted and waterproof liners zipped in to cut the wind. Still, the cool air finds its way up my back or down my neck.

None of this stops us from camping. Chileans love outdoor recreation, and we have no trouble finding dirt roads leading into radiant autumn-hued forests, stirring up leaves on the ground as we pass.

One evening, we set up the tent in an empty campground beside a beautiful lake. Dave builds a campfire, and we watch it grow brighter as darkness falls.

"Oh," Dave says. "I wanted to tell you about this really cool experience I had today. I was riding along and noticed a shadow on the road just in front of me. A huge bird was just above my head. He followed me for a long time, and I followed his shadow. It was like we were flying together."

I look into his eyes, twinkling from excitement, then suck in my breath when I see another pair of eyes down by the lakeshore reflecting our campfire. Stepping away so my pupils can adjust to the night, I make out the shape of a long, dark animal slinking along the shoreline. Whatever it is hesitates, alert to our presence.

"Is that a puma?!" I whisper.

"I don't know," Dave whispers back.

The animal moves on and is swallowed into the night.

Despite a large cat somewhere near our campsite, I sleep well. But first thing the next morning, I walk down to the lakeshore to check for prints. Sadly, the beach is covered in rocks, devoid of any hint as to what belonged to those shining eyeballs that night.

The place that started it all

Since entering Chile, we've seen more ADV bikes like ours as we all funnel into the narrowest part of the continent together. Most riders are heading south to north, however, where temperatures are warming up.

Our southbound route for the next few weeks will pass between Chile and Argentina several times, following *Ruta 40* and other side roads around, over, and through the 300,000 square-mile Patagonia region.

After a few days in Santiago doing bike maintenance and replenishing supplies, we take a steep, curving road high into the mountains and the border for Argentina.

Scooping my bike into a tight corner, Dave says, "I remember this road," over the intercom.

In 2002, he'd come to Argentina to climb Mount Aconcagua, the tallest peak in the Americas at 22,841 feet. I like that during our travels, we can point out the highest mountains we've each climbed.

In line at the border, I discover I've lost one of two important receipts that are proof of us leaving Chile. One must have blown away when I took my camera out to get a photo of Aconcagua. I lie to the aduana officer, claiming I only received one receipt for both of us. She insists I was given two. I pull up closer to the window, not used to fishing for documents while balancing the bike's weight on one big toe, and hand her my passport. So far, all our border crossings have been on foot. I beg myself not to fall over.

"Where is your reciprocity tax receipt?"

"My what?"

"Canadians must pay online the reciprocity tax to enter Argentina and bring the receipt!"

Shit, more receipts we don't have.

"Okay, how much is it? Can I pay here?" Embarrassment-induced sweat soaks my helmet liner. Over the intercom, Dave's asking what the holdup is.

"No, you can't pay here!" The officer sticks two fingers in her mouth and a shrill whistle brings forth another officer. This one is friendlier and speaks better English. She asks us to park and follow her to a small office with a computer. I sign into a government site and buy our way into Argentina for seventy dollars per person. Dave, a citizen of both the US and Canada, had decided to travel only on his Canadian passport. Now, he regrets not bringing his American passport as well, because the United States and Argentina have a reciprocity agreement, and there is no fee for US citizens.

"Do we only have to pay this once?"

Crossing back and forth between Chile and Argentina was going to get expensive, if not.

"Yes, it is for multiple entries."

We're able to butt back in line, which pisses off the people behind us who've been waiting in the two-hour lineup. The unfriendly female guard continues pressing me about the receipt I've lost. She isn't going to let us enter the country without it. Cars start honking. I'm desperate to get the whole ordeal over with and just ride. My anxiety must be obvious, as there's now another officer trying to help. He somehow facilitates a piece of paper in place of the lost exit receipt, which Mean Chica is forced to stamp.

Three hours after getting to the border of Argentina, we're finally free to keep going.

By mid-April, the very place that originally inspired our trip unfolds before our handlebars. Its five-syllable name appears on a wooden sign beside the road: PATAGONIA.

This stunning region shared between Chile and Argentina, with its deserts, steppes, grasslands, and the incredible glacial lakes and rivers of the Andes, has my imagination running wild about what we'll see.

Of course, the first thing I'm braced for is how windy it'll get. At certain times of the year, it's all but impossible to ride a motorcycle in Patagonia, with windspeeds exceeding seventy miles an hour. We're late in the season to be traveling south, but the time of year is in our favor. April is one of the least windy months of the year in Patagonia. If not for my broken wrist delay, we'd have arrived a few months earlier, like January, which is the worst time for wind. I remind myself that everything happens for a reason.

April or not, it isn't long before my neck aches bracing against the powerful sidewinds. Even the thousand-year-old, hundred-foot-high monkey trees are swaying. That time riding along the Gulf of Mexico…*was the wind stronger than this, or am I just more confident now?*

The trick, I've learned, is not to fight it; that takes a lot of energy. I weave like a drunk over the center line and back, letting the gusts push me around. But not too much. Oddly, I begin to find comfort in something that once terrified me; I lean into the wind like it's a friend's shoulder.

Air blasts across the Pampas plains to my right, pressing the tall grasses nearly flat to the ground. When we make a left turn, I stand for balance on the gravel road, aware of something odd. Normally, I'd feel air resistance against my chest and helmet without my windscreen to shield me. I feel nothing; like I'm going walking speed.

Later, I mention this to Dave, who uses this opportunity to bust out a math problem.

"So," he starts, "say you're riding at fifty miles per hour—you'll have a head wind, even if it isn't windy, because you're creating turbulence through speed. When you change direction, the tailwind, now behind you, matches your speed, therefore equalizing the air speed. That means the sidewind this afternoon was blowing at roughly fifty miles per hour."

"Wow," I laugh and shake my head.

"What?"

"You're such a nerd!"

"But I'm *your* nerd."

While friends and family back home are anticipating spring, Dave and I get colder by the minute riding in the southern hemisphere's autumn. We take cover from the mid-thirty temps one day and eat lunch in a culvert—the only shelter available to block us from the windchill. Short, yellow grasses flicker like flames in the persistent gale. The gray strip of pavement we've been following is ruler-straight and mind-numbingly boring. I have a lot of time to think about ridiculous things, like why is the word "acronym" so long, and what asshole decided to spell "lisp" with an "s"?

This isn't the Patagonia of my dreams. Instead of granite spires and turquoise lakes, mile after mile of prairies and grasslands are punctuated only by the never-ending, quiet highway.

I stir hot soup on the camp stove, which Dave pulls out of his bags with begrudging compliance. We don't normally cook for lunch, and he wants to keep going. But on frigid, uninspiring days like these, it's too easy to hunker down, chest to tank bag, and press on, ignoring the need to take care of our bodies. My handlebar grips and heated jacket were turned on high that day, but I still can't feel my fingers.

Like trolls cowering in the culvert, we sip our soup and start to warm up.

"Maybe we should reroute into the mountains," Dave suggests, handing the pot back to me. I wrap my hands around the stainless steel, feeling its heat through my gloves.

Until now, we've stuck to lower elevations; higher roads mean even colder weather and potentially snow. It also means repeatedly crossing between the two countries, but that now seems favorable over the monotonous, gusty plains.

At the next opportunity, we enter back into Chile and get on the *Carretera Austral*, running 770 miles through rural Patagonia. Despite its length and modest fame among overlanders, the highway—which also goes by the less grandiose name of *Ruta 7*—is remote. The largest city along the route is Coyhaique, population just over 44,000.

In my headset, I listen to artists like Alice in Chains and Bassnectar to keep myself awake. I think back to that day in Dave's room when we stared at the map on his wall, and how that has morphed into the very thing I'm now living daily. How daunting it felt then. How daunting it still feels, even though all I'm required to do each day is get up, ride, and go to bed. It's the in-between stuff that can be tough, but also exciting. How many people want to leave their lives behind and travel the world, yet something—fear, money, family, responsibilities—keeps them from the dream?

Is this a dream? I'm uncomfortable a lot lately. Either my ass is numb or my back is throbbing or my head hurts…I long for the days when being on two wheels will be more soothing, meditative, fun. *Yes, fun. That's what I miss!*

Extreme temperatures—both hot and cold—present ongoing challenges. At home, I'd never ride so close to heat exhaustion as I have the past few months—or let myself freeze, as is the case now. Traveling inside a vehicle, I could alter the environment with air conditioning or heat, but on a motorcycle, only mental fortitude works.

The cold makes me tired and cranky. Dave and I bicker, each feeling the other should meet our needs. Yet oddly, we're more united than ever in our shared discomfort. The rigor of long-distance travel is something few can commiserate with, and it bonds us despite the downsides.

One thing that helps is the chance to decompress in our helmet bubbles. If one of us starts out in a bad mood, we're soon rolling along in our own little worlds, almost forgetting the other person is there—an escape you can't look forward to inside a vehicle.

While daydreaming—or night dreaming, since it's getting dark—I see Dave's brake lights snap on.

"I just hit a jackrabbit," he says. "I'm going to go back and make sure he's not suffering."

Dave walks the lonely highway, searching left and right before heading off into a field. He stops and looks down.

"It's dead." He calls over to me. "We should probably get off the road."

I agree this is a sign. We left a gas station an hour earlier, thinking we'd easily find somewhere to camp, but mile after mile of exposed grasslands and private property kept us riding well into the night.

A farmer's field is our only option. We enter through an open barbed wire gate then roll along the spongy ground littered with cow patties, which our tires flick into the air. Burning shit fills my nostrils when feces stick to the hot parts of my bike and smolder. Finding some small hills for a wind break, we set up our tent without permission. In the dark, I see nothing resembling a home or building anyway.

I jog around to stay warm. We ate earlier at the gas station. All I want now is to crawl into our nylon home—flimsy, but shelter nonetheless. Packing for our trip, Dave said I'd regret bringing my bulky sleeping bag, rated to -4°F.

Not so far.

Pre-dawn, my bladder nudges me awake. I intend to deal with it then jump right back into my cozy cocoon for more rest before committing to the day. I unzip the tent fly and my heart skips when I see a few inches of snow covering the ground.

Hoping to make light of it, I lean close to Dave and whisper, "Get your skis."

"Huh?" Turning over, he wipes his eyes awake.

I spread the door open and point.

"Oh no," he groans, rising onto his elbows.

In minutes, Dave has his riding gear on and his bike running. Mine is dead. We boost it with a set of short jumper cables we carry. Along with a radiator, I need a new battery. The one that came with the GS when I bought it two years ago is worn out, and now jump-starting the Stallion on cold mornings is a regular routine.

"I'm going to check out the road," Dave says, unclipping the alligator cables from my battery and popping the plastic fairing back into place. "If it's icy, we may have to stay put for a bit."

I leave the Stallion idling and look at the dismal surroundings. *What if we're stuck here for days surrounded by cow crap and no amenities? What if the weather gets worse?* Sooner or later, the property owners will spot us; I hope they're sympathetic and kind, not like the assholes who terrorized us in Peru.

Snow starts falling again, and it's hard to keep my stuff dry. I pack up in optimistic, stubborn determination. The road might be dangerous, but if I get on my bike, I can plug in my heated jacket—a luxurious thought.

Dave returns and says the road is covered in snow, but there are melted tracks from one car's tires.

"We can stay in those tracks, and it'll be just like wet pavement," he says with conviction, perhaps expecting an argument.

"Great, let's get out of here," I reply.

With no other vehicles around so early in the morning, we ride at a cautious thirty miles an hour. I have tunnel vision trying to keep my bike on the wet foot-wide track. Every now and again, I veer into dense slush and my wheels spin, shooting blood into my racing heart before I can steer out.

Descending in elevation, the pavement is just wet now with snow remnants on the shoulders. Even the sun pokes out.

As a reward for our tenacity, a roadside cabin-turned-café appears. Dave opens the door for me, and I walk into the aroma of fried meat and onions. I almost drop to the floor with gratitude when I see a woodstove with a crackling fire. We can't contain ourselves and order four meat-filled empanadas, two slices of chocolate cake, and some lemon squares. Early that morning, while Dave and I were busy stuffing wet gear into our panniers, the baker had been hard at work.

The middle-aged woman at the cash register giggles when we have trouble carrying everything over to a table. We choose one closest to the fire, and Dave goes back to order hot drinks.

A small store, a smiling face, a warm fire—it's that easy to find everything we need, even this far from home. For two hours, we sit warming our frozen toes and drying out our riding suits.

"I was pretty worried this morning," Dave says over his coffee mug.

"How so?" I know he means waking to snow, but I wait to see whether he'll express his vulnerability. I need to know he gets nervous and fearful, like me.

"I kept thinking, what if this is winter? What if the snow is here to stay?" he says. "Ushuaia would be out of the question."

I've often wondered whether aspirations can set us up for disaster—can you really have goals without expectations? Travelers are supposed to carry a cloak of armor against agenda disappointments, but it would truly suck not to reach *El Fin del Mundo* at the end of South America.

Prying ourselves from the lovely little café in Chile that cold, late-April day is so very hard, but we pull on balaclavas, tighten helmets, and go in pursuit of our hopes and dreams.

Paperwork games

Our GPS shows the border for exiting Chile is twenty miles away. Trusting the digital map, we ride along a scenic dirt track, high above a robin-egg-blue lake scattered with whitecaps. A gust of wind catches me while I'm cresting a hill, almost knocking me off my seat. I see nothing in the way of vegetation on the hills around us, nor down near the water.

The road is rough. I've recently discovered that my bike's bushings—a collar placed between the rear shock and the swing arm—are worn out. The rear end of my bike is loose and sloppy without the stability, and I feel an uncomfortable metal-on-metal *thunk* with every bump.

There's yet another issue: my chain. After so many miles, the teeth on the sprockets are ground down to nubs and the chain keeps slipping, emitting a loud *clank* when it slaps against the sprocket.

It's been difficult to find parts and supplies to take care of our motorcycles in isolated areas. Of course, two weeks earlier, while in Santiago with access to multiple motorcycle parts, we didn't stock up. At that time, neither of us needed anything, and weight and bulk are always a consideration. We also want to get as much life out of our motorcycle parts as possible, since repairs and replacements—especially for the BMW brand—are expensive.

Although we're doing some regular maintenance, like oil changes, weather conditions are deteriorating as we continue south. It's getting colder, wetter, and grittier, and these elements are taking their toll sooner than expected. I hope to find parts and new tires in Ushuaia, but that's still 1,500 miles away.

Cursing every bump and dip my bike slams into as we make our way along the track, I finally see a white building in the distance. Riding so gingerly, however, takes me another hour to get there. On approach, I look up at a flag whipping in the wind—two blue banners with a sun between. *Oh no.* Somehow, we've missed *aduana* exiting Chile and are already in Argentina, having entered illegally.

"What the hell is so hard about putting up a sign?" Dave growls.

"Maybe they'll make an exception," I say. A long shot, but the remoteness of this particular post has me hoping they'll be lax about formalities.

Opening a creaking door leading into a warm cabin, I greet the border guard.

He doesn't return any pleasantries, and after hearing we don't have the proper documentation, demands we turn right around and properly exit Chile. I dread riding back over that road with my battered bike, but there's no bargaining with the officer unless we offer a bribe, which we continue to avoid doing.

Customs is easier to find from the opposite direction. For some reason, the sign on the otherwise featureless building that looks more like a garden shed is only visible coming from the Argentina side. Without a soul in line, Dave and I get through the process quickly.

Before leaving, however, I look at my stamp. Because we've come from Argentina, the customs agent misunderstood and gave us entry stamps into Chile. I take the passports back in and after some creative Spanish wording and charades, the correction is made. I can't imagine arriving back at the Argentina post, seeing the error, then having to backtrack yet again.

Of course, it's not as bad as the time we drove 2,000 miles back to the Mexico/USA border for FMM stamps.

Dave rides faster now out of sheer impatience for our third pass over the bike-destroying road. We've already traveled 200 miles today, sixty of which were crisscrossing between two countries. I'm sure bolts are vibrating loose and welds are cracking on the Stallion.

At the Argentina border, we walk back into the cabin and stand by a wood stove to get warm while the officer glares at our paperwork.

"*¿Dónde está tu seguro?*"

We've crossed into Argentina a few times already, and there's been no mention of insurance for our bikes. Although it's risky, Dave and I rarely bother with such paperwork unless it's mandatory. Motorcycle travel forums tell many a tale of insurance companies not paying out to foreigners, and the only place we can really buy such paperwork is at borders, which isn't advisable since they're often bogus setups.

I'm trying to figure out how to deal with this demand for our insurance papers when a black Land Rover pulls up outside. Its beefy tires crunch on the gravel. The driver comes in and overhears me. He speaks English and offers to translate for the officer.

"You must have insurance," the driver explains. "They can put you in jail if you have an accident."

"No problem, we'll buy it here," I say.

"No, you were supposed to have it before you arrived."

The irony. Vehicle insurance is shoved in our faces at border crossings for countries where it isn't mandatory, but now that it is, this border doesn't sell it.

I pull out expired paperwork from home, trying my luck. Our translator shows the paperwork to the officer, explaining it's our international motorcycle insurance. He points to the VIN numbers and title, telling the officer our home insurance covers the bikes across the world, which it most certainly does not.

The guard scrutinizes the papers. I pray he doesn't notice the expiry date of several months ago. We all wait in anticipation as the man's brow creases deep lines into his forehead. He's exasperated, but the friendly driver's calm demeanor smooths things over. Finally, Dave and I are again permitted to enter Argentina after promising we'll buy vehicle protection at the first chance. We never do.

The officer is only doing his job, but traveling has us trying our luck more than we would normally—even though the consequences can be worse in a foreign land.

I know Spanish!

At a gas station in northwestern Patagonia, a handsome, broad-shouldered Argentinian man comes over to us.

"*¿De donde?*" he asks.

"Canada."

Mario is in his early fifties. His English is decent, and after twenty minutes of chatting, he invites us to stay with him and his wife in San Martin de los Andes.

I wonder what it is about us that draws a stranger. We've had more than our fair share of kindness in our travels: Sheffy lending his van and keeping my bike stored after I broke my wrist; Neil and Linda taking us in during part of my recovery; random offerings of food, accommodation, or help in any way we need from people who've known us for mere minutes. Why do they care?

Of course, we can hope for—and maybe even expect—such treatment from family and friends, or even friends of friends. But when someone you don't know offers something so personal—like an invitation into their home—it's mind-blowing, when you really think about it. These gestures we've experienced throughout our travels give me a renewed sense of wonder for each day and an inspiring hope for humanity.

How would sleeping in a stranger's home play out back home? "Oh yeah, we met this dude at a gas station and went to his house."

"He could be a murderer!" they'd say. "Or what if he robbed you?"

And what if *we're* the murderers? What if *we* rob *him*? These people are putting faith in us, too. There are no guarantees either way, but if Dave and I don't seize these moments to interact, then why travel in the first place?

Mario's wife, Carolina, welcomes us inside. After a filling meal of barbecued steak and garden potatoes, she prepares yerba mate.

Yerba is a tea made from the twigs and leaves of a holly plant species native to South America. It's served in a cup called a gourd, or *mate*—a calabash fruit plant that's been hollowed out and dried. When people drink yerba from a gourd, it's usually through a straw called a *bombilla*, which has a filter on the end to keep out tea debris.

The first time I had the tea was at a friend's in Revelstoke. A world traveler herself, she liked to serve her yerba out of a thermos, flavored with soy milk and honey. I drank it that way for years afterward.

I watch Carolina make the tea. First, she packs the gourd about two-thirds full of yerba leaves. Next, she adds a little hot water to help insert the *bombilla*, tilting it just so. She explains this is the best angle for ensuring a debris-free sip. Topping off the gourd with more hot water from a thermos—never boiling, or it'll burn the leaves—Carolina passes the gourd around. We each take a sip. The tea tastes acrid—much stronger than I'm used to. Dave later describes it as steeped cigarette butts, and he's not wrong. But I enjoy the caffeine hit and even feel smarter after drinking yerba—one of its many benefits. I'm able to carry on a conversation with Carolina, who doesn't speak English. This is a significant moment for me, realizing how much conversational Spanish I've learned over the past few months.

Adding to the energy jolt we get from the yerba, Mario passes around *Fernet*—a liqueur that tastes like cherry cough syrup. *Fernet* is a drink Argentinians love faithfully. They mix it with Coke, which makes the cocktail far too sweet for either of us, but Dave and I partake to be polite.

We stay with Mario and Carolina for three glorious, relaxing days. Despite the feasting and drinking, I sleep soundly in their spare room. My body is desperate for the restoration and nightly platters of red meat that help rebuild my weary muscles.

San Martin de los Andes is a picturesque town of 23,000 situated alongside a lake and surrounded by forest. Its downtown core reminds me of a much-less-crowded Whistler, BC, with attractive sports shops selling the Patagonia outdoor brand and all kinds of recreational toys for climbing, skiing, and mountain biking.

Before staying with Mario and Carolina, Dave and I had taken a breathtaking side road through columns of rocks poking out of deep-green forests overlooking glacier-blue lakes. We love this area so much we talk seriously about moving here sometime. Mario is building himself and Carolina a modern house in a spacious suburb. New construction is popping up everywhere, and Mario expresses to Dave the need for skilled contractors in town. As a writer, I can work remotely, and what better place?

We know, however, there are more places ahead that we'll fall in love with. We haven't even left the Americas yet.

I'm drawn to both Carolina and Mario at the end of our time together, having become like family to each other, but something sad I've learned about traveling is you're constantly in "goodbye" mode. You'll meet some of the best people you'll ever know in your life, but these people are almost always gone forever after you leave.

The road ahead

The Andean mountain range and Patagonian region crisscrosses over both Chile and Argentina, but the former country gets more of the rugged land-scape. As we move farther south, Dave and I discover more about the Patagonia we've come all this way for.

Unique ecosystems and national parks have been established in both countries to preserve the pristine wilderness of the region. We are already seeing some of the rich flora and fauna. Guanacos, which look like small llamas, skip across the wide-open steppes. We see the endangered ostrich-like, flightless birds known as rheas that can sprint up to thirty-five miles an hour.

Jagged peaks, cavernous valleys, and ice-blue glaciers beg for explora-tion, but we don't have the right gear. That's okay; just seeing the landscape in real life leaves me breathless. No matter where we are in the world, mountains make us feel at home. Although Dave and I have mo-torcycles and traveling in common, it's nice to share something quiet and peaceful together.

Our first date, almost two years ago now, was ski touring near the Mount Baker ski area, an hour from Bellingham and an easy border hop from Vancouver. After several hours of hiking uphill with our skis on, we topped out on Coleman Pinnacle for a great lunch spot before skiing back down. Baker's volcano was in full view that sunny spring day—so close I felt I could reach out and touch the top. I took off my skis and dashed behind a tree to pee. When I walked back to Dave, I was surprised and impressed to find him laying out a picnic spread in the snow, with expen-sive cheese, crackers, salami, olives, chocolates, and even two little plastic cups of red wine. He'd told me not to bring lunch on our date, but, always a Girl Scout, I had some granola bars in my pack. This was much better.

I can't say I knew Dave was *the one* on that first date, but there was no question something special was brewing in the high-altitude air that day.

Harsh winds remain a constant companion, hitching a ride and pushing me around. Updrafts sneak under my helmet, tugging painfully at my chin strap and forcing me to adjust its position on my head. The Stallion never feels fully in my control in this kind of wind, but I have a much lighter grip on the handlebars than I used to.

Late fall is settling in, reminding us we're on a tight timeline before winter. The cold is draining, but the wild scenery and smiling locals bring light to our days. In contrast to other countries we've ridden through, where drivers seemed to be trying to kill us, Argentinian and Chilean motorists honk and wave out open windows, cheering as we pass. Our adventurous undertaking is celebrated here in a way I've been missing, and the jovial greetings bring me happiness.

The first time I learned about Patagonia was through a photo. I was nineteen and obsessed with rock climbing when my parents gave me a National Geographic calendar for Christmas—a dozen pictures of dramatic mountains from around the globe. Something about June's image, taken in Torres del Paine, Chile, was spellbinding. The photo almost seemed fake. Pointy rock walls thousands of feet high rose like giant canine teeth, severe and striking, into a cloudless sky. In contrast, an unruffled turquoise lake sat in the foreground, fringed with lush plants and delicate purple flowers looking more fragile than spun glass. When I stared at the photo, I heard waves lapping the shoreline and felt a soft breeze rustling the hairs on my arms. I was born near the Canadian Rockies and knew natural beauty like this, but something about this scene called to me.

In my early twenties, I did a three-month solo road trip through the western US. The Patagonia photo was taped to the canopy in the bed of my truck, along with similar images I'd ripped from magazines, creating a sort of wallpaper of desire. I'd lie on top of my sleeping bag in the back of my Jeep Comanche and stare at the Patagonia picture, daydreaming of a life I hoped was in my future; a life that would afford me the chance to travel somewhere like that. If I was lucky, I'd also find someone who wanted to travel to these places with me.

A gust of wind snaps me back to the moment. We turn off blustery *Ruta 40* and head west on Highway 23 toward El Chaltén. I gasp when the road tapers to a fine point in the distance and at the end stands a foreboding mountain vista. The granite is so sheer it looks sliced by a knife. Glaciers drape themselves like white blankets where the terrain has a gentler angle. To my left, a tongue of ice licks the shores of *Lago Viedma*, milky blue with glacial silt. My calendar image is in another park, but this view is equally as thrilling because I'm *right here.*

In the communal kitchen of our hostel in El Chaltén, we cook rice and beans with fresh red onion and avocado, then dive into a delicious bottle of Chilean merlot for dessert. The wine is top-shelf quality but cost only four dollars.

Excited to be here, we take an off-bike day the next morning and hike thirteen miles into the Fitz Roy cirque, then over a pass into the valley below Cerro Torre. Everywhere I see illustrious peaks serious mountaineers the world over come to scale. Although I'm a climber, I can't imagine getting up the smooth, flat walls—where are the holds?

Using my body for something other than sitting feels great. My limbs lose their stiffness, and my neck is more in line with my spine, instead of straining against the wind. Dave usually takes some convincing to go on a hike, preferring skis or a mountain bike for the downhill, but right now he's in awe seeing up close the famous mountains we've only heard about.

Despite the windy, cold, cloudy days, fall, in my opinion, is the best season to be in Patagonia. Warm autumn colors make even the grayest of days vibrant with red, yellow, and orange trees contrasted against the gunmetal rock walls and shimmering blue lakes. Mystifying color schemes show that nature never clashes, and every layer just adds more beauty.

We trek under the rocky behemoths into a flame-red forest so vibrant it reflects off our faces as if we're standing near a campfire. Hiking has been instilled in me from youth. As a kid, I dragged my feet along the trails with a scowl, following my parents to lakes, rock fields, and bear-infested bushes almost every summer weekend. Why did I need exercise? I was eight! My reluctance grew as a teenager when I wanted to be with my friends at the mall, not yodeling in a forest to scare off grizzlies. At switchbacks, my sister Vanessa and I looked for the plastic-wrapped candies placed on top of a log or rock—bribes my parents left on the trail to get us up to that alpine lake or ridgetop.

Little did we know how grounding these weekend rituals would be as we became adults. True nature lovers now, Vanessa and I thrive outdoors. She has made a career out of landscaping and horticulture. I've spent most of my adulthood hiking, climbing, skiing, and biking—the things in life that help me breathe. I'm forever grateful to be the offspring of two mountain-lovers who made me strong and resilient, like the last autumn leaf to fall from a branch or the tree rooted into place miles away from others like it.

Our feet ache when Dave and I return to town twelve hours later. Limp-walking to the hostel, we pass an old log cabin repurposed as a restaurant.

"Hungry?" Dave asks.

"Hell yes!"

Inside, a dozen tables are covered with crisp, white tablecloths and spotless silver. Each place setting has several forks and three different wine glasses. We're trail-weary and look it but get the best seat in the house beside a wood stove in the center of the small dining area. Dave offers me the chair closest to the fire. Feeling heat sink into my back, I open the menu and almost cry in elation. Twelve-ounce steaks, garlic bread, tiramisu, red wine—affordable and delicious-sounding, we order it all. The entire day has been celebratory. We're truly in the trip's essence now; mountains, meat, wine—what else do we even need?

"Hey, we're only 600 miles from Ushuaia," I say, holding up my glass in a toast. "It feels so…within reach now, doesn't it?"

Dave smiles and clinks my glass. I'm loved and in love; we need more days like these.

When we leave, rising stiffly from our chairs, Dave can barely walk. The muscles in his legs have seized hard as rock. I try not to laugh on the way back to the hostel when he steps on or off a curb, moving his legs like they're solid, unbending blocks of wood.

"You need to drink more water, babe," I say.

"Yeah, I know…"

El Fin del Mundo

Closing in on the world's most southern settlement, the Stallion is almost unrideable. Once-pointy sprocket teeth are worn off after 15,000 miles since leaving Canada seven months ago. My bike sounds like I'm trailing newly-wed cans behind me. Links slip over the dull disc, unable to grip anything. They clack and clang, and I think the chain will someday snap—a potential deal breaker as that could jam and damage or destroy the engine.

After the intense beauty around El Chaltén, it's dismal getting back into the monotony of riding forever-straight roads again and worrying about my ride. Pavement is scarce, and the washboard gravel crashes my teeth together and beats a dull, constant pain into my lower back. When I stand on my pegs to relieve the strain in my spine, it isn't long before my knees can't take the repetitious hits either. I curse the broken wheel bearings and seriously regret not forking over the cash for top-of-the-line suspension, like Dave did. I *only* spent $1,500 on my aftermarket rear suspension—a lot of money for small cushions that aren't really doing their job.

Dave's experience building out 4×4 vehicles taught him to buy the best suspension he could afford. Now, he rides well ahead of me with confidence, barely changing position whereas I'm wrestling in my seat, trying to find the same comfort he has.

"You need to ride faster," Dave's voice comes over the headset. "That way you won't feel the bumps as much."

The warm, fuzzy feeling from our romantic meal in El Chaltén is gone. He's been saying this mantra to me for months.

"I don't *want* to ride faster," I retort. "And don't tell me what to do."

Ball-bearing gravel is not a confidence-inducing environment in which I can will my brain to "ride faster." But as the miles roll by under my worn-out tires, I rationalize that skimming the crest of bumps, rather than scooping down into them, is more comfortable. I visualize the waterskiing analogy: when the boat increases its speed, the skier pulls up out of the water. When it slows down, the skier sinks. The dirt road does roll smoother under my tires going from forty miles an hour to fifty, but I draw the line at going past fifty-five. Getting more confident to ride faster will be my Achilles heel on this trip.

Because of the repairs needed, we discuss storing my bike somewhere and riding two-up the remaining 350 miles to Ushuaia. On these roads, that could take days. Neither of us loves this idea; taking a passenger and all our gear on one bike would be a compromise for both of us—but the important thing is to get to Ushuaia. I've learned well the age-old adage that it's the journey that matters, not the destination. But sometimes I beg to differ.

That night, I toss and turn. Ushuaia is a significant milestone for me— I want to accomplish it myself, not by hitching a ride. Like summiting a mountain, I might have a climbing partner on the other end of the rope, but it's me and me alone lugging myself to the top. That's why getting there is so rewarding.

In the morning, I tell Dave I want to push my bike. "Not literally," I add.

He's relieved that I won't be riding on the back, but we're both crossing our fingers there will be no significant roadside repairs or breakdowns.

Before we leave, Dave removes two links from my floppy chain, which adds more tension to the sprocket that drives the bike forward. Hopefully, this will increase its lifespan until we can get parts somewhere.

My Patagonian calendar image is within reach. I ache to do the 100-mile detour to Torres del Paine, where it awaits me in a real-world setting, but I can't afford the extra miles on my failing bike. Leaving with temps in the low 30s, I mope about losing out. *When will I ever be back here?*

A border for Argentina/Chile comes and goes. Another materializes two hours later in reverse. They're quick exits and entries, and we're back in Argentina after a choppy ferry ride across the Strait of Magellan. Seasick and green, we swing cold, stiff legs over our saddles without talking, eyes on the prize. It's go time. By this evening, we'll be at the southern end of the world. If either of us is concerned about the gathering storm clouds on the horizon, we don't mention it.

We're within fifty miles of Ushuaia when the tedious flatland views are replaced by the arrival of stubby forest trees so dark green they're almost black. Their bristle-like branches reach away from the wind like arms trying to escape an attacker. The tallest tree stretches just ten feet high and offers little protection against the wind gusting at thirty-five miles an hour.

By 6:30 p.m., we're still on the road—and also heading straight into the storm. After 300 miles of gravel, the paved highway should come as a relief, but good roads attract traffic, and suddenly everyone is driving into the port city. Oncoming vehicles whoosh past on the wet roads. Transport trucks edge a little too close. Riding in the dark is scary enough, but with no center line or shoulder markings to alert drivers of lane positioning, I have a hard time seeing where to go.

Fat raindrops spatter my helmet, and headlights reflecting off each drip create a disco ball effect in my vision. I have my visor down to keep my eyes from watering in the wind, but when it gets wet, the tiny scratches in the plastic turn into smears, like with bad windshield wipers. I lift the shield, but the sting of icy shrapnel hurts, so I snap it closed again. Because I can't see more than three feet in front of me in the sideways rain, I slow to twenty-five miles an hour. The speed limit is sixty. I'm putting us in a dangerous position and am not at all confident drivers can even see us until they're right on our tails—Dave's worst nightmare. He once explained to me that's why he rides faster; to stay away from everyone else. He's behind me now with his hazard lights blinking to alert cars since my own four-ways no longer work—just another flaw on what Dave's now regularly calling Frankenbike.

The only good thing that happens when the rain turns to snow is that most people slow down. We rise collectively in elevation to reach Garibaldi Pass at 1,476 feet, and snow piles up on the side of the road. I want to get off the bikes, but we're both soaked to the bone, risking hypothermia. A bitchy wind punch shoots me toward the snow-filled shoulder and my heart races, anticipating a crash, but I steer out of it.

Dave's voice startles me in my helmet.

"How're you doing?"

"I can't...no talking."

All my concentration is spent keeping my bike upright. I haven't been this scared since the winds in Mexico, which were no big deal in comparison.

Brake lights from other vehicles paint the rock walls red beside me. When a car passes me, I see the occupants staring back at me with comical O-shaped mouths in a silent gasp. *What are they doing out here?* they're probably asking while eating snacks inside their heated four-wheeled capsules.

USHUAIA—35 MILES, a highway sign reads, yet we're still high in the mountains. Ushuaia's at sea level.

"We're going to make it," Dave says. The voice of reason in my head. Literally.

As though his words have nudged the powers that be, we begin a long, winding descent, and the snow turns back into rain. I stare at taillights lining the shores of where the Atlantic and Pacific meet and allow myself to daydream. *Maybe Dave has booked us a nice hotel as a surprise. I hope it has a bathtub! Do they sell champagne at the end of the world?*

At last, Ushuaia surfaces as a series of lights in the distance. It looks much larger than I expected for *El Fin del Mundo.* Tears fill my eyes, and it hurts to swallow. *If I'm this emotional just getting to Ushuaia, I might pass out and die if I actually finish this trip.*

Riding a motorcycle to the bottom of South America seemed unfathomable when we first set off from BC seven months ago. It felt even less likely, given everything that happened in between: a broken bone, a three-month hiatus, mechanical breakdowns, relationship ups and downs, more than a dozen border crossings, and ruthless weather. My mouth spreads into a righteous smirk. Not only did *I* make it to Ushuaia, but so did the Stallion. I lean down and pat my steed's flank.

"Thank you." My love for this rattling, clanking machine is strong—two wheels that have taken me to the world's end. "Now, will you take me the rest of the way?"

On April 24, almost four weeks later than we'd planned, Ushuaia welcomes us without fanfare at 8:30 p.m. I think somehow our feat should be noticeable to everyone: the drivers stopped beside us at a light; the family walking down the street. This milestone is life-changing to me—like if I look in a mirror, I'll see a different person staring back.

But we can't find a place to stay. Dave doesn't have a surprise up his sleeve, and I'm disappointed with the anticlimactic sentiment. Without anyone or anything to keep my balloons inflated, they pop and drift limply to the ground. I'd placed too much expectation on this day. And Dave.

I come from a family that makes a big deal out of accomplishments, big or small. When my sister or I do well at something, my parents show praise and admiration. They often award us with thoughtful gifts. Dad is especially crafty with the element of surprise and loves planning special occasions.

For my sixteenth birthday, he showed up at my high school under the guise of taking me out for lunch. I'd just gotten my learner's license and was hoping he'd let me drive to the restaurant. Dad and I shared an adoration for cool vehicles; I used to sketch Lamborghinis and Ferraris as a hobby, and he liked to photograph classic cars.

I met Dad outside. He squeezed my shoulder and said, "Ready for lunch?"

"Yep!" I smiled up at him.

Walking toward the parking lot, Dad stopped beside a white Mazda Miata with its top down.

"Wow, nice car, eh?" he said, running a hand along the side of its spotless exterior.

I glanced around for the Miata's owner, worried someone was going to yell at him for touching the car. When he opened the driver's door and slid into the black leather seat, I was mortified.

"Dad!" I squeaked, "what are you *doing?*" Looking up the street, I noticed some of my friends watching. My cheeks burned.

"Get in, buddy," he said, "I told you we were going to lunch, right?"

"Ya, but whose—"

"Get in," Dad's eyes twinkled. "This sweet ride is ours for the day, and we're going to Banff!"

On the way home after our lunch date in the mountain town an hour away, Dad let me drive, even though the insurance would have been void if anything had happened.

I cherish my upbringing and thought this was how everybody behaved when they cared about each other. It never occurred to me I might be setting myself up for disappointment later in life when such thoughtfulness wasn't shared in my relationships.

"We can stay here," Dave says walking back from a run-down house offering rooms for the night, "but there's no restaurant close by. Do you have anything in your panniers for dinner?"

I swallow an outburst of anger. Dave and I have lived and breathed motorcycle travel for over four months now—longer if we count the first day of planning. From our second start date of December 15 in Quartzsite, Arizona, we've ridden 14,593 miles to Ushuaia, passing through thirteen countries: Mexico, Guatemala, El Salvador, Honduras, Nicaragua, Costa Rica, Panama, Colombia, Ecuador, Peru, Bolivia, Chile, and Argentina— all to get to the southernmost tip of the Americas.

And now I have to *cook*?

"No, I don't have anything for dinner and I sure as hell don't feel like cooking after all *that*." I gesture back toward the highway. Dave checks the GPS. His lack of excitement irritates me.

"Can we try something closer to the city?" I suggest, looking at the quiet street. "I don't want to jump on the bikes every time we need to go somewhere over the next few days."

"Sure," Dave says, more with resigned exhaustion than acquiescence. "There's a hotel we can try downtown."

By the time we get a room, unload our bags, shower, and go out in search of food, it's almost 10 p.m. I've talked myself off the ledge and reined in my hopes and desires. For now. Our hotel is one of many buildings positioned tier-like on a steep hill a few blocks from downtown. Although it's dark now, we'll wake up with an ocean view, and that counts for something.

The road outside the hotel is shiny-wet, with temperatures hovering around freezing. At the same time, Dave and I scuff our feet on the surface. If traveling the globe together by motorcycle isn't enough proof we're riders to our core, subconsciously testing for icy road conditions must be. I laugh at our mutual observance, and Dave slings an arm around me.

I never like acting like a tourist, but the next day, my camera is stuck to my face like an extension of my nose. Ushuaia is ringed by weathered, craggy peaks, their rocky ledges holding snow like cakes dusted with icing sugar. No wonder it took so long to descend to sea level; the mountains rise straight from the water's edge. A sign tells us that Antarctica is just 600 miles to the south from where we stand, and 1,600 miles to the west is Hobart, Australia.

Determined to celebrate on some level, I buy a bottle of merlot called *Del Fin Del Mundo*. Later, we go to a nice seafood restaurant and order lobster.

Dave still hasn't said much about us reaching our first big trip milestone together. This journey down the Pan-American Highway—considered one of the world's greatest road trips, traversing nearly 19,000 miles from Deadhorse, Alaska, to Ushuaia, Argentina, or vice versa—is worth celebrating. Driving or riding the Pan-American Highway is on many an overlander's bucket list, and we've just covered a significant portion of it.

I don't know what to do with Dave's subdued excitement. My own happiness seems excessive, so I downplay it; though truly, I want the moment to matter to him as much as it does to me. We'll never have it exactly like this again. I want to hear him say he's proud of me—of us. But maybe reaching Ushuaia isn't such a big deal. After all, we still have a long way to go—another year and a half, in fact.

Back in our hotel room, panting from the steep walk, I open the wine while Dave is in the lobby booking another night. Earlier, I posted on our blog that we'd made it to Ushuaia and so had my bike.

An email from Dad is already in my inbox: "Hey buddy…just been re-reading your *Fin del Mundo* blog, and it made me think of your trip. The whole scope of it. What an amazing adventure. All the regular adjectives fall way short of addressing the immense scope of this once-in-a-lifetime venture. There are words in a song that apply to you now in this moment of your life—"Today" sung by the New Christy Minstrels back in the folk song days of the early sixties and covered by John Denver in the seventies. Mom and I still remember the words, which are about living for today and in the moment, and not yesterday's glory or tomorrow's promises. Never forget this wonderful time in your life, Heather. It will remain special forever. We are proud and happy for you both, sucking it up and getting the very most life is offering. Be thankful!"

I hear Dave's footsteps in the hall and wipe my face dry. I want to show him the email and say, *See, this is a big deal!* But I know Dad's words won't mean as much to my boyfriend as they do to me.

Calendar worthy

We've been keeping an eye on the weather report and are ready to turn around after three days in Ushuaia. The only way out is back over the snowy highway we came in on. I'm nervous. Winter is here, and it's the one time in my life I remember saying, "We need to go north for warmer temperatures."

I've had zero luck finding parts for my bike, which is perplexing since so many adventure riders come to Ushuaia, and that would justify a good motorcycle shop. One mechanic suggests turning my rear sprocket around so the worn-down "teeth" face the other way. Any margin of longevity is a plus at this point, so we take his advice.

My stomach flip-flops thinking about repeating the ride over the wintry pass, but we get lucky with two things in our favor: daylight and sunshine. All that remains of the storm are some melting mounds of snow on the highway shoulders. Otherwise, the pavement is bone dry—a total contrast to seventy-two hours ago.

Dave and I have yet to make up our minds about what's next for us. We've ruled out riding to Buenos Aires and flying to Africa, as originally planned—mostly because Buenos Aires is 2,000 miles away from Ushuaia, but also due to our indecision about Africa: a hot, risky part of the world to travel by bike.

After chasing seasons for the last several months, we've realized that weather is also an important factor when creating our route plan. We want to ride through Alaska and Russia and initially planned those destinations for the end. However, summer in the far north lasts only so long—two months, at most—and that's not enough time to cross the world's largest country and enjoy the Great White North, as well.

In El Chaltén, we heard about a four-day ferry leaving from Puerto Natales to Puerto Montt, in Chile. Taking the cruise would get us back north and close to Santiago, where we could fly almost anywhere. It would also save 1,000 miles of wear and tear on our bikes, keep us out of the winds, and give us a new vantage point from which to admire the scenery.

Since we're heading west to the large city of Punta Arenas, I'm elated when Dave suggests renting a car and driving into Torres del Paine to find my calendar photo. The ferry, which is the last crossing for the season, leaves in two days. We'll be cutting it close trying to fit in that side trip, but I think we can swing it—*if* we catch the once-a-day sailing from Porvenir at 2 p.m.

A rough dirt road and strong winds make for slow going into the charmless portside town. We arrive at 2:21 to see the boat getting smaller and smaller out on the water.

"Dammit!" I bark.

With only one day to spare before the ferry leaves Puerto Natales, missing the Porvenir boat means Torres del Paine is off the table. Again. Now I'm just sad. I seem to be living off nothing but pouts and tears lately.

I remove my helmet while Dave searches for a place to stay. The wind catches my hair and whips it skyward like a little tornado. I struggle putting it back into a ponytail.

We kill time in a café that's oddly chic for what the rest of Porvenir suggests. I catch up on posting to our blog while Dave drinks several cups of espresso, impressed with the bean quality.

In the end, I'm happy for some downtime. Writing and editing photos inspires and encourages me more than I can comprehend at the time. Summarizing our trip highlights our progress between updates and allows me to see the bigger picture—that we're doing something few people do. I'm grateful.

At 2 p.m. the next day, we board the ferry from Porvenir to Punta Arenas. When we dock in the city, I set out on foot looking for a hotel. When I return, defeated and sweaty, Dave's talking to a young Latino on the street.

"This guy knows a shop selling BMW parts," Dave smiles.

"Really?" I look at the stranger with hope. "Do you think they'll actually have parts for my chain?"

We'd gone into every motorcycle store we'd seen over the last several weeks. I wasn't sure things would be any different in Punta Arenas.

Giving up on accommodation for the moment, we ride to the address the young man gives us. The shop is still open. I cross my fingers.

"What year is the bike?" the owner, Serg, asks Dave.

"2010," I reply.

Serg looks surprised. *What?* I want to challenge, *it's my bike.* I may not know how to fix it, but I know its model year.

Walking over to a shelf, Serg pushes some items out of the way then pulls out two boxes. Handing them to Dave, he says, "Here you go."

Dave sets the boxes on a table and turns them over to read the specs. "These'll work," he says.

Forking over $200 to be rid of the *clankety-clank* in my chain has almost the same effect on my tense shoulders as an hour-long massage.

Our home that night is a guesthouse with a host who loves baking. I shove muffins into my mouth the next morning while Dave—still uninterested in teaching me how to fix anything—replaces my chain and sprocket. He has to work along the side of the house, which is also the area where the family dog shits. Dave kicks the drier piles out of the way and kneels carefully.

I'm lucky to be traveling with someone mechanically inclined, but it makes me feel overly dependent—a thought I keep to myself. After so much of my life spent single, it's nice to let someone else take the reins for once. But I like taking charge, too. I yearn for a more challenging role, but with exhaustion comes laziness. In a reluctant way, I'm content to just let Dave take care of these things. For my part, I've at least learned Spanish, so it's easier to communicate with people.

Before leaving Punta Arenas, we go to the ferry office to book tickets for the crossing from Puerto Natales to Puerto Montt, leaving the next day—April 29.

"The ferry has been postponed to May 1," the ticket agent tells us.

I looked at Dave and beam.

"Torres del Paine!"

After reserving our spot on the ferry, we ride off on a crisp, sunny afternoon toward the national park. The air is chilly, but I manage to get my heated jacket set to an ideal temperature. My bike purrs. I no longer sit clenched in fear of hearing a metallic *clang!* that might be the chain destroying my engine. *This is what riders talk about: the thrill and Zen from riding a motorcycle.*

It's late in the day when we get to the park entrance. Unlike North American national parks, there isn't another car or tourist in sight. A warden sits inside a small cabin by a lit woodstove. I ask him about the park fee and camping and am surprised a three-day entry is sixty dollars per person.

"We don't have three days," I explain. "Can we get a twenty-four-hour pass?"

The warden shakes his head. I leave the cozy cabin and walk back to Dave.

"It's sixty per person for three days."

"Wow," he says. "Is there a day rate?"

"Nope."

"Well, it's your call. I know this place means a lot to you."

"Let's camp outside the park and think about it."

We backtrack and follow a trail up a grassy hill with a flat spot at the top. I go looking for wood scraps in the sparse forest. Returning to camp in the late evening light, I drop my load of sticks to grab my camera. Our red tent is backlit and glowing with the setting sun. Across the valley, glaciers have a pinkish hue, and a large lake below is calm and flat. The bikes, parked side by side, look as though they, too, are enjoying the view. Now stopped for the day, I savor the time to take as many pictures as I want.

"I think we can save a hundred and twenty bucks. I'm happy with just this view looking into the park," I say, warming my toes against the fire and sipping whiskey, like any good Canadian.

We put thought into almost every dollar spent, and paying more than our daily budget for a daytrip through Torres del Paine seems excessive.

But when the fresh morning air hits my face and I look up into a perfect blue sky, I reconsider. *What was I thinking last night? I've dreamed of this place for two decades!* My mom's voice comes into my thoughts—*"It's only money..."*—and seals the deal.

When I traveled to South America in my twenties, I never got to Chile or Argentina. I'd planned to, but my backpacker's budget was far less than fifty dollars a day. Those countries were too far—*el fin del mundo*.

Now, I'm here. *Oh my god, I'm here!*

We pack up, smothering the fire circle with water and dirt. Back at the park gate, I find the same warden in the same position by the same woodstove. I wonder if he's been there all night, dozing by the fire's heat, feet propped on his desk. I pay the fee, knowing it's going to be worth it.

A loop circling over 100 miles takes us through the national park along shimmering, lapping lakeshores. Rock faces stand thousands of feet high and are topped with summits covered in white, prickly hoarfrost. Cottonball clouds catch on their pointy tips and stretch. Although calm down below, the wind is fierce up high.

Torres del Paine has many impressive granite towers within its 700 square miles, but three spires in particular are what the park is named after. The "towers of paine" (*"torres"* means "towers" in English, and *"paine"* is the word for "blue" in *Tehuelche*, the language of a group of South American Indians) are roughly thirteen million years old, formed from magma. Also known as "Cleopatra's needles," as British explorer Lady Florence wrote in her book *Across Patagonia*, the pinnacles can be reached in a full day's hike, which we don't have time for. Los Cuernos—"The Horns"— is what we're looking for and expect to find on our loop tour.

Operating a motorcycle is not conducive to swivel-headed sightseeing. The scenery passes by too fast when you also need to keep a diligent eye on the road. I come to a sliding stop in the gravel, almost missing the glorious offspring left behind after centuries of ice ages and powerful winds.

There it is—June 1996.

You haven't aged a bit, I almost say. But what's a quarter century when you're already a few million years old?

Sliding off my seat, I walk toward the view, hearing the *ting, ting* of my engine cooling behind me. Twenty calendar years later, I'm staring at those charcoal-gray rock walls, created by a timeless event known as erosion. They're just as sheer and mind-blowing as I imagined, as is the dark green carpet of small shrubs leading to the Caribbean-blue lake waters cradling the base of the granite crown.

Dave walks up behind me. I think about hiding my tears but don't. He understands.

"We almost didn't make it here," I smile.

I'm not just talking about our decision to pay the park fee or gaining extra time with the delayed ferry, which now feels like stars aligned by a universe in my favor. I'm talking about mechanical issues, the lateness of the season, the life-threatening near misses...

Dave tells me to stay as long as I want and walks off in discovery. I sit and stare, pulling at a long piece of grass that feels dry between my fingertips. I want to engrave every detail of the mountain faces, every wave from the wildflowers—into my memory. Somewhere in the last two decades, I'd lost the calendar image, but now I can take a real-life photo.

With goosebumps prickling my skin, I bring my camera to my face. The click from the lens sparks an epiphany. *This* is my celebration, here among the magic. Ushuaia is just a city. A boring city. There, I was forcing the actualization of my achievement, wondering why it wasn't forthcoming. I hadn't known the moment would find its way to me; that I would be over-come with the sense of my—*our*—accomplishment in a place far truer to my character than somewhere filled with traffic and buildings. A place I'd always gone to for answers—*nature*.

I take several photos nowhere near the quality of that National Geo-graphic image, but I'll cherish this moment forever. Half an hour isn't long enough—hell, I want to build a cabin and stay for life—but the time I have is more than I thought I'd get twenty-four hours ago.

We slowly complete the loop, stopping to appreciate and ingest every-thing we can before it gets covered up with darkness. I'm grateful Dave indulged me by coming here and that he'd loved Torres Del Paine just as much as me.

After all, riding to Patagonia was his idea.

A bottle of Chivas & several dying cows

Our bikes are lashed down tight with ratchet straps on the Puerto Natales ferry. Dave and I sit through orientation and frown at the part where we sign a "no alcohol" agreement. *What the hell kind of cruise is this?* But five minutes later, half a dozen Latino truckers are pouring hard liquor straight into plastic cups with no mix. We soon learn the agreement is more of an "if we don't see it, you don't have it" technicality.

In our six-by-six berth, Dave and I keep a modest collection of Chilean wines in our windowsill, which hugs the bottles perfectly. Alongside the merlots and cab sauvignons is a bottle of *Chivas Regal* we'd found in Puerto Natales, of all places. *Chivas* is the favorite whiskey of our Idahoan friend, Neil. Earlier, I'd sent him a photo of the bottle strapped to the back of my bike and had already received a reply praising my priorities.

I try to wait until at least 11 a.m. each day before taking a plastic cup filled with booze to the outside deck, where most of the boat's sixty or so occupants gather—not so much because it's a great viewing platform, which it is, but more because the other end of the boat stinks like rotting flesh.

Cows—at least a hundred of them, wretched and seasick—are being shipped north from Argentina to be butchered. Parked inside trailers on the dock, they sway side to side, moaning. Some have already died during transport and lie rotting in the heat after landing in their own excrement and puke. It's enough to turn anyone vegetarian. I love steak, but it's hard to think of my medium-rare T-bones suffering like this—all in the name of food-chain greed.

Although the change in transportation for getting ourselves from A to B offers a unique and spectacular way to see coastal Chile, the stench is overwhelming on this utilitarian World War Two-era boat. Dave takes to calling it a ghetto cruise. Despite the smell, however, the hardest part of the four days we spend aboard is deciding whether to play board games or watch the movie showing in the theater.

Dave and I are more relaxed than we've been in months. Although I had high hopes the sailing would be more like an Alaskan cruise (not even close), the scenery is comparable: Glacial tongues drip into the Pacific, and rocky ridgetops rise high above our heads. Some of the straits are so narrow we all rush outside to witness the captain maneuver through the impossibly snug slots covered in rocks and trees. Some of us stretch out hands out to see if we can touch land.

During the sailing we see whales, penguins, and dolphins—all of which are announced over the intercom.

The cruise costs $400 total. The food served on board is basic and hard to eat indoors because of the dying-cow stench filtering through the cafeteria. Still, it's cheaper than riding 1,200 miles back to Santiago. I'm more than happy to leave winter and the wind behind, but I'm sad to say goodbye to incredible Patagonia.

During our time off the bikes, Dave and I talk about what's next. We're still on the fence about Africa since neither of us does well in extreme heat. We also know it will be risky at best to ride south to north through the continent and into Europe. Our route could go up the west coast from South Africa to Morocco, but I was in Benin, Togo, Burkina Faso, and Ghana in 2007. Although it was a cool experience, I have little desire to revisit those heavily populated, urban areas.

My dream has always been to do a safari in eastern Africa. Dave is on board with that idea. We can ride as far as Kenya, but then things get tricky for getting into Sudan, Ethiopia, and beyond. Also, the second half of our trip requires more document logistics, like tourist visas we'll have to apply for weeks—sometimes months—in advance. It's hard for us to plan that far ahead.

We dock in Puerto Montt the first week of May, feeling refreshed and excited to get back on the bikes. Six hundred miles later, we're back in Santiago.

While making dinner in our hostel's small, communal kitchen, Dave and I come to a spontaneous-traveler decision. The next day, our motorcycles are boxed up in a cargo container en route to the USA.

To touch the land

USA

The headlights on the Navajo woman's car light up a run-down mobile home and two smaller outbuildings, caved in like crushed pop cans. There isn't a single light on, inside or out. My stomach sinks. I'm sure Dave's thinking the same thing: *this looks super sketchy*. I hope we aren't about to be robbed. My gut tells me we're okay, it's just a weird-feeling place.

Broken glass glints at my feet. I wonder if any has lodged into my tires after I rode up the dusty driveway. I see the shells of several hundred spent rifle bullets and wonder if we'll need a rake or broom to make room for our tent.

After claiming our beloved two-wheeled companions from Los Angeles customs, we spent several weeks riding north along the Backcountry Discovery Routes in Arizona and Utah, sewing up the gap we'd missed out on the year before because of my injury. Now, we're in the Navajo Tribal Park near Monument Valley, following a thirty-something woman we just met, who offered us a place to stay for the night.

"No one'll bother ya here," she says. "I have lots of land. You can just camp…anywhere." She waves a hand through the air.

It's after 10 p.m. Dave and I had an exhausting day on the Utah BDR and were getting desperate for a place to wild camp when the woman pulled up beside us in her Impala.

"That's really nice, thank you," I say, unsure where she and her companion—an old man, chin-to-chest-tired in the passenger seat—are staying.

"So, my house is a few miles from here," the woman says, standing beside her car. "But this is also my land. Me 'n' him will leave ya'lone."

Good, I just want sleep. "We won't be botherin' ya at all. We'll leave." They don't leave. "But do ya mind if we kick it here for a little while?"

She walks around the Impala to open her trunk.

"Do you drink?" the woman asks, popping her head out from behind her car, looking hopeful.

"Oh no, thanks very much." I'm also hopeful. That I'll be asleep soon. "We're really tired and would just like to set up our tent, if that's okay?"

The old man grunts and shudders. I think he's having a heart attack, but he settles back into place. Our host looks disappointed in my answer. I feel guilty turning down her invite—especially since she's just offered us accommodation for the night—but I can barely keep my eyes open.

"Sure," she shrugs and slams the trunk closed. "You'll be safe here, don't worry. If ya need anything, I'm the first house two miles down on the left."

The Impala creaks back to the main road, stirring up the warm, herbaceous scent of fresh sage from the bushes that wipe the sides of her car. I love the smell; it reminds me of adventure.

With the car gone, we're alone in the dark with thousands of crickets and a zillion stars. I let out a sigh of relief and start laughing.

"What the hell was with that old guy?" Dave says, turning on his headlamp.

The unfamiliar situation we've found ourselves in makes it hard to fall asleep. But the night passes without issue. The woman is just like all the other nice people we've met who want to help travelers in need and offer something she's proud of.

In the words of Nina, the seventy-year-old rider we met in the Atacama Desert, I'm a worrier, and sometimes life scares me. Yet here I am, traveling the world, seeing the best of it all every day: the kindness, empathy, and love. Why is it these observations seem so much more prevalent while traveling than at home? Are our senses more heightened? We are taught from childhood to fear strangers to keep ourselves safe. Do we notice the good in people more when we're traveling because we're so far from family and friends that strangers become our refuge and comfort?

When dawn wakes me with a hot, orange glow inside the tent, I scramble out to a view of epic proportions and stare, speechless. Dave wraps his arms around me as the sun makes its way down two prominent monuments called The Mittens—isolated buttes over 800 feet high, with steep sides and a flat top. Each one has an "appendage" of sandstone sticking out that looks like a thumb, hence their name.

The property where we stayed last night may have dilapidated buildings, but this morning we're greeted to a million-dollar view. As designated land under the Navajo Nation jurisdiction, the tribal park's intent is to eternally protect and preserve local monuments and recreation areas for the Navajo Nation. What a privilege it is to be here—a privilege money can't buy yet granted to us at no cost, thanks to the generosity of a complete stranger.

"Look at this place!" I finally speak.

"I know. I'm so glad that woman offered to help us out."

Once again, a stranger has come to our aid. Had we not thrown caution—and first impressions, based on the rough-looking buildings—to the wind, we'd never have seen Monument Valley from this vantage point.

Dave walks over to his bike to pull out our camp stove for coffee. "Shit."

I look over to see him bend down by his flat front tire.

"Well, I guess one of my concerns actually came true," I say.

Most Improved Rider of the Year

Eight months earlier, while my wrist was mending and Dave was making his way south to Arizona alone, he attempted to ride Lockhart Basin, a difficult off-road section along the Utah BDR filled with boulders, sand, and darting geckos. The narrow canyon is steep and barely wide enough for a Jeep or ATV. Few take two wheels in there; especially dual sports loaded down with gear. Unless you're Dave Sears.

Mr. Sears, however, grossly overestimated his ability to get through Lockhart Basin by himself. He dropped his motorcycle six times in one-eighth of a mile. Determined to make it to the top, he tried again and again to get over the rocky, loose ground. Every time he dropped his bike, he had to remove all the luggage and heave the 500-pound beast upright. He crawled along by mere feet an hour, exhausting himself. With a storm darkening the late afternoon and the very real possibility of a flash flood in the canyon, Dave finally gave up and returned to the small town of Moab just before dark.

If there's one thing that eats at Dave's psyche, it's unfinished business—especially unfinished business that's just within reach. Lockhart Basin might have thwarted Dave once, but he wasn't about to let it happen again.

Now, Dave spreads a map out over the seat of his bike.

"Okay, so this road we're camped beside will take us to a Utah BDR junction. Lockhart is about fifty miles from there. If you're not feeling it, we can turn around. Or I can get your bike through."

No amount of rationalizing on my part will rein in Dave's commitment to taking another stab at Lockhart. He's trying to be nice and give me an out, but I know he's praying I'll find the equivalent of some male anatomy and say yes once I've gone all that way.

"I think it'll be much easier going down than up, like I did last year," Dave barters, "but it's your call. I'm actually kind of nervous, too." Maybe he's figuring out that validating my anxiety is the key to my heart.

His soulful brown eyes shine with anticipation. Or is it trouble? When I first showed a photo of Dave to my Nana, she *tsk-tsk'd* and said, "Well, he looks rather mischievous." I took this to mean "untrustworthy," but when Nana met Dave a few months later, she batted her eyelashes at him, always a flirt and "rather mischievous" herself.

Stuffing my sleeping bag back into its sack, I say, "Okay, let's do it."

"Really? You sure?"

"As long as *you're* sure you'll get my bike through the sections I don't want to do."

I'm admittedly curious about the trail that took down my boyfriend six times. Outside of Lockhart, Dave hasn't dropped his bike more than two or three times on the entire trip so far.

After filling our tanks at a remote desert gas station, we turn onto the BDR connector. Within minutes, we come to the first technical section: a series of ascending rock ledges filled with loose red sand and gravel. Something like this would have stopped me in my tracks when I first learned how to ride off-road. Even with a whole continent more of experience under my belt now, every bit of me is screaming *no;* and we aren't even close to the canyon yet.

Dave goes first. I watch him buck and lurch up the ledges. *He's going way too fast!* But speed is the only way to make it over obstacles on a motorcycle; if the suspension is doing its job, it'll lift and provide maximum cushioning. Braking before the obstacle forces the suspension to compress and therefore slam into things—something I'd experienced often, due to the chickening-out factor. I start internalizing Dave's way of thinking: *Momentum is key.*

Dave stops and gets off his bike to come help me. I dearly want to use my Dave Safety Net and let him ride the Stallion through, but I need to work up to Lockhart, which means starting now.

I keep my brain from overfiring—no easy task—and aim for the top. The skid plate that covers and protects the undercarriage of my bike scrapes against the ledges with a jarring *screeeeech*. Rocks kick out behind my rear tire and crash down the slope like out-of-control bowling balls.

When I pass Dave, he's clapping his hands.

"Wahoo!" I scream once I've found flat ground again.

Never would I have imagined I'd ride something like this after breaking my wrist. There was a time I didn't even want to go over a parking curb.

For the next few hours, the terrain is more of the same. I get better and better at not thinking about it and just twisting the throttle back. When we stop to rest among flowering cacti and red rock walls, Dave says, "Where's the rest of the band, because you've been riding like a rock star!"

I groan at his lame dad joke. *"No entiendo."* I smile, using the Spanish term for "I don't understand."

"Oh, you *entiendo*, all right. Come on, I've been thinking about that one for a while and couldn't wait to tell you."

This does make me laugh.

Dave's pun is dorky but lifts me sky high. Too often, terrain like this has scared me senseless and Dave gets impatient, not knowing how to handle my fears and his own. This day, however, we're a team, encouraging each other along as equals. Something has clicked inside me. The feeling is familiar, like the first time I rolled my kayak upright or learned the difference between skiing powder versus resort snow.

We decide to camp just above Lockhart and tackle it fresh the next day in the cool morning air.

Despite riding strong the day before, standing at the top of the basin, my stomach drops.

"No way. Nope." I cross my arms.

The canyon starts with a drop off a three-foot-high rocky step into a constricted gully littered with boulders and a faint line in the sand gouged out by tires. Bits of broken brake lights and fenders are scattered about—telltale signs of other vehicle casualties. I see how approaching the slot in reverse, like Dave did last year, would be next to impossible for bikes like ours.

I park at the top and remove all my luggage, which will allow the bike to sit higher off the ground. Clearance has been an issue on the Stallion, and in rough terrain, I often feel its belly skimming the ground. Even a fraction of an inch could be the difference between riding up and over something or high centering on the skid plate. Taking off the aluminum panniers also makes the bike slimmer. Dave won't have to worry as much about slamming into rocks. Hitting a boulder with a pannier is how I broke my wrist, after all.

On seeing Lockhart again, Dave's face is pale, his speech short and curt. I try not to distract his concentration with too many questions, like: *What. The actual fuck. Were you thinking?!* I can't fathom how he ever thought this was a good idea to do solo.

"I have butterflies," he tells me.

Great.

Before we can stew about what carnage might befall us in this birth canal of a trail, Dave gets on my bike, grimacing. I don't know if his facial expressions are because he hates riding the Stallion or he's imagining his demise.

Dave inches toward the rock step. It's not a dead drop; as we say in mountain biking, "it rolls." But once he goes past a certain point, gravity will take over, and he'll be committed. There's no way to get my bike out if he can't ride the rest of the basin, but it's smart to take mine first in case Dave needs to ride his out for help.

I turn my camera onto *record.* Just as Dave's about to enter the canyon, he loses his nerve and skids to a stop before the drop. Keeping the bike balanced, he shouts at me to help push him back uphill.

On the second attempt, I watch, breathless, as he rolls toward the edge again. One second later, I hear a sickening screech echo through the basin as the skid plate slides over the rock, flicking out sparks. Dave is in the canyon, rubber side down. He rides out of sight.

I grab one of my panniers and cradle it to my chest like a forty-pound baby then speed-hike after my boyfriend. The trail is easier to negotiate on foot. Once inside the canyon, I catch a glimpse of Dave cresting a steep, smooth boulder, the Stallion rearing on its back tire. Just when I think he's about to fall over, the front wheel touches back to the ground and Dave's again out of view.

We meet up fifteen minutes later when Dave's walking back for his bike. He hugs me and says, "I never in a million years would have guessed we'd do this trail together."

I appreciate him saying "together." Dave's clearly doing the hardest and worst parts himself. All I need to do is ferry my luggage through. He's starting to understand that if he wants me to join him in these kinds of places, he has to meet me part way. The unspoken compromise is him helping me with my bike.

From a better viewpoint, I film Dave bringing his bike down. Aside from a few skidded slides here and there, he stays on course. *He's such a great rider.* My thoughts are a mix of envy and pride.

Later that afternoon, we arrive in Moab. After showers at the rec center, we find a pub and order nachos and bottomless Arnold Palmers—a delicious iced-tea/lemonade concoction we drink to rehydrate.

Dave toasts me with a sweating pint glass and declares me *Most Improved Rider of the Year*—an easy prize to win when I make up fifty percent of the competitors.

Into the wild & overgrowth

Canada/The Yukon

Following a logging road for several miles out of Smithers, BC, Dave stops by an old wooden sign that reads TRAIL. He points into some prickly shrubs budding with wild roses. An overgrown single track leads off into who knows?

"Look, it's even got directions!" he says.

I glance at the sign, which has an arrow scratched in by someone's knife, and sigh. Dave grins. He's busting with excitement. I'm content to stay on the perfectly safe gravel road, surrounded by purple fireweed and white daisies waving in the breeze. The air has a vanilla aroma this time of year. It doesn't smell like epic adventure, it smells like peace and quiet.

Back in Santiago, Dave and I had decided a summer in the Yukon and Alaska was calling us. After making our way north from Utah, we spent some time at Dave's dad's in Arlington, Washington. Now, my bike is in better shape to gallop north. The radiator patch from many miles back in Peru held, so we left it alone. Along with some maintenance to his own bike, Dave rebuilt my forks, added a new air filter, spark plugs, fresh tires, and foldable brake and clutch levers, which keep them from breaking when the bike is dropped on its side. All of this cost a bunch of money; however, the hope is for fewer issues on the road ahead. Will the Stallion be easily bribed with expensive gifts? We'll see. There's still a long way between where we are right now, in west central BC, and our northern-most destination in Deadhorse, Alaska.

Dave thinks I've been resting on my laurels. Ever since Lockhart Basin in Utah, he's decided we can take things up several notches. Inspired by a YouTube video, he zoomed into Google Earth a few days ago and scouted a "shortcut" from Smithers, BC, to Terrace, BC, over Telkwa Pass. I'm more confident riding through river crossings and over rocky surfaces than I was six months ago, but Telkwa is like shaking all that up in a jar, dumping out the contents, then being asked to ride over it all on a unicycle.

Dave's eyes are on me. He hasn't gotten back on his bike yet, hopeful and waiting for my okay.

"Fine," I breathe, starting my bike. Curiosity and remote mountain scenery always suck me in.

Getting through the cluster of bushes isn't too bad, and the trail opens up afterward. *This is going to be easy!* But it's not long before the track becomes overgrown again, with steep up and down sections at frequent intervals. My front tire hits embedded rocks, forcing unplanned wheelies. I ask Dave to take the Stallion down a loose rocky section, and he wipes out partway. He's never crashed my bike before. Heaving it up, he continues while I hike after him. Alone, I pick handfuls of fat blueberries as a reward.

Ugh, what is that smell? It's…disgusting!

Steaming excrement lies in prideful plops left on display every hundred meters down the trail. Digested berries simmer in the hot mess where flies feast, the smell a combination of wet dog and old fish brought to boil. I can't tell if it's grizzly or black bear scat—we're on the crest between forest and alpine, so it could be either.

I call out, "Hey bear!" every few feet until I find where Dave has left my bike.

Alerting wildlife is something I'm used to, having grown up with parents who loved hiking in the Canadian Rockies. I honk my horn maniacally to alert the animal, but its little *beep beep* sounds pathetic.

Despite our bike engines making some noise, the bear could duck into the trees and wait for the commotion to die down, then re-emerge between us, back onto the path of least resistance. It's our responsibility as humans to make ourselves known in wildlife country. A startled bear might attack.

Years ago, I was hiking with two friends in Revelstoke. When we left the trail and bushwhacked through a thicket of blueberries, I lagged back, stuffing my mouth with the juicy, purple orbs and collecting some for later in a baggie. Turning to face downhill after hearing a twig snap, I saw the bushes shaking below me about two city bus lengths away. There was no wind or tall trees; only a bear was squat enough to stay hidden in there. I called out, and my breath left me when a grizzly stood on its hind legs and looked straight at me. I screamed to my friends, who were ahead but within earshot. "Bear! There's a bear, there's a bear, there's a bear!" Every inch of me was poised to run, but with grizzlies, the advice is to play dead. I couldn't imagine getting down on the ground, waiting for this beast to decide what to do with me. The grizzly started approaching, unfazed by my loud voice. I assumed it was a female because of her smaller size, though that did nothing to calm me—a grizzly is a grizzly. She was close enough for me to see her mouth stained with berry juice and hear her grunting with the effort to reach me on the steep mountainside. I turned away, terrified, and got ready to lower myself to the ground, hoping my backpack would offer some protection from the attack. I took a moment to be grateful that my last breath would be in the mountains. Bushes crashed around me, and I expected to feel her jaw clamp down on my head. Instead, I heard my friends yelling and glanced behind me to see them waving their hands around like lunatics. The grizzly took off.

Who knows what might have happened that day had I been alone. Seeing a grizzly is an extraordinary experience, but I don't want to upset a wild animal like that again.

We see no bears this day at Telkwa Pass, even though my skin is on high alert, prickled with goosebumps. I'm sure the bear saw us, though. For the most part, wildlife steer clear of humans. I don't blame them.

An emerald-green lake has us thinking about a lunch break, and we ride onto the beach.

"I hope the road gets better," Dave says, unbuckling his riding boots to let out his steaming feet. Refraining from commenting about the trail's difficulty, I strip, walking along sun-warmed pebbles into the freezing water.

Immersing myself slowly at first, I watch a not-too-distant glacier melting into streams that run down the mountain into the lake. Knowing I'll appreciate it later, I do a quick dive, then gasp when I resurface. Retreating to the beach, I revel in the feeling of the cool mud squishing between my toes and my long hair dripping down my back. I sit on top of my jacket, hoping it'll at least stay damp for a bit.

Dave rolls up his pants and wades into the lake. With his back to me, I see dried perspiration lines crisscrossing his dark merino wool T-shirt. We've gone quiet, listening to the water lapping the shoreline. Stops like these are always far too short. I want to fall asleep in the peace and quiet for hours. When I'm in fight-or-flight mode for most of the day, these moments help me cleanse the stress.

When an engine buzzes nearby, I scramble to put on some clothes seconds before a couple in their sixties roll onto the beach atop their all-terrain vehicle—a more appropriate form of transportation for Telkwa Pass, with four wheels for balance.

"Wow, you guys must be having a hard time with those monsters," the man chuckles, gesturing to our bikes.

"Yeah," Dave nods. "It hasn't been easy. Which direction did you come from?"

"The same way as you. We noticed your tread patterns in the dirt."

"I guess you can't tell us how much worse it gets then," I say. "Unless you've been here before?"

"We have been here before, but I've never seen the trail in such bad condition."

Telkwa suffered a tough winter. The resulting runoff from snowmelt caused soil deterioration that dislodged rocks and boulders onto the trail in landslides.

The couple carries on. Soon, they're climbing a hill at the end of the lake, where we're headed.

"We should get going." Dave packs up his lunch.

Fifteen minutes later, I'm longing for that swim again. The broken mountains have spilled over our path, leaving behind rocks the size of toaster ovens. In a steep uphill section, I'm not carrying enough momentum, and my rear wheel spins in the loose ground. I start to fall over, but with a strength I don't know I have, my muscles strain to keep my machine upright. Balancing on tiptoes, I rock forward and back, blasting the throttle, which just digs a deep hole behind me. At the same time, the front tire tunnels in, with nothing solid to roll over. Sweat drips down my temples inside the full-face helmet, and I fear destroying my bike in the middle of nowhere. Even a smaller dirt bike would have a hard time here.

Dave's F800GS has more torque than my 650, which tractors him up the steep, loose bits. More comfortable with speed, he stays afloat to the top. Despite all the rocks and hills, my most significant barrier is being scared; I still worry about breaking another bone. I try to channel the rock star persona from the Utah BDR, but that seems like the memory of a good dream, rather than reality.

When Dave returns to help me, he revs the 650's underpowered engine while I stand in the sketchy zone behind the rear tire, pushing. Rocks spray my legs like bullets, leaving welts through my riding pants. I keep the visor down on my helmet. At last, Dave shoots off, the tail of my bike lashing fish-like.

Once we get through the rockslide, there's little relief for miles. Alder branches slap me in the face and arms while I ride through the thicket. Dave takes the Stallion over difficult areas I won't ride. After two hours of hot, exhausting work, we've only covered six miles.

The ATV couple has turned around to get back to their truck.

"You guys need some help?" asks the man, pulling up alongside us and seeing only one bike.

"Sure," Dave says. "You can save me walking back to my bike."

When the three of them drive off—Dave sitting side-saddle beside a cooler on the back—the sudden quietude stills my beating heart. Moments ago, all I heard was a revving engine and my own cursing. Now, I sink into an almost immediate meditation. I notice the sound of a creek nearby and then whiskey jacks and chickadees. I'm standing at the base of an old avalanche path, where trees and shrubs have been sheared from their bases by the razor's edge of moving snow. New life pokes up in the form of wildflowers and green saplings. Bees and butterflies flit through the colorful vegetation.

Before we left my parent's place in Revelstoke and were interviewed by Canada's CBC radio, the host asked what we thought we'd encounter. Dave replied, "I expect we'll feel the lowest of lows and the highest of highs."

Some bipolar days, we get both.

Merlot in a plastic mug

I steer around a bison weighing four times my motorcycle, hoping I don't startle him to the point that he'll charge me. Passing within a few feet, I'm in awe of how relaxed he is, just lying there on the tarmac, covering the yellow center line with his massive body. If we hadn't already threaded through at least fifty of these guys lazing along the quiet Stewart-Cassiar Highway, I might have mistaken him for dead. But there they are—buffalo ahead; buffalo behind—like cars parked wherever they please. The roadside grasses are too hard to resist, and the warm, black pavement the perfect spot to nap and digest.

Bear scat is another common sight, surprising me with its frequency. Piles litter the shoulders where the omnivores walk at dawn and dusk—

the preferred time of day to roam for food. Black bears are easy to spot, since they're more prolific. We watch them dash across the road or nose through bushes looking for berries. With only a few dozen vehicles passing by daily, wildlife use the roadways for easier travel. Or slumbering.

Aside from the ribbon of tarmac, nothing but wilderness stretches for miles. Woods, mostly, and mountains far in the distance. The weather this far north is cool for the end of July, with highs in the upper fifties. It's like riding in Patagonia, only without the winds. Also, like Patagonia, we find warmth and comfort in cafés and gas stations, which often have fresh-baked cinnamon buns or apple pie at the counter, made with love in nearby Indigenous villages.

With well-paved roads, an abundance of camping options, and no language barriers, northern travel is downright pleasant. The only thing problematic in such remote locales is a mechanical breakdown.

Something's off on Dave's bike; he feels it while riding down a bumpy backroad. When we stop to set up the tent, he takes apart his rear wheel, revealing broken wheel bearings, now in pieces on the ground. We're thirty miles up a logging road near Atlin, an isolated community in northwest BC, and we're down one motorcycle.

Leaving everything at the campsite, including Dave's bike, we ride two-up on the Stallion into Atlin and the visitor center. Dave calls around for tow trucks, which will have to come out of Whitehorse over a hundred miles away, since there's nothing in town. A truck coming from the city and towing back will cost $800. Dave tries rental trucks instead, and on the third call, finds something for $170, with the first 250 miles free. Now how to get Dave to Whitehorse? Riding my bike that far together isn't feasible, and I need transportation to get back to camp before dark.

Inside the small visitor center, I ask around. An older couple is willing to give Dave a ride. He climbs into their RV, ready to share his day with a small, yappy dog and chain-smoking retirees from Idaho. Watching them pull away, I'm glad for once it isn't my bike causing trouble.

I'm about to ride back to camp when I realize I now have hours of time for myself. The tent and Dave's broken bike are safe; we've asked a couple camping and canoeing by the lake to keep an eye on our things. Giddy, as though I have a surprise day off from work, I sit in a local café for hours, writing blog posts and drinking lattes. Later, I walk around town looking for a food store, seeing only a handful of people on the streets. A tourist destination for fishing, hiking, and backcountry skiing, Atlin is a peaceful gold-mining town with a population of fewer than 500. Residents keep to themselves. Visitors respect that and do the same.

I buy a bottle of wine and a bag of salt and vinegar chips, excited to get "home" and relax by the lake.

Riding an adventure bike is a workout, but my mostly healthy diet of veggies and lean proteins has been replaced with convenience foods like rice, pasta, cookies, and chips. They're the easiest calories to come by and require little prep or refrigeration. Neither of us is gaining weight, though. In fact, Dave has lost over fifteen pounds due to food boredom (not enough variety and flavors), and despite a drastic change in diet, my weight is the same as when I left home. We're certainly eating some of the best food of our lives at times, but on average, the menu is anything we can put together while living out of a tent or what we can find roadside.

In camp, I use water from the lake to wash the only three pairs of underwear I have with me, then hang them and other laundry on a piece of cord we carry for hanging food in trees to keep it away from animals. While the loons call out over the water, I stare at the campfire I've made and drink the merlot from a plastic tea-stained mug. It's heaven.

Because he was concerned about the Stallion's reliability, Dave had encouraged me to look for another motorcycle in Arlington, before we headed to Alaska. I don't want a different bike. I know Dave's fun is compromised because of my mechanical malfunctions, but I've sunk a lot of money into my Frankenbike. Plus, it has sentimental value; I want to finish my trip around the world on the same bike I started with. I don't like shiny motorcycles and want something that looks like it's been somewhere. No—*everywhere*.

Contrary to what others may think—mostly men commenting on our blog and social media—a BMW GS is ideal for me and this trip. A heavier bike is safer on the highway and keeps me from being tossed around by wind and passing semis. I can't imagine riding a bike without a windscreen, either, which smaller bikes rarely have, and I need something off-road capable that can jump onto dirt without issue. At times, I've wished for something lighter, like when I'm riding in sand. However, we aren't on a dirt biking trip; we're traveling a huge distance in countries with varying road surfaces, but roads nonetheless—not trails. We also carry about 100 pounds each in gear, tools, food, clothing for all weather, and camping equipment. Our GSs saddle the heavy loads easily, which again, small bikes don't; plus it means we only need to carry one set of tools for one brand.

"I'm on this trip for the fun of it," Dave told me at his dad's, while the ratchet wrench in his hand clicked around a bolt on my frame. "If I had to ride this thing," he said, making a scoffing gesture toward my bike, "I wouldn't be having fun. When the fun part is taken away, what are we doing this for?"

Good question; *was* I having fun? Perhaps my mountaineering years were helping me not give up on the Stallion. I have the drive and tolerance for suffering and can adapt to what I have. But whether intentional or not, Dave was teaching me something: I didn't have to settle for discomfort.

A diesel engine interrupts the sound of lapping waves, and my serenity vanishes. It takes me a second to recognize Dave behind the wheel. Putting down the window, he calls over to me.

"Check this out!" I hear a faint motor whine, then notice the Ram 1500 lower a few inches. "I can operate the axles on adjustable air suspension, with the push of a button."

It's a nice truck, but I'm kind of bummed Dave's back so soon. I was enjoying the solitude. Now I have to share my wine. He starts fiddling, enamored with bells and whistles. Having access to a vehicle after more than 200 days of motorcycle travel is a novelty—even if it's just a rental.

"How are we going to get the bike in the back?" I ask, making no moves to help.

Dave gets in the driver's seat and backs up to an embankment a few feet high behind him. Using the ingenious suspension feature, he adjusts the truck's bed height to that of the grassy mound. Then he walks over to his bike and looks at me.

I stifle a sigh; he's helped me with the Stallion numerous times.

"All I need you to do is help me balance it," Dave says. "I'll do most of the pushing."

Together, we shove the GS up the slope and into the truck bed. With a few handlebar cranks and some muscle, it's positioned for tying down. Easy.

I start dinner. While I'm stir-frying a chicken breast I bought in Atlin, along with some onions and broccoli, a woman who'd been canoeing on the lake comes over to ask if everything's all right. As it turns out, she knows an ex-motorcycle mechanic in Whitehorse and gives us his number.

When we arrive the next day in the Yukon's capital, Dave calls the man. We're invited to work inside his home garage. He also introduces us to a machinist who can make the part for Dave's wheel. Without the help of these people, we'd be waiting weeks for things to get shipped this far north.

While the bushing is being made, Dave and I walk around the city. Whitehorse has a great visitor center filled with mining artifacts and information about what to see and do, like dog mushing tours and gold panning—all of which sound interesting, but we're on a budget.

We've been staying with friends of my parents, Joan and Don. Joan worked with my mom and dad in the '60s at a backcountry lodge in BC. They've kindly offered us a room for a few days while Dave deals with his bike.

I take advantage of city amenities and stock up on non-perishables, toilet paper, and little travel soaps and shampoos. After deep cleaning our camping stove and dishes and doing another load of laundry, I catch up on our blog. I'm so far behind, I'm writing about weeks ago in Utah.

Thanks to our meeting the woman with the canoe, Dave's bike is rideable again in just a few days. We're back on the road after saying goodbye to Joan and Don. There's a chance we'll meet up with them again for some camping, once we return from our second biggest trip milestone.

Permafrost & dead toe cocktails

In 2016, the Northwest Territories town of Inuvik was Canada's northernmost road-accessible point, thanks to the formidable Dempster Highway, one of the country's toughest roadways. Riding north from Whitehorse, the Yukon's capital, we stop to fill up after a day and a half of riding. Our general rule on such roads is never pass an opportunity to add fuel, even if it isn't necessary. The next place could be closed or out of gas altogether.

Unpaved and remote, the Dempster begins south of the gold rush town of Dawson City and ends 458 miles later in the arctic village of Inuvik. It is considered one of the most scenic roads in the world—the epitome of overland adventure, with just three gas stations. There are even fewer auto shops at which to fix flat tires, blown radiators, shattered windshields, etc. All that comfort-zone stuff is traded for unpopulated space and wild, quiet beauty.

Riding the Dempster Highway will bring us into Inuvik and a northern end-of-the-Americas milestone.

The station isn't a retail location, meaning no one is around to manage the transaction, as it's mostly intended for commercial fleets with company credit cards. We're having trouble, so a guy waiting in a Toyota Tundra comes over.

"Sorry," I say, using the universal greeting from a Canadian, "our card isn't working."

"Let me try mine," he offers.

His works, so we let him go ahead of us. When he's done, instead of cutting off the supply, the man hands the pump to Dave. "Fill 'em up," he smiles. "It's on my company."

We're surprised and try to repay him in cash, but he declines. After wishing us good luck, he drives off. Fuel in Canada's Great White North is expensive. At that time, it was over three dollars a liter, as opposed to a dollar and sixty cents in Vancouver. Although filling two motorcycles isn't much compared to a thirsty Tundra, the generous donation is appreciated.

Climbing over the Ogilvie mountain range, it's easy to imagine how storms can affect the Dempster any time of the year. With little to stand in its way—trees don't grow tall in this climate—rain will turn the road surface into an unruly mess. For now, it's bone dry, which creates another issue: dust. Regular-sized vehicles are one thing, but when the haul trucks pass, they leave behind a whiteout that disguises potholes, rocks, or other cars. We need to slow down or even stop to let the dust settle, and I have a realization that perhaps the reason my bike seems to have more issues than Dave's is because I'm often following him, eating his dust, so to speak. That grit gets into moving parts and can cause breakdowns more frequently. I've always noticed that in drier places, because my throat hurts more and my nostrils are dry. I never thought of what it might be doing to the mechanics.

I scan the slopes and plains often, hoping to see bears, moose, or caribou. I'm finally rewarded with mountain sheep on a fan of scree. We pull over to watch, hearing only the distant clink of shale being flicked from under their hooves.

Lunch inside a no-frills hotel in Eagle Plains gives us an opportunity to warm up from the cool spring-like temps. When I inquire about milk for my tea, the owner—also our server—tell us his food truck didn't come that week. Dave's hamburger is a reconstituted frozen patty, and my grilled cheese is made with processed cheese slices. The food is what you'd expect when it has to come in over hundreds of rough, unpaved miles. Good enough.

These seldom-seen signs of infrastructure along the Dempster hold a certain charm, despite the dreary architecture. I read somewhere that the

Eagle Plains staff are more than just restaurant and hotel workers—they are beacons of light in the storm, a warm soul to hug when people go off the road or come inside creeped out because they haven't seen another human being in hours, sometimes days. The Eagle Plains hotel has been known to house stranded visitors and will even let people sleep on the floor if all the beds are taken.

We encounter wind and rain riding to Inuvik. Calcium chloride—a mix sprayed onto the road to keep it from eroding into hard ruts from heavy haul trucks—covers our bikes. When the chemical solution gets wet, it becomes seagull-shit slippery and splashes up everywhere, settling into a pottery-like concrete wherever it lands. There are no carwashes along the Dempster. They'd be useless anyway. We carry on looking like we've run into a cement truck.

Four hundred miles north of Whitehorse, Dave and I cross the Arctic Circle. The day is clear, for the most part, but dark clouds boil in the distance and a frigid wind cuts through our suits. Those hot days of riding in the tropics are distant memories, and my body aches from the cold. I shrug my shoulders to work out the kinks and stomp my feet to get blood to my toes. Everything hurts from long days riding along bumpy gravel, but I'm happy, remembering a time not so long ago when I could barely ride off-pavement for even a few miles. In reaching the Arctic Circle, we've ridden over 300 dirty, muddy miles. My body is adapting after nine months on the road, and I'm improving as a rider, even if it doesn't always feel that way.

The arrival into Inuvik—which, like most far-north towns, was built for industry, not tourism—is disappointing in contrast to the scenery we've seen along the Dempster. I'm convinced, however, that the largest town north of the Arctic Circle must have some endearing qualities.

We register at a campground in the city's center and set up our tent on a wooden platform. Nothing in this climate is built on the ground due to permafrost. This is so that any heat emanating from whatever the item or structure is doesn't, over time, start to melt the permafrost and sink.

I have a hard time imagining it gets cold enough here to permanently freeze the ground, when the sun is still shining on us at 10 p.m. It's now August, when the north experiences twenty-four hours of daylight. In winter, it's the opposite. In fact, a December 2016 weather chart recorded the sun rising in Inuvik at 12:51 p.m. and setting at 2:36 p.m. on the first of the month. On the fourth, there were just forty-six minutes of daylight.

From December 5 on, the graph just says, "down all day" in the sunrise/sunset category. I've always wanted to experience living in the Yukon or Alaska year-round; would I go crazy and leave early or acclimate and want to stay forever?

With so much daylight, seeing the northern lights—an ethereal phenom I was hoping to witness—isn't possible yet. But according to the sun chart, it will start to get darker at night within the next month.

After buying some cinnamon-apple muffins at a sparse farmer's market, we stop at Inuvik's visitor center and learn about the Igloo Church a few blocks away. *Our Lady of Victory* was built as a replica of the historic snow houses from eras past. However, there was method behind the design. The round structure prevents any damage that might come from frost heaves. As such, it's the only building in Inuvik that isn't built atop pilings. Instead, the church sits on a bed of gravel, which stops the building's heat from warming the frozen ground underneath.

Not yet finished with touristing, Dave and I walk to an old hockey arena that's been converted into a giant greenhouse. The gardens are owned by locals, who pay for dirt plots. Groceries are outrageously expensive this far north. A carton of milk is ten dollars Canadian, and a wilted head of lettuce is six dollars. Growing food seems a resourceful option, but how does anything thrive during the months that only see a few hours or less of daylight? I want to know if they use grow lights, but there isn't anyone around to ask.

Back at our campsite, we talk to Germans who've ridden bicycles to Inuvik from Vancouver, BC. It's taken them months to travel the 2,000 miles. They are young, fit, and happy. Every visitor to Inuvik has a story to tell. They all come here via the same direction, whether by car, canoe, or two wheels. Seeing an RV or camper trailer is especially impressive—the Dempster is not easy on vehicles.

After three days in Inuvik, we turn the bikes around and head back toward Whitehorse, hoping to spend a few days hiking in Tombstone Territorial Park. Our hopes are thwarted when heavy rains come and stay. Most of our time is spent in the tent in the Tombstone Mountain Campground.

Our boredom cure is the park's visitor center a quarter-mile walk through the forest from our site. We pass hours sitting there by the fire, drinking complimentary Native herbal teas and reading books from the extensive library.

Despite getting soaked in the night by the small pool forming under our sleeping bags, the downtime is welcome—and made better by a chance reunion with Joan and Don. We ran into them two days earlier when they were driving their truck and camper along the Dempster on a hiking trip. Sadly, they were heading back to Whitehorse due to the weather forecast. When I mentioned Dave and I were going to try and wait out the storm but were running low on groceries, Joan said she'd drop off some extra food in the bear-proof bins at the campsite.

We found the bag later, after a wet hike. Inside was a traveler's dream buffet: three different cheeses and crackers, homemade granola, salami, nuts, and other tasty items. Joan's note read: "Heather and Dave. Enjoy!" It was like receiving a care package in the mail and made us smile.

Without bear-proof food bins—which are made from steel, have latches that need opposable thumbs to operate, and are installed in almost every mountain campground—food storage is tricky. We don't have a vehicle to lock things away from animals and rodents, and trees in the Yukon aren't high enough to hang things off the ground. Sometimes, we have to get creative; I once dangled our food bag off a bridge over a river. Another night, I double-bagged everything odorous and put it in an outhouse. Gross, but better than a grizzly getting into our Tasty Bites.

For times when we can't use a rope for keeping food away from bears and other critters, I carry a plastic three-gallon bear vault. We picked this up in Vancouver at an outdoors store. The see-through, incredibly sturdy plastic container has a screw-top lid that must be squeezed past stoppers to open. It's designed to roll away from anything trying to paw at it. If a bear gets hold of the bin, it will just spin from its grip. This, in theory, is supposed to frustrate or bore the animal until it wanders off, looking for lower-hanging fruit. The food storage company has YouTube videos showing a grizzly bouncing up and down on the vault, trying to break it open. After a few hours, he's unsuccessful and moves on.

The bear vault is supposed to hold enough groceries for a week, but that volume estimate is generous. Fitting not only all our food inside, but anything smelly, like shampoos, toothpaste, gum—even mosquito spray— is impossible. I cram in the stuff most concerning—like smoked oyster tins and my pomegranate lip balm—and store everything else for the night inside our panniers. That will never stop a grizzly from clawing through, so we park the bikes far away from our tent and hope for the best.

The container is twelve inches high and nine inches around. It's awkward to pack into my pannier and takes up all the room.

"This thing is just annoying," Dave grumbles.

I'm the one who carries it, but it annoys him that it doesn't annoy me enough to leave it behind.

"I don't care. I don't want animals coming near our tent."

I have a hard enough time falling asleep without worrying about every snap, crackle, and pop in the bushes. Dave thinks I'm overly paranoid about bears; we've seen dozens in our northern travels, and so far, we've never had one come near camp. Not that we know of. However, I have PTSD after being charged by that grizzly in Revelstoke years ago, and the memory resurfaces whenever I'm sleeping in bear country.

Three days later, we're still waiting for the weather to break at Tombstone. I walk over to the visitor center with my laptop and use the free time to calculate our distance traveled to date. From Quartzsite, Arizona, to Baja then mainland Mexico, Central and South America, back to Santiago, through the States and Canada, then up to Inuvik, the total is 26,681 miles—more than the equatorial circumference of Earth by almost 2,000 miles. And we still have three more continents to go.

Strolling back to our soggy tent, I pick ground cranberries at my feet and eat them from my rain-soaked hand. Surrounded by natural, innocent beauty, it's hard to believe anything bad is happening to Mother Earth. This is why I love to immerse myself in nature—a head-in-the-sand tactic against the harsh reality that we humans are destroying the world. I couldn't survive in a place without flora and fauna, mountains and glaciers, lakes and streams...a true hippie at heart. What can you expect from a girl named Heather whose parents baptized her under a tree with river water?

During my forest wander, I daydream about living with Dave when our travels are over, envisioning a big garden with flowers and veggies I can use in our meals. Maybe we'll even get a dog. I want to cut back on consumerism and my part in the pollution chain, and I think how nice it would be to ride two wheels—powered or pedaled—more often than I drive a vehicle. But will I stick to these goals when I get home? When the convenient luxuries I've gone without for two years tempt me again?

The rain finally eases enough for us to make a move the next morning. We pack our sopping tent and leave quickly before another storm comes through. Our hiking plans are thwarted, at least until we can return sometime in the future.

A few hours later, Dave and I are in Dawson City and learn the Dempster Highway has just closed indefinitely due to a washout. We made it out just in time.

To celebrate, we pay five dollars each for the privilege of drinking a Sourtoe Cocktail—a shot of liquor with a severed human toe in the glass.

As the story goes, a man suffered from frostbite during the Yukon's prohibition years, sometime in 1918. To prevent gangrene, his brother chopped the toe off with an axe, and the appendage was then stored in alcohol as a keepsake. Fifty years later, a captain found the jar in an abandoned cabin and decided to start a club. There was only one requirement to join—you had to take a sip from the toe jar.

"You can drink it fast," says a skinny man with a white captain's hat in front of me. "You can drink it slow. But your lips must touch that gnarly toe."

I wonder if he hears that repeatedly in his dreams, since he must recite those words countless times a day for all the tourists.

I look at the tumbler in my hands filled with an ounce of whiskey and a detached toe. It isn't the original toe; as another story tells, some guy who was a bit of a spoilsport came into the Dawson City bar in 2013 and purposely swallowed the toe. Since then, however, there have been several donations—which is perhaps the weirdest part about this whole Sourtoe Cocktail history.

To get a certificate for drinking the Sourtoe Cocktail, both Dave and I allow the shriveled digit to touch our lips and leave the bar with our names on two documents proving we've nibbled a dead human toe.

Day drinkers & blasted undies

Alaska

The Great White North is a fun place to get into trouble, and we trail the Yukon shenanigans across the border into Chicken, Alaska, population twelve.

After window shopping in Chicken's only store, I find Dave straddling a stool in Chicken's only bar.

"So," he looks at me. "Are you gonna do it?"

The interior of the bar is the kind of dark that's always dark, no matter the weather or time of day. Having just walked inside through the narrow wood-framed doorway from the bright summer's day, I wait for my eyes to adjust.

"Do what?"

He points to the ceiling, low and covered with used baseball caps, lewd posters of girls, and the not-so-subtle remnants of female underwear. *Great, another panty ceiling...*

The fabric is shredded, like they've been shot out of a cannon. Which they actually have been, it turns out. The bar is known for blowing up women's undergarments and tacking them to the ceiling. I instinctively feel mine creep up a little between my legs, as if to say, *please don't blow me up!*

Dave's ordered himself a beer and sits with his hands around the glass. I reach over, take a quality-check sip, then order one for myself. Above the crowded supply of liquor bottles, cop badges are nailed to the shelves. I hear the sound of a rutting moose, then realize it's someone's ringtone.

We haven't come to Chicken intending to destroy underwear. We just happened by while traveling along Highway 5 after crossing into Alaska from the Yukon. However, a few other patrons in the bar are watching me expectantly, and I'm always game for a good story.

Outside, I unearth one of my three valuable pairs of laundered underwear from my panniers. Taking a moment, I admire a twelve-foot-high chicken statue designed out of old metal school lockers. The statue can be seen from all directions, given that "town" is only one square block encircled with a few log buildings. I guess if you live in Chicken, you have to get creative about bringing in tourism.

I bring my green thong—already rough-looking after several months in the saddle and shower-handwashing—back into the bar, thinking about Coco in Baja and his panty ceiling. What's different now that I'm willing to leave behind a contribution? Maybe it was because Coco seemed kind of pervy, whereas the bartender in Chicken is aloof and disinterested.

Matt, as I've heard him called by locals sitting in the bar, is extracting gunpowder from shotgun shells because he's out of cannon powder. Using a long stick and looking like this whole charade is beneath him, he reaches out to grab my green undies. Using the stick, he tamps them down the foot-long steel tube. Dave and I, along with two curious day drinkers, follow Matt outside, where he places the gun in the middle of the vacant parking lot, pointing it away from people and other valuables.

While Matt's prepping for launch, four bikers ride in on Harleys. Their throaty engines cause my beer bottle to tremble on the picnic table. *Where did they come from?* The road Dave and I took to Chicken was gravel—not a friendly surface for cruiser Harley Davidson motorcycles, and Chicken is far from anywhere in any direction. The four riders go in to order drinks, then come back outside to watch the action.

Everything is ready to blow. Matt lights a match to a wick hanging behind the cannon like a rat's tail, then steps back several feet. The wick sparks, sizzles, then dies and falls out. No boom.

Muttering about not being paid enough for this shit, Matt walks back to the cannon, re-tamps, and tries again. The second and third attempt to ignite my lady garment fail as well.

"Maybe your underwear's damp!" yells one of the Harley riders, eliciting a cacophony of laughter.

"Or too ugly; not enough spark in those panties, ha!" says another.

"I doubt anyone has wet panties around you guys," I say, "unless it's pee from laughing at your motorcycles."

Silence and then another round of laughter; it's hard to ruffle feathers in Chicken.

My thong finally explodes on the fourth try and comes fluttering down like leaves. The crowd cheers and everyone moves back into the bar.

Inside, I add the fabric remains to the ceiling while Dave tries to win a bet with one of the bikers to see who can deadlift a cannon ball with one hand. It's not Dave. I strike up a conversation with a long-haul trucker and tell him my dad drove Greyhound buses for over thrity years. Road Life is a culture of its own, and I understand well the trucker's sadness at leaving his kids and wife behind for days on end; Dad felt the same, even though Mom was an independent woman who respected his living and enjoyed some time to herself. I have fond memories of her playing ABBA and Fleetwood Mac cranked to eleven on the house stereo while she cleaned or tackled one of her many craft projects. Her beautiful singing voice cascaded into my bedroom, lulling me to sleep. A night owl in her younger days, Mom often waited up to greet Dad when he came home, even if it was three in the morning. I always thought that was sweet.

"I'm ready to call it a night," I say to Dave several hours later, already feeling a headache settling in.

Since anything goes in Chicken, we set up our tent in a corner of the parking lot, near our bikes. Scooting into my sleeping bag, I hear one of the bikers say, "Well, I didn't come this far to spend the night sober," and a raging party begins, lasting long into the night. Still, I sleep well, dreaming of multicolored underwear falling around me like snowflakes.

Years later, a feminist I knew pointed out that ripped female clothing on bar ceilings is sexist. At the time, blowing up my underwear seemed funny and anecdotal to traveling in a northern frontier country. But in hindsight, I could have thought this over. Bars—where women are often harassed, or worse—should think about what this suggests. I don't consider myself a feminist, but I'm definitely not comfortable with women being objectified or pigeonholed.

Chicken is chilly the next morning. I squirm out of the tent, trying not to wake Dave, and walk over to my bike, thinking about my battery issues. *I wonder if it'll start?* Nothing happens when I turn the key. We're 270 miles from Fairbanks, which has a BMW dealer, but that's a long way on dirt roads.

Another milestone awaits us in Alaska—several hundred miles of remote wilderness called the Dalton Highway, which will take us to Deadhorse, Alaska—the farthest road-accessible point in the US. These roads to the ends of the earth are never easy on our bikes, and mine needs more TLC before I'm confident riding it to the top of America.

"Babe," I say to the tent, "my bike won't start. The battery's dead again."

A deep sigh, followed by the sound of Dave unzipping his sleeping bag. It never occurred to me to ask his opinion before I bought the used bike off Craigslist. Maybe I should have, since he's mechanically inclined. But as someone who cherishes her self-reliance—and who's been single for so long—I'm used to doing what some consider "man jobs" by myself—something else my dad has instilled in my sister and me. We were taught how to change the oil, tires, and spark plugs in our vehicles. We learned to drive stick shifts and how not to put up with bullshit from anyone. Dad did not raise damsels in distress—though at the same time, he is wildly protective of his "ladies," and we can always count on him. If I'm being honest, these are the same qualities I'm searching for in Dave. It irks me that he isn't open to teaching me more about bike mechanics and that I'm reluctant to ask because it'll likely lead to an argument.

I'm realizing more and more that my beloved Stallion has flaws that may be holding me back. Its low clearance has me regularly bashing my skid plate into embedded obstacles, and even though it's low to the ground, it's still hard for me to get my feet down because my custom seat is so wide. The smaller 19-inch front wheel (compared to Dave's 21-inch wheel) forces my bike to auger into potholes and ruts. Both my wheel rims have dents from hitting potholes and rocks, and now the Stallion has a disconcerting wobble at speeds over fifty. Replacing wheels is expensive—about $2,000—so I just ignore the problem.

These subtle differences between my bike and Dave's make a huge difference at the end of the day, but I don't know what to do about it at this point. An F800 like Dave's, with its higher clearance, larger front wheel, and more power, feels like too much bike for me. I'm not sure I'm ready to control such a beast, but I do like the BMW brand—especially for a trip like ours.

My mind tallies up the cost of kitting out the Stallion to make it more reliable for the next leg of our travels. A new radiator is top of the list; the epoxy crack repair won't last forever. And it would be wise to replace the wheel rims.

When Dave gets the Stallion running, I let it idle to warm up, but it stalls twice just leaving Chicken. Thinking the battery just needs more time to charge, I venture forth. For the next 200 miles, the Stallion lurches like

I'm riding one of those mechanical horses for kids at the mall. I can't get into fifth gear, but fourth revs the engine too high.

Dave hooks up a diagnostic tool we have. The computer suggests something's wrong with the stator (a coil of wire that generates electricity). This could be a never-ending issue or another costly, vital repair, or both. And if the dealer in Fairbanks doesn't have what I need in stock, that means a long wait.

I can feel Dave's irritation. He wanted me to get a different bike when we had more options in the lower forty-eight, but I'd dug my heels in. I'm attached to my bike and all its dings, dents, and scratches from our many ups and downs together. A smattering of stickers on the fairing and panniers tells the story of where we've been: Baja, Peru, Patagonia…I'm in a relationship with the Stallion and I don't want it to end. What choice do I have? It will take time to find another bike capable of such a long journey—time we don't have—and I'm not about to buy something brand new.

Reaching through the thorns

After gassing up in Delta Junction, I engage the clutch to snap it into second, but the engine lugs and stalls again. My round-the-world ride won't even go another mile.

"Fuuuuuck!"

I've deployed the Helmet Scream release before. It usually makes me feel better. But this time I may have popped a vein.

Putting on my hazards, I ride slowly along the shoulder, letting drivers pass me. Dave's voice booms into my helmet.

"What are you doing?"

The sore throat I woke up to is turning into something worse, with body aches and a foggy brain. I'm miserable after hours of coddling the Stallion along, and edgy anticipating my boyfriend's tolerance for derailments like this.

"What do you *think's* going on?" I fire back. "You've been with me all day."

"You can't ride like this on the highway."

"Oh my god, Dave, I'm trying to get *off* the highway. Why are you so impatient?"

"Hey, don't be pissed with me; I'm not the problem here."

The condescending tone irks me to boiling point. I turn into a vacant parking lot. When Dave pulls in, I can't hold back.

"You know, it wasn't too long ago that *your* bike broke down and I did everything I could to help."

"I'm *always* helping you, and I'm getting tired of your stupid bike causing us so many issues."

I feel like someone just gut-punched me.

"You're not *always* helping me. Do you have any idea how exhausting some of these days are? Yet, I still follow you wherever you want to go!"

It's not something a lot of women would do. I explain this to Dave—not that he seems to notice.

If I wasn't tired and sick, I might have understood Dave's roundabout way of expressing concern for my well-being. But there's a fine line between chivalry and arrogance. Like many self-governing women, I'm fighting an internal tennis match between giving in and losing my hard-won independence. I thrive on blowing past my boundaries, but doing it day in and day out for months on end is taking a toll.

Now that we've spent so much time together, Dave and I are circling the blackberry bush of our relationship. Neither of us wants to reach through the thorns for that juicy morsel—glistening in the sun, fat and full of nutrients, yet just out of reach. It looks delicious and inviting, but the path through the prickles is rough.

I stomp off and sit on some grass, recalling a painful memory from a few months earlier. We were traveling near the Tetons, a mountain range in Wyoming where I'd done some climbing in the past. Dave was impatient with me for taking too long to photograph something. Lashing out, because the place meant a lot to me, I took off on my bike. Dave did not follow. After about fifteen minutes, I stopped by a river when my tears made it too hard to see properly. Dave rode by some time later, saw my bike, and pulled over. Both of us were too stubborn to make amends, and the debate escalated. Suddenly, Dave stood up and said he was done—with me and the trip. I was stunned, watching him walk away. Flashes of everything we'd accomplished together—and had yet to accomplish—swarmed through my brain. *Should I run after him or just let him go?* In the end, I did something I've never done with other boyfriends when it got this bad: I asked Dave to stay so we could talk things over more calmly.

If we'd broken up then, where would we be now? Would we have each kept going on our trip of a lifetime, or would it be too lonely without each other?

I think of suggesting to Dave that we take a week apart for some alone time; maybe we just need a refreshing break. Then I remember we have only one tent, and I have no maps or GPS. *And what if my bike breaks down…*

I'm tired. I hate fighting. I have no idea if the man I've become so attached to understands me. But I stand up and walk through those imaginary thorns toward Dave, ready to reach for the juicy antidote that might fix this.

I coax the Stallion a mile back to where we fueled up earlier. The station owner lets me leave my bike in his garage overnight. I grab some things I need then get on the back of Dave's bike. For the first several miles, I hold onto the luggage rack behind me, still reeling from our fight. I don't know what to do about my bike troubles now, but either way, the stress it's putting on our relationship and the trip is a problem I can no longer ignore.

Leaning forward, I wrap my arms around Dave's middle. He reaches back to give my knee a squeeze.

Someone I used to be

There's nothing like a familiar face to ease tension, and my longtime friend and climbing partner, Ed, is that face.

Ed lives in Fairbanks, an hour away from where my bike is currently broken down. He's been expecting us, and within moments of seeing him and his wife, Jill, along with their kids, Vera and Thomas, I sink into the joy of hanging out with an old friend.

I first met Ed in California while on a solo road trip through the US in my early twenties. After climbing Mount Shasta together, we formed a solid friendship spanning miles and years. Although we lived in different countries, Ed and I managed to meet in various locales to climb, like our time in Peru when we summited Mount Huascarán.

The last time I was in Alaska—and had seen Ed—was fourteen years ago in 2002, when we climbed a remote peak in the Alaska range. Reuniting with him now reminds me of when I was fiercely independent: road-tripping for months at a time, picking up work here and there, answering to no one and nothing.

My fight with Dave, or at least its intensity, was likely the aftereffect of me pining for the person I used to be and not embracing how I'd changed and the person I was becoming. I missed that girl. But I had to let her go if I was going to share my heart with someone.

Dave and I borrow Ed's pickup the next morning and rent a U-Haul trailer to retrieve the Stallion from Delta Junction. Three hours later, we're at Outpost Alaska—the BMW dealer in Fairbanks. Like an anxious parent awaiting the outcome of a kid's surgery, I watch through the workshop window. Brad, the mechanic, works around my disemboweled bike, trying to locate the issue.

Dave puts his arm around me. "Everything'll be okay."

The gesture is comforting. I know he wants that bike gone for good, but he also understands my dilemma.

Brad finds us a few hours later in the lounge, which is not unlike a hospital waiting room with tea, coffee, and a TV to help people forget how much time is passing by. I almost blurt, *How's my baby, doc?*

"The problem was diesel in the fuel line," Brad says. "It's common in the north, 'specially if you get your gas somewhere remote."

What isn't remote up here?

I trust Brad has been thorough, but his conclusion doesn't make sense. Dave and I always fill up from the same pump, and his bike is fine.

I ask about the high RPMs. Brad tells me he pulled a new fuel injector from a demo bike and transplanted it into mine. All the lines are flushed now, and he's filled the tank with new gas.

"It runs great now," Brad says. "You should be good for the Dalton."

I've gotten away with a $200 dollar repair but wonder if the Stallion isn't just behaving for now.

Back at Ed's, I forget about any troubles and embrace some time off, relaxing with a book, going for walks around Fairbanks, riding bicycles to pick blueberries, and making pies. It's all well-needed and well-deserved. Unfortunately, I've developed a full-on flu. I'm embarrassed being sick in Ed and Jill's home and sit far from everyone during dinner and in their living room, using up all their tissues and trying not to cough.

Dave and I exclaim over the sockeye salmon Ed cooks one night. He and Thomas had gone on a recent father-son fishing trip on the Copper River, and the freezer is stocked. The fresh catch just endears me to northern living even more.

Woman against machine

A week later, with both me and the Stallion feeling better, Dave and I aim the bikes toward the Dalton Highway—destination Deadhorse, Alaska. This will be a four-day, out-and-back excursion, so we leave gear we don't need at Ed and Jill's.

The Dalton starts eighty-four miles north of Fairbanks and ends 414 miles later in Deadhorse. Some long-distance motorcyclists claim to have ridden Prudhoe Bay to Ushuaia, or vice versa, but the industrial community of Deadhorse is as far as we'll be able to go on two wheels. Prudhoe Bay itself, sitting 300 miles north of the Arctic Circle, is a US government-protected oil field. Tourists can visit but only after a security check and paying seventy dollars for a chaperoned bus ride to the Arctic Ocean's edge—something we aren't planning on doing.

The forecast shows dry weather for the next five days, before another rainstorm is predicted. Time is of the essence. Road crews use the same calcium chloride mix on the Dalton as the Dempster, and Dave and I want to be back in Fairbanks before the road turns to goo.

A twenty-one-point checklist in the visitor's guide for driving the Dalton recommends items like two full-sized spare tires for all vehicles, extra fuel, a CB radio, and plenty of groceries. There are limited medical and cell services along this meandering gray ribbon laid on a blanket of red, gold, and green vegetation. Some people think the Dalton isn't worth the risk or hassle. For us, it offers another opportunity to traverse a remote mountain range leading to the top of the continent—just the sort of thing we're after.

Haul trucks and anything else passing in either direction stir up so much dust, I feel the grit between my teeth, even with my visor down.

I have cautious optimism regarding the Stallion. It's running better than ever on the hard-packed, bumpy road, so I turn my attention to the tundra, hoping to spot a grizzly or caribou. Due to the short summer season in the north, tree growth is stunted. Evergreens grow in patches six or seven feet high, rarely taller. There's little to obstruct my view.

The Alaskan pipeline—one of the world's largest pipeline systems, transporting Alaska North Slope crude oil from Prudhoe Bay—can be seen from nearly all viewpoints. It follows the road like the world's longest waterslide park, carrying oil to Valdez, where the precious resource will be shipped to a convenient location near you.

We're hard pressed to get scenic shots without the rusty, 800-mile-long pipe in the way. But it's cool to see; we are, after all, on the highway leading to North America's largest oil field. Hundreds of haul trucks cruise up and down the Dalton every day, carrying the equipment, materials, and supplies needed this far north.

The Dalton is marked by numbered mileposts indicating distance traveled. At 115, a large wooden sign in a pullout tells us we've crossed the Arctic Circle again—this time in a different country. Most people never get to do that once, but we'll be crossing this latitude four times in our northern travels, counting our returns.

At a visitor center we're happy to find in the middle of nowhere, Dave and I talk with another rider coming back from Deadhorse. He's not encouraging. We've had two days of sun, but the storm is coming early. I notice the blue sky clouding over, and we still have more than 200 miles until Deadhorse.

"Also, there's lots of construction," the rider tells us. "They're raising the road. It's piled up with loose, deep river rock and filled with surprises. I went down a few times. So did some of the guys in a group ahead of me."

Shit.

The rain starts fifty miles later, and the Dalton turns into melted peanut butter. Thirty-six miles before Deadhorse, construction crews stop us. We sit freezing in the rain until a man in a high-vis vest takes pity on us and invites us inside the company vehicle. With heat blasting through the vents, he tells us stories about growing up in a small Native village nearby in the Brooks Range. He says he loves taking his grandkids fishing and hunting, teaching them how to live off the land. I enjoy the pride beaming from his eyes.

Too soon, we are back on our wet wheels.

The Dalton Highway is being raised eight feet, because the permafrost underneath is shifting and causing issues on the driving surface. Essentially, the road is sinking. Piles of round rocks the size of shoes and soccer balls have been used to add height before getting topped off with gravel. With the ground in constant flux, pavement is out of the question.

Dave and I follow a pilot truck through the extensive construction zone. We're first in line, and without heavier vehicles ahead to tamp down the rocks, our fully loaded bikes sink in and lurch forward, wheels looking for purchase.

The rocky section finishes after a few miles, and we pick up speed again. I'm jackhammering along the still-rough road at forty miles an hour when my engine suddenly shuts off. I coast to a stop on the shoulder while a long-haul truck riding my tail passes, spraying me with a mist. I make the dire mistake of dragging my glove across my visor, leaving fine scratches in the plastic and a clay-like haze that disorients me. I lose balance and start falling to the left, but then like magic, I stop. *What the hell?* Pushing up my scratched visor, I look down and see the side stand firmly planted on the ground. I investigate and realize a spring has vibrated loose and the stand has dropped, cutting the engine when it activated the sensor. This is to prevent riding away with the side stand down, which could make a rider crash.

I radio Dave, who hasn't seen me pull over.

"Failure to connect. Please try again later."

I curse. Rain beats down on my helmet. Part of me is relieved this is a minor mechanical issue—nothing a little baling wire can't fix. Still, the actual parts would be better. I walk down the road to see if I can find anything that looks like it belongs to my ailing steed.

Dave comes back, and we work together on the impossible task of spying gray parts on a gray road. Miraculously, he finds the spring, which is half the assembly. The other half is a very thin plate, and we never come across it. Dave uses baling wire to keep the side stand up, tricking the sensor so my engine will run. Unfortunately, now I have no side stand for parking.

The last six miles into Deadhorse are dismal. Another construction zone impedes our access—so close yet so far. Again, a pilot car ushers us northbound. Before leaving, the driver rolls down her window.

"It's not good ahead," she says. "The road is really, really bad..." She waits a few beats, perhaps expecting us to turn around. I stare at her until she shrugs and sets off at fifteen miles an hour.

The slow pace makes it hard to keep my motorcycle balanced, as Dave is forever pointing out to me. This time I have no choice. I curse when my front wheel continually plows into the road debris while the rear slides around on the wet rocks. It's like trying to ride across blocks of ice on a melting lake. Ahead, an orange sign reads: MOTORCYCLES USE EXTREME CAUTION. I almost laugh.

Deadhorse finally appears in the low fog. Unlike Ushuaia, where the city was a pleasant surprise, Deadhorse is definitely unpleasant. Still, I want to drop to the ground and kiss its murky, oil-laden streets.

We pull up to the lackluster Prudhoe Bay Hotel hoping for lunch. I put my tiptoes on the ground and wait for Dave to come over and hold the handlebars, then I slip off my slimy seat. I hope no one is watching; now

I can't even get off my own damn motorcycle without someone's help. With nothing solid to lean the Stallion against, Dave heaves the bike up on its center stand, usually reserved for something like changing a flat tire or oiling the chain, as it balances the bike square in its middle.

The food inside the hotel is not bad. Over a lunch of seafood chowder and chocolate pie, Dave asks what I want to do. The weather gives the day a gloomy feeling, making this trip milestone not as celebratory as the others.

"Would it be terrible if I wanted to turn around and go back after lunch?" I say.

Since getting to the actual top of North America involves an expensive bus tour, I don't think there's much left to do here. But that means forgoing a chance to see the Arctic Ocean.

"Not terrible, but are you sure you don't want to stay just for a night? I can see how much it is for a room."

"I guess. I'm just nervous about riding back over that shit show of a road to get out of here."

Dave goes to ask about room costs, which seals the deal to leave. Although the price includes meals in the buffet-style cafeteria, rooms are $117 *per person*. The Prudhoe Bay Hotel is nothing fancy, but the cost to bring supplies to the ends of the earth are huge. That, unfortunately, gets passed on to visitors.

I have no regrets leaving Deadhorse, wanting very much to get back to the sections along the Dalton where nature is prolific and refreshing and there aren't piles of rocks to steer through. Just like I've done many times before in sports—like kayaking down a raging river or jumping into a ski line where I can't see the bottom—I just want to get the scary parts over with as soon as possible.

Dave helps me get back on the Stallion, and I take off. The hardest section is right after leaving town, and somehow it's gotten worse. My bike lashes about, the rear tire excavating rocks and carving its own way in the loose ground. Not a single pilot car is in sight, so I increase my speed from thirty miles an hour to forty-five. A lurch and I'm nearly flung from my seat but stay aboard. Then, almost before I'm ready, we're out of it; ten sketchy miles done in a matter of minutes.

After the rider at the visitor center said he and some other guys had gone down "a few times," I was sure I would, too. That I hadn't crashed going in to Deadhorse only made me more convinced I would on the way out. I thought it was just luck that kept me upright the first time. But when

I pass over it all again without losing control, I truly realize how my mental and physical riding skills have improved over the last 24,000 miles.

As a reward, the rain stops and wildlife emerges. We have our first grizzly sighting and watch as it stalks along under the pipeline. A few miles later, an owl sitting on a tree branch low to the ground captures my interest for several minutes. Caribou herds dance like ballerinas across the tundra, too far away for a good photo but not so far that we can't enjoy them. The rugged beauty and remoteness of traveling along the Dalton is contrasting; here is a place where nature carries on as if humans don't exist. Yet, the Dalton is an industrial gateway, bringing fuel to millions of people, which in turn is ruining our environment.

Two hundred miles later, Dave and I are halfway back to Fairbanks. We think about pushing it the rest of the way, but an idyllic-looking campground calls for us to slow down and enjoy the Dalton a little longer.

Dave sets up the tent in the almost-vacant campground while I wander off to photograph the vibrant fall brush.

Later, we sip whiskey and toast another trip milestone. As I've learned after Ushuaia, celebration doesn't always come at the exact moment of success. Like good wine decanted and left to breathe, sometimes it's better to wait a while.

Throwing a leg over my seat the next morning, I give Dave a thumbs up and turn the key.

Nothing.

This time, jumping my bike doesn't work with what we have. Dave flags down another camper with a truck, and we're able to defibrillate the Stallion back to life on the third try. I start riding but soon smell something like burning hair. The dreaded warning light for my radiator comes on again, and my pants are covered in something wet. Inspecting, I find calcium chloride from the sludge caked into the radiator vents, which is stopping my bike from breathing. Using twigs, I scratch away at the residue, now set like concrete. Dave sacrifices his water bottle and scoops from a stagnant, sulfur-smelling pond. He splashes the radiator to loosen the clay, and I get out my toothbrush to flick off what I can. This reveals a second crack, which is why all the coolant has leaked out onto my pants. Dave adds water through the overflow cap. Until then, I had no idea an engine could run without coolant, but water does the trick. Now, with that and the vents opened more for airflow, my bike is running. However, it's only a matter of time before the water drips out, leaving the radiator dry as a bone. I ride until the warning light comes on again, stop, top up the rad with water, let the bike cool down, then keep going. I need to do this every thirty miles or so. All the messing around tests not just Dave's patience, but mine as well. On the plus side, there are plenty of blueberries to snack on while we wait.

For easier access, I leave off the plastic fairing that covers my rad, strapping it on top of my luggage. The rain is back, seeping into my suit and turning the road slick. I'm cold and weary from trying to keep my bike upright while also wondering when it might quit for good. I have a lot of time to think. A decision must be made.

Dave stays behind after one of our stops to give me a head start. The next section is mostly downhill. I cut the engine and coast where I can, managing almost fifty miles before needing a top-up. Pulling into the gas station, I have the depressing realization I can't dismount the Stallion without a side stand or my boyfriend. I pull up close to a concrete roadblock and lean the bike against it, gingerly easing myself off.

Four teenagers sit in a Jeep Cherokee, staring at me.

"Is that your bike?" one calls over.

"Yep."

"Wow, it's awesome!"

I look affectionately at the Stallion, braced against the concrete, its innards exposed from the missing fairing.

"Can we get a photo of you beside it?"

I laugh. "Sure."

Two guys come over to shake my hand. I love my bike even more then for all its crazy-looking, unfancy glory. The Stallion is a true workhorse, doing its best to get me back. I've put it through enough.

Holding on & letting go

In Fairbanks, we return to the Outpost Alaska dealership. These last few weeks, the Stallion has been like the hero in a movie who keeps getting shot and run over and attacked yet drags through until the end.

Brad tries to revive my bike, but it isn't looking good. I've sunk several thousand dollars into modifications and have repaired or replaced parts when I could. Yet, the Stallion has rejected it all like bad organ transplants.

I await Brad's final prognosis. Dave wanders around the dealership. He calls over to me, suggesting at first, then insisting, I sit on a new F800GS on the showroom floor. The bike is intimidating in its perfection: too shiny, too pretty. I don't want pretty. I want rough, rugged, and hardy. I can't imagine putting this beauty on some of the roads we travel over.

"There's no way I can touch the ground on that thing."

But I can. The bike already has a lowered seat and lowered suspension—unheard of straight from the factory. And it still has more clearance than the 650.

"There's no way I can ride this. It's too big."

But I can. When I take it for a test ride, the bike is agile, responsive, and comfortable.

I'm running out of excuses.

Brad informs me that trying to repair my baby is not going to work with our schedule. I need a new radiator shipped, as they don't have one in stock. That will take weeks and cost almost three times what it would in shops to the south. The stator is also toast, as the diagnostics test suggested, and will cost over $1,500, plus other immediate repairs or replacements. This doesn't include new wheel rims. Plus, all the money in the world won't give the Stallion better clearance.

We've already had one major delay in our travels. I don't want to create another waiting for parts.

Walking back to Ed and Jill's, Dave and I talk about the pros and cons of repairing the Stallion versus buying a new bike. I have to hand it to Dave; he doesn't interject his opinion and lets me figure it out for myself.

Hammering the last nail into the wooden crate containing my round-half-the-world motorcycle feels like I'm putting it to rest in a coffin. In a sense, that's true; my poor old workhorse is dead, and in an ironic twist, its last trip was to Deadhorse, Alaska.

I'm having Outpost ship the Stallion home, where I'll decide its future later.

I give the crate a pat, then turn and smile. Before me is the 650's replacement. A salesman named Justin Kleiter holds the keys. I stride over to the F800 I test rode the day before and take my receipt from Justin, already signed on the dotted line. My trip budget is shattered, but better that than my travels.

I can't be prouder; I've advanced to the next level of dual-sport riding. I deserve this bike.

That evening at Jill and Ed's, I pop open a bottle of prosecco and watch the bubbling flow splash over the moose droppings on the lawn. Everyone cheers—even Dave, man of subdued excitement. No doubt he's anticipating many wonderful things, like the lack of roadside repairs, and possibly a girlfriend who rides bigger, better, faster, more. Time will tell.

I'm too excited to get my new bike on the road, even though I know the first scratch or ding will feel like a knife to the heart. I've always shied away from expensive, flashy things because I usually break or damage them. Also, I don't like looking pretentious or showy—especially when we're traveling in places where people have next to nothing. I don't mention my new purchase on our travel website, writing instead that I "found a replacement." It feels uncomfortable to brag about buying a brand-new motorcycle.

Before leaving Ed and Jill's for good, we have another interview with CBC Radio. Sparkling wine, radio interviews, and a flashy new bike—at times, our travels sure seem glamorous.

Northern lights & rainy nights

Dave's snoring cuts through my sleep like the exhaust brake of an eighteen-wheeler. I glare at my slumbering boyfriend before deciding to get up and pee, since I'm now awake. I turn off my headlamp when I squat—not that anyone can see me, it's just a habit. Now enveloped in darkness, my eyes adjust to something spectacular. The night is aglow.

I pull up my pants and run back to the tent.

"Babe," I whisper, "come see this." Nothing. I shake him a little. "Dave." More aggressive shaking. I don't want to scare him but know he'll hate to miss this. "It's the northern lights!"

Dave finally stirs.

"Can't I just see them from the tent?" His voice sounds like he swallowed dry cornflakes then chased them down with whiskey and cigarettes.

I pull the tent flap aside.

"Holy shit." He fumbles for his camera.

We had found a trail off the road near the Denali National Park boundary and set up our tent that evening in a dry, flat spot surrounded by blueberry bushes and a view up and down the valley.

Looking skyward now, I watch as green, blue, and violet lights swirl—like Technicolor cirrus clouds against a black velvet night. Dave photographs the celestial scene using a tripod and some pro-photographer tips about timelapse he recently learned from some van life travelers. He shows me the results on his screen, and they're fantastic.

Both of my hopes for this part of the trip have come true: to be up north long enough to experience both twenty-four hours of sun and the northern lights. Two more life goals achieved.

After all the excitement, I sleep fitfully until a pale light on the tent walls indicates morning. Throughout the night, clouds have come in, and they hang low now in the valley. I love falling asleep to the sound of rain on our tent, but hearing it when I wake up sucks. Escaping into a warm, dry vehicle isn't an option for us to avoid autumn's sogginess. All our stuff is wet now, and the tent won't dry out until the next warm, sunny day.

Before leaving, Dave gets a text from a guy we met at the Outpost Alaska dealership. Joseph and his girlfriend, Kim, from Texas, are traveling on two bikes as well. We are planning to ride in some of the same areas so had given them our number.

Dave replies that we'll meet them in Seward, on the Kenai Peninsula. We ride in that direction over the beautiful Hatcher Pass, but the rain is back in buckets. Luckily, we recently had some bluebird days along the Denali Highway after leaving Fairbanks so I could test out my new ride. The perfect weather allowed for unobstructed views of America's highest peak. Denali was bathed in sun when Dave and I rode past; it's the same mountain backdrop that was in Dave's profile picture when I decided to email him for the first time twenty-eight months ago. Now, he points out the route he climbed in 2002.

From a single email to sharing moments like this. It's crazy and wonderful what taking a chance will bring you in life.

On the Seward Highway, faster speeds drive water up my sleeves and down my neck. I'm having a self-pitying day, feeling cold, wet, and miserable.

"I have to stop," I radio Dave.

We steer into a pullout. I get off my bike, feeling the pool of rain collecting in my crotch make its way down my legs and into my boots—like pee but not warm. Despite a "waterproof" riding suit, heated jacket, and heated handlebar grips, I'm freezing in the sub-fifty-degree weather. A few weeks earlier, I had purchased an oversized rain jacket and pants to wear over everything for added protection. I pull that out now, cursing myself for not doing that before I got soaked.

Weather is our constant companion, invited or not. It rides with us, clinging to our pant legs and getting all up in our faces. We have to accept our travel mate even though it never offers to buy us a beer or do the camp dishes.

"It's chilly," Dave understates.

I don't answer. Being cold makes me grumpy. I want to be draining the hot water tank in a motel shower somewhere. Pulling out a balaclava— the first time I've needed one—I battle to drag it down my face while trying to keep my long hair back.

"For shit's sake!" My stiff fingers don't close tightly enough to grasp the hairs tickling my eyes and nose. I resort to smearing my hands over my face in frantic swipes to curb the itchiness.

"Swing your arms around," Dave offers when he sees me rubbing my palms together for warmth. We jump in place and act like windmills to get more circulation going. Dave comes over and bear-hugs me.

"You're like a marshmallow," he laughs. "Ready?" He's already getting on his bike. "Let's go find our friends."

Despite being cold and wet, I truly love my new bike. It's a big motorcycle and takes some getting used to, but riding the F800GS is energizing rather than exhausting. I never visualized myself capable of handling something so nice or intimidating. This bike starts every time I turn the ignition. And everything works—*all the time.* I hadn't fully realized how much of my focus and energy had gone into praying for good performance from the Stallion. Now that I have something reliable, I'm free to concentrate on the actual act of riding.

Dave is in better spirits too, since he no longer has to jump-start my bike or pull out tools every day. I'm nervous and excited to see how the bike—and I—perform off-pavement. I'm not sure when that will be. Our northern travels are coming to a close, since it's now the end of summer. We've talked about riding some more BDRs in the US, but I'm eager to leave the Americas.

We enter the café in Seward. Joseph is a large man. He rises to greet us, then asks what we want. "My treat," he says. Soon, I have a hot mug of green tea warming my freezing fingers. I want to capture its heat and take it with me for later.

"What do you think of the rain?" Joseph asks. "Nothing like a wet crotch, huh?"

He's a barrel-chested, cuddly bear of a man, with kind blue eyes and long, gray hair pulled back into a ponytail. Kim is a pretty blonde with bright eyes that shine when she talks about the two of them riding down to South America.

"After that," she says, "who knows?"

The couple are in their mid-fifties. I sense they're also in a new relationship, judging by the brief information we glean about their ride from Texas to Alaska. They speak like two people who don't quite know everything about each other but have embarked on a long, challenging journey and maybe—just maybe—sometimes question what they've gotten into. I know that feeling.

We sit in the café, hoping the skies will clear. Our riding jackets are hung on the backs of our chairs, dripping.

"I think we need a mop," I look around for one before someone wipes out in the puddles, but the barista is already on it.

We wear four different riding suit brands among us, and everyone is soaked, even though we've each spent a lot of money on good gear. On days like these, it's impossible to be outside and not get wet.

We stay in the café for two hours while the rain continues to come down hard. Kim and Joseph are heading to Anchorage, where they have a place for the night at a friend's. Our original plan was to keep riding south along the peninsula, but looking at a weather app changes our minds. We ask Joseph and Kim if they want to meet in Anchorage in a few days, then ride to Valdez together. We make that plan, then Dave and I splurge on a hotel for the night.

After a seafood dinner, we walk back to our room and watch cable TV. It's total luxury. Heat, a movie, hot showers…and my new ride parked outside, waiting to whisk me off to another day of adventure.

Our tent and gear hang around the room. We crank up the thermostat to 80°F. By morning, everything is bone dry, including our parched mouths.

A new life over caribou stew

Shelly stirs a bubbling pot of caribou stew I can't wait to try. Beside the pot are oven-fresh cheddar biscuits. Her small modular home smells of rosemary and baking yeast.

"Thank you again for letting us join Kim and Joseph staying here." I pet Shelly's Australian shepherds, Maple and Sage, with nostalgia. "Your dogs are the spitting image of my parent's dog."

Joseph and Kim mentioned we were coming to Anchorage, and Shelly insisted we stay with her, too. She's a sweet, middle-aged widow who lost the man she married far too soon.

"It's so nice to have people in my house again," she says. "When my husband died, I couldn't get out of bed for months. I'm just starting to re-emerge into life again."

The five of us sit at a small kitchen table. I glance around Shelly's home. She has a framed photo of a moose silhouetted against an orange sunset.

"What an incredible shot," I say, not yet knowing Shelly is a wildlife photographer and took the photo. She has another prize picture of a grizzly chasing a crow. "Unbelievable," I say to no one in particular. My companions are busy drinking and talking.

That Dave and I were invited to stay overnight at Shelly's sight unseen is proof of her generous heart. I admire her kindness mixed with hardcore sturdiness. A rifle hangs in the kitchen, and she knows how to use it. After her husband died in a car accident, Shelly had debilitating pain from her sciatic nerve, which in good humor she calls her "psychotic nerve."

"The joy in my life for things like food and photography left me—I thought for good. That's why I just love having you all here."

She steps around her kitchen with familiar ease, and her resilience moves me since her loss is still so raw.

Shelly talks about their life together.

"We'd go hunting all the time, and we both loved being outside. I miss him."

I sense the pain talking about a husband she loved as two adventurous couples sit before her. Yet Shelly's eyes shine with the flicker of a soul that wants to get on with life—as though the transformation is happening right then and there. She makes piles of food—more than we can eat. It's a symbol of her vibrance returning. We crowd her modest home, but Shelly assures us there's room—not only for us, but whatever gear we want to bring in to dry or launder.

Kim, Joseph, Dave, and I, along with the dogs, sleep on the living room floor that night, snug beside a crackling woodstove. I stare at the moose photo until my eyes drift closed.

"I'm coming with you," Shelly announces in the morning, after feeding us biscuits and gravy.

I look at Joseph and Kim, as if they have the answer for her spontaneity. The four of us are outside packing our bikes for Valdez.

"You've all inspired me to live free and without attachments. I want to drive with you to Valdez. I can take your stuff and here—" she points to a cooler—"it's full of beer and elk sausage. I gotcha covered!"

"Woohoo!" I call out. "Shelly, you're awesome. And I'm not just talking about the cooler contents."

Maple and Sage jump into the back of Shelly's GMC Yukon. We're quite the entourage now: Shelly and her dogs, Kim and Joseph, and Dave and me.

Our third day of riding and driving all together is Shelly's birthday. We're just as thrilled to help this warm-hearted lady celebrate fifty-two years on earth as she is to have us with her. At our campground that night, Joseph walks over to the office/convenience store and comes back with an improvised birthday cake: two chocolate Ding Dongs layered on top of each other with a matchstick stuck in the top.

Shelly is gleeful and claps while Joseph lights the "candle." We all sing happy birthday.

She meant to travel with us just for one day and hadn't even packed a toothbrush. But it was seven days before Shelly returned home to restart her life anew. Months later, I sent her an email to check in. I hoped her life was going well. She assured me she was finding happiness again and that Kim was actually visiting her in Anchorage at that moment. I asked if I could buy a copy of her moose photograph. A card she sent along with the 5×7 framed photo—which she refused money for—read: *Heather and Dave, you've inspired me, free spirits! Best of luck on your journey!*

That photo hangs in my office today.

I'm not a motorcycle smuggler

I'm nervous approaching the US/Canada border near Tok, Alaska. I'm a Canadian citizen bringing a US-plated vehicle across the border.

"Don't worry," Dave assures me. "It'll be fine."

I worry anyway and am frustrated that neither of us thought this through when I was buying the bike. Dave reasons that because the bike is continuing to other parts of the world, we'll have no trouble explaining this. I'm sure there will be a problem.

The customs building is a pleasant log cabin nestled under a cluster of quaking aspen trees. Pulling up to the window, I flip open my visor and smile, ready to answer the officer's questions.

"Nature of your trip?" she asks, taking my passport. I see her nametag says Beth.

"Travel." I answer. She waits for me to elaborate. "My boyfriend and I have been traveling through the Yukon and Alaska for two and a half months."

"Pull ahead so I can see your plate." I push forward on my tiptoes without starting the engine. "So, you're Canadian but on a US bike," Officer Beth states.

"Yes."

"Why?"

"My other motorcycle broke down and left me stranded. I needed a replacement to get home."

She hands me a neon-orange piece of paper and tells me to go inside.

Here we go.

Joseph and Kim are still with us after Valdez, which turned into four days of nonstop rain. Our plans now are to travel logging roads through BC to the US border before Dave and I go back to Washington, where we'll prep for the second half of our trip.

Everyone but me sails through the Tok border crossing. Our friends are waiting on the Canadian side. Dave tells them to keep going, and we'll catch up with them later.

"Whenever you import a new motorcycle from another country," an officer named Devon scolds me, "you have to pay import fees." That would amount to a few thousand dollars, based on the retail price of my new bike.

"I'm not importing this bike, sir. I'm traveling with it, and we won't be in Canada for longer than two weeks."

Officer Beth, who'd taken my passport earlier, comes over with it in her hand. Tok is a quiet crossing, and she's probably bored. Officer Devon continues.

"What do you mean, *traveling with it?*"

I communicate to the three border guards now staring me down that my boyfriend and I sold everything a year ago so we could travel around the world by motorcycle.

"We hear this all the time," Beth interjects. "People tell us they're just traveling on through to the US, then they bring contraband into our country. How do we know your bike isn't going to end up on a farm somewhere, unregistered, without plates?"

A farm?! I want to shake her. *Would I spend $11,000 for a farm bike?* My sexy dual-sport machine, with its ABS brakes, 800cc engine, heated handlebar grips, computerized dash, and USB plugins, is made for the incredible adventure I have in mind. Putting a bike like this on a farm is like keeping a border collie in a city apartment.

Having a US-plated bike will also present a problem for me when our travels are over, for the same reason it is a problem now. I'll have to import it into Canada when I come home. But that is far off in the future. I am not going to pay the fee now. I'm being honest about passing through Canada, and they don't believe me. Out of principle, this makes me more stubborn than usual.

"We have a travel website," I offer. "You can see our proposed route and even hear a CBC interview about where we're going next."

Since I've replaced the Stallion, Dave and I are much more confident traveling farther afield. We've decided—hot weather be damned—that we can't leave Africa off the list. Cape Town is our next destination. I say as much to the now-four border guards gathered shoulder to shoulder behind the counter.

"What's the web address?" Officer Devon asks reluctantly. I pull a business card from my wallet. The three guards group together into a small room with a computer. I joke with Dave that maybe they'll read some of our blog posts and "like" our Facebook page. He doesn't laugh. We sit in a row of chairs, waiting.

"What if we change the bike's title to your name?" I suggest.

"It's Saturday," he says, head in hands. Dave doesn't like being derailed at the best of times—even less so when we're traveling with others. Perhaps he's also embarrassed because my gut instinct was right about this being a problem. "We won't be able to get that paperwork from the dealer until Tuesday."

Most motorcycle shops the world over are closed Sunday and Monday. I glance at the time. Outpost is already shut down for the day.

If we're sent back into Alaska, it's not the end of the world. We both had a great time in the north, made extra special with abundant wildlife sightings. I think back to an experience one morning after riding into the abandoned Kennecott Mine in McCarthy. We were eating breakfast in camp, surrounded by thick aspen and poplar trees dropping their leaves, when a loud clacking sound came from the forest.

"Heather, look!" Dave whispered. A bull moose walked by not twenty feet away, snagging his antlers on tree branches. He rubbed the points on his head like they itched as bad as mosquito bites. I'd never been so close to something considered more dangerous than a grizzly. I held my breath, more from awe than fear.

Pulling back to the present in Tok, my brain races with options. I can stay on the Alaska side and fly myself and my bike to Washington, thereby avoiding Canada altogether. But that's expensive, and my travel budget now has a huge dent in it.

I'm nervously tapping the side of my water bottle when Dave gives me an irritated look. I recall one of our first arguments. I was doing the same thing, keeping time to a song I liked. He asked me to stop because he didn't like the sound. I told him he was anal. "You're so hard to please!" I finished.

"That's why I chose you," he retorted.

I stop the tapping and sit upright with an idea. "Hey, we could take the ferry to Bellingham!"

"Nooo, we can't. The boat still goes through Canada customs. Besides, that costs three grand, which is more than the cost to import your bike."

"Okay, I'm just trying to help. I did mention my concern about crossing the border with the bike, and you said—"

"Heather, not now, okay?"

I fold my arms and turn away. We sit in silence, waiting for the border guards to decide what to do with us. An idea ping-pongs around in my brain, but before I can articulate it, Officer Devon returns, and the thought is gone. They want proof of flight reservations to Cape Town, referenced in our CBC interview. I don't understand how that verifies anything; plane tickets can be bought and canceled.

"We don't have our flights yet," I say.

Then Dave speaks what my brain was trying to formulate earlier.

"Would it be possible to get something in writing that says we need to be in and out of Canada by a certain date? Sort of like truck drivers and their route logs?"

Devon seems embarrassed he hasn't thought of this already. He pretends to think for a moment then grabs a pen and begins filling out a form.

"Sign here." He spins the carbon paper pad toward me. "By 11:59 p.m. on September 17, you better be back in the US with that bike—" he points outside—"or there will be a warrant out for your arrest."

We have five days to cover 2,000 miles.

Dave and I catch up with our friends and camp our last evening together. Since we need to blast back to Washington, our plans to ride backroads through BC with Joseph and Kim are off the table.

To make the distance, Dave and I average hundreds of miles a day down the Alaska Highway into BC. Flying down the road at seventy miles an hour, we don't see much, but we do have a well-timed meeting with a migrating caribou herd wandering beside tranquil, fall-blazoned Highway 97.

Abiding by the Canadian government's demand, we roll up to the Canada/US border on September 17 at 10:47 p.m., with an hour to spare. I cross into Washington with my US-plated motorcycle.

No one asks questions. The guards are more interested in my cool bike than my passport.

Placing color images in this book was cost-prohibitive, so my solution is to bring you our travel photos digitally. To see color images for each country, scan the QR code or visit Photos under Riding Full Circle on my website, heatherleawriter.com.

Is any of this *real?*

USA/Canada

The second half of our trip is logistics-heavy. We need to arrange travel visas and continental flights, for starters. My thought is to spend two or three weeks organizing in Arlington, then get back on the road. Dave has other plans, however. He informs me one evening that he's picked up a contracting project in Seattle for six weeks. He didn't discuss this with me before accepting the job, and I'm pissed.

Dave borrows his dad's truck to drive me to Revelstoke and visit my parents, then returns to begin work.

Soaking up hugs, home-cooked food, and all the other perks that come with visiting family makes me soften toward Dave for his impromptu decision. I need the rest and relaxation. We never get enough time to unwind while traveling.

Dad and I take the dog for a walk and talk about how things are going. I appreciate hearing that he's proud I've seized this opportunity in life.

"Some people never leave the town they're born in, Heather, let alone their own countries."

I reflect on all I've seen in the past year and the people we've met: people of diverse cultures, colors, and income levels, often typecast by xenophobes confined in their closed-minded cocoons. It breaks my heart that some of the kindest, least superficial people on earth are stereotyped because of others' ignorance. My hope is to use my travels and my writing to show that the world's people shouldn't be feared. There are two sides to every story, and news and social media favor drama. We're all just trying to survive, to love, and to be loved back. As humans, we protect our sense of place and our hearts. Sometimes it seems the easiest way to do that is to attack what's different or unfamiliar.

One afternoon over a game of Scrabble with Mom, I admit the trip is harder than I anticipated, and that Dave and I are having challenges.

"Oh, Heath, you're being too hard on yourself. It's normal; you're falling in love and trying to travel around the world at the same time. Either one on its own is a lot to handle, and you guys have so much on your plate dealing with both for two years. You're still getting to know each other."

She's right.

Nostalgia flashes me back to the early weeks of Dave and I dating. "I love you," he said one night. "You don't have to say it back; I just want you to know." His words made my heart leap in fear and excitement.

Later, when I told a good friend I was in love, it sounded careless and like I should have kept it secret. I second-guessed his admission and my own reply that I felt the same. We'd only just met. Maybe it only felt like love because we were planning an incredible adventure together. But was any of it *real?*

Nobody cares about your white privilege

I stay a week with my parents, then drive myself back to Washington in my Ford Escape—the one thing I haven't yet sold. Four wheels feels weird after so many months on two. Traveling over mountain passes, I deal with early winter snowstorms and am exhausted by the time I get to the border six hours later. My slow pace has put me in Sumas at 10 p.m. I use free Wi-Fi at the Tim Horton's donut shop on the Canadian side to call Dave on Skype. I've long ago given up paying for a cell phone plan, since I no longer live anywhere.

"I can't wait to see you," Dave says, making me smile. We haven't been apart for more than a few hours in seven months. Maybe the weeklong break has been good for us.

I want to be done with the drive. Even with tens of thousands of miles under my belt, the seventy miles separating me from Dave seems too far.

I move up to the border window and give the guard my Nexus Pass—a special card I'd been vetted and fingerprinted for because of frequent Canada/US crossings before I'd even met Dave. A friend and I used to love going to Bellingham when I lived in Vancouver, and the Nexus lane meant we didn't have to wait in long lineups.

After a few pointed questions, the officer hands me a bright orange card and keeps my coveted Nexus.

"Sorry, what's this for?" I ask politely.

"Just park over there, ma'am, and go on inside."

What's with me and borders lately? I'm frustrated with the interruption between me and bedtime.

Inside, a different officer motions for me to approach the desk. I see my Nexus card in his hand. He's a large man, fit and frowning.

"It appears you cross the border quite frequently," he states. "Why is that?"

"My boyfriend lives in Bellingham, sir." I give the same response I've used every time I cross the border to see Dave and never had an issue. I follow rules—at least for things like this—and respect authority.

"Where do you live?" he asks.

"At the moment, my boyfriend and I are traveling around the world, so—"

"Where do you live?" he demands again.

Just answer the question. Don't overtalk. "I gave up my apartment in Vancouver so I could travel for two years." Hopefully that'll make sense, and I can go.

"So, you have no ties to Canada then."

"I wouldn't say *no* ties." I smile, keeping my voice even. "I'm just returning from visiting my parents in BC. I have investments and other money in a Canadian bank. And I pay Canadian taxes, of course."

"What do you do for work?"

Do not tell him you're not working and that you sold your business.

"I'm a freelance writer."

The officer has yet to look me in the eye. Instead, he stares at a computer in front of him. I want to know what he's looking at. *Have I been flagged despite following the requests in Tok? Is there now a warrant out for my arrest?*

"So, you have a job where you can work from anywhere and you don't pay rent or own property in Canada. Is that right?"

"I travel but not for work." *You're not even making sense! Shut up and just answer his questions.*

"That's not what I asked. Do you have a place you need to be for work and/or do you pay any utility bills in Canada?"

"I do not. However—"

"What I'm hearing is there's nothing keeping you from entering the US and staying…maybe shack up with this boyfriend? Work under the table?"

I see myself through his eyes and I'm getting a bad feeling. I don't fit into whatever box he wants me in. Liquidating my life looks like an attempt at illegal immigration, and waiting on the other side is my American boy-friend. Honest, normal adults work and pay a mortgage or rent. They don't sell everything and travel—how irresponsible and careless.

"I have a travel website." I'm grasping at straws; it sort of worked in Tok. "If I can connect to Wi-Fi, it could help—" I almost say *it could help you understand* but figure he won't like that. "It might help verify my story."

"Your *story?* What…are you making this up as you go along? You are a writer, after all."

Wow. "No, sorry. I just meant our GPS tracks are uploaded to the site. They show where we've been over the last year." *So does my passport,* I think about pointing out. "I'll be leaving the US in a few weeks to go to Africa," I add, emphasizing "leaving the US."

"Great. Let me see that flight you've booked to Africa then."

Oh no. "We don't have our flights booked yet."

"Well, let me see the website." He's enjoying himself.

"Sure. Can I get online?"

"This isn't an internet café. Show me on your phone."

Oh. My. God. "My phone doesn't have data, sir."

"Why's that?"

"I canceled it last year when I started traveling."

"You seem reluctant to stay in your own country."

"No, I love—"

"Wait here." He leaves to go inside a windowed room and talk with another officer. I get my hopes up, thinking surely the other officer will be more sympathetic.

When the first officer returns, he growls, "You're denied entry into the United States. Please get in your car and return to Canada. This," he flicks my Nexus card into a tray behind him, "is being revoked due to abusing your privilege."

There's no longer a need to keep my composure, and tears drip down my face. I'm not going to change this guy's mind, even though I'm certain something's been lost in translation. We may share a language, but at this moment we're worlds apart. When I turn to walk away, he says, "One other thing: the next time you try and cross into the United States of America, you better show us you're going to stay in your own country. Bring a rental agreement or property title, along with credit card receipts and bills paid for six months prior to that date. Until then, your file has been flagged."

My frazzled brain can't catch up to what just happened, like I've been hit over the head by a heavy book titled, *So, You Think You're a Privileged White Girl?* How ironic that travelers are so concerned about traveling to developing worlds, yet I've just had my worst border experience right here at home.

I do a U-turn back to Canada, sobbing in my car. After a few minutes, I call Dave again, driving close enough to Tim Horton's to get a signal without having to go inside. The box of donuts I bought him earlier sits on the seat beside me.

"What's wrong?" Dave asks right away. I've been detained for well over an hour, and he had no way to reach me.

"I couldn't get in!" I screech. "The border guard denied me entry for six months! I didn't even do anything wrong—and he took my Nexus." I drag my sleeve across my snotty nose, releasing my inner child.

"Sweetie, calm down." What person on the face of the earth likes being told that in such moments? "What happened?"

I relay the story, which is getting worse in my head by the minute.

"Where am I supposed to go now?" I'm homesick for my parents' cozy house I just left, which seems more like a week ago now. I also want to be in my boyfriend's arms, even though I loathe needing a savior.

"Can you call anyone?" Dave asks.

"What? You're okay that I'm here with nowhere to go?" This night is drawing on far too long.

I don't like this "me," vulnerable and weak, distressed and dependent. The Heather I know—or at least want to be—would put on her big-girl pants and find a hotel with a pub. Instead, I'm frozen by helplessness. *What does my denied-entry issue mean for our trip?*

"Okay," Dave relents, "I'll use my dad's truck and come up." I see the weariness on his face; it's almost midnight. "Can you find us a hotel for the night? Once you're settled, email the address and room number. I'll see you soon."

Finding a cheap motel near the border, I get into bed with all my clothes on. I'm too tired to think straight but can't sleep so I grab the TV remote. *What about flights through US destinations? We'll have to arrange everything direct from Canada.* Then my stomach sinks. *My bike! All my gear!* How will I get everything here from Arlington? Dave can bring up my stuff, but he can't ride two motorcycles—especially one not registered in his name.

You're getting ahead of yourself. I try to relax and find something funny to watch.

At 1:30 a.m., I hear a soft knock on the door. Now that Dave's here, I can finally sleep.

Drowning in red tape

Sometimes the best-laid plans are like rugs on a hardwood floor: They slip out from under you, and you're flung off in another direction. If you're not dead or injured, you now have the choice to rearrange the rug and take another step.

The momentum of the trip has become the framework for my life. I'm disoriented without its excitement and guidance. After losing hold of my purpose yet again, I hop among couches and floors in friends' homes and apartments in Vancouver. Revelstoke is too far for Dave to visit with his contracting job in Seattle. I see him on weekends, like when we first dated. The abrupt derailment from traveling and my loss of freedom to cross into the States depresses me even though—or maybe because—it's out of my control. I pine for the day we're back on the road.

Six weeks have passed since we returned from Alaska, and we're not even close to ready for Africa. While my friends work all day, I write and busy myself with trip logistics. It helps me stay on the trip, at least mentally.

The first year was easier to plan; all we had to do was get on the bikes and ride south to Ushuaia. There were border crossings, of course, and flying over the Darién Gap. But aside from a few visas, traveling between countries in the Americas required minimal advance planning.

The second half of our journey to Africa, Europe, and Russia is a whole different story. It will involve considerable documentation and planning. I look at my to-do list: *malaria pills and vaccinations; flights for us and bikes to Cape Town; find crates for bikes...*

We also need a *carnet de passage* for each bike—a booklet several pages long that lists every country a traveler with a vehicle plans to ride or drive through. The carnet contains identifying information connecting the vehicle to its owner, so people don't take advantage of the black market, for example. It allows us to cross international borders without paying customs or import charges. Like a passport, entry and exit stamps are placed in the carnet on the page with the corresponding country, all of which must be predetermined by the traveler and shown at border crossings. Upon returning home, the carnet is presented at the place of origin as proof the vehicle is still in the possession of the owner, and a hefty deposit is refunded.

Few countries around the world require a carnet, and my research finds much debate about whether motorcyclists even need one—many riders have traveled without it. Still, others have gotten stuck or been denied entry into certain countries.

After my recent border issues, it seems like a good idea to cover all bases.

Dave and I need to plan what countries to include in the carnet. I don't like the idea of a fixed route; what if we want to deviate and visit another country? We've done enough traveling by now to appreciate a whimsical change of course. I can see this being at least one reason why overlanders don't bother with the carnet.

Through lengthy discussions about Africa, Dave and I decide not to go farther north than Kenya. A Sudanese visa will take nine weeks to issue, and, in 2016, the Government of Canada travel advisory website suggests travelers "avoid all travel" to Sudan anyway. Gone are hopes of riding the length of the continent into Europe. We can choose a more common route via Morocco, but having already traveled in western Africa, I want to see a different side of the continent. Also, we're hoping to do a safari, and southeastern Africa is the best place for that.

We settle on arriving in Cape Town, South Africa, and going as far as Nairobi, Kenya. From there, we'll fly to Europe. That's all we need to know for now. Selecting six other countries we want to visit, Dave lists them on the carnet forms: Lesotho, Botswana, Zimbabwe, Malawi, Zambia, and Tanzania.

The carnet deposit is almost $4,000—a percentage calculated by the value of our bikes, which my brand-new ride inflates. The idea of carrying this highly valuable document around with us for the next year is nerve-racking.

Dave takes over the carnet details so I can work on getting Russian visas—a mind-boggling process that becomes the second biggest mishap in our trip for the chunk of time it steals.

Russia isn't scheduled on our route until next summer. It's only November now. But we need to send away our passports for the visas while in our own countries. To make things more complicated, my Canadian passport expires within six months of when I want to arrive in Russia. This isn't allowed, so I need to renew it before doing anything else—an annoying task that has me paying extra to expedite the process before crossing my fingers and sending everything off in the mail.

Since we can't go far without passports, that means no traveling for now. The estimated time is three to six weeks. We kick ourselves for not starting the visa application before leaving for Alaska, when something like acquiring our invitation letter could have been working in the background.

This is another time suck. Visitors need an invitation letter issued by a Russian travel agency or a hotel. We're just not those types of travelers, so I'm unsure how to handle this. Overlanders said Russia would be the hardest country to get into, but I still didn't expect such a convoluted process. I begin filling out forms for a tourist visa. The only other option is a business visa, which doesn't apply to us. After hours of research, I find no way to get around the single-entry, thirty-day limit for tourists. I call a Russian consulate in Montréal, Canada, and explain to the agent that we'd like more than thirty days to get across the world's largest country and need more than one entry.

"We hope to ride from Moscow to Magadan, which will take months," I tell him. We also want to visit Kazakhstan and Mongolia, which means re-entering Russia.

"Do you have your invitation letter?" the consulate agent in Montréal politely asks over the phone.

"Can you tell me more about that?"

"You can ask anyone. They just need to be okay signing for you, and you'll need to send them all your personal information, like passport numbers, etc."

"Hmm." I don't love this idea. "And how do we get around the thirty-day limit for tourists?"

"Are you a business?"

"No, we're just traveling."

"Are you sure?"

"Well, I'm planning to write a book about our trip. Russia would of course be included. Does that count?"

"So, you're a journalist and your boyfriend's the photographer—sounds like a business plan to me."

I laugh. "Really?" A multi-entry business visa application will give us 180 days in Russia over one year, and we can come and go as we want within that timeframe. "Perfect!" I literally clap. "But there's still the invitation issue."

"You said you're riding motorcycles? There is a nonprofit rider organization in Russia. I'll give you their email. Perhaps they can help."

I jot down the info and thank the agent for his creative thinking. Excited, I type a hasty email to the rider organization, the Night Wolves. You can't really go wrong with nonprofits, and I'm forever impatient these days.

In the email, I gush about long-lived dreams of visiting Russia and my career as a "journalist" (I usually say, "freelance writer," but semantics…). Only after pressing *send* does it occur to me to Google "the Night Wolves."

An image pops onto my screen: an edgy-looking dude in leathers shakes hands with President Putin. Continuing my search, I find a 2015 article from a well-known magazine. The edgy dude is called the "Surgeon," and he's the Night Wolves' leader. The nickname comes from his past occupation as a dentist. In a photo from the article, his Herculean stature emerges from a smoky background like some kind of czar astride a matte-black motorcycle. I find it hard to imagine this apocalyptic man's hands inside someone's mouth—unless he's pulling teeth for torturing purposes. With a sinking feeling, I read a quote from the Surgeon about not wanting to meet any foreigners, as they won't write anything good. He mentions his distaste for America, Europe, homosexuals, liberals, and traitorous fifth-columnists. The Surgeon is not only good friends with Putin but has a fondness for Stalin as well.

There's no way to stop my already-sent email. Although I haven't given any personal document information in the email, I did include our website. My overactive imagination sees a headline: "Two Naive Travelers Offer Themselves to Putin's Angels."

While trying to figure out what to do—*Um, Dave, sorry but we can't go to Russia now*—my inbox pings with a new message telling me that email has bounced. I let out a deep breath. What a stroke of luck! The motorcycle gang's email must have expired or changed. They'll never know of us. I can sleep tonight.

The potential of a Russian motorcycle gang as a host family gives me an idea. I contact BMW Russia and receive an email for their customer relations agent. She's willing to grant us invitation letters for our visas if we promise to do a travel presentation at the dealership when we arrive in Moscow. I agree immediately. Finally, something is moving forward.

A few days later, I receive an email from someone in the motorcycle industry who asks to remain anonymous. He's willing to pay for our visas—over $1,200 Canadian. This is another happy surprise that makes me sure the universe really wants us to get to Russia.

The invitation letters will take over a month to process at the Federal Migration Services office in Moscow. We need them back before we can then again send them off to the embassy for the visa placement. It's mid-December now. At best, we'll see something by the end of January.

Trying to make the best out of the extra time, I do a travel presentation one evening to a welcoming crowd of ADV riders at the BMW motorcycle dealership in Burnaby. I've gone through my notes and put together some trip statistics for the audience. After nearly 35,000 miles through fifteen countries—including Canada and the US—the stats are interesting:

Flat tires: Heather 0, Dave 2

Tire swaps: 16 (due to expired tread)

Nights in a tent: 126 (25 paid)

Nights in hotels/hostels: 95

Nights with family/friends/strangers: 98

Nights on a boat/ferry: 4

Top speeds: Heather 88 mph; Dave 102 mph (Salar de Uyuni)

Hottest day: 102.2°F (Colombia)

Coldest day: 14°F with windchill (Patagonia)

Highest riding altitude: 15,662 ft (Andes)

Longest day: 541 miles (Boise, Idaho, to Arlington, Washington)

Stolen items: GoPro off Heather's bike (Colombia/Ecuador border)

Money paid in bribes: zero (not counting the angry Peruvian men)

Because we were new riders from the start, I kept track of how often our bikes hit the ground. Dave had eighteen, six of which were while riding solo in Lockhart Basin. The Stallion had gone down forty-three times—mostly on difficult terrain when I didn't have enough momentum. No crashes were at speed, thankfully.

Doing the BMW presentation puts it all into perspective. I broke a bone and got back out there. My former motorcycle sucked at times, but I sucked it up. Countless miles were spent uncomfortable in extreme weather, with my sore body, with relationship woes—and I'd ridden on without giving up. Seeing what I've already done makes me confident to get back out there. I can't wait for the next leg.

When Christmas arrives, I'm tired of couch surfing and mooching off friends, so I move back to Revelstoke to enjoy the holidays with family.

Five weeks later, a FedEx truck pulls into my parent's driveway with a much-anticipated envelope. Inside are our passports, complete with Russian visas. I jump up and down, almost hugging the delivery driver. It's been four months since Dave told me he was going back to work for six weeks and I'd pouted about taking so much time away from our trip. Four months since I was denied entry into the US by a border guard who didn't have the imagination for a life like mine.

I call Dave.

"The passports are here! I'm booking our tickets to Cape Town today."

DIY stress

I find direct flights from Vancouver to Heathrow in London, which means I can bypass the US. Next is getting the bikes to Cape Town. Because the Vancouver airport is closer than the Seattle airport, Dave plans to bring our bikes into Canada. A shipping company in Vancouver wants $500 per bike just to crate them for the flight. Hoping to save a grand, Dave decides to build the crates himself but finds out he needs special wood treated for contamination because the crates will go overseas. Luckily, a motorcycle shop in Maple Ridge, BC, has metal frames large enough to hold our bikes and gear. All it costs is a box of Tim Horton's donuts.

Dave brings the frames back to Arlington and packs up the bikes. Extra steps are taken since I can't come to Washington, and it's all on Dave's plate. He takes care of my bike and gear, which I haven't seen since October the year before.

With my accumulating list of border problems, I'm overly anxious the day he drives across the border. The cargo flight leaves Vancouver airport at 11 a.m. the next day, which means the bikes must clear customs before 4:30 p.m. that afternoon. If the bikes aren't through by closing time, they'll miss the cargo flight, and we'll need to reschedule our own flights.

At 2:30 p.m., Dave texts to say he's leaving Arlington. Half an hour later, I get an email from our impatient shipping agent asking me to inform her when Dave has the bikes at the airport cargo warehouse. Dave needs to be in two places at once within the next hour: Canada customs and an office in Delta that has our "dangerous goods" labels and airway bills for the bikes.

I sit in my parents' kitchen in Revelstoke, biting my nails to stumps. Another text comes from Dave. He went to the wrong border crossing, at Peace Arch. Because of the carnet, Dave had to import the bikes to eventually export them and should have been at the commercial truck crossing ten miles away. He was already in the lineup so had to enter Canada, do a U-turn and enter back into the US, then drive to Aldergrove and re-enter Canada. All this time, my motorcycle is coming and going across international lines, increasing the chance Dave will get questioned about trailering the bike through the border without its owner present.

I've asked Dave to tell me the very nanosecond he crosses into Canada, but an hour passes and I don't hear from him. I try to relax, but after so many months removed from our travels and everything that's gone wrong in between, this could be the final straw that will blow it all apart. I leave a message on Dave's phone reminding him when customs closes. He knows, but it makes me feel better to repeat myself.

When 4:30 comes with no word from Dave, I call the office with our "dangerous goods" labels and ask if there's any way they can leave them outside under a rock or something.

"Oh, don't worry, there's always someone here late—we'll wait for him," says a blessed soul on the other end. "Just have him call us when he arrives."

There's nothing I can do about customs closing, but if Dave at least gets our motorcycles to the cargo warehouse at the airport, he can go back in the morning and get them through customs. My next call is to Vancouver friends who are happy to let him crash in their spare room for the night. Trying Dave again, I get his voicemail. It's 5 p.m.

It doesn't occur to me what we've been putting our bodies and brains through, planning a trip like this. I send out an extra prayer to the universe that neither of us will get sick or have a nervous breakdown.

Finally, my phone buzzes around 5:30.

"Hi," I say, breathless. "Whathappenedwhereareyouhowdiditgo?!"

If I could hear my thoughts, I'm sure they would sound like a rapper scratching vinyl.

A deep sigh comes from the other end. Dave's either pissed off or very tired.

"I got through the border. The biggest issue was the carnet de passage."

"What? So, not my bike?"

"No one even looked at the trailer. They were all distracted with the carnet and which page to stamp." It's imperative we have this documentation for leaving the country, as that's part of the deal for getting our deposit back. "In the end, the US stamped me out on the wrong page, so I had to go back across the border on foot, show them the right page, then walk back into Canada, and have the officer there stamp me in."

"Oh, thank god. Sorry, that was insensitive. I'm just glad you and the bikes got across."

I sleep like a surgery patient under anesthetic that night. In the morning, a message from Dave tells me he went to the airport early. The bikes are through customs and will make their flight to Cape Town.

Heather riding Telkwa Pass in British Columbia.

Heather's crash in Idaho. The boulder shows a dark scratch where the pannier rode up and over the rock before breaking off.

Lunch with Linda and Neil in Sandpoint, Idaho.

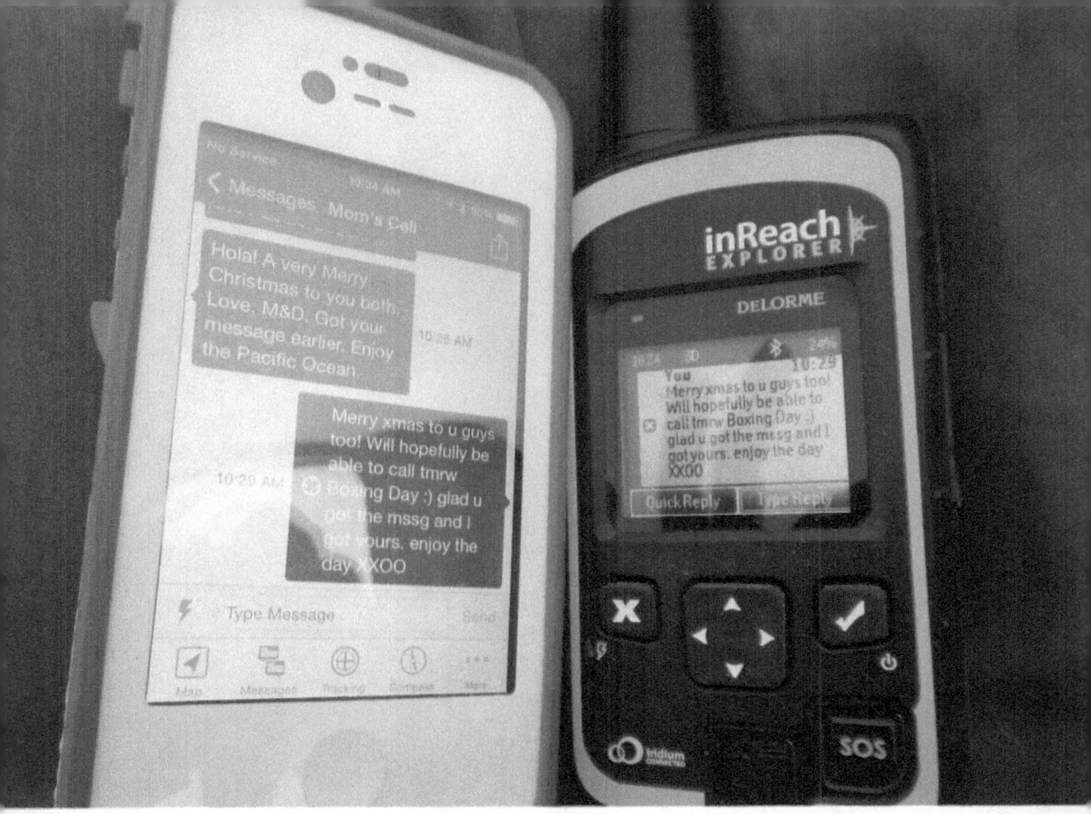

Delorme had an app that allowed us to use the iPhone's keyboard to type and send messages through InReach, even without service. This was far easier than using the InReach keyboard.

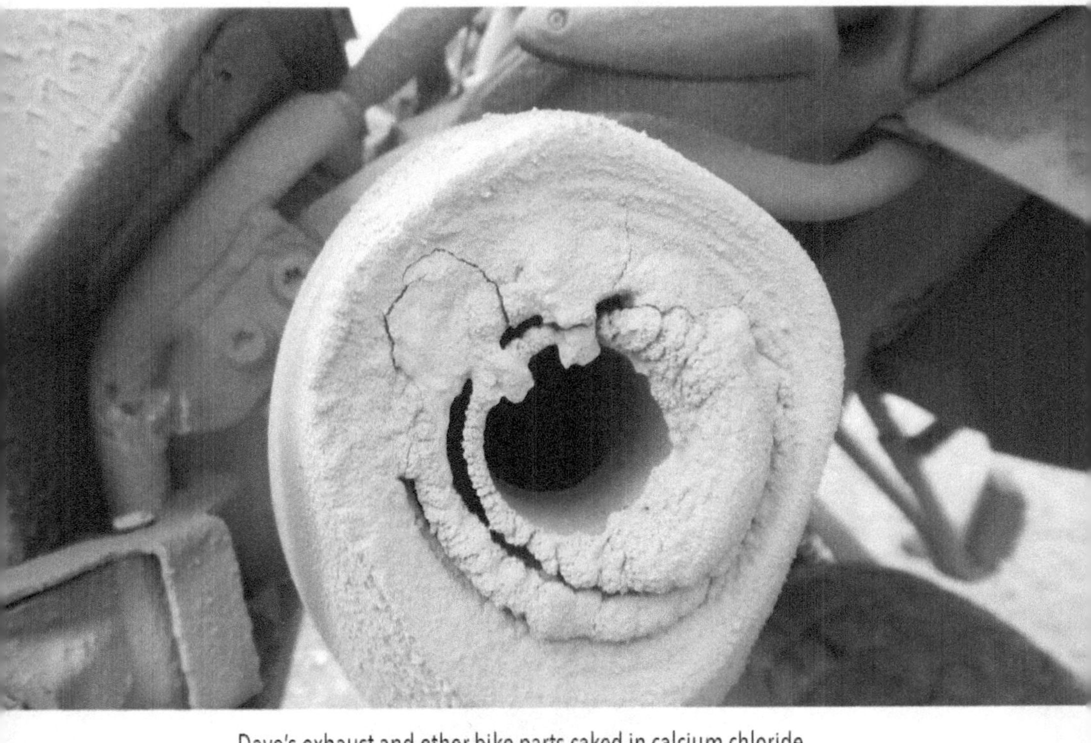

Dave's exhaust and other bike parts caked in calcium chloride.
Dempster Highway, Yukon.

A stunning grizzly seen in Alaska.

An adult male moose, or bull, in camp near McCarthy, Alaska.

Dave and his F800GSA in front of Denali (Mount McKinley) in Alaska. Dave climbed this mountain—the highest in North America at 20,310 ft—with his friend Andy in the early 2000s.

The "calendar image" in Torres del Paine, Chile.

Camping on Navajo land on the border between Utah and Arizona.

Heather paraponting in France.

A giraffe in the wild. Namib Desert, Namibia.

Zebra and oryx in southern Africa.

Heather handing out stickers in Lesotho, Africa.

Incredible Sossusvlei, Namibia.

Heather's bike stuck in African mud.

Heather riding in Mongolia.

A flat spot in Heather's wheel rim, caused by a pothole in Mongolia.

Dave riding the dusty roads along Russia's Trans-Siberian Highway.

Dave, filthy and happy after hundreds of miles on remote, dirt roads.

Oskars from Adventure Team Latvia.

Al teaching Dave and Heather the Cyrillic alphabet.

Nalichniki window framing in Russia.

Heather holds an Alaskan king crab in Russia.

YEARTWO

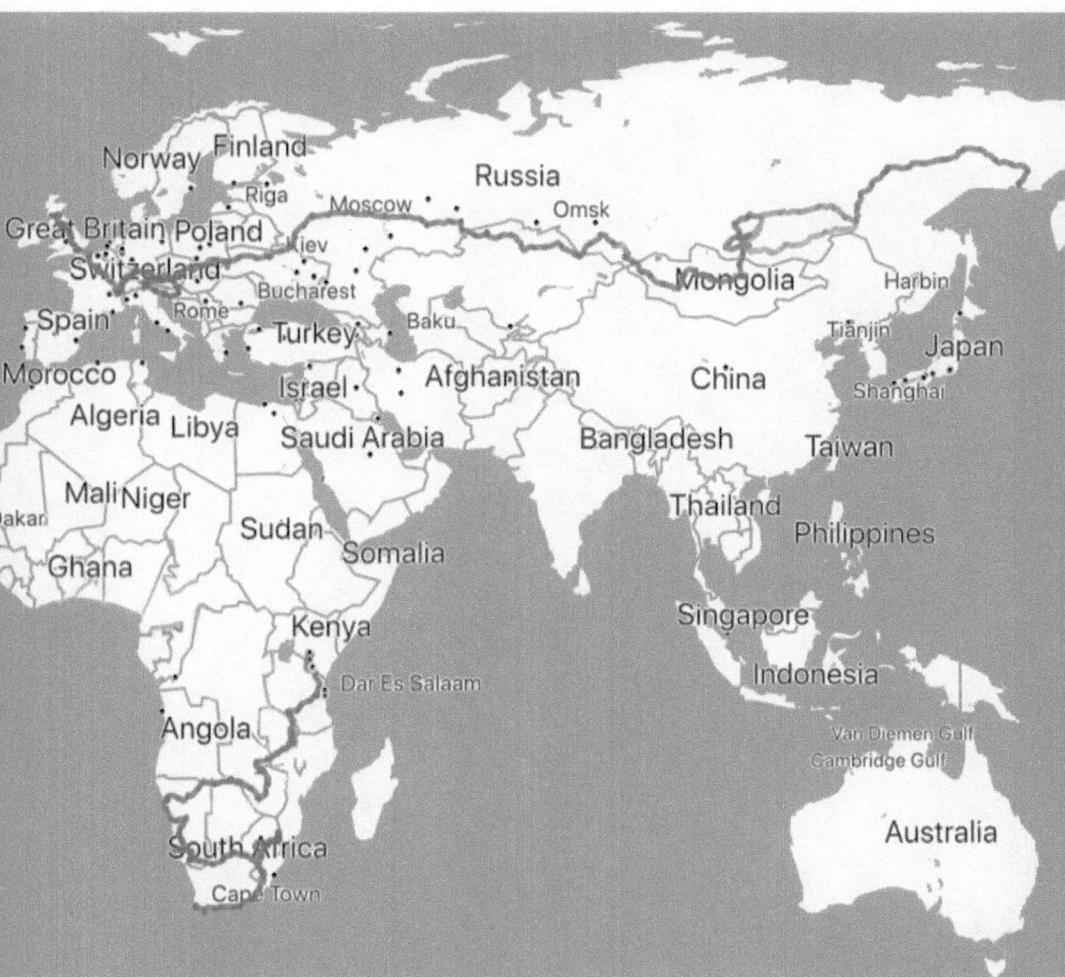

ROUTE MAP

Wine & warnings

South Africa (Part 1)

Africa—with its bloodred sun, sky-high giraffes, and boiling heat—burrows into my heart like a wood tick and calls me to its intense, wraithlike power. I've loved this continent for as long as I can remember, though I'm not sure how or when it all started. Perhaps it was while watching the movie *Out of Africa* with my mom as a kid, or my friendship with an Ethiopian girl in elementary school. Maybe it was the budding-traveler's cliché—flipping through National Geographic magazines showing people, places, and things I wanted to see in real life.

In 2007, I traveled through Ghana, Togo, Mali, and Burkina Faso as a backpacker. I met locals and other travelers during those three months but mostly traveled alone. At first, the absence of a friend or partner was intimidating—though I knew no other way of traveling—and I'd hurry back to wherever I was staying before dark, heeding countless warnings. For the first two weeks, I made sure I was back at my hostel before 6 p.m., when the sun went down. Bored and yearning to go out and explore the country when it was at its most lively and intoxicating, I could no longer keep myself from the very intrigue I'd gone there to find. I gave fear and guidebooks the middle finger, opening the door for the exploration and curiosity living inside my soul.

Instead of sitting in front of a fan in my room doing crossword puzzles, I ate street meat off wooden skewers. Nothing was more delicious. I went to a nightclub with young Ghanaian locals and danced until four in the morning. Nothing was more exhilarating. Sitting in the back of a 4×4, I bounced across the desert for eight hours from Bamako to Timbuktu, with a scarf over my face to keep the dust from coating my lungs. Nothing was more adventurous.

Africa does come with a price, though. It can be frustrating as hell. I once sat on a bus for several hours before it even left the station, just to save my seat. Food and drinks were brought to the bus windows by women who balanced everything on their heads. When I had to go to the bathroom, I asked my seatmate to watch my stuff and prayed the bus wouldn't leave without me.

Africa is not a place for proactive, impatient minds arriving with an agenda-filled "where there's a will, there's a way" mentality. There is plenty of will in Africa but not always a way, and go-getter travelers will soon be rocking in a corner if they don't lighten up.

I'm curious how I'll feel about Africa coming back a decade later. But more so, how will Dave manage the heat and disorder I know is forthcoming? I'm anxious but optimistic. I can't wait for what the continent will show us.

When we land in Cape Town, it's not the Africa I imagined in my geographical ignorance. For example, there are a lot of white people around; I've sometimes mistaken South Africans for Brits, Aussies, or Kiwis because of their lilted accents and light skin color. The city itself is also a surprise. It reminds me of Vancouver, with the ocean lapping at skyscrapers against a mountainous backdrop. Cape Town is modern, clean, and breezy, and I already love it.

After leaving Vancouver twenty-seven hours ago in a snowstorm, we arrive to summer in February and an urban playground calling for exploration. I'm elated to be traveling again. Now that we've finally left North America and Dave and I are together, I feel settled and calm. Oddly, I'm more comfortable these days when I'm somewhere unfamiliar.

I don't remember what changed our minds to come here, except that we both knew Africa was a must, no matter how hot and hard it got. We're here during the rainy season, which isn't a big concern; the showers can be intense and tremendous, but they're over in a few hours and are often a welcome relief from the heat.

Our Airbnb host's name is Edu. He picks us up at the Cape Town airport for ten dollars—a small price to pay for the seamless transition from airport to accommodation after a long flight. Although our bikes left a day and a half before us, they won't arrive for another thirty-two hours.

Edu takes us back to the house he shares with his wife, Arinda, in the suburbs. Their home is spacious, well kept, and has a pool. By North American standards, the neighborhood is upper class. Our room is attached to the ground floor of the house, with its own entrance through French doors. The room itself is small—a queen-sized bed, two nightstands, and a tiny bathroom—but the entryway opens onto a secluded, terra-cotta-tiled patio and a manicured lawn that looks inviting for bare feet.

One dead giveaway Cape Town isn't in Europe or somewhere like home is the cost of things. Before leaving Canada, Dave reserved the classy Airbnb for just twenty-nine dollars per night. A cab ride costs a few dollars, and groceries are cheap if one shops in local markets and not the large, air-conditioned superstores that make Cape Town seem like a rich, first-world city at first glance.

Edu and Arinda invite us for dinner, where generous quantities of South African wine fill four tall-stemmed glasses. A young, Black server brings us our meals—hearty vegetarian peanut stew with fresh garlic, ginger, and collard greens in a rich tomato-based broth.

Between bites, Dave and I tell our hosts where we plan to travel in Africa. They heavily caution us about going off the beaten track to some of the villages and mountain roads. This is disappointing, as that's exactly where we want to go. With no desire to hear about kidnappings, rapes, and other atrocities, I thank Edu and Arinda for the warnings and change the subject.

"Where else should we visit while in southern Africa?" I ask.

This starts a more pleasant conversation about safari tours. We're encouraged to see Kruger National Park and Okavango Delta, if possible.

"By the way," Arinda says when Dave and I are heading back to our room for the night, "Cape Town only has ten weeks of drinking water left. If it doesn't rain soon, we will have a drought. For this reason, don't flush the toilet if it's just urine, and please be conservative with showering. Place a bucket in the stall to collect the water so we can use it for our garden."

We're happy to oblige and appreciate the beautifully landscaped yard even more.

It's a relief to receive notice two days later that our bikes have landed and we can claim them at customs. This is the longest point-A-to-point-B flight they've had, with many more rules and regulations to follow.

Dave and I take a cab to the airport late in the evening. Unlike at the US/Canada border, stamping the carnet de passage in South Africa is a smooth process, because officials are used to seeing such documents. We clear our two-wheelers from customs in minutes then spend a few hours on the cargo loading dock uncovering the bikes from their metal homes. Wrapped in see-through plastic, they look like aquariums with big bike-shaped fish inside. I'm so excited to reunite with my girl and to again feel the joy of riding a motorcycle; it's been so long!

I get busy removing the plastic while Dave takes apart the metal frames with a screwdriver; there are no electric or battery-operated tools available. With the frames dismantled, Dave starts putting parts back together, again by hand. To decrease volume and size, he removed the windshields at home and put them on the crate floors, wrapped in our riding suits. He also folded the handlebars back toward the seats so they didn't stick up.

The cargo office is closed now, but a few workers have stayed to watch, more entertained by us than by whatever else they had planned after their shift. By 10 p.m., the bikes are whole again. We place our panniers—which also traveled on the floors of the crates—back onto their racks and return to the Airbnb.

Penguins & other surprises

Reunited with the luxury of our own transportation again—something I never take for granted—Dave and I ride to Table Mountain, one of Cape Town's most iconic landmarks, and hike to the 3,563-foot summit.

Leaving gear on our bikes is often left to fate. Through the Americas, Dave and I used aluminum hard cases that could be locked with a key. For Africa and beyond, a sponsor has given us soft bags to try. They aren't lockable and can be cut into, although not as easily as it might seem. I like the look of the lower-profile bags and think they're safer on difficult terrain, where I don't want a hard case mowing over the back of my leg. In the coming months, I find a lot to like about using soft bags versus hard cases and stick with them for the rest of my travels.

For our hike up Table Mountain, I've brought different shoes, so I place my riding boots on the rear luggage rack, covering them with my riding jacket. This is all protected by a large, cabled net locked to the rack. I secure my helmet to my handlebars with another cable and a combination lock. Neither cable is easy to cut, though given enough time and ingenuity, anyone can break into anything.

We climb a well-worn trail high over Cape Town and False Bay, watching miniature city life below. From the summit of the flat-topped mountain, we look over the other side into a totally different world. The mountainous slope is covered with impenetrable vegetation all the way to the water, as though Table Mountain is a massive breakwater shielding the city. Clouds whisked by the wind skim off the peak and cascade downward like waterfalls, meeting the moist ocean breeze. A winding road below follows the curvature of the mountain, between rock and water.

"We should go ride that," I say, and Dave agrees.

A gondola saves our knees on the way down. Back at the bikes, all our gear is where we left it.

The coastal road at the base of Table Mountain leads us along a turquoise peninsula to a beach town. Here, we're astounded to find a penguin colony—something else I'd never have associated with Africa until now. The birds are adorable and entertaining. Looking like footballs with wings, they hop off rocks onto the sand and make me laugh with the hilarity of their sporadic, awkward movements. When jumping off rocks or logs, their flippers stay stuck to their sides, unflapping. They drop like a dead weight, landing flat-footed before waddling off, now manically flapping their wings. This seems backward to me, but what do I know about penguins? I thought they only lived on icebergs.

We follow the same road to where the Indian Ocean meets the Atlantic at Cape Agulhas and experience a bonus trip milestone we hadn't planned on—reaching the southernmost tip of Africa. This is the first "end of the earth" for my new bike. I love traveling to earth's edges like this. Having grown up in landlocked Alberta, I moved steadily west as an adult until I hit the ocean. I've stayed for years in that remarkable place where the sea and mountains meet.

When we ride back toward the city and around Cape Town, people call out to us from their cars.

"Excuse me! Please, where are you from?"

One driver pulls up beside Dave while we're stopped at a traffic light and gives him a fist bump. These are the flash-in-the-pan moments I so badly want to capture on film, but it's impossible to know when such encounters will occur. Our Bluetooth radio headsets, in addition to playing music, can also shoot video. However, I rarely use mine to film, and Dave uses his even less. I don't want 16,000 hours of footage to edit once I get back from two years of riding around the world.

While we ride, I notice how comfortable it is to be back in the saddle, especially when I'm not worrying about a malfunctioning bike. My F800 is the gift that keeps on giving. It still excites me, even after all the downtime over the past few months. I hope the feeling continues and that I'll feel more connected to my travels—and Dave, since I can now keep up.

On our last day in Cape Town, I don't want to leave. Edu and Arinda are familiar now, and I'm intimidated to venture into the unknown wilds of Africa. But by mid-February, we are finally back on the road of adventure.

 Placing color images in this book was cost-prohibitive, so my solution is to bring you our travel photos digitally. To see color images for each country, scan the QR code or visit Photos under Riding Full Circle on my website, heatherleawriter.com.

Baboons & pineapples

Lesotho

Lesotho—pronounced *le-soo-too*, not *le-so-tho*, like I botched at first—is a small country of 11,583 square miles. On a map, it looks more like a state or province, but Lesotho is an independent country, surrounded on all sides by South Africa, like a donut hole.

Dave and I can't miss riding one of Africa's highest roads to Sani Pass. Poorly maintained and scenic, it's exactly what we're looking for.

Unpaved, sweeping switchbacks take us higher into the mountains, remote and beautiful. Other than two Toyota Fortuners traveling behind us, there is no one around. The scenery is so picturesque that in one hour we've only ridden ten miles due to all my photo stops.

At this altitude, the hills are carpeted in what looks like mown grass. Shrubs dot the landscape, and tall rock chimneys crumble off the top, leaving debris piles like cookie crumbs at their bases. Everything vees into a wide valley with a thin, running creek.

I ride ahead to photograph Dave coming toward me from a distance. It isn't the toughest road I've ever ridden, but I need to pay attention to embedded rocks and the occasional deep rut from water erosion. The unpaved switchbacks would be treacherous in heavy rains, but for now, things are dry.

When I remove my helmet, the only sound around me is bubbling water—like something recorded for an app used to calm anxious people. The soft, delicate resonance mingled with the grandeur is both bewildering and comforting. *How am I lucky enough to do something like this with my life?*

I hear Dave's engine approaching and get into position, snapping several shots as he passes by. Because I'm pitching stories to magazines, I've invested in a better camera for the second half of our trip—a mirrorless

Olympus with a 14–150 mm zoom lens that produces high-quality photos. The Olympus is more professional by far than my Nikon point-and-shoot. I still carry the Nikon, though, because it's waterproof.

I'm walking back to my bike when something rustling in the bush catches my attention. My first thought is *snake!* Then I see the source: A baboon family sits in a field of yellow flowers above me. Dave has continued riding, so the adorable scene is for my eyes only. I bring the camera to my face, resisting the urge to take the littlest one home with me.

At the top of this winding road of baboons and other African mountain splendors is Sani Pass. In more arid months, the surrounding area is bone dry, the mountains beige with dormant foliage. I'm glad to be here at a time tourists tend to avoid. So far, the rain showers haven't stopped our progress, and the moisture has delivered a special beauty few get to see. The photographer in me is bursting with excitement. I stop yet again for an epic shot of Dave riding into a turn with the vibrant valley spread below him and the Indian Ocean over a hundred miles in the distance. Encroaching cloud cover gives the thriving slopes dramatic shadowing. The shot is calendar worthy, in my not-so-humble opinion, but a photographer can only take credit for so much; subjects add the real value.

At a viewpoint, I wait for Dave, who backtracked for the photo. Pulling out a snack, I laugh, remembering how I ended up with an entire pineapple in my bag. After leaving Cape Town, we had stopped at a fruit stand to stock up. An elderly Black woman dressed in a pink apron, with a swath of mauve fabric wrapped around her head, picked up the prickly orb and showed it to me.

"How much?" I asked.

The price in South African *rand* equaled one dollar—reasonable, but we'd never eat a whole pineapple before it went bad in the heat. I asked the old lady if she could cut it in half. She didn't understand me, but a younger woman came out of the shack nearby—her daughter, maybe— and spoke to her in another language. Over thirty Indigenous dialects are spoken in South Africa, and although English is common, few elders have learned it. The old woman nodded, understanding the translated request. I expected her to find a knife and start slicing. Instead, she shuffled to a barbed wire fence and began sawing the pineapple back and forth. Watching her hands moving so close to the rusty spikes made me cringe. *She's going to get tetanus because of me!* Before I could say we'd take the fruit whole, the job was done. She returned, sloshed the pineapple with bottled water, and presented me with both slices. There was no sense in arguing. I smiled a thank you, took the two halves wrapped in a used plastic bag, and found space inside my food pannier.

At Sani Pass, I snack on the most delicious rust-infused pineapple I've ever tased. One of the Toyota Fortuners we saw earlier pulls over, and a couple in their sixties gets out. Rentia and her husband, Stoffel, live on a farm in Bethlehem—a free state province in South Africa a few hundred miles away.

"I always thought Bethlehem was in Jerusalem somewhere," I say.

"Well, yes, there's one there, too," Rentia smiles. I like her accent; there's a British inflection with what sounds like a little German. The couple's first language is Afrikaans, which originated with the Dutch settlers who arrived in the Cape of Good Hope in the seventeenth century. Afrikaans is commonly spoken in South Africa and uses German vocabulary.

The second SUV arrives—friends traveling with Rentia and Stoffel—and everyone implores Dave and me to stop for a beer in Africa's highest pub at the top of the pass.

"Yes, do come!" Rentia claps.

"Let us celebrate your travels," Stoffel adds. "Our treat."

An afternoon storm is approaching when the six of us reach the pub at 9,436 feet thirty minutes later. Before going inside, I glance down the valley, where dark clouds are fast swirling upward. A heavy rain starts seconds later, like in the movies, and I run toward the door Dave's holding open for me. I'm grateful for the cozy stone-and-wood shelter. While my South African pilsner is being poured at the bar, I watch shepherds walking by outside, dressed in the national wool blanket dress and balaclava cap. The men disappear into a low-ceilinged grass hut, round like a yurt, where smoke churns through a chimney flue into the damp air.

Turning from the window, I look around the pub, where a dozen other patrons sit—all white, including the six of us. Most are using their phones with what must also be Africa's highest Wi-Fi. I read some of the "art" on the walls: *Guys: No shirt, no service. Girls: No shirt, free drinks.* Another one reads: *We don't serve women, you must bring your own.* Bars are the same everywhere—or maybe this one's Americanized on purpose. Do the shepherds come in here, or is this a place that alienates them—Western culture infiltrating their homes and lives?

Stopping for a midday beer isn't something Dave and I normally do, but it's only getting windier and wetter outside, so it's time for a break.

Inside, a wood fire crackles in the corner, keeping us warm and dry. At the advice of Rentia and Stoffel, we settle in to wait out the storm and, with time to kill, get to know each other. Learning about our new friends isn't easy, though; they only want to hear about us, and they continually fire out questions, like: *How did you two meet? What made you decide to sell everything and travel around the world? How do you like Africa so far? Do your mothers know you're doing this?!*

A group of five other riders comes in, shaking rainwater from leather jackets like dogs emerging from a lake. They've come up the opposite side of Sani Pass, where the road is paved. In the small space, we can all hear each other, and Dave and I soon have a wider audience asking us the same questions as our Bethlehem friends.

Three hours later, the sun is back. As we're putting on our riding gear, Rentia hands me a card with their address.

"If you're in our part of the country, do call us."

We promise to.

A bathtub reckoning

We follow the five bikers out, and they invite us to join them at a place they've rented for the night in a nearby village.

When planning our route back home, I wondered about where we'd sleep in Africa—especially in places where camping is dangerous due to wild animals—but in just three hours, we've already found options. I'm always glad in times like these that we haven't pre-booked a hotel.

I love the idea of experiencing rural life in Lesotho, so we tag along with the other riders. On the descent, it soon becomes clear they're on another level, racing each other on the unobstructed pavement, leaning away from hairpin corners and almost touching the road with a kneecap. Their bikes are like ours but with smooth street tires. Knobby treads, like Dave and I have for going off-pavement, aren't dependable at such speeds and angles, though I'm leaning more now than I did a year ago. I have the feeling these guys regularly "drop a knee" even on their daily commute. The thrill of tipping a motorcycle into the centrifugal force of gravity is not only addicting but the correct way to ride. At first, this technique felt to me like forcing the bike almost into a crash. But when I got used to counter-steering—pushing on the left handlebar to steer the bike right and vice versa—riding became a whole different mind game.

We're a posse of seven now and stir up the village of Molumong when we ride through to find the guest house. Kids chase us as far as their little legs can manage, then fall to the ground laughing. Dogs bark at our plastic-clad heels. Faces appear in windows and doorways to see what all the commotion is about.

The guest house sits overlooking part of the Molumong Valley, and its exterior resembles the rest of the village housing: stone with a thatch roof and wooden doors. The inside, however, is modern–minimalist, with bold colors on the couch cushions and bedding. Clean, bright-white walls give the whole place a beachy feel.

Norma, the host, corrals three teenagers to find our group some beer. They slump off, taking their time (teenagers, like bars, are the same everywhere) and return half an hour later, helping each other carry milk crates filled with tall brown bottles. I'm in for a long night, so I grab a bottle and head back into the house for some downtime. Even as last-minute invites, Dave and I have been given the best room, with a double bed and a deep soaker tub.

I debate between a nap and a soak, choosing the latter. Filling the tub, I remember Edu and Arinda telling us how precious water is in South Africa. Is it the same in Lesotho? The region seems lush and water rich, but I shut off the taps once the tub is half full. Sinking in, I relax with my beer and use the windowsill beside me as a shelf.

Outside, I hear Dave laughing with the guys, all from Durban, South Africa. He's helping them set up for a barbecue—or *braai*—with steaks sourced from the village. I both admire and am envious of Dave's ease around people; he captures interest even though he doesn't demand attention. When we first met, Dave told me he was an introvert, but he's become more outgoing over the last year.

As someone who usually loves socializing and who's had many friends in my past life, I'm experiencing something entirely different. I'm the one turning inward. At first, my female friends seemed genuinely excited about my wild adventure, but by my second year away, only a handful have kept in touch. Time and distance do that to friendships. Maybe some of these people find it hard to identify with what I'm doing: I'm not settling down; I don't have any career aspirations. Or maybe I'm becoming a different person through these adventures and my relationship with Dave, which is getting tighter and more defined by the day. I'm grateful for the friendships distance never seems to affect: Debbie used to be my boss but is now my best friend and one of my favorite adventure buddies. Gillian is another long-time pal I've had since high school. We can go years without talking to each other, then just pick up the phone one day out of the blue. Then there are people I've known for years, commenting on our blog and social media—subtle connections that mean the world to me. I think it's just more that I'm missing female connection.

The morning after a night of beers and roasted meat, Dave and I say good-bye to the Durban boys, who need to get back for work. I feel so fortunate to be taking two years off to explore the world, while day after day, people return to their careers and families after quick weekend getaways.

Dave and I aren't trust fund kids or lottery winners. Through hard work, commitment, and a willingness to let material things go, we're making the dream happen. It's a triumphant feeling to have such agency in life, but we will be back in the grind soon enough. Two years is a long time, but it isn't forever.

Leaving Molumong, we discover more villages just like it with the help of our GPS and make a conscious effort to go slow, wave, and lift our visors so people can see our smiles. Some villagers are uncomfortable or surprised by us, while others are so excited they drop everything to chase us on foot.

When people don't return our waves or smiles, I'm on edge, remembering the conversations with Edu and Arinda in Cape Town about unwanted visitors getting kidnapped, raped, or beheaded. I know these horrible things happen to innocent travelers who have likely just wandered into the wrong place at the wrong time. We stay vigilant, but after meeting seventy-year-old Nina almost a year ago in the Atacama Desert, I'm trying not to let *what ifs* ruin my adventure. Experiences only happen when we take chances.

Between each village, scenic plateaus stretch to the horizon, and the wind blows all day long. Grasses grow short and stubby, and it's easy to spot sprinting herds of *bontebok,* an antelope species. Long-tailed widow-birds remind me of Steller's jays back home, only they're mostly black and trail twenty-inch-long feathers, more visible in flight.

The backroads we favor over main highways mean rougher rides and a heightened sense of adventure. When wet, the orange dirt turns to slick mud and makes for extra-slow going. The difference between a wet and dry road can mean the difference between utter misery and sheer fun.

My low-fuel light comes on late one afternoon while we ride through a small hamlet in Lesotho. I ask two women balancing baskets on their heads where I can get gas, realizing this is a stupid question; not only do the women not understand me, but the village doesn't even have electricity. Everybody gets around either on foot or bicycle.

Several kids run alongside us, and the older one understands English. "Wait!" He dashes off.

The other kids stare at us. I want to appear friendly, so I dig out a baggie of stickers in shapes like stars and unicorns and pass them around. The children don't know what to do with the colorful pieces of paper, so I demonstrate by peeling the backing off, then sticking one on my face. Their musical giggles make me smile. Now they all put stickers on their faces. Dave pulls out his camera and takes some shots on his digital camera, which he then shows the kids. Their eyes grow wide seeing their on-screen personas. Although digital cameras are an excellent advancement in technology, I wish for a Polaroid so we can leave each of these kids with a photo. Do they even have pictures of themselves or family members? It could truly be decades earlier than 2016 in the village that day; nothing defines it as the twenty-first century, which is what I love most about traveling through these parts of the world.

A group of men return with the boy who told us to wait. We can get fuel in the next town, thirty-five miles away, they say. I find it amusing that half a dozen men came to tell us this. Everyone wants to see the strange foreigners.

Waving goodbye to the now-larger crowd, we roll away and soon encounter heavily eroded roads. I get through a creek crossing but fall off trying to climb the other side and need Dave's help to lift the bike on the wet, slimy rocks. After that, the road flattens out, but the muddy ruts hold on to rainwater. I drop my bike twice more but can pick it up by myself.

By the third time, however, I'm exhausted, and Dave is out of sight. I've just passed a teenager and an elderly woman who I assume is his grandma. Seeing my struggles, they come over. I have my ass pressed into the seat with my left hand on the right handlebar and my right hand gripping the luggage rack. This is the best technique I've found for lifting my bike, using my legs and supporting my back. The young man and the old woman position themselves on the other side, and the three of us heave, grandma taking her fair share of the weight. I shake their hands, laughing in awe. Incredible moments happen in the blink of an eye.

Again, I wish I could capture it all on video and wonder if I should have also invested in a drone. Those hovering cameras are becoming hugely popular for overlanders these days. Instead, I have only my memory to relive these experiences and my words to rewrite them.

Dave's waiting up the road. I often stop for photos or pee breaks, so he's not concerned that I took so long. When I tell him an African grandmother just helped lift my bike, he laughs and says, "Wow, they make 'em tough here."

There's no fuel in the next village, but I make it all the way to the South Africa border, which is already closed for the evening. A more pressing matter now is where to sleep. We can't backtrack with my tank on fumes.

I approach some officers standing outside to ask whether it's possible to camp here until the border reopens.

The officer smiles and says, "No problem. Welcome to South Africa!"

Your feet stink like cheese

It's tough to have any concerns about sleeping at a border crossing when you're fenced in with razor wire. I relax with the feeling of safety and try to find us something for dinner. The officers, dressed in dark green slacks and matching tucked-in shirts, observe us. Mostly they just stare at our bikes. A shepherd on his horse also watches from the other side of the chain-link fence. I want to photograph him, but he trots away before I get the nerve to ask his permission.

I look at our surroundings; we're high in the mountains again, and the view is beautiful.

"Imagine asking to do this at home?" I say to Dave, thinking about the last American border guard I encountered.

Although we hadn't planned to camp and didn't have much in the way of food, our cobbled-together dinner is surprisingly good: ramen noodles, Peri-Peri sauce, fresh carrots and broccoli, and hard white cheese. The *pièce de résistance* is *droëwors*—a South African dried sausage flavored with coriander and other spices. *Droëwors* are like meat sticks but much tastier and not full of nitrates and MSG or whatever else is in that crap at the gas stations back home. Stirring the soup on our camp stove, I realize today was a "free" day. We won't get to a gas station until tomorrow, so I didn't spend any money on fuel. We're camping for nothing and didn't have to buy extra groceries or eat out. Free days balance our costs when we try to stick to our budget of one hundred dollars a day. Especially after someone buys a new motorcycle.

With little to do once it gets dark, Dave and I go into the tent early. This is our first night camping in Africa, and we're surrounded by men with guns—in a good way. I'm happy to be under the stars again—until I smell something nasty.

"Dave! Move your riding boots. They're right by my face and wafting into the tent." Our gear is tucked under the tent's vestibule for the night, secure and sheltered from weather. "It's like a mix between Swiss and parmesan cheese!"

"But you like cheese," Dave provokes.

"I like cheese, but I don't like out-of-context smells. People eat tuna, but if a person smells like tuna, you're not going near them, right?"

"Are you saying I smell like tuna now?" Dave raises his eyebrows. He loves teasing me when I'm trying to be serious about something that isn't all that serious.

"No, just cheese."

"But it's not me, it's my feet!"

Enclosed in plastic boots all day, Dave—or his feet—can't help it. But the smell is pungent and sinks deep into my nostrils. My feet smell, too, but not as bad; at least that's my opinion. The euphoric act of removing our boots at the end of the day and putting on flip-flops is something I always look forward to. There's no easy way to clean or dry out a pair of riding boots except to leave them in the sun on days we don't use them, which isn't often.

"Come on, they're not *that* bad," Dave says, trying to cuddle.

"Yes!" I burrow inside my sleeping bag. "Yes, they *are* that bad!"

"I can't even smell them."

"Of course *you* can't!" Dave's dulled sense of smell sometimes comes in handy—like during the time he worked for the National Parks Service and had to clean outhouses—but not for when I'm trying to tell him something stinks and he doesn't believe me.

"I can put my actual feet on your pillow. Here—" Dave starts to unzip his sleeping bag.

"Get away from me!" I screech.

Dave hushes me, breathless from laughing. "Those officers are going to come running over here with their guns drawn."

Gin & tonics in Bethlehem

South Africa (Part 2)

After the shortest border commute ever, we're stamped back into South Africa the next morning and soon find a gas station. By then, my tank is almost fifty miles into its reserve tank, sucking on fumes.

A few days ago, I sent Rentia and Stoffel an email saying we'd love to take them up on their offer to stay there. We fuel up and for the next forty-five minutes, travel through Golden Gate Highland National Park, passing under sandstone cliffs hundreds of feet high with overhanging rock at the top. Their shape reminds me of muffins. They're colored in ocher and orange layers, like some of the rock walls in Utah. A mineral I don't know the name of seeps down the walls, staining the cliff faces with its ink-like substance.

It's one thing to visit a (literal) wonder of the world like Machu Picchu—familiar through photos yet still awe-inspiring in person—and quite another coming across something out-of-this-world beautiful without planning or knowing about it. This to me is the essence of adventure: to explore and discover what isn't already plastered all over the internet. To experience raw wonder, firsthand.

Golden Gate is a climber's dream. I want to stop for one of my favorite pastimes—scouting routes—but I'm also content watching it all pass by from my seat.

We hit pavement again and pick up the pace. Something feels off; I'm working hard to keep my bike on course, and my handlebars aren't steering well. I pull over and shut off my engine, hearing the unmistakable sound of air escaping from my first-ever flat tire.

Dave heaves the bike up on its center stand and stacks two level-ish rocks under my skid plate. This impromptu "jackstand" will prevent the bike from teetering forward. He gets out some tools and removes the wheel, letting additional air out of the tire to make it more pliable. Putting the wheel flat on the ground, he breaks the bead by standing on the rubber, which then peels away from the rim. With small tire irons that look like spatulas, he slips the rest of rubber off the rim to expose the inner tube so we can find the hole and patch it.

We have no shade from the 80°F sun. I stir an electrolyte drink mix into water while Dave looks for the puncture by dribbling water and a little dish soap over the tube. We watch for bubbling and soon see where the air is escaping.

"I can't figure out what caused this," Dave says. "There's no puncture in the tire itself." Investigating further, he discovers a sturdy foil sticker on the inside of the tire. Over time, it rubbed into the tubing, causing the hole. This probably happened when we aired down our tires for going off-road. Tires ride better over uneven surfaces when they're more malleable, and we regularly stop to air up and down, according to road surfaces.

"What a stupid spot to stick that," I opinionate. Had I been going highway speed, the hole could have spread and blown the tube. The thought of a blowout scares me. In a car, you have three other tires to keep you on the road, but if one blows on a bike, you're almost guaranteed to crash.

One piece of gear we carry is well worth the extra bulk—a travel-sized air compressor we can hook up to the bike's battery and inflate much more quickly than by hand pumping. The compressor isn't only for fixing flats; we also use it to top up the psi for pavement after airing down for dirt roads. Dave powers on the compressor now to fill up my patched tube. Because of handy tools—and my boyfriend's now-expert skills in swapping out motorcycle tires—we're back on the road and cooling down through air flow within half an hour.

We arrive at Rentia and Stoffel's to the wagging tails of six dogs of various sizes, shapes, and colors, and a horse swishing its tail in greeting. Dave and I are led to the spare room, where a housekeeper is snapping the duvet tight.

"Liesbet," Rentia says to the Black woman, "This is Heather and Dave. They'll be staying with us for a little while. They're from Canada and are riding around the world on those motorcycles." She points out the window. "Can you believe that?"

Liesbet smiles and takes our hands warmly.

"We'll leave you two to get freshened up," Rentia says.

I let Dave have the first shower while I strip down to my underwear, pulling the duvet back to lie under the ceiling fan. I feel slightly bad for disrupting the tidy bed but, unshowered, it doesn't seem right to lie on the cover itself. Pale yellow curtains curl and flap at the open windows. The floors are a dark polished wood that squeak with every step throughout the farmhouse bungalow, built in 1872. The house is well loved and well kept. I'm already looking forward to a good sleep in a real bed.

Lying there, I think of how African culture for the more well-to-do, and even for the lower-middle class, means having house and yard keepers. These helpers seem to be treated well, but it's not something I'm used to or have ever had in my life. I'm hesitant to ask Liesbet for anything, like a towel or glass of water. Ironically, I'd feel fine asking Rentia or Stoffel. It's part of the culture, however, and I'm out here in the world to learn about other people and how they live.

Later, Dave and I join our new friends outside on their pretty green lawn. The yard looks out over the pasture with the horse. We're in farm country, drinking gin and tonics, fresh with lime and heavy on the liquor.

Stoffel's blue eyes shine. "You both clean up nice."

"Better than when we arrived, I'm sure," Dave says.

Bethlehem had recent flooding from rains, and we'd ridden through the *Liebenbergsvleirivier* overflowing onto the road just before their house. Our boots are soaked through and drying now in the sun so they don't smell any worse—like cheese, for example.

Lifting his glass, Stoffel says, "This will ward off malaria." He pronounces the *w* as a *v*.

"Which?" I ask. "The limes, tonic, or gin? I'm hoping the gin."

"Well, it's the tonic, but who can drink it without the gin?" Stoffel laughs.

Later, I look up what malaria prevention has in common with G&Ts. Tonic water does contain quinine, an important anti-malarial ingredient, but one would have to drink seventeen gallons for it to be effective. By then, you'd have other things to worry about than just malaria.

For two days, it pours. Dave and I stay put, grateful for shelter and friendly hospitality. Rentia and Liesbet cook large, delicious meals that we devour at the family table. There's always a home-cooked South African food, like *pap*—a porridge with an unfortunate name—or *biltong*, made from meat marinated in vinegar and spices and then hung to dry. *Biltong* is like beef jerky in texture but tastes different from *droëwors*. Since the family runs a beef and dairy farm, there's plenty of both food groups, and Dave and I are only too happy to sample everything. Dave is in love with this meat-loving country, and so am I. Lately, I feel perpetually tired, and my joints and muscles always ache. We both have consistent cravings for iron-rich protein and are several hundred nutritious calories in deficit compared to the energy we exert.

Rentia and Stoffel's kids stop by often with the grandchildren. One evening, Liesbet's two younger kids come over to play with them. I've come to see Liesbet is part of the family, not a servant. She's respected, and no one orders her around. She exudes the kind of happiness that can't be faked. The family appears well regarded in the area, employing cheerful farm and house workers, and their property is a welcoming, heartwarming place to be.

When I'm not napping or socializing on rest days, I create blog posts. I love writing them but often get behind, and posting becomes a monumental catch-up. I try not to let more than a week pass before finding Wi-Fi, but that isn't always possible. Dave could go the whole two years without ever communicating with the outside world, but sharing stories is ingrained in me, and our website is a way for me to connect with family and friends.

I'm diligent about keeping notes, which I thumb into an app on my iPhone at the end of each day. When I have Wi-Fi, I copy and paste those notes into a Microsoft Word journal for backup and to help me with accuracy in my posts. I enjoy taking the extra time for this task, even when I'm dog tired.

On our fourth day in Bethlehem, Stoffel surprises us by lending his pickup, which in South Africa is called a *bakkie,* pronounced *buck-ee.*

"You really can't leave South Africa without taking a safari in Kruger National Park," he tells us.

Showing what greenhorns Dave and I are when it comes to safari-ing, I say, "but we have the motorcycles."

Stoffel looks concerned. "The lions and cheetahs will eat you in minutes! Motorcycles are not allowed on safari. You need the enclosed vehicle. Take the bakkie. We'll send you with some food and a bottle of gin. For the malaria, of course!"

Nana bird

Kruger National Park is one of Africa's largest game reserves, at 220 miles long and forty miles wide. Rentia and Stoffel say our chances of seeing the Big Five—lions, leopards, rhinos, elephants, and buffalo—are high.

"I still can't believe they gave us their truck for five days," Dave says, driving north along Highway 17.

"I know. And that cooler?" The insulated box is plugged into a 12-volt outlet in the bed of the truck and is full of steak, cheese, milk, and all the fixings for G&Ts. "They're so generous. I really hope they do come to Canada so we can repay their hospitality." One of Rentia and Stoffel's sons lives near Vancouver, BC.

I look to my right and smile at the casual way Dave holds the steering wheel—calm yet alert, with his left hand on the gear shift. I'm comfortable enough to fall asleep in a vehicle with him, which is saying a lot. My dad—whose career was driving—gave both my sister and me a strong foundation for driving. As such, I'm a nervous passenger if I don't trust who's at the wheel. The trouble is, so is Dave; I rarely get a chance to drive when we're both in the car.

After ten long hours as a passenger, watching the wipers slapping away the heavy rain, we find a campground near a small town just outside of Kruger National Park. What a difference a vehicle makes. A day that long on the bikes would have been exhausting. We've paid close to fifty dollars in tolls, but with two bikes, it would've been twice as much. And of course, being sheltered from the weather is a huge plus.

Our twenty-five-dollar campsite includes a large gravel pad under an awning that fits both the bakkie and our tent. A tidy red gravel path leads from our site to a brick building with toilets and showers. The grounds are clean and peaceful.

While Dave and I walk our sleeping bags and other items between the truck and tent, we talk about the animals we hope to see and photograph. I've seen elephants—in Mole National Park while backpacking in western Africa—but they were the smaller variety. I really want to see the big guys.

I'm about to head to the showers the next morning when I notice the red light blinking on my InReach. It's a message from Mom telling me Nana has died.

The day before my flight to Cape Town, I'd gone to Kelowna, where Mom had been visiting Nana in hospice care. I was able to say goodbye, though I didn't let on that I was there to see her for the last time. Nana and I talked about my travels instead, and she made me promise to send her my safari photos.

Dave and I feared losing a loved one during the time we were away. I was sure it would be my grandpa, who'd just turned 103 that February, but he was still kicking. Despite fading away, Nana, 93, still had her cheeky sense of humor. While I was visiting her, the doctor was checking her heart, and she told him to watch where he put his hands, with a glint in her eyes. Nana was a flirt right up to her dying days.

Nana would have loved an African safari. She hadn't been able to travel much in her life and, like me, had a wanderlust soul. She always said she liked living vicariously through my travels. In my early twenties, when I told her I was going to Ecuador, Peru, and Bolivia for three months, Nana went to her library and checked out books on all three countries. I always appreciated her desire for continued learning, even as a senior and later as an old woman.

A surge of sadness hits me when I realize Nana's gone now and will never see my safari photos. I'm also sad for my mom, who often drove two hours one way from Revelstoke to Kelowna through winter storms just so Nana wouldn't be alone in her hospital room. Nana could be hard to get along with at times, and her judgments and criticisms were hard on those who loved her. But losing your own mother is never easy, no matter what the relationship. Mom doesn't expect me to come back for the funeral, but I'm upset I can't be there for her. At least she has my dad and her siblings nearby.

"Nana died," I tell Dave. He wraps me in his arms, and I cry. The air is muggy, but it's stopped raining. Frogs and crickets croak and chirp, even in the broad daylight. Later, we make breakfast, pack everything up, and drive into Kruger National Park.

"Holy shit, look at the size of that *shit!*" Dave gets out of the truck. I take a photo of him standing beside several piles of elephant dung three times the size of horse poop. We haven't seen the giants yet, but they must be close. I'm pulsating with excitement.

An African safari can reach the tens of thousands, depending on how luxurious you want the experience to be. Up until meeting Rentia and Stoffel, we were trying to figure out how to budget for the side trip. Now, our only costs are diesel, camping, and park entry fees.

Passing by the elephant's digested leftovers, we carry on along the red sandy road, devoid of people and traffic.

"I hope we see some animals," I say again, wistful.

"I'm sure we will." Dave reaches over to squeeze my hand. "How are you—"

"Look, a giraffe!"

Dave stops, and I jump out of the bakkie. While setting up my camera for a photo, a car comes along and grinds to a skidding halt.

"Get back in your car!" A woman yells through her window, opened just a crack. "For god's sake, are you crazy?! There are lions everywhere!"

We haven't seen lions or any other human-eating predators yet, but she's right. There's a reason we're in a vehicle and not on our bikes. I get in the truck. She drives off shaking her head.

"Stupid tourist move," I say, hunkering down in my seat.

Dave and I grew up around bears and scoff at people who get out of their cars on mountain highways when they see one wandering in the ditch. Grizzlies, for example, can hit thirty miles an hour in a short sprint.

"Guess we also risked our lives back there for a photo of shit, too," Dave replies.

I snap a quick shot of the giraffe from inside the truck, but by now it's meandered off to flick out its long, prehensile tongue and snip a leaf from a tree. I think it's odd no one at the park gates mentioned staying in our vehicle at all times or that there aren't signs every now and again as reminders. Having grown up in North America, I'm used to frequent, sometimes overzealous cautions and caveats. Africans seem to get by just fine with actual common sense.

The advantage of being the passenger is that I'm free to scan the landscape. On our first day, the horizon is dead flat in front of us. Heavy, navy blue and gray clouds hold back a wall of rain, leaving streaks in the sky. In the foreground, acacia trees and buffalo thorn bushes poke above long, lush cattail grasses waving in the breeze. While we crawl along looking left and right, up and down, I keep noticing a bird the size of a large robin. Maybe it's a different bird every time, but my mind wants to believe it's the same one flitting from branch to bush, chasing us.

"Okay, we have to get a photo of that bird," I say to Dave. "It's Nana. This is her way of joining us on safari."

"Sure." Dave doesn't question my sanity—at least not out loud. He rolls to a stop and reaches back for his Canon. Photographing wildlife is one of Dave's hobbies, and he brought along more camera gear for this part of the trip, anticipating a greater diversity of wildlife. "Wow, you should see this bird close up," he says from behind the big lens. I grab the pair of binoculars Rentia let us borrow.

"It's gorgeous," I say. "In bird life, I think it's more often males who have coloring, but I still like thinking it's Nana." The lilac-breasted roller turns to look right at me. Its colors are incredible—an iridescent rainbow of feathers. "That's totally Nana. She was just like a bird herself, always dressing in stylish clothes with beautiful patterns." I smile. "This makes me happy. She's here with us."

I don't believe or not believe in reincarnation, but today it feels true and is helping me. *This is the real thing, Nana. You deserve more than just photos.*

By the time we pull into a campground later that evening, we're overwhelmed from all we've seen: monkeys, baboons, kudos, dik-diks, zebras, wildebeests, impalas, and big-ass elephants. The bird life was also plentiful. Aside from the lilac-breasted roller, we've seen spurfowls, hornbills, ostriches, storks, and vultures.

"I took over 500 photos today." Dave is looking at his camera that night in camp, flicking from one image to the next. I make gin and tonics and hand him a glass.

"To Rentia and Stoffel." We toast. "And to ward off malaria, of course." I try to mimic Stoffel's accent.

"Wow, that's strong!" Dave says after sipping his drink.

"So are the mosquitoes."

We waited to purchase malaria pills until Cape Town after reading that we could get a local doctor to write us a prescription and the medication would be much cheaper. Edu and Arinda, our Airbnb hosts, had a doctor friend who was happy to write us each a scrip, sight unseen. We saved over $300 buying the vaccine in Africa, and it was all legit. Neither Dave nor I noticed any side effects after being on them for months, which I was grateful for. I'd heard horror stories of travelers having psychotic episodes and other bad outcomes with some malarial brands.

Campgrounds in Kruger National Park are protected by tall, electric fences and gates, so nights are spent sleeping peacefully under the stars, listening to lions, monkeys, and other nocturnal creatures. This is not the height of the tourist season, so we don't have people camped beside us. It all feels very surreal.

You're kind of a boner kill

Our second day in the park shows us less wildlife, which might be due to a change in terrain. The park is large enough to have several different eco-systems and has turned from wide-open savanna into rolling hills and deep valleys, making it hard to spot anything if we don't know where to look. Because it's the rainy season, the wildlife are well hydrated and not con-gregating. We come across several watering holes hoping to witness some *Planet Earth*-type action, but they're mostly empty. We have yet to find the lions that are supposedly *everywhere*, as the female driver shrieked at me. A family of cheetahs lounging under a baobab tree catches my eye, and we also see crocs and hippos after stopping for lunch at a lodge overlooking a river.

We're determined not to leave before seeing the last of the Big Five and sign up for a sunset driving tour. This, we're told by the park rangers, is the time of day when the lions like to come out, since it's cooler. Climb-ing onto the bus, I'm surprised the vehicle is only a few feet off the ground and open air, with just a canopy overhead. No steel and glass to protect us from claws and teeth. I let Dave take the window seat.

It's not long before we spot a lioness trotting down the road toward us. The driver stops, and we all elbow each other out of the way to get a better look. Hot on her tail, a randy male is closing in. Lions will fornicate up to forty times a day. They don't have a mating season, though when there's an abundance of food, sex is more likely. I'm nervous how close our driver is getting to the male. He does a U-turn and tailgates the big cat trotting after his lady friend. Every now and again, the lion glances back at the driver as if to say, *Can ya give me a little room here, buddy? You're kind of a boner kill.*

I snap more photos but leave most of the photography to Dave, with his multiple lenses and camera bodies. He takes some incredible shots, which I proudly post on our blog and social media pages.

Later, still on the guided tour, we come across a male elephant in *musth*—the Urdu word meaning "intoxication," defined as increased tes-tosterone production and heightened aggression and sexual behavior. This period in a bull's life happens around the age of thirty and lasts just a few days. A male elephant in *musth* can be very aggressive, and the giant is now blocking the road. Our safari truck is large enough to hold twenty people but feels dwarfed by the enormous animal. A charging elephant can reach speeds of twenty-five miles an hour.

The driver begins revving the engine to scare the elephant off, causing the bull to flap his ears. He lets out a rowdy trumpet, and I cover my own hearing appendages.

"I hate humans sometimes," I mutter to Dave when the driver starts honking along with the revving. This is hair-back adventure but also feels like animal harassment. "Does he have to do that?" I say a little louder, receiving some nodding heads and sympathetic sighs from other passengers.

"TIA," one woman says.

"What's that?" I asked.

"This is Africa."

Five days later, we're still reeling back in Bethlehem. Where else on earth can you see such a variety of animals all in one place (that isn't a zoo)?

We say our sad goodbyes to two people who already feel like family. It's never easy to express our heartfelt thanks to people like this in our travels. All we can do is say, "We hope to see you again!"

A detour to a screensaver

Namibia

The temperature remains hot well into the night. For days now, we've been riding in mid-90s. I don't know if we've gotten used to the higher temps or if the dry heat is just less intense than humid heat. Either way, Dave and I seem to be putting up with it better than in Central America, when we contemplated not coming to Africa at all because it's too hot.

As predicted, the opportunity to change direction on a whim presented itself. Namibia wasn't included in our original plans for Africa, and we didn't list the German-colonized country on our carnet de passage. However, several people said we couldn't leave Africa without going to the Namib Desert and the Atlantic coast—and why travel if not for spontaneity?

When I learn Namibia is also home to some of the world's largest sand dunes, I implore Dave to take the 780-mile detour west. It doesn't take much convincing when I mention most of the roads are unpaved.

At our campground that night, I get ready for bed by going straight to the showers to stand under the cold water. I try to do this whenever possible because cooling off gives me a better night's sleep. But by the time I return to the tent, I'm already sweating again. Too hot to get inside my sleeping bag, I lie on top, but some mosquitoes have gotten inside and start biting our exposed flesh. We don't have any insect spray, so we take turns getting up in the night to slaughter as many as possible before falling back to sleep in exhaustion.

It's hard for me to drift off with all the commotion, but also because I'm nervous that we've come all this way and won't be able to cross into Namibia. We're still on the South African side and haven't tested our luck with a country that isn't listed on the carnet.

As (almost) always, I didn't need to worry.

At the border the next day, we learn our carnet is good for all southern African countries, so we're permitted to enter Namibia without issue. I'm excited to get into the heart of the country and see all its glory. But first, the bikes are thirsty.

Border towns in developing worlds are usually undesirable places, and this one is no exception. Run-down, with dilapidated buildings and dry, dusty roads, it's an unwelcoming welcome to Namibia. I pull up to the pump and kill the engine, keeping an eye on half a dozen drunk, loitering men, old and young—I swear one's barely a teenager—who perk up when they see us. They wander over, and one reaches out to stab a grimy finger at my dashboard gauges. I work hard not to slap his hand away and tell him that's rude. There's no point. Another man saunters over to Dave. With drooping eyelids, he lays a hand on my boyfriend's shoulder and asks how much our motorcycles cost.

"I can't remember," Dave says.

We get this question a lot in Africa. It's everybody's business if you're in public with something flashy. This kind of attention is what concerned me back home, but we're used to it now. When traveling, you can get beaten down by certain cultural nuances, but it's futile to impose your own ideals. At first, I found the questions unnerving, until I accepted them as not only part of the culture but also how people strike up a conversation. If I say, "None of your business" and add that the question is disrespectful where we come from, that would be offensive to *them*. Usually, I ignore such questions or make something up, like our bikes cost $500 each.

Like Torres del Paine in Chile, Sossusvlei, Namibia, is another place I've dreamed about but never thought I'd actually get to. The sweet-potato-colored dunes in Namib-Naukluft National Park look like a giant has pinched them into piles in the world's largest sandbox. When contrasted against a brilliant blue sky, the scene is otherworldly.

Getting into Sossusvlei, a UNESCO site, means riding over 200 miles through the Namib Desert on isolated gravel roads covered with intermittent sand traps. Just like when a blizzard drifts snow over a highway during a storm, the same happens here with sand and wind. Runoff from floods leave perpendicular ditches gouged into the road as well, which fill up with "sand surprises." There's no way to know how deep one of the traps are until you're in it. Sometimes it's only a few inches, sometimes a few feet.

My dislike for loose ground shifting beneath me isn't abating; if I'm not dealing with marbles under my wheels, it's the sand surprises that catch me off guard, making me curse with the fear of crashing.

Of course, Dave's solution for everything is to use more speed. On this road, I'm tensely averaging forty miles an hour while chanting my mantra: *Never ride faster than your angels can fly.* Today, my angels are slow-asses like me, and we're all fine with it.

Despite my hopes, Dave and I are still butting heads over pace: him riding faster to keep up the momentum and me riding slower to anticipate the unexpected. He's pushing me now to speed up. I'm increasingly annoyed at his persistence. I would never force someone to go out of their comfort zone on a motorcycle. My reflexes are improving after so many days on the road, but they're still slower than his and always will be. I want to be a better off-roader, but I do not want another broken bone or worse—especially way out here.

I hit a sand patch without warning and feel my rear wheel kick out. *Whoa, that was close.* Paying more attention, I notice the road surface fades from light beige to a pale orange ahead—a sand surprise indicator. I have less than a second to brace for the next one, which I again hit too fast—or, as someone might say, not fast enough. The back end of my trusty ride swerves. Panic shoots through me while I wait for the bike to gain traction. *Phew.* I'm back on track with a pounding heart—a reminder that I'm doing something risky yet thrilling. The last time we'd ridden so much sand was in Baja with Brenda and Ruppert, over a year ago.

Dave's a mile or more ahead, but in the vast landscape, I can see him—or at least the cloud of dust behind his bike. I try to relax and even pick up my speed as, for the moment, the sand has been replaced with hard-packed clay. Taking in my surroundings, I'm astonished to notice zebras to my right—a "dazzle," as they're called when appearing in a group. When zebras gather, their stripes blend and camouflage, making it harder for predators to single out just one. We saw several zebras in Kruger National Park, but out here, where the gray gravel road meets the orange desert floor and there isn't a soul around, this dazzle is really...dazzling.

I hit another sand patch, and then another and another. They're short-lived but long enough to cause disruption in my speed as well as my spirits. I loathe the feeling of losing control and reason that slowing to ten miles an hour will be less painful in a crash. That speed, however, makes things worse. My bike swerves even more with every patch I hit, causing me to stab toes to the ground for balance.

Dave—relentless and having a great ol' time flying down the quiet road—is in his element. I doubt he even sees the oryx we've just passed. I stop to catch my breath, watching Dave plant his butt back in his seat to check for me in his mirrors. He pulls a U-turn.

"What's up?" he asks, trying to conceal his irritation.

"I hate sand! I can't do this, it's too nerve-racking."

"If you want to see Sossusvlei, this is the only way there."

Will I care about missing the basin of dead trees photographed for National Geographic and posing as screensavers on millions of computers?

"Just go faster." Dave's mantra is irking the hell out of me.

"I'm going as fast as I want to go," I breathe through my teeth.

"But you need speed to skim the surface of the sand. There's no other way to ride it. You're far more likely to fall off or drop your bike when you're going so slow."

"You've never mentioned that before," I mock sarcastically. "So, I guess crashing is also better at high speeds, too, when my body is tomahawking across the desert? Also skimming?" Dave's mouth twitches with a laugh he's smart enough to hold back.

Either I need to get comfortable with—or at least accept—the bike lashing around beneath me, or I'll be stuck riding pavement forever. I bear down on the next sandy section, keeping my speed at a lofty-for-me fifty miles per hour. It's still not fast enough to skim, and my tires slide out a little, but it feels less dramatic. A grin pokes through my grimace. *This is kind of fun.* Going against logic, I twist the throttle even more, increasing my speed to sixty. I cut through the next sand surprise like a water-skier and cheer like a sports fan.

The rest of the day is filled with more *aha* moments, and I'm flying high when we finally pull into Sossusvlei. I'll never forget the feeling of staying afloat and in control with the thrill of speed. It really is magical. I finally get it—the "it" all riders must feel when crossing the threshold of beginner to advanced. It's all gelling with my new bike, which I love more than ever. Now I just need to remember this sensation the next time fear takes over.

Dave and I stay overnight in an almost-vacant campground at the gates of Sossusvlei. Few people want to travel so far over such rough roads just to see piles of sand, so only a handful of 4×4s—and no other motorcycles—are in camp. We sit in the dark drinking G&Ts. The small campground store has ice, and the cubes crack now in our plastic cups.

"You did well today," Dave says. "You're really good at digging deep and getting through something, even when you're scared."

He rummages in his bags for a snack. I laugh when he pulls out the pork knuckle he had two nights ago at a restaurant in Aus. It arrived as big as a Thanksgiving turkey, and he couldn't finish it. "Are you still gnawing on that thing? Isn't it rancid by now?"

"Nope." Swallowing, Dave says, "It was huge! Did you see how much deep-fried goodness was on there?!"

"Yes, babe, I was there, remember?"

"Oh, were you? I couldn't see you over the pork knuckle."

I laugh hard into the warm night air, then catch my breath. Above the dark Namib Desert, the sky is bright with a gazillion stars. I know nothing about astronomy but wish I did now. Since the Northern Hemisphere holds more landmass, ninety percent of humans live north of the equator, where light and air pollution obscure so much of the sky. Here, in the Southern Hemisphere, we're far from even the smallest town. In the flat expanse of the Namib Desert, I see more stars than I knew existed, and the ones I do know, like the Milky Way and the Southern Cross, are brighter and more prominent than ever.

"Even though home is over thirty thousand miles away, we're still under the same sky, more or less," I tell Dave.

"Well, that's not technically true…" I let him mansplain the universe to me while I enjoy the rest of my drink, only half listening.

Motorcycles aren't allowed in Sossusvlei beyond the park entry. A few years ago, dirt bikers rode all over the dunes, which are considered sacred, so now motorized bikes and all-terrain vehicles are banned. It only takes one asshole…

Our choices are to pay fifty-five dollars each and sit on a tour bus or try hitching a ride. There are a few private vehicles parked in the lot, but when we ask around, no one has extra room. Dave and I sit in the shade of a camel thorn tree and debate what to do. No way did I come this far to let a technicality turn me around.

I spot an older couple and stalk them with my eyes as they walk toward a rented bakkie. The back seat appears to have plenty of room.

"Hi," I call out. "Would you happen to have two extra seats and be will-ing to take us into the park? They won't allow us with our motorcycles."

They agree.

Getting into the back seat of the truck, I'm immediately aware of the air conditioning. Even sitting in the shade, it's damn hot out there.

During the forty-mile drive into the bigger dunes—some higher than 1,000 feet—we spot an abundance of oryx, Namibia's national animal, chosen for their handsome looks and elegant resilience to harsh desert life. Their tall, pointed horns are shaped like a V and protrude from the ani-mal's skull like a unicorn in striped, menacing spikes. Unlike other antelope species, both male and female oryx possess horns. The way to tell the difference is the male points are shorter and thicker.

The Swedish couple is happy to stop for photos, but I restrain myself from jumping out of the truck every five minutes with my camera. Our surroundings present magazine-quality scenery: a single green bush con-trasting against the rich orange landscape, footprints leading to the top of a sand dune, quiver trees baking in the blazing sun.

The last miles to the trailhead—where we've decided to do a dune hike together—is sandier and bumpier than anything we've experienced out on the road. I hit my head a few times on the truck's ceiling before adjusting my position so I don't break my neck. I'm glad we're not on the bikes or inside a bus.

The four of us hike up a dune until we reach its spine, our shoes and socks full of sand. The Swedes are out of shape and have me worried we might need to perform first aid for heat stroke. But they plod along at a conservative rate. Dave forges ahead. I'm somewhere in between, savoring the alone time at first, but the heat is blistering and the sun sears my flesh, covered in 110 SPF sunscreen. I wear a hat but can't tell if it makes me hotter or cooler. I don't like sun in my eyes so leave it on. Maybe hiking in the Namib Desert at high noon wasn't the best idea.

At the ridgeline, I stop in my tracks. Rivers of sand swish down the steep incline under my feet. In the basin below, flanked by dunes on all but one side, an open pan of dry, caked earth holds the scorched remains of acacia trees, dead now for over 600 years. Due to the arid environment, the trees have never decomposed, but they haven't produced anything green in cen-turies. The white, clay pan—*Deadvlei*, meaning "dead marsh"—was formed after the Tsauchab River flooded from rainfall, which once allowed for vegetation. In time, the sand dunes changed their shape and form from the wind, blocking the river and cutting off the water supply.

Sossusvlei means "dead-end marsh," but nothing in the parched landscape before me remotely resembles swampland. The thick, blackened acacia limbs reach for the sky, looking like tall, headless humans with arms outstretched. The bright blue sky, vibrant orange sand, and charcoal-gray trees are a stunning combination of color and shadow. I feel the pull of emotion, which I always do after working hard to get somewhere incredible. These are the images I want to capture forever. I'm grateful I bought a better camera. Popping off the lens cap now, I frame the dead wood set against the dunes for a backdrop.

Coming to Sossusvlei is by no means easy, but if it were, the crowds and garbage would be just like at home in some of our national parks. Sossusvlei is still pristine, with little population throughout its 19,216 square miles.

The immense scope of the Namibian beauty—its remoteness and exoticism shown through photos on our website—have our followers gobsmacked. We're truly out there in the world, seeing what some only see in magazines or travel websites. And it doesn't end in Sossusvlei.

Yum, is this crocodile?

Riding up a steep road the next day, I reach the top and look back to admire the view of a green plateau with pinkish-beige hills popping out in the distance. There's no one around but the two of us. I think the rainy season is the best time of year to go to southern Africa: fewer tourists, lush vegetation, and rain to keep the dust down, yet there's still plenty of sun.

Cruising along the hard-packed dirt road at sixty-five miles an hour, I glance to my right and watch in awe as a giraffe keeps pace with me on my bike. *Let's race*, I imagine him saying. Later, on a slower section, we stop to watch a mango-sized tortoise crawl across the red gravel. Even the intensity of the heat doesn't distract us from taking in everything we're seeing— more game than people, more flowers than cars.

Stopping for some rest days in Windhoek, Namibia's capital, we lodge at one of the coolest accommodations so far. Urban Camp is in the middle of the city for convenience but is designed like a safari camp, turning it into a quiet oasis against the hustle and bustle. Leaving the sleeping bags packed, Dave and I splurge on renting a canvas safari tent with real beds off the ground. An outdoor shower encircled with bamboo rods for privacy is a luxurious addition. In the open-air restaurant/pool area, we gorge on the free breakfast, stocked generously with fruit, meat, bread—and even a full bar, for anyone wanting to start their day off with a mimosa or three.

With our gear and bikes somewhere safe, I'm unencumbered in my sundress and flip-flops and carry just my camera bag when we set out for Joe's Bar and Grill, famous for its well-prepared exotic meats. I order a sample platter with grilled kudu, springbok, zebra, crocodile, and oryx. The crocodile is chewy, but everything else is seared, cooked, and salted to perfection.

I've always respected non-meat lovers or anyone wanting to eat a certain way, but food restrictions while traveling around the world would be tough. I'm grateful that I can eat whatever I want. Trying something I've never tasted before is one of my favorite parts about traveling and getting acquainted with different cultures.

When Dave tells me he was once a vegetarian, I almost spit out my charbroiled kudu.

"That must have been for a girl," I say.

"It was. I also used to shave my legs when I was a road cyclist."

"What?! This is too much. Where's the hairy, carnivorous man I know and love?"

I've already had my second flat tire—a slow leak coming from the patch we used to repair the first one—so Dave sets out the next day to look for a spare we can keep in our emergency stash.

With some blissful downtime, I sit in Urban Camp's restaurant, enjoying the upbeat African music coming from speakers in the room. Throughout much of Latin America, and now in places we've been in southern Africa, music is usually played too loud through distorted speakers blasting out the windows of vehicles or through the doors of shops and shacks. Now, the speakers above my head are clear and at a perfect decibel level to enjoy the intricate rhythms and drums, the latter of which play a central role in many African traditions. If I had a musical talent, I'd play the drums. I get that from my dad, who, while he's waiting for his toast to pop up, uses the cutlery to tap out tunes with on-point cadence.

I upload hundreds of photos and update the blog, taking advantage of the fast internet connection. While doing so, I drink a beer, and then another, which makes me sleepy. The music follows me out to the pool, where I find a lounge chair in the shade and drift into a nap. No matter how much rest I get, it never feels adequate, and the lack of restoration for my body is taking its toll. Aside from constant sore joints and muscles, my brain seems overly taxed, and I have a hard time concentrating some days. I'm grateful not to be working at something mentally demanding, like a job, but I'm starting to wonder if something's off—something more than just overexertion. Like many women, I'm gripped by abdominal cramping each month, but mine are getting worse. I've upped the dose on my over-the-counter painkillers. The pills make my stomach acidic and give me heartburn, but it's far less painful than menstrual cramps. My female friends are missed most during these times, and although Dave is sympathetic, nothing replaces the commiseration from another woman who gets what I'm feeling.

Despite concern over how my body is suffering on this trip, I'm having a lot of fun lately. The F800 builds up my riding confidence, and I love feeling the improvements almost daily.

Dave and I are integrating into full-time travel as a lifestyle, going more with the flow. It was so worth coming here; southern Africa is striking, glamorous, mysterious, colorful…I'm loving this side of the continent, so different from my previous experience in western Africa a decade ago. Although exciting in its own way, that side doesn't have the extent of scenery and wildlife that add exhilaration to our days.

Dueling dynamics & coastal skeletons

Filling our tanks in a small town on our way to the Skeleton Coast, I spot familiar faces. We met Magnus and Tina in a campground a week earlier. They are also from Sweden, like the couple we hitched a ride with into Sossusvlei. The thirty-somethings are road-tripping around Africa with their young daughters: seven-year-old My (pronounced *me*) and four-year-old Ella. While camping one evening, we noticed their rented 4×4 truck and rooftop tent—an elevated sleeping platform mounted on top of the truck that opens like a tent.

"Hey!" Tina greets now. "Great to see you again!"

I'm happy for a chance to be off my bike for longer than a quick fuel-up and walk over to her while moving some tension out of my shoulders. Adorable and bubbly, My and Ella bounce in their seats and stare at me. When I catch their eyes, they burst into giggles.

We decide to continue traveling together, since we're all heading to the Skeleton Coast. Tina and Magnus have a cooler, so we pick up some meat for a *braai* later. On the way to a beach Magnus has in mind for camping that night, we stop at a seal colony—a spectacular sight that smells awful. Gray, blubbery bodies numbering in the tens of thousands *ork ork* their way up and down the Atlantic coast as far as the eye can see. I remove my helmet and hear them farting and belching then cover my face with my shirt. Not even the fresh sea breeze can dilute the stink.

Bacteria and fungi can thrive in the moist environment of a seal's fur or skin. While the smell is off-putting to the human nose, it has a purpose in the animal kingdom, helping seals recognize each other and communicate within their social groups. Also, the strong scent deters predators or competitors from approaching too closely.

"This reminds me of childhood!" Dave says, taking exaggerated deep breaths. Dave spent some of his youth growing up on Quadra Island in BC, where his house overlooked rocky islands filled with these stinkers.

The babies are cute, of course, and watch us with sad eyes, perhaps hoping we've come to rescue them from their smelly elders.

We don't last long at the seal colony, especially when one drags itself after Ella and makes her cry.

Although we've had dry, hot weather lately, we soon come across a large section of mud covering the road in front of us. Two vehicles—a small pickup and a car—are stuck, with three men trying to dig them out. They're shoeless, with muck up to their calves.

Magnus waits for us to cross first with the bikes, since their truck has a tow strap if we need it. I've never tackled something this deep before and carefully line up my bike for what I hope is the path of least mud-filled resistance. Dave blasts by on my left, impatient. He chooses a different line, and now I question my choice. The second I commit, a tanker truck—sitting idle on the other side—starts moving. *He's taking my line!* Too late. I change course in the thick slop and immediately get sucked into much deeper slop. My rear wheel spins and flicks globs into the air. No amount of throttle will get me out. *Dammit, where's an African grandmother when you need one?* Waiting for the winch, I save my energy and slip off my seat. I don't even need to put down the sidestand—the bike's glued upright.

Dave's walking over to me at a fast clip. I think he's coming to help me and say, "Good job for trying," like that time in the mudslide in Ecuador. I get ready for a high-five, but instead he says:

"What were you thinking? Why did you choose that line?"

I stare at him.

"Why are you so upset?" I hiss, keeping my voice low. I don't like arguing or being reprimanded in front of people. "At least I tried!"

No one else seems bothered; Magnus is already pulling out the winch with a smile on his face, no doubt excited to put the rescue gear to use.

I avoid eye contact with Dave, rage brewing. One minute, he admires me for digging deep; the next he's giving me shit for digging deep!

We continue to yell-whisper retorts at each other in a full-on lover's quarrel I hope is going unnoticed. I do not like the man I love right now.

Magnus brings over the tow strap. He and Dave wrap the rope around the frame by my forks, then Magnus puts the truck in reverse while Dave and I guide the F800 out upright.

With no time to feel sorry for myself, I pick mud out of my hair and clean my hands with my water bottle. Dave has ridden my bike to the other side, and is now taking the lead in a rescue effort on another stuck vehicle. Sure, he's happy to assist *them*... Everywhere, people are helping each other get unstuck. My and Ella are out of the truck laughing and flinging mudpies at each other. The carefree scene and teamwork would warm my heart except it's frozen cold toward my boyfriend at the moment.

After a few hours, during which Magnus and Dave save the day for several stranded motorists, we get going. The hustle and bustle allow me to ignore Dave. I leave without a word to him. For each negative thing about him, there are a dozen I love, but the condescending side can be hard to take.

I ride fast, dirt lobbing from my tires, sometimes pelting me in the shins. It's satisfying to see the clumps whip off and roll along the road in my wake. If only my bad mood could be tossed off as easily. I have an intense urge to keep going. *Let him worry about me.* Instead, I slow my roll. Fifteen minutes later, I see him in my mirrors.

When Dave pulls up beside me, he acts like nothing happened.

"Tina and Magnus stopped for a photo," he says.

I stay quiet, watching the wind drift sand across the road. I'm not ready to let Dave off the hook yet. My willingness to try anything, even if I'm not successful, is something I like about myself. That and my resilience, which comes from my mom. She could have two broken legs and would still drag herself across the finish line.

The Skeleton Coast is austere, haunting, beautiful. My camera is focused on the water, where three abandoned ships ran aground at the turn of the twentieth century. The vessels are stuck in the sandbar and listed to the side, wrecked and rusting.

This part of the Atlantic coast is prone to thick fogs that can roll in for months at a time, along with storm-force winds. Chaotic weather was often the reason for the shipwrecks—some of which date back to 1530. The Skeleton Coast is named in part after the decaying remains of the shipwrecks, but there are also tales of the discovery of sun-bleached human bones from those who jumped overboard after realizing they'd run aground. I can only imagine how disheartening it must have been for anyone who survived the wrecks to swim ashore only to find nothing but an endless, waterless desert awaiting them.

It has a remote, harsh feel but is actually home to surprising desert wildlife, like springbok, seals, hyenas, and even lions. The Skeleton Coast is also named for the whale and seal bones that once littered the shorelines due to the whaling industry and seal hunting.

Although some websites claim there are thousands of shipwrecks in this area, we only see the remains of three large boats above the water. The area with the most shipwrecks runs over 300 miles from Swakopmund to the Angolan border. As with many places worth seeing in Namibia, the Skeleton Coast is hard to get to, and that works to our advantage. I expect to see a few other tourists around, but it's just the six of us. And three locals—a woman and two men. They're hoping to sell us little handmade wooden trinkets. *Where do these people come from? Where do they live?* We haven't passed a town for hours. There's no vehicle nearby and nothing but white sand and the exposed road stretches for miles along the water. The young entrepreneurs aren't pushy salespeople, but they're visibly disheartened when we all shake our heads at their efforts to make a few dollars. I want to explain it's not that what they're selling isn't worthwhile—I'd love to have something as a souvenir of the Skeleton Coast—but I just don't have the room. The three go back to sitting in a circle beside a tuft of desert grass, shielding their eyes from the sun and wind, watching us.

Before we leave to head east and away from the crashing, roiling sea, Dave comes over and puts his arm around me.

"I'm sorry," he says. "I was an asshole, and I've been feeling bad about it all day."

I soften. At least he's not afraid to apologize.

While the Skeleton Coast is an interesting side trip, I look forward to getting back into more lush territory. At a dusty junction with nothing or no one in sight but the lanky heads of two loping giraffes, we say goodbye to the Swedes. They're scheduled for a safari in Etosha National Park, and Dave and I are heading northeast.

I congratulate Tina and Magnus for giving their girls such a memorable education. Not all parents would be comfortable taking young ones traveling through Africa. It's reassuring to see a family so open-minded. This type of exposure will shape My and Ella as they grow older and hopefully encourage them to travel as adults.

The value of enough

Over the next week, Dave and I make our way across the Caprivi Strip—a narrow slice of Namibia that points like a finger toward the far northeastern corner of the country. The odd colonial fabrication was an attempt by German Chancellor Leo von Caprivi to connect land via the Zambezi River. He neglected to consider Victoria Falls, however, so the slim strip—varying from twenty to over sixty miles wide—stops at Katima Mulilo, the Zambezi region's capital.

The border town is still 500 miles away. We had planned to ride most of that along the Zambezi River, but flooding has us rerouting. We arrive in Katima several days earlier than expected. The rain hasn't reached this far, and dust clouds puff in front of my headlight as I follow Dave in our search that night for a place to stay. From what I can already see, the city is a dump and feels like somewhere we want to pass through fast. Coming in at night always makes a new place feel scarier.

We have to wait in Katima for several days for some bike parts that are being shipped. Usually, we aren't too picky about where we spend one night, but multiple days in a dull place is soul crushing. I swerve through glinting shards of glass and rotting garbage. So far, Katima is the least attractive place we've been in Namibia.

Our GPS search for a motel leads us to a dirt parking lot. The building is still under construction, but I have a feeling it's been like this for years. They're charging thirty-two dollars a night—higher than we've paid for much nicer accommodation, but I'm too tired to argue. After dragging our bags up the exterior stairs—two trips each—I go to take a shower. The water doesn't flow unless I keep my hand on the knob that activates the showerhead. No water whatsoever comes out of the taps in the sink, and the toilet only flushes half its contents.

Happy to remove at least some of the dust and grime from my body with a face cloth, I step back into the room.

"Don't get your hopes up," I say to Dave.

At the front desk, I inquire about another room—at least one where the bathroom works. I haven't seen another soul around, aside from a few staff, and our bikes are the only vehicles parked in the lot. The young receptionist is pleasant and shows me a room two doors down. The first thing I do is check the functionality of everything in the bathroom: the toilet flushes, one tap works in the sink, and the shower has better spray.

We transfer our belongings down the hall. Even the internet works now, because we're closer to the modem in the front office.

Our motel room comes with free breakfast, served to us each morning in a small dining area off the kitchen downstairs. The receptionist—also our server—brings over trays stacked with white toast, milk, tea, coffee, eggs, and fruit. Her name is Sonnet. She even remembers what we leave on our plates and doesn't serve it to us again the following morning. This, I hope, is for cutting down on food waste rather than any sort of special treatment.

A connoisseur (snob) of fine coffee, Dave misses his espresso machine back home but is adapting well to the powdered granules in its place. He loves saying, "Pass the bowl of coffee" then grinning at his own hilarity.

Sonnet brings us an extension cord on the second day of our stay. It's meant for the knee-high fridge in our room. At first, I don't understand why we need the extension until I see that the fridge—enclosed in a compartment made exactly for it—has a cord that is just a foot shy of the outlet on the counter. My carpenter boyfriend has a lot to say about that oversight.

"TIA," I reply. There have been many "this is Africa" moments since we first heard the phrase in Kruger National Park.

Oddly, Dave and I begin to enjoy our disheveled home away from home, even venturing out to walk the dusty streets. Katima feels far more friendly and safe in the daylight, and the motel staff are so nice that they make me smile every day. Dave strikes up a friendship with the maintenance man and lets him sit on his bike. The two speak together in laughter-filled, flowing conversations. I enjoy watching the easygoing nature between my American boyfriend and the dark Namibian—two men from very different worlds.

That evening, we position the floor fan to blow at us lying in our single beds. Sipping cold beer from our little fridge, I think of how we've adapted to the motel despite how it looked at first. Choices are nice, but too many can spoil humans rotten. In the end, there's nothing wrong with good enough.

I'm almost sad to leave after our fourth day in Katima. The bike parts have arrived, and Dave has everything assembled in under an hour. Before leaving, I find Sonnet and hand her a twenty-dollar bill as a gesture for taking care of us. She looks astonished. It only occurs to me afterward that it might have been the equivalent of a week's pay for her, or more.

Nothing to trade but some denim

Botswana/Zambia/Zimbabwe

An elephant trumpets close by, and I almost run into a pack of snorting warthogs dashing across the road. Botswana's Chobe National Park is the first game park we've ridden through fully exposed on motorcycles. We enter the park after crossing from Namibia into Botswana, and no one seems concerned to send us on our way. I hope there aren't any lions or cheetahs around. I'm glad I recently opted out of purchasing a zebra-skinned rug for a cushy layer between my butt and seat.

Namibia was extraordinary—totally worth the detour. Now, as we make our way back toward the eastern part of the continent, Botswana is another wildlife-rich country, but we are only passing through for two nights. Victoria Falls is our next destination, on the border between Zambia and Zimbabwe.

The town of Victoria Falls itself is a culture shock: touristy, expensive, and busy. Dave and I are lucky to find a hotel with a fenced-in patch of grass where they allow us to set up our tent for a fraction of the cost. Anyone who might take an interest in going through our stuff will have to enter the hotel first, as the fence is tall, with spikes at the top. Still, it's not ideal security-wise, so we keep everything on our bikes under the lockable wire nets, just like when we park somewhere to go hiking or into a restaurant.

Setting out on foot for the falls, we walk out of the hotel lobby and are immediately swarmed by local buskers selling anything from sandals to wood carvings to used clothing. They crowd us on the sidewalk until we can barely get by. I have a brief idea how it would feel to be famous; it's unpleasant.

"No, thank you," I say a dozen times before reaching the main road.

One of the more interesting items being hawked are Zimbabwean trillion-dollar notes. They aren't fake but rather a clever businessperson's vision to get a better return on the country's defunct currency. The years 2008-2009 were devastating for the country; there are reports that the monthly inflation rate reached an estimated 230 million percent.

When the Zimbabwean dollar was introduced in 1980, it was more or less on par with the US dollar. But in 2017, a $100 trillion Zimbabwean note—that's fourteen zeros—equaled about forty cents. So, if a hawker can sell me some trillion-dollar bills for a couple US dollars, that's a pretty good return on investment.

After a forty-five-dollar lunch, we pay thirty each to enter the park.

At 350 feet tall and 5,604 feet wide, Victoria Falls is considered the largest sheet of falling water in the world. Since it's still the rainy season, the falls are very full. In seconds, we're covered in a thick-as-fog upspray created from the water crashing into the ground below. Even at our campsite almost a mile away, we could feel the mist on our skin. Mixed in with the tropical vegetation and the mini rainbows here and there, the enormity of the waterfall is stunning. With all the moisture in the air, however, we have a hard time getting close enough for good photos. Dave drapes his rain jacket over his head and pulls out his zoom lens, capturing what he can.

We leave the falls looking like we've been through a car wash and walk back into town, continuing to fend off hawkers. A solo busker approaches us with beautiful wood carvings. He's more subdued than the others. I'm sympathetic for how hard life must be for him trying to sell trinkets to impolite, ignorant tourists. The young man shows us his items for sale. I tell him they're really beautiful but that we're traveling on motorcycles and have no room. He tries another tactic, saying he'll take clothing instead of money. We again politely decline.

Walking back to the tent, Dave's lost in thought. When we get to our bikes, he digs around in his luggage and fishes out a pair of clean jeans he barely wears.

"I'll be right back," he says.

Fifteen minutes later, he returns emptyhanded.

"I told the guy I didn't want anything. The jeans were just a gift."

The next day, as we're riding out of town, we see the young man on the sidewalk, selling his wooden carvings. He's wearing Dave's jeans.

TIA & it's okay

Malawi

Over the next month, Dave and I ride around Zimbabwe, into Zambia, and eventually Malawi—countries in stark contrast to South Africa and Namibia. Still scenic and filled with lovely people, the poverty is much more prevalent in the sense that infrastructure and services are next to nothing. In its place are people without shoes, villages without electricity, societies without the benefits (and the burdens) of modernism and materialism.

I want to see it all: rural, rugged, unruly Africa. It's not always pretty, it's not always fair—or even sane—but TIA.

There's little distinction between backroads and highways now as we ride north on one long, chaotic, unkempt, potholed throughfare used by everyone and everything. Our days are monotonous trying to put in the miles again. I entertain myself by watching road life, where villagers travel by foot or bicycle, carrying impossibly heavy loads on their heads or on the back of two-wheelers that groan and squeak while pedaled. I want to buy the baskets I see commonly used everywhere and take one home, but I don't have room. They are made from traditional fibers, and the materials—sourced from local habitats—include African bamboo, ilala and fan palm, sisal leaves and fiber, and banana leaves. They're beautifully colorful and strong, and they come in all different sizes.

A vehicle passes too close to some roughened men who look like they've been working in a coal mine. I wince, but no one scatters, putting full trust in the driver. At home, cars would be honking for these men to get off the road, and the men would be swearing at the crazy driver. Here, everyone shares the road, despite obvious dangers.

Something else we notice—also common in Mexico, Central and South America—are piles of branches on the road. This is a way to alert traffic that there's an accident or broken-down vehicle ahead, forcing people to slow down when they need to move around them. If the wood looks dry or scattered, we can assume the obstruction was cleared some time ago and someone just forgot to pick up the branches.

I think I see one of these piles moving. When I get closer, I see it's an old man with a load of firewood strapped to his back. He looks like a walking bush, and I laugh to myself until I'm beside him. The poor guy is severely stooped and wears plastic sandals that are worn to scraps and only cover the balls of his feet. It's heart wrenching. I feel self-conscious passing by him with all my gear and a bike totaling in the five digits.

Despite what appears to me as an utterly desperate way to live, everywhere people smile and are friendly—even though the chaos seems to make it more likely their loved ones will be taken out by a speeding truck at any minute.

These near misses are common. Too common. I begin to think of Africans living in these areas as having like charges, such as when you try to touch the ends of magnets together but there's a subtle force pushing against the connection. It's the only explanation for how anyone here makes it past infancy. Even Dave and I seem adopted into the life-saving phenomenon. I lose count how many times someone comes ripping around a hairpin corner on bad suspension, hits a pothole, and goes over the center line before reeling it in.

My fight-or-flight mode never shuts off. Our safest position is down the middle of our lane, where we hope to stay clear of pedestrians and animals to our right and vehicles crossing into our path on the left.

Every dozen miles or so, we pass through a village, and the speed limit changes from fifty miles an hour to twenty. Getting from A to B here is a slow, tedious process, but it gives me a chance to observe more closely. I admire the roadside villages, with their mud huts and peaked thatch roofs. They're built round and clustered in circles to cut the winds whipping across the exposed, wide-open terrain.

I watch a woman walking along uneven ground with a thirty-pound bucket of water on her head. By the end of the day, my three-pound helmet feels as heavy as a bowling ball. I'm amazed how these women keep their balance—and some even have fabric-swathed babies on their backs.

The kids are adorable, their round, brown faces turned to watch us roll by. They're initially surprised, perhaps never having seen anything like us roll through their homestead. But their bright, beautiful smiles and little pink palms wave with gusto. At first, I wave back to every single one of them. I don't know how the Queen of England did it with all the waving. My biceps and shoulders are nearly coming out of their sockets. I remember that I have a horn and use it in a friendly *beep, beep* tempo for greetings the rest of the day.

To travel through this part of Africa, where so many are so poor and have little to no access to clean water and proper sanitation, is troubling. I want to help but have no idea where to start. How would I decide who gets the money? If we want to buy someone a meal, there are no stores or restaurants. And what would be the point if it's just one meal among thousands?

It's overwhelming. There's a guilty part of me that's glad to just keep moving on.

By nightfall, we're off the road and out of danger. I welcome the reprieve from negotiating traffic bedlam. Food and fuel have been difficult to find, and camping is not a good idea, but we find a luxury hotel in the more touristy area along the shores of Lake Malawi. The owner lets us set up our tent for a small fee and asks us to eat in his restaurant. With no other choice for dinner, we're happy to oblige.

Walking back to our tent after dinner, we watch a lightning storm slashing away on the other side of the water. Lake Malawi is big—360 miles long by forty-five miles wide—so the storm is a long way off, yet it feels close enough to touch. The sporadic flashes light up naked bodies bathing in the lake—fishermen who live along the shoreline. They don't seem concerned or surprised to see a white couple walking in the dark, perhaps because of the tourist accommodation close by. Despite being one of the poorest countries in the world, Malawi has a national park located at the lake's southern end where clear waters shelter colorful fish, and diving and boating are popular for those who can afford it.

The convenience of camping on the lush grounds of a fancy hotel, however, doesn't come with a no-wildlife-encounter guarantee. While walking back from the shower house, I almost run smack into the hip of a hippo. The squat, wrinkled beast doesn't like my headlamp shining in its eyes and lumbers off. *Phew!* Seeing a hippo in the wild is like seeing a grizzly bear—both are massive and neither likes to be surprised. It's hard to sleep that night knowing the 2,000-pound behemoth is roaming around on the other side of our flimsy nylon walls.

Before leaving the next morning, I walk back to the lakefront to watch fishermen stringing large nets. In a few hours, they will use a rowboat and head out for a daily catch. Sadly, net fishing in Lake Malawi has caused a severe food resource depletion, but with few options, the locals continue to do it.

Our cash is running low, so we stop at a bank machine, where the lineup stretches down the street. After forty-five minutes, it's finally Dave's turn. He's only able to extract fifty dollars from both of our cards, and our banks at home will charge a foreign fee of five dollars just for the convenience. We're really only getting ninety percent of our money. Fifty dollars won't get us far, even in Malawi, but we try to stock up with US currency whenever possible, since it's what most countries now accept.

I'm ever vigilant at ATMs and banks. I stay with the bikes but keep an eye on Dave, too. Any opportunist with ill intent knows we're walking away with enough cash to feed an entire village. In 2017, more than half of Malawians live under the international poverty line of one dollar and ninety cents per day. For some, one hundred dollars is two months of wages.

Long days in the heat and the sometimes-depressing scenes around us suck our energy. For every hour I love traveling in Africa, another hour is spent dealing with its lack of order and calm. I'm starting to look forward to when the rest of the continent will pass under the belly of an airplane heading to Europe.

After one especially trying afternoon riding over bumpy roads, my throbbing headache is unbearable. I take two Tylenol, but the migraine is too far advanced and doesn't go away until I throw up in a cold shower.

In our room later, Dave asks what I'm writing. Reciting my notes, I read: "Today I avoided a few head-on collisions, dumped my bike doing a U-turn on the highway, waved at 700 people in gusty winds at highway speeds, saw a lot of blood coming from a flayed toe after a guy on a bicycle was cut off by a car, and walked a few miles in the heat trying to find a grocery store." I point to Dave. "You had to pick up my dumped bike, also avoid head-on collisions, help pick up the bicycle of flayed-toe guy, which weighed a ton because he had a rice bag full of rocks or something strapped to the back, then perform first aid on him and fix his bike. Oh, and we rode 273 miles."

"Huh," Dave says, "I wonder why *I* don't have a headache."

For the love of reggae

Tanzania

Sometime after leaving Zambia weeks earlier, I began to notice very dark skin mixing with lighter tones. Hookah pipes appeared in restaurants, and the morning, afternoon, and evening calls to prayer filled the streets. The chant, coming from speakers attached to nearby mosques, to me signifies foreign travel more than anywhere we've been so far—the soundtrack for our real-life movie.

During three months of riding through Africa, we've passed through a variety of cultures and religions, but none as alluring as Islam—the second-largest religion in the world after Christianity.

In Tanzania, Islam makes up just over thirty-four percent of the population, and in Zanzibar, where we're currently headed aboard a ferry for an off-bike excursion, ninety-nine percent are Muslim.

The first and only Muslim country I've been to before now was Mali in 2007. That was my first time wearing a head scarf and taking off my shoes to enter public places. In Timbuktu, I was invited to stay with a family and can still feel the heat of embarrassment when the husband asked me to cover my bare ankles. I was sitting on the floor wearing sandals and capri pants, eating from a big pot with the entire family. My long-sleeved shirt seemed modest enough, but I hadn't considered the rest of my exposed skin. The only other bottoms I had were shorts, so I reached over and pulled the top sheet off my sleeping mat, which made the kids laugh. Inexperienced or not, in that moment, I felt like a true traveler.

Perhaps it's naive of me to put so much faith into the idea that travel can change the world. Yet how many conflicts might be resolved by simply knowing both sides of the story? Had someone not kindly pointed out my error, another person might have been insulted and gotten angry. There are many stories of ignorant tourists ending up in jail due to cultural mishaps.

Watching the emerald-green Indian Ocean pass under me between Dar es Salaam and Zanzibar, I think, *what if schools were structured differently?* What if every student had the opportunity to choose a place on the globe and stay with a host family where they could learn about a nation's religion, food, and what they do for fun? Such opportunities exist in some schools, but only for those who can afford to send their kids away. What if foreign home stays were mandatory, like math or biology?

A choice my parents made for me when I was twelve was, I believe, the catalyst for my adventurous spirit. Probably at their wits' end after signing me up for countless extracurricular pursuits I never stuck to, they enrolled me in a marching band called the Calgary Cavaliers. Not musically talented, I was one of those girls who threw a tall pole with a flag on the end into the air, then caught it to twirl behind my back. After months of practice and fundraising, I traveled with the Cavaliers by bus all over the US for a summer, performing at football games and in town parades. I felt so independent and lucky doing something few kids my age had the opportunity to do. And America was so action packed, unlike boring Canada (I thought at the time). That summer, time stopped long enough for me to appreciate that people lived differently than me. Yet time also flew by so fast that when I got home, my parents said, "Really? Only *one* postcard?" I was gone for two and a half months and had licked just one stamp for Canada.

Dave and I spend three nights in Zanzibar snorkeling (me), relaxing (also me), and receiving fist bumps (Dave) from Maasai men walking by us on the beach. The purpose of coming to Zanzibar—and our hostel in Paje—was to get away from the madness of Dar es Salaam. We've applied for our Kenyan visas and have to wait about a week.

The beach holiday was my idea. Dave, the swimming-and-hot-weather-hater, is not too excited. I convinced him to go to the island when he saw photos of the wet bar and tree-house-like accommodations at our hostel.

Unfortunately, when we arrive, the quaint, subdued refuge shown online is a full-on party scene. Loud, poolside speakers play reggae—Dave's least favorite music.

"Maybe they turn it down at night," I suggest, hopeful.

The music plays eighteen out of twenty-four hours a day. Dave is pretty much rocking in a corner by the time we leave, and my ears ring for weeks.

Before catching the ferry back to the mainland, we spend two nights in Stone Town, the former capital of Zanzibar known for its spice and slave trade in the nineteenth century. This Muslim city comes alive at night, and we walk for hours through narrow cobblestone passageways, ducking into art galleries and spas. In the main plaza, we barter over the cost of seared-meat kabobs in the night market and fan our tongues at the eleven-spice marinade. Ordering fresh-squeezed cane juice, we watch the long, fibrous stalks get cranked through a press to produce juice in a plastic cup. These perennial grasses grow two to six meters tall and are a good source of antioxidants and vitamin C. I watch Dave take a hesitant sip, think about whether he likes it, then gulp down the rest.

Although we've had some serious ups and downs, I've discovered something about Dave: When he commits, he's there to stay. It's hard to hide who you really are when you spend 24/7 with someone under challenging circumstances, and we've each seen plenty of unattractive and undesirable traits in the other. But Dave's resolute love for me is something I've never felt from anyone outside of family. I'm letting him in. Maybe that's why I haven't always recognized myself lately; Dave is one of very few people I let my guard down around, and I'm changing. We don't have it all figured out yet, but we're learning how to be together.

We return the following day to Dar es Salaam and check on our Kenyan visas. They're ready, so we can get back on the road. I don't feel as rested as I'd hoped, but I'm excited for the next phase of our travels. We'll soon be in Nairobi, where we'll once again deal with the logistics of crating the bikes for a flight. After several months in disorderly Africa, I'm looking forward to orderly Europe.

But unbeknownst to me, Dave has quite the African finale up his sleeve.

Beauty in the breakdown

Having climbed Mount Aconcagua and Denali—two of the seven highest summits of the seven continents—Dave isn't about to pass up on a third. Kilimanjaro is the highest mountain in Africa. It rises 19,341 feet straight out of the coffee and banana plantations near Moshi, Tanzania.

"Kili" is also the world's largest freestanding mountain, meaning it's a straight shot starting from 2,300 feet all the way to its conical volcano summit. This is unlike Denali or Everest, which are given a buoyant lift on the shoulders of subalpine ranges.

When we decided to ride through Africa, Dave and I discussed climbing Kilimanjaro. As we got closer to making the decision—and my body was feeling more trashed—I put the idea out of my mind.

But it turns out to be top of mind for Dave.

After so long sitting on a motorcycle, I'm not sure we're in good enough shape to climb a mountain, but we really have the ideal scenario. Dave's uncle has a friend named Peter who lives in Moshi with his wife, Rose, and they welcome us to stay in their home. Peter and Rose have two houses on their property behind an electric security gate, and we're set up in the smaller of the two, reserved for guests. The furniture is sparse and the white-tiled floor immaculate. As always, I feel guilty bringing in our dusty, soiled gear. Peter insists we make ourselves at home.

Settling in, I ask Rose if I can do laundry, thinking that with two homes and a security gate, the middle-class family must have a washer and dryer. Rose tells me to bring her our bag of dirty clothes. I don't want her going out of her way to load our stuff into the washer. I can do that. But Rose is insistent, so I leave her with the bag and carry on with my cleaning spree. When I walk into the yard to shake out our tent on the grass, I'm mortified to see Rose elbows-deep in a plastic tub of sudsy water, scrubbing Dave's cheese-smelling socks. I rush over.

"Oh no, Rose, please let me do that!"

A shy, kindhearted woman, Rose is taken aback, perhaps thinking I'm angry that she's washing the socks the wrong way or something.

"I thought you might have had a washing machine," I say, knowing how ignorant I sound. "You know? Those machines that spin and wash the clothes?"

After a lot of *I'm sorry*-ing and *what-I-meant*s, Rose and I start to understand each other and burst out laughing.

I take over, and Rose shows me how she washes larger, heavier items like jeans. First, a dunk in the soapy water and a vigorous scrubbing over a washboard, then a dunk in a second tub to remove the soap, and finally several dunks in a third tub of clear water. It's a great arm workout. We work quietly together, standing up off our little stools to hang dripping clothes on a wire strung between two banana trees.

Dinner is just Dave, Peter, and me. Rose eats behind a closed kitchen door with another woman who I think is their house helper. Eating without Rose seems odd after she's prepared the delicious meat stew for us, but in many parts of Africa, it's tradition and an act of love to serve the husband or men first.

Peter is a reverend. As with most religions, he's an ambassador of faith and is in a position of power to judge sinful behavior and spread calm and hope among his people. But he also seems like a down-to-earth, modern guy. It's not as if he asked to see our marriage certificate or anything, and we are strangers in his home. I want to ask him questions, but pointing out that Dave and I are "living in sin" in the house right next door or asking whether Rose can come to the table might make me seem even more daft than the washing machine comment.

When Dave tells Peter we're thinking of climbing Kilimanjaro—"the impossible safari," in the region's tribal language of Chagga—Peter gets excited. He knows of a reputable guiding service who can take us.

Being guided up the mountain is mandatory and part of the permitting system. It also ensures local employment. Since we have somewhere to stay, Dave and I don't need to worry about our bikes or gear, either. With all these logistics in place, it makes sense to go up the mountain. Still, I resist. All I want lately is to relax the minute I get off my bike until the minute I get back on.

As usual, I promise to "sleep on it," which usually means not sleeping at all and instead lying awake most of the night, overthinking. What's the issue? All we really need to do is pay our money and start walking uphill. The porters will carry everything we need, like tents, sleeping bags, and food. Dave and I only need light daypacks for water and snacks.

A big reason I'm hesitating is the cost. It's not cheap to climb Kiliman-jaro. We'll have to pay $830 each just for the park/permit fees, then an additional $750 per person for the guided climb. Really, it's a small price to pay to access one of the Seven Summits; Mount Everest comes with a price tag between $50,000 and $75,000.

Also, there's the concern of weather. It can be 90°F in the valley bottom and just 40°F or colder at the top. Big mountains create their own weather patterns. The peak might be soaked in rain or even snow while people are wiping sweat from their brows in Moshi.

I toss and turn then chastise myself. *Why are you overthinking this? You decided to ride a motorcycle around the world in two seconds flat!*

On the morning of April 15, we leave Peter and Rose's house in a van with eleven strong, lean porters and two guides. I'm shocked so many locals are employed just to take a couple of white folks hiking for six days. It seems ironic, because the more people we have with us, the more food, and therefore weight, these guys must carry. But it's also nice to help provide jobs—even temporarily—for thirteen men who might be feeding families.

After a hearty lunch of hard-boiled eggs, fried chicken, and fruit, Dave and I start up the trail with Kidu, the main guide, and his assistant, nicknamed Good Luck. I'm floored when some of the porters catch up and I see one of them carrying a propane tank strapped to his back. Another balances a folding table on his head and carries a bag in each hand.

Remembering our not-so-awesome "guided" climb up Volcan Acatenango in Antigua, I wonder if we'll again be eating ramen noodles and foraging for our own firewood. But we soon find out that Peter has made an excellent recommendation; this climb is an entirely different experience.

At the end of each day, our tent—supplied by the guiding company and much roomier than the one we've been using—is set up for us on arrival, sleeping bags laid out inside. Two bowls of hot water are placed at the door alongside a bar of soap and a washcloth for cleaning up. The dining tent—large enough to stand in and with an actual table and chairs—seduces us with nutrient-rich snacks and meals. Everything is set out just for the two of us, and it was all brought up on the backs and heads of eleven happy, smiling, singing men. Somehow, even though Dave, Good Luck, Kidu, and I leave an hour before the porters each morning, they get to camp well before us.

Given that we're being waited on hand and foot, Dave and I are more convinced than ever that the next five days will be a cakewalk. We cover a very doable average of five miles a day, carrying lightweight packs and secretly feeling that the pace is too slow. We know, however, that our lungs will acclimate better to the high-altitude air at this pace, and we need to be patient. Kidu and Good Luck remind us constantly, *"pole, pole,"* which rhymes with "slowly, slowly," and means exactly that in Swahili. Too often, climbers succumb to cerebral or pulmonary edema, which is when the brain or lungs fill with fluid from pushing too high too fast.

The first three days are easy. Each morning, noon, and night, Kidu tests our oxygen levels with a finger clip. If our heart rate and blood pressure aren't optimal, we'll be sent down the trail. We've never been monitored like this before, and I enjoy tracking the numbers. Of course, Dave and I turn it into a competition.

"What's your oxygen percentage reading?"

"Ninety-two."

"Ha! Mine's Ninety-six."

You can't argue with science.

Calorie-rich meals fill our plates daily: sausage, eggs, and toast for breakfast; sandwiches, eggs, and chicken for lunch; soup and salted popcorn as snacks before dinner, which is usually a meat and vegetable stew, rice or pasta, and fresh fruit. Plenty of hot and cold liquids keep us warm and hydrated. I'm impressed with the cook, who prepares everything while sitting cross-legged in a small tent, his hands rapidly moving in and out through the door flap toward steaming pots on an outdoor burner.

The scenery and environment on Kilimanjaro are different from anything I've seen in my mountain life. Huge plants called *groundsels* rise several feet on thin stalks only six inches in diameter. They sprout wide and wildly at the top into what look like massive pineapples. On lower slopes of the volcano, red, sword-shaped flowers called *gladiolus watsonioides* and *impatiens kilimanjari*, shaped like tiny elephant trunks, bloom bright with color in the rocky landscape. Dave takes a photo of me standing beside a giant heather plant growing well above my head. I've never seen this flowering brush so tall. At home, they are just tiny buds that sit in small clusters in the alpine, almost flush to the ground.

I feel more energized than I have in weeks, maybe even months. Dave also seems to have an extra hop in his step.

I wake at 12,975 feet on the morning of our fourth day, anticipating our summit push. Like every mountaineer everywhere, I'm praying for clear skies when I unzip the tent fly. Instead, it's dark, gloomy, and wet outside. I dunk my hands into the bowl of hot water to warm my fingers. Sitting with my sleeping bag still wrapped around my lower half, I look around for the summit, but it's obscured by low-hanging clouds. I hope we haven't paid this much to see nothing at the top.

Before leaving my warm bedding, I fish for every bit of clothing I have. Because we have limited space on the bikes, Dave and I have improvised our climbing attire for this trek. Back in Moshi, I removed the quilted and rain layers from my riding pants and brought them along. This is the first day I put them both on over my hiking pants. I find my long-sleeved wool top and pull it over my wool T-shirt, under which is a tank top. Next, I add my favorite piece of gear—a puffy down jacket. It's not raining anymore, so I leave my waterproof jacket in the tent. Grabbing my hat, or toque as we Canadians say, I plunge out the door to the breakfast tent. Dave is already there, having beaten me in the getting-dressed game. He's sipping a cup of powdered coffee.

Seconds after my butt is in the chair, Riziki, one of the porters, brings me black tea just the way I like it: brewed strong and heavily laced with cream and sugar. My England-born mom has bequeathed me her love of tea. I've never been a regular coffee drinker.

"Breakfast is soon!" Riziki says, already covering the doorway with the canvas flap to keep our body heat in.

Kidu gives a soft tap at the door.

"Good morning," he says, gently taking my finger for the oxygen test then moving over to Dave. We both pass. "Our plan today," Kidu continues, "is to hike to summit camp—five or six hours, not including stops. Then we have a hot meal. I strongly suggest afterward you sleep, even though it will only be late afternoon. We will rise around midnight and climb to the top, weather permitting." Kidu crosses his fingers. I cross all of mine and my toes.

A lot of summit attempts start in the middle of the night. Colder temps keep rocks and other debris glued to the slopes, and leaving early means climbers can maximize daylight. In this case, there's also another reason: Leaving at midnight will allow us to reach the summit at dawn. Watching the sun rise below you is always an incredible experience.

Ascending that day, the landscape changes from lush plant life to rock and ice. We don't need full-on climbing gear for this summit, like ice axes and crampons, but if it snows, the steep slopes will be challenging in our lightweight hiking shoes.

Perhaps we should have thought about training a little before scaling one of the world's tallest mountains. We're athletic in general, and riding every day still requires a lot of fitness, but hiking at altitude uses a totally different set of muscles. Dave and I are starting to feel the effects of lower oxygen levels, and we both have headaches, despite constantly hydrating and going slowly.

Arriving in the summit camp at 15,331 feet, I immediately go to our tent for a nap. Two hours later, around 6 p.m., I'm woken from a dead sleep by Riziki telling me it's dinnertime. I roll over to see Dave rubbing his eyes awake. I didn't even hear him come in.

Unzipping the tent fly, I almost cry. Snow covers everything in a white blanket. It isn't deep, but it is enough to make me think that climbing to the summit is out of the question. We don't have the right footwear to be slogging up a mountain in the snow.

Wet clumps slide off the tent flap when I push it aside. In the kitchen tent, I hardly eat a bite—a side effect of my body using its resources to adjust to the rarefied air. I try not to think about what climbing Kilimanjaro has cost us financially, and now we won't even make it all the way.

Dave and I say nothing to each other. He looks even more remorseful than I feel. I leave a large pile of food on my plate and am about to go back to the tent when Kidu pops inside.

"The weather isn't as good as hoped for," he says, "but we will attempt the climb tonight."

"Really?" Dave and I look at each other.

"Yes, it will be fine. Not much more snow is coming. Eat then sleep. We leave at midnight sharp."

After learning we're ascending, not descending, I stuff as much food in me as I can stomach so I'll have enough calories.

The next five and a half hours pass slowly. I want to fall back asleep, but I'm buzzing with excitement and trepidation. Does Kidu know what he's doing? Earlier, I glanced at the steep slope out of camp, and it looked potentially deadly if one of us missed our footing. I lie still, listening to Dave's gentle snoring, and try to barter with my body: *You need sleep and nourishment, or you won't be able to summit.*

Just as I drift off, Riziki's voice beckons me from my dreams.

"Time to get up," he calls softly.

Waking for the third time in twenty-four hours—and now in the middle of the night—is impossible for my brain to comprehend. I can't think straight, and my eyes keep shutting. Dave leans over to pull on shoes that barely cover his ankles.

Kidu meets us in the kitchen tent and tests our heart rate and oxygen levels again. Despite feeling half dead, we both have healthy readings. At midnight on the dot, five of us leave camp, our headlamps lighting the way with a soft glow off the snow and rock. Good Luck, Kidu, Dave, and I plod forward, along with one other porter who wanted to join us "just for fun."

For the first while, I feel as expected for having had just a few hours of on-and-off sleep and then asking my body to climb a mountain in the dark. Four hours in, around the 16,000-foot mark, my head starts to hurt—common at high altitude. I think about asking Kidu for some pain killers but don't want to get drowsy.

Again, I negotiate with myself: *Focus on the next landmark, nothing further.* I can't fathom going another 3,000 feet, despite trying this mind trick athletes sometimes use to make forward progress. *Come on, you've done this before.* I've woken up many times for an alpine start in the single-digit morning hours to start huffing uphill with a heavy pack. Today, I'm carrying just a day pack with water. Like a light turning on, my body recognizes the slow torture I'm about to put it through and begins to rise to the occasion. We slog uphill behind Kidu, who chants *"pole, pole"* and *"hakuna matata"* ("no worries") every so often. The scree slope is steep and rocky, but there's no more snow falling, and what's left is only a few inches deep.

Although I'm hiking uphill, I can't get warm. My down jacket is zipped to my chin, the hood drawn tight around my face. It's 15°F, a shock to our systems after spending the last eleven weeks in weather over 90 degrees. My head aches worse now, and my stomach feels like I've swallowed some of the rocks on the trail. I want to barf, or cry, or shit myself, just to feel some release, but I keep all fluids inside except pee; they're vital to staying hydrated and sustained.

To pass the time, I guess how many footsteps it will take me to get to my chosen landmark, then start counting. I feel some sense of satisfaction when I'm correct to within a step or two.

Every few minutes, I scan the slopes below for Dave. He's a few switchbacks behind me and Kidu, and he's suffering. Good Luck hikes with him, but I'm getting more concerned about my boyfriend; I've never seen him struggle like this before. Back in oxygen-rich Moshi, we joked about our lack of training for this climb, but it's the opposite of funny now. It doesn't take much fluid to enter the brain or lungs and become an emergency.

Kidu and I wait on the trail for Dave and Good Luck. I appreciate the rest, but my legs can't hold my weight anymore. I sink to the ground and roll onto my back, feeling like an Everest climber but knowing this is nothing like what they endure. That mountain is close to 10,000 feet taller, way colder, and a hell of a lot more technical.

I can just make out the silhouette of the summit above, where the sky is still dark without a single star. Kidu informs me we have only a mile to go, but there's still 1,300 feet of elevation left before we get to the highest spot in Africa.

When Dave arrives with the other guide, I smile and say, "Looks like you have good luck following you everywhere you go."

Dave doesn't laugh. Instead, he bends at the waist, and his heavy breathing makes me nervous.

"Are you okay, babe?"

"Yeah," he breathes.

After a few minutes, Dave walks over to some large boulders. I think he's peeing, but he braces himself against a rock. I walk over and put a hand on his back. The porter has taken Dave's lightweight pack, because every little bit helps. When I get closer, I'm alarmed to see tears streaming down Dave's face.

"I've never been so exhausted in my life," he says. "I don't think I can go any farther."

When Dave climbed Aconcagua and Denali, he was younger, but he also spent more time acclimatizing—weeks, in fact. In hindsight, the four days we spent climbing to this altitude may not have been enough. I don't want to push Dave in a way that risks his health, but I know he'll regret giving up on the summit if he turns around now.

"It's okay," I say, "just give yourself a few minutes. We can wait here as long as you need."

We can't, though. It's too cold, and we should keep moving.

Dave starts to cry openly, no longer holding back. *Oh my god, does he need medical attention? Is he having a breakdown?* I'm about to call Kidu for help when Dave says, "I just…really wanted the summit to be special. For us."

"Hey," I rub his shoulders. "I get it." Or at least I think I do. I'd been complaining again about doing too much riding and not enough time off the bikes. Dave is trying to show me he listens. Still, his reaction seems over the top; is he that upset about how much we spent to reach the summit and not getting his money's worth? Is he embarrassed? "I don't want you hurting yourself just to get to the top."

We hug, and Dave buries his face in my neck.

"You're so strong," he says, surprising me with the vulnerable compliment. I feel some relief that his reaction seems to be coming from a rare but intense feeling of letting himself down, not anything requiring emergency attention. But the raw emotion catches me off guard. Dave is taking this climb far more seriously than me.

"Do you want to go down?" I ask, hoping he'll say no.

"Yes."

It's the most dejected I've ever seen him, and now I have a selfish thought. I want to keep going.

"I'll go tell Kidu," I say. "For what it's worth, you're the strong one, making this decision to go down. It's a smart call." I wait a beat then ask, "How would you feel if I keep going? I may not make it, but I want to try."

Dave nods. "I really want you to keep going. You'll love it up there. Mountains are your happy place."

And yours, I want to add.

Walking back to our guides and porter, I tell them Dave wants to descend.

"But I'd like to keep going," I say firmly.

Kidu stares at me with a question on his face. I'm about to defend my decision when I realize he's actually looking behind me. Without a word to any of us, Dave is walking. Uphill. Altitude sickness can affect people's judgment, and I wonder if Dave is confused about what he just told me. Or thinks up is down.

The three of us follow in silence. Sometimes it's just a matter of breaking past the mental barrier.

I trust Kidu and Good Luck, who don't feel Dave is suffering from anything more than extreme fatigue. As mountain guides, they see people working through mental roadblocks all the time and have a sixth sense for when someone's pushing too far or just enough. That, after all, is why people do these things—to test their upper limits of strength and become stronger in doing so.

When Dave slows to a crawl and my own crawling is slightly faster, he steps aside to let me pass. But he keeps walking. At this point he feels worse than any of us, yet he's found something deep within to motivate himself. I'm impressed.

Finally, half an hour later, we're on the summit ridgeline—all five of us together and not another soul in sight. The slope is less steep now, and the sky is turning into the pale pink of dawn.

"No clouds!" I cheer.

The sun hits my back, and it feels like the temperature just went up 30 degrees. Dave visibly perks up. We're within a few hundred easy feet of the summit. I'm fixated on the wooden sign that will confirm we're the highest humans in all of Africa and in many parts of the world at that very moment.

Oh my god, we're doing it!

When there's no more mountain left to climb, I turn to Dave for a hug, but he stops me. It's then, at 6:45 a.m. on April 19, 2017, that I learn why Dave pushed himself so hard.

Taking my gloved hand in his, he says, "I was going to get down on one knee, but I can't right now."

He laughs, and I start to cry. Hugging me to his chest, Dave whispers, "Will you marry me?"

It's been three years, almost exactly to the day, since Dave and I met. On our first date backcountry skiing together near Mount Baker, twelve hours passed in the blink of an eye. Now, on top of another volcano—and just like when Dave asked me the first big question that would change my life forever—I reply an exuberant "yes" before he even finishes the question.

We hug for so long our legs give out and we almost fall over. Kidu and Good Luck come over to give us high fives and take our photo in front of the Kilimanjaro summit sign.

"I was waiting for a time when she was in an oxygen-deprived state of mind," Dave jokes, back to his old self.

I want to stay on the roof of Africa and savor this life-changing moment longer, but we're all very cold.

The descent takes a fraction of the time it took to climb up. I feel like I'm floating and force myself to stop running downhill. In a swift two and a half hours—compared to six on the way up—I'm already back in camp. Dave's behind me, favoring an old knee injury that flared up on this climb. At the tent, I kick off my frozen solid shoes and nestle deep into my sleeping bag. I'm grateful for the time to myself to take it all in. Not only did I just summit the highest peak on this continent, I also received what must have been one of the best—and loftiest—marriage proposals on earth.

Dave and I have talked before about what to do when our life on the road ends and we go home. Living in two different countries poses a considerable challenge, and a shimmer of anxiety comes when I think about it. I will likely be the one leaving my home country. As a writer, I can work from anywhere, and Dave already has clients and contacts for his carpentry business in Bellingham. I push the nervous thoughts from my mind. These are discussions we can have later. For now, I want to coast on the endorphins. When I was single, I wondered if I'd ever meet someone I'd want to share my life with, let alone marry. Once I was nearing forty, with no long-term relationships under my belt, I was starting to think there was something wrong with me.

Yet here I am. With someone who shares my thirst for adventure and pushes me to challenge myself. And hopefully I do the same for him.

When Dave flops into the tent an hour later, we snuggle together and drift off to sleep. It's 10 a.m. We've accomplished enough for the day.

Peter and Rose are overjoyed to hear we got engaged on Kilimanjaro. When we say goodbye to them on their driveway a few days later, glowing and recovered from the climb, they're each dressed in their best clothes to see us off. This is a formal occasion to them, and it touches my heart that we're treated like honored guests. Earlier, Dave and I went shopping and left two bags of groceries as a gift in our room. I know if we handed the food to them personally, they'd refuse.

I'm strapping luggage to my bike when Rose hands me a package. I recognize the spices inside. One afternoon, I was walking between the two houses and noticed a mat in the backyard with piles of drying cinnamon sticks and cardamom pods.

"Do you use those to make your delicious chai?" I asked Rose.

"Yes," she answered. "Yesterday, I harvested the plants in the forest, and now they will dry."

Every afternoon during our stay, Rose called us over for tea and cookies in their living room. I've had chai tea before, but nothing tasted as rich and creamy and wonderful as Rose's home-brewed version.

I gratefully accept the spices and carry them all the way back to Canada months later. When I try to replicate Rose's chai at home, it's never as good.

The time is now!

Riding away from Moshi, we have views of Kilimanjaro—the first time we've been able to see the whole mountain rising out of the savanna. I smile again, thinking about Dave's proposal and how hard he worked to make the moment special.

Following the smooth, recently tarred pavement, we both must be daydreaming as two policemen standing on the shoulder ahead catch us off guard.

Here we go again. I steel myself for a battle with corrupt cops or questions about how much our bikes cost. We'd been flagged down a lot lately for illegitimate speeding fines that couldn't be proven. Mostly, we pretended to care, then rode off. The fake cops had no radios or even a chase vehicle.

Now, however, a broad-shouldered officer walks over with a legit-looking radar gun. He shows us actual photos of two speeding motorcycle riders. They look just like us. I want to ask if there's some way I can have the photos. Dave and I have no shots of us riding together. *Can you text those to me?* I almost say.

Under the photo of Dave, I see "72 kmph." My speed is just slightly less. Looking at where the officer is pointing, I read a sign: 15 KMPH. *Holy shit.* At home, such a speed discrepancy would get our bikes impounded and our licenses revoked. I'm nervous about how this will go down. There's no arguing our way out of this one, and the officers have radios and a police truck, so we can't just ride away.

I follow Officer Jesmond over to their setup beside a massively thick-trunked baobab. Now I understand why these stakeouts are always behind trees or buildings: for shade from the blazing sun.

Jesmond pulls a sheaf of papers in front of him. Flipping to a blank form, he fires questions at me:

"Where do you live?"

"Canada."

"What is the make of your motorcycle?"

"BMW F800GS."

"What year?"

"2016."

"How many childrens?"

What? "None."

My answer stops Jesmond mid-scribble.

"Nine?"

"No, none. Zero." I hold my thumb and forefinger in an O.

What do kids have to do with getting a speeding ticket?

Jesmond drops his pen and looks me up and down. We're off the record now.

"No childrens? How old are you?"

Wow, point blank. Okay then.

"Forty-three."

"And no childrens?" he scoffs. "What's wrong with you?"

I'm not offended. Most of our days are spent learning how other cultures operate, and I don't mind enlightening this middle-aged man on mine.

"There's nothing wrong with me, sir. My husband—" I stop briefly, enjoying how the word feels on my tongue "—and I have decided to spend this time in our lives traveling instead of chasing after kids. Where I'm from, this is accepted and common."

The officer *tsk-tsk's* at length, unimpressed with my explanation. He looks over at Dave casually eating a granola bar.

"You tell your husband the time is now. *The time is now!*"

I stop myself from calling over to Dave, "Hey, the officer is demanding we have sex *right now!*"

Jesmond fills out the rest of the paperwork, blowing air through his teeth and shaking his head the whole time, like he's just heard the world is flat or something. Finally, he presents me with an official ticket—seven dollars per speeder. Not bad for going more than quadruple the speed limit.

The "last" African hurdle

Kenya

Nairobi is our last destination in Africa. Here in Kenya's capital, we're all business, hunkering down on the challenging task of flying our bikes to Europe.

We know TIA, and nothing happens fast in Africa—especially if someone doesn't feel like working that day. This has been evident when trying to get travel visas; at border crossings where officers take three-hour lunch breaks; with banks that close at random times of the day; and restaurants, campgrounds, and hotels that say they're open but are, in fact, shut tighter than a jar of pickles. Having our own transportation is a huge advantage, but we have no control over almost everything else, including the logistics of getting two big motorcycles out of Africa.

Dave started looking for a shipping company weeks in advance. After three attempts to find something affordable, we settled back on our first option—a company with a couple of reviews saying they've dealt with foreign motorcycles.

Initially, the only issue is cost—$4,862. In cash.

Although we have more direct options into Europe, like London or Amsterdam, Dave has a good friend in Scotland, and I have one in England. We've decided to fly the bikes to Glasgow.

Classified as dangerous goods, the bikes will go on a separate cargo plane and are scheduled to leave the day after our passenger flight out of Nairobi. Normally we wouldn't leave before our bikes, but we'll still be here to see them through customs. After that, they're secure and there's no point hanging around without them.

Our passenger flight leaves in seventy-two hours. We arrange with our shipping agent, Irene, to begin crating our bikes for air travel, which is included in the fee. She sends a rep named Joshua to our Airbnb, and he leads us to a back-alley café overly decorated with Coca-Cola advertising.

"This doesn't look—"

"I know," Dave finishes. He asks Joshua what we're doing here. "Where's the shipping warehouse?"

"Here! This is Irene's sister's boyfriend's cousin's place," Joshua answers with a wide, reassuring smile. "It's very fine!"

Joshua is dressed in an olive-green suit, and his black hair is short, tight, and curly, cropped nicely around his neck and ears. He does look professional, but I'm not convinced of this operation. Especially when two older men pull up in a beat-up red pickup. They begin to unload warped and twisted oak two-by-fours—the bulk of which overburdens the tiny truck so much so that the wheels are buried up in its bed.

I want to call Irene, who hasn't been the most reachable person now that she has our money, which we'd gathered and stockpiled in various places on our bikes and persons over the past few weeks. There's nothing sketchier than showing up in Nairobi with almost $5,000 in cash.

"Where is she?" I look around the littered, spraypainted alleyway, half expecting Irene to pop out from behind the garbage cans. I'm naive to think she'd be here doing any dirty work; she's in a skyrise in Mombasa, probably ordering people around, stroking a hairless cat with her long, manicured nails.

A man in jeans and a Nike T-shirt stares at our bikes from the alley, grabbing his crotch like he wants to mate with them. He rolls a toothpick back and forth across his ample lips, making sucking sounds.

"And where do the bikes stay overnight?" Dave asks.

"Don't worry, don't worry," Joshua declares, beaming. "They go inside the nice café. We do this so many times!"

"Really?" I raise my eyebrows. "You lift 500-pound motorcycles up that stairway there and—"

Dave gives me a "be nice" glance.

"We'll come back tomorrow with the bikes and help with the crating," Dave says. "And everything needs to be fumigated, right? Will there be enough time to do all that and get them through customs?"

"Sure, sure." Joshua looks disgruntled now that we don't trust his competence.

I consider postponing our passenger flights to ensure the bikes are dealt with first, but we do have a twenty-four-hour cancellation window.

Thirty-six hours before our flight, we are back at Irene's family ghetto café. Before my already-doubting eyes, Joshua pulls out a measuring tape. He uses chalk to mark the length of our bikes on the ground, then measures the gap. I'm skeptical. Joshua writes a number down on a piece of paper and hands it to one of the two old men from the red truck yesterday. The man, who looks exactly one hundred years old, looks at the paper and begins cutting the oak two-by-fours with a hand saw. It takes two hours to make one crate. The men do not use a single power tool. Everything is measured and then the heavy oak is hand sawn. Nails get hammered in manually. It's an unexpected work of art, but Dave and I are impatient with the slow pace. Dave aches to do things more efficiently, and I know he's dreaming about the dozen drills he has in storage back home.

I hop from foot to foot, wishing I'd brought my laptop. I had no idea we'd be here for several hours; it only took fifteen minutes to crate the Black Stallion with power tools and a hydraulic lift back in Fairbanks, Alaska.

Twenty-eight hours before our flight, both bikes are finally boxed and ready for fumigation, but it's 6 p.m. now and that office is closed. We have to wait until morning. Dave and I leave the ghetto with Joshua's assurance that the crates will be loaded onto a flatbed truck and kept in a secure building overnight. I think this is the most trusting we've ever had to be. They have our cash and our bikes; who's to say they won't put them on a truck and drive them off to sell on the black market?

Dave and I cross our fingers and go for pizza.

Twelve hours before our flight, Joshua picks up Dave, and together with the driver, they leave in the flatbed loaded with two large wooden boxes I hope contain our bikes.

Dave's gone all day. I sit in the Airbnb chewing my nails and reading his email updates to me complaining about how everything is taking forever. There's no forklift at the fumigation office, because TIA, so Joshua spends an hour wrangling up nine men who agree to lift the crates—which, with a motorcycle, riding gear, panniers, and all that oak, must each weigh close to half a ton now—out of the back of the truck. Then the crates are pried open to be fumigated (I wrapped all my clothes and cooking gear in extra plastic) and heaved back onto the truck.

Our twenty-four-hour cancellation policy came and went at 10 p.m. the night before. Even with prepping weeks in advance, flight arrangements and logistics are always last minute and stressful. To distract myself, I write a blog post.

In the eighty days since landing on the continent, Dave and I have ridden over 7,000 miles through nine countries: South Africa, Lesotho, Namibia, Botswana, Zimbabwe, Zambia, Malawi, Tanzania, and Kenya. We endured heat exhaustion and high-altitude sickness; avoided head-on collisions and other near misses; deflected corrupt cops and border guards; paid a thousand dollars in travel visas, road taxes, and mandatory insurance; and paid sixty dollars in traffic fines.

It's intense. It's all encompassing. But this is Africa. With its poverty, disorder, and corruption, Africa can be hard to love, yet it also makes my heart soar. The stunning beauty, people, and experiences will never leave my memory. Nothing feels quite as foreign or adventurous as three months of traveling through contrasting climate zones with an astounding diversity of environments, economies, historical ties, and government systems. Africa will always live in my heart as the place where I took my first safari, raced a giraffe across the Namib Desert, improved my skills in shifting sand and corrugated gravel, climbed the continent's highest mountain and, most memorable of all, got engaged.

Despite the warnings, I never feared the people here. In all of my travels, I don't recall a society who smiles as beautifully and wholeheartedly as Africans do.

I'll be back, but in this moment, I can't wait to be gone.

Dave finally comes through the door at 7 p.m. Since most of our gear is packed with the bikes, we only have carry-on bags. We grab them and run to the street to hail a cab.

Where are our bikes?

Scotland

Through the wonder of jet travel, Dave and I are whisked from developing-world limitations to first-world conveniences in eleven hours and thirteen minutes. I'm still thinking of the orphaned boys and girls I saw wearing only one shoe or dirty, ripped clothing. And those we stayed with, who'd be considered low-income or downright poor where I live. What if they could be transported into another world this fast, leaving scarcity, famine, and disease behind in a flash, like we can?

Landing in Glasgow, we take a train to Edinburgh three hours away, then meet up with Dave's longtime friend, Andy, in a pub. Every surface seems made from black walnut or mahogany. Its dark interior creates a warmth that is enhanced watching my fiancé reunite with his old climbing buddy. It's such a nice feeling to see someone familiar when you're so far from home.

Andy and Dave worked at an outdoors store in their twenties and have had many mountain adventures together, including summitting Denali. Somewhere along the way, Andy met his wife, Rachel, and they moved to Scotland, closer to her family. They have one son: a ten-year-old named Francis.

Andy congratulates us on our engagement. After a couple rounds, the three of us take a bus back to the Heins' house, where Rachel and Francis are expecting us. Over dinner, we answer questions about how things are going so far.

"Welllll…" Dave and I chuckle and look at each other.

"We were naive about how demanding it would be to ride almost every day for two years," I say. "I want to go way off the beaten track and explore, but the minute I see a tough road section ahead filled with mud or embedded rocks, I know the amount of energy it's going to take, and I waver."

"Then she drops her bike," Dave rolls his eyes, "and I have to hike back and pick it up…"

"Not always," I defend, "but, yeah, I do go down a lot, which is not only tiring but demoralizing, too."

"But surely you're both becoming fitter, better riders each day?" Andy says.

"Definitely," I agree, telling them switching to the F800 was a game changer. "But I don't feel like I'm recuperating well, even on rest days. This isn't the kind of tiredness that resets after a good night's sleep. It's bone-deep fatigue. At least for me."

"Are you eating well? It must be hard to find all the nutrients you need when traveling," Rachel says.

I nod, swallowing a hearty sip of wine. "It is. We eat a lot of starchy, processed carbs. They're easy to come by and don't go bad. Dinners almost everywhere we go in the world are chicken and rice or fries. And very few vegetables. But we've also had some of the best food of our liv—"

"Oh!" Dave cuts in. "Did I tell you about the pork knuckle I got in Namibia?"

"Come on, babe, I don't think we need to go on about that!" I laugh. "Luckily, we're not picky eaters or allergic to anything. I can't imagine being gluten free or vegetarian; that would be really limiting."

It's cathartic to be with good friends and talk honestly about how long-distance traveling really feels. I make a point of listing some highlights, like when a stranger arrives at just the right moment; turning a corner in the road to find breathtaking scenery; how it feels when I master my motorcycle on difficult terrain; and the moments when I realize I'm one in a million or more who gets to do something like this in life.

"And what about the motorbikes?" Andy asks.

"Yeah!" Francis perks up, "when do they arrive?"

"We should get an email in the next day or two," Dave says.

That day or two goes by with no confirmation that the bikes have even left Nairobi yet. Dave calls the cargo airline and learns that Irene "forgot" to pay them. The bikes missed their flight. I feel sick to my stomach. We handed over thousands of dollars in cash and left our bikes behind on another continent.

"How could we be so stupid?" Alone in Andy and Rachel's townhouse, I use every swear word in my vocabulary. "Our bikes are probably for sale right now on the Nairobi black market!"

"People can't just walk in and take something from customs. You know that."

Dave is using that voice that might just push me too far. I know he's thinking the same thing, even though he was there with the carnet throughout the process.

Grabbing my laptop off the couch, we use Skype to call Irene, who conveniently leaves the video off, claiming a bad internet connection. She reminds us she's a very busy woman and that forgetting to pay the cargo company was a mere oversight. "They will be on the next flight, May 8," she says dismissively.

"What?" I screech. "That's ten days away!"

We're doing a presentation at BMW Edinburgh the day after tomorrow. Part of the talk is showcasing our round-the-world bikes and how we pack our luggage. Now, along with her hairless cat, I imagine Irene's Cruella-like nails gripping a bottle of expensive red wine while she forgets to do things like work.

Dave hangs up after threating that if we don't get confirmation from the cargo airline right away that payment has been made, he'll fly back to Nairobi and show up at Irene's sister's cousin's boyfriend's whatever's café and come looking for her. Irene probably thinks we won't spare the expense, but those bikes are our whole world right now.

"Mother of a shitload of assholes," I cry.

Dave spits out his English breakfast tea.

"You're really getting creative with the swearing there," he says. "Is one curse word just not enough for you anymore?" I start laughing through my anger. "Let's just see how May 8 goes."

Adding forty-five dollars to our Skype credit, we call Irene and the cargo company every two days to make sure everyone is staying on track. I don't care if we seem uptight; a lot of money and value are at stake.

May 8 comes and goes. Nothing from the cargo agent. Nothing from Irene. Another phone call informs us that, yes, the payment was made, however, the bikes are still not on any flights to Glasgow. The holdup is confusion over the bike owners (us) having a US address when the cargo (our bikes) is being sent to the United Kingdom.

This time, it's Dave who loses it.

"Why wasn't this mentioned at customs?" he demands.

I'm glad the Hein residence is empty during the day due to work and school schedules so we can have our daily TIA cursing rants.

Dave's able to show the cargo agent our carnet de passage through the video call. Traveling around the world by motorcycle is done by far more people than I thought, but it's still rare enough that not everybody understands what we're doing and why. The carnet helps explain our address dilemma, and the agent promises the bikes will fly at the next available opportunity. But he can't tell us when, since they're now on a flight waiting list.

Evenings with Andy and Rachel are our stress reprieve. We drink too much, laugh a lot, and tell stories. Dave and I apologize for overstaying. We've been in their home for two weeks now, unfolding the pullout couch every night, smack in the middle of their living room. Being able to stay with friends during this debacle and not paying for a hotel is a huge help and makes the circumstances a lot more fun. For us, anyway; I'm sure our friends want their living room back.

On weekends, Andy and Rachel take us camping, hiking, and to the climbing gym. Coming straight from the heat of Africa to spring in Scotland, Dave and I are wimps in the chilly highland winds. Most of our clothing is with the bikes—including my cherished down jacket—so we borrow sweaters and hats.

On May 10, we receive an email with an air waybill listing two items for pickup in Glasgow.

"They're here!" I shout to Dave, who's in the kitchen making his morning coffee.

We take the train three hours back to the port city, excited yet nervous; there's always a risk the bikes have been damaged in transit. Did the handcrafted wooden crates hold up?

At customs, a clearance agent named James deals with our paperwork.

"I've not seen anything like this in all me forty-seven years workin' 'ere," he says, scratching his head about the carnet.

Of course, this means James has no idea how to release our bikes to us.

"Awfully sorry, but could you come back in two hours?" he asks.

"Can you at least tell us if the bikes are here?" I ask.

"I don't know what's 'ere, lass, but for two large wooden crates weighin' several hoondred pounds."

I want to see with my own eyes, but that info will suffice for now.

We walk for forty-five minutes and only find a gas station, where we buy packaged sandwiches. Dave decides we should take a bus back to the cargo agency. He's hungover from a night on the town with Andy. While we sit on a bench waiting for the bus, a prostitute plunks down beside me and unapologetically snorts a line of coke off her grimy wrist. A crackhead standing behind her and missing most of his teeth hollers, "Give me shome of that fucking shtuff!"

I can't wait to have our own transportation again.

Back at the agency, James greets us with, "Awfully sorry mates, but there's a wee problem with the carnets. They…emmm…don't appear to be legal here?"

"Carnets aren't even needed for the UK," Dave says. "I just showed them to you to speed up the importing process."

James explains that because "United Kingdom" isn't printed on the documents, it isn't legal for him to release our vehicles to us. Dave argues back that, again, if the UK doesn't require a carnet de passage then why would the country be on the list?

"Ah yes, well, there's someone who'll know 'ow to deal with this, perhaps," James says, "but she's not 'ere until tomorrow."

"Of course she's not." I slap my forehead.

Dave and I have been at the agency now half the day. It took us three hours and a hundred dollars to get here by train. Adding the cost of going back to Edinburgh and returning the next day—at fifty dollars per person, each way—we consider getting a hotel but settle on renting a car. James, feeling "awfully bad," drives us to the rental agency and offers to pick us up when we return the car. James is a good chap.

Somehow, overnight our bikes are released from customs; someone talked to someone who talked to someone, and we find out the next morning we can retrieve them. Thrilled, we drive back to Glasgow, drop off the rental, and get into James's car. When he lets us into the warehouse, Dave and I rush to the crates. The solid oak boxes are completely intact. As the squeaky sound of nails being pulled from wood fills the air, I have tears in my eyes. I've missed my girl.

Jewelry from another man

England

Despite setbacks, we are back on the road by mid-May. After crossing into England, we arrive in Penrith to visit a friend of mine. In the late nineties, Jenny and I both had jobs at the Alpine Club of Canada in Canmore, Alberta. Not only did we work side by side, but we lived, cooked, and adventured together as well. When I was let go because they could only keep one of us on, and Jenny was chosen, I felt like my life had crumbled: I no longer had a job or a place to live, and my best friend wasn't around anymore.

Uncertain what was next, I got into my Jeep Comanche and used everything in my savings account to fund a climbing road trip around Washington, Oregon, and California. When Jenny moved to England to marry a Scottish mountaineer she'd met at the ACC, we barely saw each other again. But every now and then, we'd check in.

It's great to see her now, waiting for us on the street in her Penrith neighborhood. She's wearing one of her ubiquitous weird T-shirts, which reads something like: "Elvis is my other husband."

During our visit, Jenny, Martin, and their kids, Isla and Lewis, take us hiking and climbing. My old friend and I hang back on the trails with our arms over each other's shoulders, laughing at the same dumb stuff we used to, which usually leaves everyone else confused. I've needed this heartwarming catch-up with her and am sad to leave just five days later.

Riding away from Penrith into the hills, we come across England's highest pub at 1,900 feet. It isn't much of a day for views, and the pub is closed, but there's a takeaway window. Dave orders *chippies* and beef pies, and we eat at a picnic table.

A handful of street riders show up. I have a conversation with an older man, Ron—a happy, excitable person exclaiming over everything around him. As often happens with strangers when you allow yourself to welcome them in, our conversation merges into more than just small talk. When I mention how Dave and I got engaged, Ron yells across the parking lot to his friend.

"Harry!" Ron motions for me to follow him. "These kids got engaged on Kilimanjaro! Harry!"

Harry is over by our bikes, talking with Dave.

"Harry!" Ron is still yelling even though we're right beside them now. "This young man proposed to this young woman on the highest mountain in Africa! And they're traveling around the world on the motorbikes. What a journey!"

Dave and I chuckle at being called "young." Ron's enthusiasm is infectious. I'm laughing again when he enlists a man he doesn't know—who is mid-leg-swing getting off his Ducati—to take a photo of the four of us. When the rider shoots only one, Ron demands he take more. After another shot or two, the man hands Ron back his camera and walks away, shaking his head.

An invite is extended, and suddenly Dave and I are on a day-long adventure, following Ron and Harry to all the cool spots within a hundred-mile radius. We stop at castles and ruins, hitting up ice cream and coffee shops along the way. Ron and Harry never let us pay for a thing.

During lunch, Ron inadvertently insults a café owner by bringing in takeaway fish and chips. The owner looks pointedly into Ron's lap—where our new friend is hiding the greasy paper bag—calls him cheeky, then tells him to eat elsewhere. Ron leaves to eat his meal at a bus stop.

Before going our sperate ways later that afternoon, Ron goes into a gift shop and emerges with a velvet box, which he presents to me without a word. Surprised, I open the box and find a beautiful hematite bracelet.

"It's good luck for your travels," Ron tells me. I'm touched and give him a hug.

"Thank you, Ron. Whenever I wear it, I'll remember you."

"I think that's what he's hoping for," Harry winks.

Riding off, I'm still smiling when Dave's voice comes over my headset.

"You seem to have a way with older men." I can hear the grin in his voice, but I do think it's ironic that the only piece of jewelry I've received while dating Dave has come from another man. Dave did not present me with a ring when he proposed. I didn't expect one. It's safer to leave the bling behind while traveling. Also, it leaves things open to get creative. I'd recently had the idea to combine my Nana's wedding ring and another one I'd inherited of her birthstone into a band when I got home. I think she would have loved that.

Are you going to barf?

France

My tandem pilot and I are strapped together—me in front, him behind, like some kinky getup. A series of thick straps weave through my legs and around my body, more robust than a climbing harness.

"Whatever you do, don't trip," he says.

I'm nervous and nauseous, receiving a lot of instruction from Benoit on how to master the perfect liftoff. Basically, it comes down to *do not trip*.

Karen, a friend I know from Revelstoke, BC, has been staying with her friend in the Alps nearby. She photographs us getting ready with a smile on her face like it isn't the last time she's going to see me. This is comforting. Dave is thirty feet away, getting the same instruction and probably feeling the same stomach-clenching fear and excitement.

The time arrives for our launch into the abyss. An impatient thrill-seeker, I want to get the running-to-the-edge part over with, both because I know how thrilling it will be and because—much like an airplane's take-off and landing—this is the most dangerous part of hang gliding.

I stand there suited up with a helmet on and my fingers crossed. Metallic clicking noises fill my ears while Benoit checks and double checks my harness, then his own. When he asks if I'm ready, I say *sure!* too quickly and loudly.

Let's go, let's go, let's go. Will there be a few seconds of freefall or will the glider catch immediately? Will it be like the time I jumped out of an airplane or that day I missed a hold while climbing and fell until the rope caught me?

Before I can change my mind, Benoit yells, "Run!" Nothing is more of a mindfuck than willing yourself to sprint toward the edge of a cliff and jump. I keep my head up, focusing on a mountain range in the distance.

Lake Annecy glimmers below like the most innocent thing in the world. In the final seconds before we lift off, I'm overcome with terror and my legs almost collapse like wet noodles. *Don't trip!*

Then, there is nothing but air and the sound of my mind being blown. A nanosecond of freefall sends my heart into my throat before the current catches us and lifts the hang glider. *I'm flying!* Tears blur my eyes, both from the wind and emotion. My breath is gone. I want to cheer, but it comes out as a squawk, like when I try to scream in my dreams.

We turn so I can see Dave and his pilot gliding nearby. Together, we whiz over trees so close underfoot I think I might stub my toe on the evergreens. I see the house where we are staying with Karen, surrounded by a pasture-green landscape and rugged peaks. I think about her and why she's here in this beautiful place, healing.

Karen has been living in Montmin on and off for a while now, getting her life back together. A few years ago, she and her husband, Jean-Luc, sold everything they owned—like Dave and I did—and bought a sailboat. They were planning to travel around the world and live on their boat.

One night, while docked in Ladysmith, BC, just after purchasing the sailboat for their journey, Karen's husband dropped dead from a heart attack.

Karen's story is awfully sad, but I've always admired her for what she did next, which was to try and stay the course on their mutual dream—even while navigating what must have been terrible heartache. She enlisted in courses on how to sail and fix the boat, but, after giving it her all, Karen decided the adventure was no longer for her without Jean-Luc. She sold the boat. Karen continues to travel and despite this grief, she always seems to have a quick smile and kind word for anyone and everyone she encounters.

Benoit lets me take the controls. I turn the wing left, then right, left, then right, feeling like the world's biggest autumn leaf fluttering to the ground. My pilot takes back the reigns and calls over my shoulder: "Do you want to do some spins?!"

"Yes!" I shriek.

Autumn leaf turned whirling dervish, we corkscrew through the sky, going faster and faster with every turn.

I'm a bird, I'm flying, I'm doing the coolest thing ever!

I feel the bile rise and try to swallow it by covering my mouth with my hand.

"Are you going to barf?" Benoit's French accent makes everything sound sexy, even a word like "barf."

He jerks me to the right and leans far left. Out comes my breakfast croissant. I watch it cascade down to the traffic below and think I see some drivers turning on their windshield wipers.

Benoit keeps things pretty vanilla for the remainder of our forty-five-minute flight. When we come in for a landing over a large, green meadow, I'm instructed to keep my knees up but not so much that they punch me in the teeth when we skim the ground.

I'm still nauseous when I walk over to Dave, but a smile covers my ashen face. Dave is also beaming.

"That was awesome," he says. "How did you like it?"

"I puked."

Dave bursts out laughing.

Naked strangers

Switzerland/Austria

Now a year and a half into our travels, I'm noticing a subtle tickling for routine: daily yoga practice, vegetables in my fridge, the same bed and pillow…yet my curiosity for what's around the next corner is still strong. It's been almost two months since we've been on a dirt road or camped in the wild. Europe is fun, easy travel, but it feels too much like home, with everything you could ever want just a credit card away.

On Europe's smooth, fast motorways—rife with expensive tolls—Dave and I easily clock hundreds of miles a day. One, the roads are good and most countries do not have border crossings. Two, we're on a time crunch again. Like Alaska, Russia has a short summer window, and we have a few thousand miles to go before getting to the world's largest country.

In Neuchâtel, Switzerland, we visit my cousin. Alison was born in Canada, but she and her husband, Daniel, born in Altishofen, have lived in Switzerland for years. I don't see Alison or their two boys, Leo and Eliot, often. It's nice to spend time with this busy family, hiking in the Alps, eating expensive but delicious fondue, and taking funiculars—a cable railroad that operates at very steep grades of up to 110 percent, or a 47-degree angle. The roadway up to their house feels more like a narrow cobblestone trail. It's almost vertical, and Alison walks seven-month-old Eliot in a stroller with a sling attached to the handlebars, in case the buggy gets away from her.

Dave is perplexed how tradespeople get around on the steep, narrow roads. I think of the work vehicles he's had in the past: large 4×4 trucks with hitches to drag trailers full of tools. He wouldn't make the first bend in a road here.

After a week at Alison and Daniel's in real beds, we are more rested when we leave for Austria, where friends I used to river guide with show us how to sauna Euro-style. I read somewhere that sweating naked—as opposed to being covered up somewhat in a bathing suit—allows the body to detox better. I'll subscribe to almost anything at this point that might make me feel more energized, so I happily enter the steaming wood shack and remove my towel. Dave is not overly comfortable and leaves his towel draped over his middle. I let the heat take me to boiling point, hoping to release all the inhaled diesel fumes, burning plastics, and other airborne toxins I've ingested while having my face exposed to road life. I also hope to calm my mind and tap into that parasympathetic system everyone's talking about. Unfortunately, the body doesn't know the difference between good stress and bad—meaning the heart races and adrenaline kicks in whether you're hang gliding over the French Alps or being chased by crazy Peruvian men on a motorcycle.

The sauna experience is lovely—in the woods, by a crystal-clear stream—but I can only handle so much heat. After fifteen minutes, I leave to dunk my beet-red body in the creek. Dave follows, using me as a gauge for what's considered a polite amount of time to be crammed in a room with nude strangers. With our bits modestly exposed, we pass a young, muscular guy lying spreadeagle in the sun, hands clasped behind his head. Dave still has a death grip on the towel covering his lower half.

It's mid-June when we roller-coaster through Germany, Italy, Croatia, Slovenia, Slovakia, and Czechia. Never have we crossed so freely from one country into the next. Thanks to the European Union and European Free Trade Association, we ride through open borders belonging to the Schengen Area—twenty-six countries among which travel is regulated to be frictionless, regardless of nationality.

These more mountainous roads are twisty and steep—a way to see how my riding has improved. I lean more into the bends and apply less brake. I'm better at cornering and have the proof when I look at my new pavement-specific tires, which we put on in Scotland, knowing we'd be riding tarmac for thousands of miles before Russia. The little rubber tags that stick out of the sidewall on new tires are scrubbed off in places, which means more rubber is contacting tarmac—an exciting rite of passage for a motorcyclist.

Travel is stress-free in this part of Europe, with little concern over how to find gas stations or grocery stores. If we need anything for ourselves or the bikes, we can find it. Although I'm eager for Russia, I take time to appreciate this ease; in eastern Europe, fewer people will speak English, and amenities will be scarce again.

Something I do not miss from the developing countries we traveled through is being stared at everywhere we go. I've tried to overcome this annoyance as a traveler—it comes with the territory if I want to explore off the beaten track—but it can be overwhelming. I do realize that if Dave and I blended in with everyone else, we wouldn't have met some of the great human beings who enhanced our days.

In Europe, we don't stand out. Our BMW-branded bikes are common here, and so are our white faces. We're just like everybody else. I'm enjoying the comfort of being inconspicuous and just riding. We still have fun interactions with people at gas stations and grocery stores because it's clear we are travelers. It's just less intense and tiring, and most people speak English.

Another plus for being back in the first world is the roads are free of wandering humans and livestock, and potholes are basically non-existent on the smooth, paved roads.

Dave and I are staying in a pleasant paid campground in Czechia after a long day of riding. I'm grateful I don't have to socialize tonight and can go to bed when I want. We've been staying in people's homes nearly every night for well over a month now. I've loved the quality time with familiar faces, and the cost savings on restaurants and hotels has been a huge bonus. But it's tough to always be *on*. Sometimes, I just want to read a book in a quiet place, then go to bed at 8 p.m.

Does anyone speak English?

Poland

On a busy freeway outside of Kraków, Poland, I scan ahead through the congestion of semis, then sit back in my seat. I can't find Dave.

Did I pass him? Was he pulled over and I didn't see? I stop on the shoulder and wait several minutes. No Dave.

Although the freeway is busy and fast, we're following a remote connector out of Poland's second-largest city to the Ukrainian border, with little in between but farms and prairies. If all else fails, I'll catch Dave at the crossing, but he won't go that far—another 300 miles—without finding me first. *Will he?* I unzip my tank bag and check for messages on InReach. Nothing.

The inactivity—about fifteen minutes now—makes me restless. If I get online, I can sign in to our InReach account and see if Dave's behind me or ahead. The problem is, where do I find Wi-Fi?

Riding a few more miles, I see a small town in the distance, well off the freeway. I merge toward it, thinking maybe I'll find an internet café. That optimism leaves my brain the minute I see people traveling down the main road on horse-drawn carriages, nineteenth-century-style.

I pull into a gas station and go inside.

"Does anyone speak English?" I ask around.

"I do."

I turn to face a young man in his twenties. After some explanation, I ask if I can use his cell phone as a hotspot. He agrees. Pulling out my laptop, I sign in to our account, and there on the screen is a little blue dot showing me Dave is ahead. Way ahead. My immediate reaction is *that jerk* until I zoom in and notice he's at least stopped in what appears to be a large pullout about twenty miles away.

Shoving the laptop back into my pannier, I offer the young man a few dollars for using his data. He asks for a photo with me instead. I don't want to be rude but am anxious to get to Dave before he second-guesses himself and moves. Twitching with impatience, I pose while someone from the small crowd that's gathered takes the shot. Before anyone else gets the same idea, I quickly jump onto my bike and leave.

Covering the distance quickly, I'm glad to find Dave is still waiting in the pullout. He doesn't notice me at first and is typing a message on his InReach when he hears my bike.

"I'm so glad to see you," he says. "I wasn't sure if you were ahead or behind me."

I tell him how I had to find someone with data to sign into our InReach account. As usual, Dave doesn't acknowledge my resourcefulness. Instead, he says, "We should get going, since we've lost a lot of time."

Dave sets out, and I'm back in the position of follower, not leader. I will myself not to start an argument; these little moments I have alone are proof I can fend for myself, and that has to be enough.

Over the headset, Dave says we must have gotten separated when he passed a semi. He doesn't like riding behind big trucks. Motorcyclists have been badly hurt or killed by flying retread that whips off when truck tires blow. Judging by the amount of shredded rubber along the road, that happens a lot here.

Although Dave pulled onto the shoulder to wait for me to catch up, I was likely obscured by a different truck, passing in the left lane, unbeknownst to either of us. After some time, Dave kept riding, thinking I must be ahead, but I'd merged off the freeway by then.

I remind myself to talk to Dave yet again about riding closer together. Sometimes we need to have the same conversation more than once for something to sink in.

For now, I let it go. Everything's sorted, and we need to save energy for the border crossing.

Crossing from Poland into Ukraine takes three hours—one of our longest yet. We arrive to half a mile of waiting eighteen-wheelers and have no idea where to insert ourselves. I tuck in behind Dave, who's riding down the right shoulder. It's well over 80°F. With each truck we pass, I feel a blast of hot air from their idling exhausts.

We go to the front of the line, as we've been encouraged to do in other countries. I'm alert for a cacophony of angry horns, but everyone seems fine with us cutting in. They're either staring at our bikes or their cell phones. When the time comes to advance to the officer's window, we are under the shade of the buildings and proceed through the well-versed motions of presenting our passports and other documents. Our line-cutting advantage is kiboshed, however, when we ask where to get our carnet de passage stamped. Another thing becoming the norm: border guards having no idea what this document is.

"Go back." A guard in charge points to the mile-long truck line. "Maybe they know how to do."

"All the way to the end?" I say.

"Yes." He shrugs because in his eyes, we're travelers and have all kinds of time.

As we get ready to move, the guard has a change of heart. He talks to someone even more in charge about letting us through to the Ukraine side.

"Without stamp," he gestures to the yellow booklet Dave's already sliding back into his pannier. I catch Dave's eye and shake my head. Tempting, but there's likely a bribe expectation, and we need the stamps or else our deposit of more than $4,000 is compromised. The carnet is really becoming a pain in the ass, and I wonder again if we even need it. After Africa, it seems we're now just carrying an expensive sheaf of papers.

Getting back in line causes a stir since the other officers don't understand what we're doing. They too order us to go to the very back of the line, which now stretches into the right lane of the freeway.

I put on a polite face and reason with the border guard. It's dangerous for us to be sitting in the sun wearing our protective gear. We'll overheat. "May we go to the front?" I ask. "We just need one stamp."

"No," he growls. "Everyone waits."

Yeah, in air-conditioned vehicles!

A second officer comes over, poised and casual.

"Where from?" he asks, eyeing my bike.

"Canada," I sigh, brushing him off as just another person who wants to gawk at us and our stuff.

Instead, he opens the gate and points us through to a window.

Back to World War II

Ukraine

When some of my family members find out I'm in the country where my maternal grandpa (*"Dzia Dzia"* in Polish) was born, they encourage me to find his village.

Bolechów was part of Poland pre–World War II until 1945, when the country's borders were redrawn. When the war started, Grandpa fled Poland to join the French allies. He eventually ended up in Romania. Carrying his belongings on his head, *Dzia Dzia* crossed a deep, cold river and was placed in a refugee camp. He lived under horribly uncomfortable conditions until he was transported by train to Beirut, where he boarded a boat to France.

Grandpa, who was posted with the Royal Air Force, eventually met my Nana in London, who was a translator/secretary for either the Free Polish government or for the British. Grandpa never saw his mother nor most of his family members again after leaving Poland. He once returned to his homeland in 1972 to try to find any remaining family, but he was not allowed to cross the border. (Many officers who returned to communist Poland after World War II were viewed with suspicion, and some were charged with espionage.) This was a heartache *Dzia Dzia* carried throughout his life.

Grandpa spoke poor English, even after living in Canada for several decades. I had a hard time understanding his heavy accent. When we'd visit him and he talked about the war, tears filled the corners of his eyes. As a kid, I didn't like hearing the depressing stories; they gave me nightmares. I wish I'd been older and offered more sympathy and attention to his life-changing experiences.

Bolechów—also spelled *Bolekhiv*, or Болехів in the Cyrillic alphabet—is just sixty miles from our hotel. Although the village isn't in our direction of travel, Dave agrees that we can't miss the opportunity to go.

I expect the village to be small but with twenty-first-century modernization. However, Bolechów is like being teleported to the era of when my grandfather was a kid. The one barely paved road through town is crumbling and filled with potholes. Traffic passes through the nondescript downtown, stirring up mini tornadoes of dust. Buildings need care, and churches appear forgotten. I'm undeterred. *Dzia Dzia* grew up poor. How he got from here to Canada (after meeting Nana and starting a family) only added to the mystique of his history.

Bolechów is run-down, but I sense happiness among its people. I must have relatives here—at least cousins removed several times over. I wish I could stay long enough to find one. How cool would it be to see someone you're related to for the first time?

So we can explore more, Dave and I park the bikes in the shade of an old church. I look up at the two-story building made of brick and mortar, wondering if Grandpa attended when he was younger.

At an outdoor market, I buy fruit and veggies from old ladies in *ochipok* headdresses who let me photograph them. I walk over to stand by a statue commemorating World War heroism and eat a plum—*Dzia Dzia*'s favorite fruit. I send him a silent message, apologizing for not listening better to his harrowing stories of escape and appreciating the hard work it took to get Nana, Mom, and her siblings to a better life in Canada.

It doesn't take long to walk from one end of town to the other. Returning to our bikes, we find two young girls taking photos of each other in front of them. One has on stylish jeans and a top, the other a girly pink dress. When we walk up, they act like they've been caught doing something bad. I wave for them to come back.

"Do you speak English?"

"A little," the one in the dress replies.

"Do you want to sit on the bike?" I point to mine.

The girl wearing jeans covers her face and laughs, but the other girl walks over without hesitation. With my help, she hoists herself onto my seat and poses for her friend to get a photo. Their shyness now gone, they ask to have a photo with me. Dave takes the camera—an old point-and-shoot that's the most modern thing I've seen in the village—and snaps off some shots.

"What is your name?" the girl in jeans asks me. "Where are you from? How old are you?"

I answer all their questions, and they take more photos of me with my bike. Dave is all but ignored. When we leave, I have a warm feeling and am very glad we took the side trip. *Dzia Dzia* would've been thrilled to know I'd visited his village, but he passed away in 2002.

 Placing color images in this book was cost-prohibitive, so my solution is to bring you our travel photos digitally. To see color images for each country, scan the QR code or visit Photos under Riding Full Circle on my website, heatherleawriter.com.

Riding Full Circle starts here

Russia (Part 1)

Dave can't stop talking about how excited he is for Russia. During our entire trip, he's been waiting for the country that will truly define adventure riding to its core, the ultimate accolade to an ADV rider's skill and grit. A country that contains his longed-for Baikal-Amur Mainline and Road of Bones.

These two iconic routes through Siberia are not so much roads as a thrash through swampland, wilderness, and rivers. The routes were brought to the attention of intrepid adventure riders through the *Long Way Round* film with Charley Boorman and Ewan McGregor. In fact, the phrase "adventure riding" is due largely to those two men. An entire industry has been built from their exciting and well-publicized undertakings, which began in 2004 and have led to books and films. It doesn't hurt that Charley and Ewan were already movie stars, too.

A handful of adventurous souls were taking long-distance motorcycle trips before Ewan and Charley rode nearly 12,000 miles from London to New York via Europe, Asia, and Alaska—but they were rarer than steak tartare. Back then, the businesses now making a ton of money from the throngs of overlanding and adventure riding enthusiasts were mere startups in someone's garage—if that. Every year, there are dozens of overland and motorcycle events throughout Canada, the US, and Europe. Six-figure camper van builds are on display, and round-the-world motorcyclists give presentations to people dreaming of such trips. Thousands of articles have been published online and in print featuring stories from the road, whether on two wheels or four.

Overlanding is huge; it's an enviable way of life. Honestly, it's why Dave and I are here—to experience firsthand what we've seen, heard, read, and dreamed about.

Dave's hoping I'll change my mind and want to ride the BAM and Road of Bones. I'm his only riding partner, after all. I'm as prepared as ever for this adventure on top of an adventure. But I'm failing to get excited about bucking my 500-pound steed along trails punctuated with mosquito-filled muskeg and ice-cold whitewater crossings.

When I watched *Long Way Round* with Dave when we first started dating, and I saw Ewan and Charley flailing about in bogs on the BAM, up to their thighs in muck, I knew it wasn't the type of riding I'd ever want to do. Not in the way Dave wanted to. Not even after almost two years of improving my skills. It's still a hard no from me.

Now that we're actually at the border to a country that was a hell of a lot of work to get visas for, I'm anxious about how it will go. I've heard the border guards for Russia are extra cantankerous and that the country itself is not welcoming. What if, after all the time and effort getting this far, one little thing—like a piece of paper not in order or a box not checked—keeps us from even getting into the country? What if they question whether we're actually a legit photojournalism team or whether we have even met the woman who helped us with our invitation letters? What if our trip's final leg and finish line leave us with a bad overall feeling for travel?

Now in line to cross into the country from Ukraine, I have butterflies and can't stop fidgeting. If they turn us away, where do we go? I have zero interest in riding back through Europe; in my mind, Russia is an absolute must for completing our journey. A true grand finale.

A semi pulls up right beside my elbow. I look up at the driver, who's yelling at me, already on edge. I can't understand his language. He waves for us to move ahead, but we're bumper to bumper with the car in front. Seeing my confusion, the driver drops down out of his truck and makes exaggerated sweeping motions in front of my bike.

I've been mentally out of it and forgot we can cut to the front of the line.

"*Спасибо,*" I say, excited to use the first Russian word I've learned, which means "thank you." It's enunciated *spa-ceebo* and rhymes with *placebo*. I wish I'd practiced more Russian before coming to the country, but I know I'll pick up some of the language while here. Learning a new language is one of my favorite pastimes.

We ride to the front. I brace myself for angry shouts and horn-honking while we pass at least thirty vehicles, but no one seems to think twice about seeing two bikes with foreign plates zip by.

We're soon stopped by a huge man whose neck merges into his shoulders—it's hard to tell where one body part stops and the other begins. He wears camouflage fatigues and a black bulletproof vest. A machine gun angles across his chest, and he grips it firmly with both hands.

I look around while waiting our turn. The crossing is similar, security-wise, to those between Canada and the US, except for the dozen or so guards milling around with automatic weapons. Concrete blocks and boom barriers covered in white and red reflective tape give the impression of serious business, as do the video cameras and watchtowers.

The male guard signals with his rifle for us to advance. At the window, we're asked for our documents. I remove my helmet and over-smile, going for the honest, harmless look. The officer looks closely at my passport, brings it up to the light, then turns it over. Flipping through every page, he scrutinizes my stamped-in Russian visa longer than feels comfortable. I'm dead quiet, dead still. I don't even lift a finger to brush away the fly crawling slowly across my cheek.

The man keeps my passport, then asks Dave for his, going through the same rigmarole.

"Motorcycle permit?" he grunts.

Dave pulls out the carnet.

The guard looks carefully through each page, then lands on Russia. He picks up his stamp, then pauses.

"You go to Ukraine?"

"Yes."

"You like?"

"Yes," I say. "My grandfather—"

"You travel a lot." It's a statement.

"We do."

"This is good. Very good." The man smiles and it changes his face so much, he's almost childlike now. "I like travel too, but I no go yet to your country. Canada. Iz nice?"

"Very nice." I relax.

"Russia also nice," the man beams. "Welcome to my country!"

I feel like we've been given the keys to a whole new world.

Our very own firecracker

Moscow was going to be our first stop, but it's well over a hundred miles away. We aren't going to make it by dark, so we get a hotel for the night, narrowly missing a rainstorm.

When we wake the next morning, it's still pouring, so we happily stay under the warm covers, reading and napping. I write in my journal about the easy border crossing and how nice Russians are so far. It's rarely citizens who singlehandedly cause political turmoil.

After waiting for the rain to die down, we're off to a late start. A few hours later, we catch the storm in the most inconvenient place—a busy freeway funneling into Moscow. My helmet visor is down to keep the water off my face, but fat drops cover my vision. It's like driving without windshield wipers. I raise my left hand to use the built-in soft blade on my gloves and clear a path to see—a futile action, as the drops return as fast as I wipe them away. Add to that the spray off the cars and trucks passing me, and I may as well be the world's first blind motorcyclist.

Coming into the nation's cosmopolitan capital, home to twelve million, we split lanes—legal in Russia—and get through the tight traffic now slowed to a crawl. We first learned of lane splitting in California, where motorcycles are permitted to ride between vehicles on freeways and other busy roadways. The idea is that it helps riders avoid risk, like being rear-ended or overheating due to the lack of airflow. In parts of the world where this is legal, local drivers are used to and prepared for bikes traveling between them and other cars. There are rules: For one, you're not allowed to ride faster than the speed limit.

Lane splitting is a practice reserved mostly for traffic jams, when no one's moving fast. When done right, it can definitely be safer for riders, although it's not hard to imagine what happens when things go wrong.

Relying on driver shoulder checks more than usual is unnerving. I like being able to split lanes, but it's intense with luggage strapped to the sides of our bikes. I still have PTSD from hitting that boulder in Idaho.

Coming into Moscow, I'm looking forward to meeting up with someone I've never met in person but who's already been a big help to us. I first met Al—short for Alexandra—on a Russian BMW Facebook page. She answered some of my questions about riding in Russia and follows our blog. We touched base the previous evening, and Al already has us sorted with a hotel and directions to meet at her garage.

By "garage" I think Al means a motorcycle or autobody shop. When we pull up to a multilevel storage complex, I'm sure we're in the wrong place. I ask the security guard to call Al, as instructed, and soon she's there in real life. Who says Facebook friends aren't real-life friends?

I take in all four feet, nine inches of our twenty-something hostess, with her light-brown, waist-length dreadlocks. She has a doll's face—creamy and flawless, with big blue eyes. Al is model-stunning, yet her tininess disarms her and makes her seem approachable. She's a little firecracker. I like her instantly.

We follow Al in her car to the fourth level of the storage facility, where it becomes clear that "garage" means just that—a place to store things securely. She opens a metal roll-up door, revealing cardboard boxes, a tall lamp, and two motorcycles: a BMW 1200 GS (her husband's) and her BMW S 1000 RR sport bike.

"You can store your motorcycles in here. It will be safest," Al says in excellent English, but trilling the *r* and pronouncing the long *i* like *ee*.

I'm relieved to be off the wet, crazy roads and have someone—especially a local—taking care of us.

Dave and I detach our luggage from the racks and put them in Al's car, leaving our valuable bikes and gear in a locked compartment for which we have no key. So much about traveling is putting full trust in strangers.

Al takes us to our hotel and talks to the receptionist.

"Okay, everything is taken care of," she says, grabbing one of my bags to take upstairs.

"When do we pay?" I ask.

"I paid already. Two nights."

Al doesn't want our money.

"Please, it's my pleasure. We live in a small apartment, otherwise, you would stay with us, of course. Anyway, the Mafia runs most of the hotels in this city. I wanted to find you somewhere safe."

I love that Al is already protective of us.

Dave and I fall into napping mode after hot showers, and I'm out cold when someone knocks on the door. Through eyes at half-mast, I see Dave open the door. The receptionist, Stev, is asking something, but we can't understand, so he talks into his phone and Dave reads the Google translation to me.

"All guests to hotel need to register as by government law."

I get up and go downstairs with our passports, confused but sure everything will be sorted out. Every country has a different way of operating, and we need to oblige—especially in Russia.

"Please give me immigration card," I read off Stev's translation app. I point at his phone and give a thumbs up. Technology is awesome sometimes.

I have no idea what he means by "immigration card," so I hand over the passports opened to the page with our Russian visas. Stev shakes his head, and soon we're each flustered. He insists I should have an immigration card and I must be misunderstanding. After thirty-nine countries, Dave and I aren't prone to losing track of important documents. We learned our lesson that time in Mexico.

I explain to Stev that Dave and I arrived by land on motorcycles, not by plane, in case that makes a difference. It doesn't.

He raises the phone to his ear and talks briefly with someone, then hangs up.

"Wait," he says in English, but it sounds like *vait*. He points to a seat in the lobby. I think he's calling a supervisor or something and am surprised when Al walks through the door fifteen minutes later.

"You don't have immigration card?" she asks me.

"No, we didn't get anything at the border except a stamp in our passports."

"Okay, this is a problem." Her brow crinkles. "You must have this. Get Dave and come with me."

The three of us—and now the hotel manager, Igor—pile into Al's car. It's late afternoon. I have no idea what's happening, but Al's handling it.

When we pull up to an immigration building five minutes later, Dave and I look at each other. *How long is this going to take?*

Thirty people wait in line with somnolent expressions. Al directs Dave and me to sit, then speaks to the hotel manager, who disappears through an unmarked door. What illicit affairs are being conducted on our behalf? It's all very exciting.

Ten minutes pass, and Igor emerges from a different door. *Is there an underground tunnel or something?* His upper lip glistens with sweat. Panting, he says, "Passports, passports…" making a *give me, give me* motion. He leaves quickly with our documents in hand.

When Igor returns a few minutes later, he gives our passports back. There is no longer any sign of sweat or heavy breathing. His chest is broad and puffed proud like a man who's just done something of considerable importance.

"So...are we good?" Nobody answers me. Al tells us to "come."

In the parking lot, Igor pats Dave on the back, like he's an old buddy. "Everything good. Everything taken care of."

I don't know how young Al has so much pull. She and her husband are involved in Moscow search and rescue, which is why we trust them, but sometimes it's best not to know too much. In Russia, there's a saying for circumstantial confusion: "Don't ask questions."

We're getting our first taste of how resourceful Russians are; they get the job done. No fanfare. Moving on.

A city of youth

I'm drawn out of another too-short nap by the ding from my phone. A Facebook message from Al tells me she's coming to get us in an hour. We've been invited to ride with her and some friends to a place called The Hill.

"Be ready," are her closing remarks.

Neither of us wants to ride around the city just for fun. All I want in the world at that moment is to stay in bed and watch TV—a sloth's life after hours to compensate for so much time on the move. But an hour later, we're reunited with our bikes, and it feels good to ride unencumbered by gear.

Al and her husband are both on the 1200 GS I saw in their garage. They lead us to the upper part of the city. The Hill, located near Moscow State University—bigger and more majestic than Ottawa's parliament buildings or even the White House—is where all the cool kids go to show off flashy motorcycles and perform street stunts.

With such youthful energy, Moscow takes on a far more liberated persona than the harsh, unsmiling place I was expecting. We order shawarma from a food truck and watch the guys (it's always guys) risking bad crashes on bare skin, hoping to impress admirers. Al introduces us to half a dozen people, all with bikes but none that look quite like ours—weathered, dented, scratched, and kitted out with costly aftermarket accessories.

Bumping the bikes up onto the sidewalk, we congregate by a waist-high brick wall overlooking Moscow. A young couple makes out beside me, and almost everyone has a cigarette between their lips or fingers. A bird's eye view of the scene could leave one thinking rebellious youth run the city.

A young man sidles up beside me.

"Is this your bike?" When I nod, he says, "Isn't it too big for you?"

I laugh. "Well, I got it here all the way from Canada, so I guess not."

Cockiness isn't my intention—or is it? I've had that question before and can't help but make the obvious point.

Completely random, yet adding to the exhilarating vibe, is a wedding party from India dancing in colorful costumes to music playing from I don't know where. It's loud, fun, and so much better than succumbing to laziness in our hotel room.

We leave The Hill at dusk and follow the 1200 GS downtown, along with six other bikes—a Russian posse with two bright-eyed foreigners in tow.

Moscow's Red Square is stunning in the azure light. I photograph the glorious Saint Basil's Cathedral, which Ivan the Terrible built between 1555 and 1561, and the outside area where Vladimir Lenin, founder of the Russian Communist Party, is mummified in a three-story tomb.

We leave the square and ride all over the city, stopping for photos, coffees, food…carefree and happy, Dave and I get back to the hotel well after midnight. We haven't stayed out that late in a long time, and it all happened without a drop of alcohol.

The Night Wolves are back

It's ironic—given how relieved I was when my email to the Night Wolves motorcycle gang bounced back all those months ago—that we end up being hand delivered to them by Al herself.

I'm not surprised that Al knows some Night Wolves members. When she hears that Dave is hoping to ride the BAM and Road of Bones, she digs through her extensive connections and finds someone who can share knowledge.

That someone happens to be from the Night Wolves.

We enter the Sexton clubhouse off a busy street, where a secret fortress greets us behind corrugated metal walls. It's like a set from Burning Man, minus the desert landscape and naked, stoned people. Huge art pieces made from scrap metal and old tires loom over us. It looks to me like everything has eyes. An indoor/outdoor bar is lined with every brand of booze known to humankind, backlit with fluorescent lights.

Motorcycles—some new, some vintage—are parked around the premises. A wooden dance floor and large steel barrels on fire beckon for a party. But it's still early.

Al suggests we sit at a large outdoor table, where two men and a scary-looking woman who reminds me of Gemma from the FX series *Sons of Anarchy* are already seated. Nobody smiles or offers to shake hands when Al introduces us. We get straight down to business.

The two men have done both the BAM and Road of Bones. In broken English, the one named Rolf asks what information we're looking for. Dave says, "Anything, really."

I'm not sure what my boyfriend's plan is for riding these crazy roads. He's still hoping I'll change my mind. I haven't. And I'm not okay with him riding this kind of terrain solo. At this point, I'm humoring him, thinking that in time he'll probably give up on the idea.

"The roads are terrible on BAM. Terrible!" Rolf says, his stoic face churning with energy. I stop myself from saying "thank you for your time" and getting up to leave.

Rolf shakes his head as though in shame. "Remote. There is no help if anything goes wrong." *Yep, okay good, let's go.* "The bridges are missing planks of wood. Some motorcycles fall in the water."

The Baikal-Amur Mainline road was used during construction of the Siberian rail line, completed in 1984. The road parallels the tracks but hasn't been regularly maintained since the trains started running. To avoid the sometimes-treacherous river crossings, ADV riders can use the tracks. Oblivious to my fidgeting, Dave asks about that option now.

"Yes, okay, you can ride on the railroad over the rivers," says the other man, speaking for the first and last time. "But the trains come fast. I would not recommend this."

In the *Long Way Round*, Charley and Ewan got across the rushing rivers with help from passing flatbed trucks. Dave inquires how common these trucks are along the BAM.

"Yes, but sometimes, these trucks they drown and then *bye bye*...your motorcycle?" Rolf claps his hands. "Gone!"

I can tell Dave thinks the men are being overly dramatic. He stares at Rolf like he wants to say, *If you did it, I can do it.* I, on the other hand, am more convinced than ever that neither of us should be exploring this road.

There's more disconcerting advice for just riding in Russia in general: "Carry $3,000 to $4,000 cash for everything you'll need. You will have to pay many people to help you."

We aren't going to take that advice. If it gets around that travelers carry that kind of money, none of us will be safe.

"Take four tires with you—two each. You won't find the right tires anywhere after leaving Moscow."

That could be true. During our trip research, I'd seen photos of long-distance riders with spare tires strapped onto their luggage. It looked cumbersome and hardcore. I wonder if I can ride with tires lashed down the sides of my bike and think it might be fun to find out. The additional gear adds extra weight and bulk of course, but a motorcycle is useless without good rubber. In the far-reaching places that capture our hearts and imaginations, there is little in the way of supplies—especially for German-made motorcycles.

Rolf advises us to ship another set of tires to Irkutsk ahead of us, saying we'll likely eat up tread on the 3,000 broken-pavement miles between here and there. Irkutsk is also a meeting point for the small pool of wild souls who want to ride the BAM, which comes before the Road of Bones when riding west to east.

In the end, the Night Wolves guys do offer some useful grain-of-salt information: Once we ride east of Moscow, there really is very little out there before Magadan, our final destination 6,300 miles away. What sometimes happens with information is it brings worry. Crossing Russia will be the longest section in our travels and the most isolated, with limited amenities. The Dempster and Dalton highways seem like baby steps compared to this.

We thank everyone and get up to leave. Where I was once terrified of encountering the Night Wolves, I now find myself wishing for a raging biker party at the Sexton clubhouse. I want to wander around with gang immunity because we're invited guests, taking photos of neck tattoos lit by barrel fires and maybe receive a fist bump from Putin decked out in his leathers—a friendly sort of *Sons of Anarchy* meets *Long Way Round* type of evening.

But all is quiet in the compound when we walk back out to the street.

Al is our tiny guardian angel, driving around Moscow—no easy feat—to help us find extra supplies, like air filters and oil so Dave can do some bike maintenance. I buy a new pair of riding boots; I didn't spend top dollar on the waterproof version, like Dave, so mine are falling apart despite my efforts to coax them to the finish line.

I've been trying for weeks to get in touch with the woman from BMW Russia who sponsored the invitation letters for our visas. I don't want to hang out in this busy city much longer, but I made her a promise. I have no idea when she wants us to do the show or even where she is.

Al takes us to the BMW motorcycle dealership, but they have no idea what or who I'm talking about. No one speaks English, and they all seem uninterested in my offer of a rider presentation. I conclude the woman has left the company. I never do hear from this Good Samaritan who helped unlock the gate to Russia for us.

100% cock

Thanks to Dave and an afternoon spent in Al's storage garage, our bikes are in great shape with new oil and clean air filters. It doesn't take much to keep them happy and reliable. This fact is not lost on me; the days of struggling with Frankenbike are still fresh in my mind, as well as Dave's. He hasn't called my new F800 any bad names at all!

With Al as our mascot, we leave Moscow a few days later. She insists on escorting us out of the city and has planned an overnight together a hundred miles east in Tankovizha (*Танковижа*), where she grew up.

Al's mom welcomes us with hugs. After changing out of our gear, soaked again from hard rains, we're invited to the main house for tea and baked goods. Al's mom is dating a Russian pop star and, like Al, speaks English well. The four of us talk about world politics, and Dave and I make everyone laugh with our Russian phonetics. All this time, we've been pronouncing a certain brand of apple juice with a label that reads *100% cok* as "a hundred percent cock." Dave has gotten much enjoyment out of asking me to "pick up some cock" at the grocery store. Al informs us now that the *c* character is actually pronounced as an *s*. So the word *juice* in Russian actually sounds like *sock*.

We're clearly having difficulty, so Al writes out the Cyrillic alphabet for us to take on the road and gives us a quick language lesson.

The Russian alphabet is mind-bending. For example, the character *b* is pronounced as *v;* a small *r* sounds like an English *g;* a small *n* is a phonetic *p* unless it's a backward И, which sounds like *i*. There are sixteen Cyrillic letters not in the English alphabet but that have the same inflection. For example, ф is an English *f;* Λ is a *d,* and Λ is an *i.*

The Russian letters *хизер* spell out *Heather* on my visa, but the actual word is "hyser." That's how everyone says my name in Russia. I had no idea "Heather" would be difficult for non-English speakers to pronounce. I've been called everything from *Eder* to *Heeher* and now *Hyser.* I don't bother correcting anyone.

Dave's name is spelled *дэвид* and translates exactly as *David*—a much easier travel name.

We pass the rest of the afternoon walking around the small village. Many houses have beautifully carved and painted window frames, called *nalichniki* (наличники). The designs are just as complex and mind-boggling as the Cyrillic alphabet.

In the seventeenth century, when glass widows started to become the norm, *nalichniki* were at first used to fill cracks between the house and windowpanes. Over the years, homeowners got creative and turned these frames into works of art to set themselves apart from other houses. *Nalichniki* often convey a person's wealth and even political stance.

Dave steps closer to examine the craftmanship. The material used for the frames is usually resinous wood.

"I see flowers, birds, and stars carved into this one," he says.

I ask how the *nalichniki* are made. Al's mom tells me they're usually built by carpenters and woodcarvers, then distributed around the country. Since people didn't have access to design magazines in the 1600s, the patterns were inspired by wallpaper, embroidery, and even soap packaging.

We're hovering around someone's window, so Al suggests we continue our walk. Stopping by her uncle's house, Dave and I take turns carrying water in buckets from a nearby stream—which is still how he gets his water—on the end of a pole carried across our shoulders. It's difficult not to spill and impressive when Al's uncle shows us how, even walking over bumpy ground and for a much longer distance than we attempt.

I'm having a blast. Interacting with locals—not just in big cities, but rural areas, too—is something I'd hoped to do on our travels. It's too easy to feel inconvenienced and avoid the unknown. *Let's get a hotel instead of finding a place to camp. Let's eat at a restaurant instead of buying local foods to cook. Let's pass right through this village or town; I doubt there's anything to see here.* I've been this person at times while traveling. I get tired and just want normalcy and ease. Travelers do need to be alert and not put themselves in risky positions. But what highlights might we have missed if we ignored rare opportunities like this one?

Right up to our final hours together, Al continues to express motherly concern that we're riding through Siberia all the way to Magadan. Outside of her network, she doesn't seem to trust her fellow countrypeople all that much.

"People get killed every day in head-on collisions. Don't ride at night," she warns. "Don't camp. There are many, many bears. They will eat you. Don't follow anyone anywhere."

Her crack-the-whip approach amuses me. Due to media and newscasts "helping" me form preconceived notions, I once assumed most Russian women were docile and the men overbearing.

Education. Knowledge. Enlightening experiences. All of this is why I love traveling. It's as much about the people as it is the adventure. In fact, I'd argue you can't have one without the other. Without trusting people, our travels around the globe would be like a child without a smile, a flower without color.

Twelve hours ahead, twelve hours behind

We leave the next morning in the rain; it's a chilly 50°F, even though it's July. I'm surprised by the tears welling up in my eyes when we say goodbye to Al and her mom. For the next week, I miss our little firecracker—not just because of her sense of humor and infectious energy, but because I felt taken care of, and daily tasks weren't as trying. Deciphering the Russian language—even with Al's cheat sheet—is hard. This is our first long-term experience with an alphabet in characters we don't understand. Normally a language lover, I'm now scratching my head when reading signs. After a while, I start to recognize words like кафе, which spells "café," but hotels and shops take more sleuthing.

After Moscow, gas stations are few and far between, and we're often close to running out of fuel. Back in Switzerland, Dave installed an auxiliary fuel tank onto my bike to help me get almost the same range he does. Now that means we run out of fuel together miles from anywhere.

As we've done on remote roads in the past, we get back into the habit of filling up at every station we come across. One evening, we pull into Kazan to look for accommodation. While Dave takes our documents into a hotel beside the highway, I watch a woman in a short, tight skirt and heels stretch to talk to a trucker leaning out of his rig. Other women dressed similarly stand with their backs to the road, perhaps to show a potentially more desirable side—or so they don't get pelted in the face by rocks and road grime from passing vehicles.

It's a cold forty-five degrees and drizzling. My handlebar grips are on high, and my heated jacket keeps my core warm. I'll be off the road and inside soon, but for these poor women, their workday is just starting. I imagine that being a haul trucker on the Trans-Siberian Highway is boring and lonely, but I have a hard time not spitting in the trucker's face and grabbing the emaciated arm of the young girl he's flirting with. What can I do anyway? Whisk her off to a better life on the back of my motorcycle?

I make a mental note to bring our sleeping bags inside so we don't have to use the sheets.

On a positive note, things are cheap again. Our room costs 1,100 rubles, about eighteen dollars. For lunch earlier, we had a hearty borscht and meat-filled dumplings so tasty that Dave's eyes rolled into the back of his head—all for six dollars.

The dreariness of the constant rain is affecting both our moods, and we're on autopilot most days: ride, eat, sleep; ride, eat, sleep. So far, the Trans-Siberian Highway is nothing like the stunning Dempster and Dalton in Alaska. The scenery is unchanging and uneventful—but forested, at least.

Such roads free up a lot of bandwidth for thinking.

While eating cheese and bread on the shoulder of a dead-flat section east of Ufa, Dave realizes there's a twelve-hour time difference between our location and home—Pacific Standard Time.

"Meaning," he says, "if we turn around and go that way as the crow flies, it's the same distance as going that way," he points ahead, "to get home."

Dave loves geeking out on stuff like this—stuff I sometimes find completely mind-bending.

"Wait. So, if I ride in that direction for an hour," I gesture behind me, "it'll now take an hour longer to get home in the opposite direction?"

"Correct."

"So, if it's noon here, but midnight at home, is it yesterday's midnight or tomorrow's?"

Dave is stumped; I've given him something to think about after lunch. Either way, we still have a long way to go. Dave's info, and the fact that Russia has *eleven* time zones, really puts into perspective the enormous country I'm about to cross on two wheels. At this point, it seems all Russia has to offer is one long-ass dusty highway from Moscow to nowhere.

Sadly, we've already seen some of the road issues people warned us about, in the form of two dead bodies. One was a pedestrian who was struck crossing the highway. Her dark-red high heels stuck out from under the tarp and eerily matched the blood around her. I wondered if she was a prostitute and thought about the young woman I'd seen talking to the trucker.

The second fatality was a driver who hit the ditch with his dump truck, likely after falling asleep at the wheel. I'm grateful he didn't hit another car. Or us. Passing the ambulance with its flashing lights, I kept my eyes ahead, but Dave later told me he saw the body slumped over the hood, halfway through the windshield.

These are grim reminders that even monotonous roads require our full attention.

The small villages brighten my mood. I admire a home painted dark brown with turquoise and fuchsia *nalichnikis* and tall sunflowers growing from a cared-for garden. I try to keep my eyes on the road while taking in scenes of daily life in these far-flung places. As always, I want to photograph everything: the boy riding his tricycle beside a chicken coop, the old woman wearing a head scarf stooping to pick carrots from her garden. How do people make their livings in these tiny, cozy hamlets? What's the typical household income? Do they even bother with money, or is barter and trade more common? The scenes are so idyllic it all seems worry free. That's probably far from true, but I feel comfortable passing through these remote, picturesque settlements.

I work to embrace the daily monotony, knowing I'll wish for it when things get tough farther east. Even though I'll avoid the BAM and Road of Bones, the New Summer Route that will bring us into Magadan isn't a walk in the park either. We talked to some adventure riders going east to west who said the Trans-Siberian turns into gravel after Tynda. They didn't even go all the way to Magadan. For us, that means 1,700 unpaved miles to reach our end point. But maybe a dirt road is better than the damaged tarmac we've been riding for weeks now, with massive potholes that come out of nowhere.

Luckily, the weather has changed. Popcorn clouds fill blue skies bringing warmer weather and happier riding days. Summer is here.

I'm thinking more often now about how it will feel to go home after two years of my life completely absorbed in our trip. I know from past travels that it'll be weird to come home and see that nothing has really changed, yet I have. It's comforting to return to familiarities like friends and family. This time, however, some big changes are ahead: I'm engaged to a man who lives in another country—a country that didn't allow me to cross its border not too long ago.

We've hired an immigration lawyer who advised me to apply for a K-1 visa. This means going back to Canada on my return and waiting about a year until I'm invited to the US. I'll have to find a job and a place to live again. After being together all day, every day, Dave and I will again only see each other on weekends.

Like a pouting teenager ordered to do chores after a night of partying, I'm not looking forward to adulting.

Come for the people, stay for the horsemeat
Kazakhstan

Dave and I are at the border between Russia and Kazakhstan, nine hours into a day of riding. In the July heat, I take our documents over to the customs office while Dave stays with the bikes. He has no shade; the mix of low shrubs and grasslands is too sparse to cast a shadow.

There's the usual rush of mostly men trying to entice me with their fixer services: overpriced vehicle insurance, inflated exchange rates for cash, the guarantee of a better crossing if I buy their expertise. Kazakhstan is our fortieth country. I'm well versed in ignoring fixers by this point. Still, they encroach, yell, even block my path. I stay focused.

Vehicle insurance is mandatory in Kazakhstan. I've done my research and know to pay no more than 7,000 *tenges*—about twenty dollars.

The fixers want 9,000 per bike.

"Twelve thousand total," I counter.

There's no argument.

I present our documents and insurance to two Kazak guards. When they see our Canadian passports, they break into a smile and give me a thumbs up.

One of the men politely asks if he can search our bags. I lead him over to the bikes and open my panniers. The officers barely glance inside before steering the friendly, broken-English conversation toward learning more about our travels: *Where did you start? Where are you going?*

The entire process to legally import our bikes and ourselves into Kazakhstan takes fifteen minutes. It's the easiest, most pleasant crossing we've had in twenty-two months. Now, all I want is to find accommodation—air-conditioned, if possible. I'm lightheaded from dehydration and need a good meal.

Since we're planning to ride across Russia for the rest of the summer, Kazakhstan is just a weeklong side trip. Both Dave and I would like to go further south into Uzbekistan, Turkmenistan, and Tajikistan, but as we're finding out, even two years to ride around the world isn't enough time to see it all. And we need to save the summer weather to reach our biggest trip milestone.

Once again, the clock is ticking, but this time it all feels less hurried, less frantic. Has it taken this long for us to relax? Or are we getting weary enough to let these last months just happen to us, a weariness that causes acquiescence? I hope we're not becoming complacent and desensitized.

Opening the throttle on a smooth, paved road, I'm almost delirious enough to imagine the tall blades of grass are waving at me in welcome. I wave back, just for fun, and see them swish to and fro in the summer breeze.

So far, northern Kazakhstan reminds me of the prairies back home. A folkloric joke about the province of Saskatchewan is that it's so flat, you can watch your dog run away for a week. But it's peaceful, relaxing. If I took a photo and said I was traveling through the middle of Canada, few would know the difference.

A small town appears, and we stop so Dave can check the GPS for that little hotel icon. We haven't set up our tent for weeks. In this part of the world, it's cheap to spend the night in a bed off the ground. Since we look like astronauts descended from space, with our full-face helmets and armored riding gear, two locals come over to check us out. After a game of charades, they realize we're looking for a place to stay. They want us to follow them in their car. My traveler's instinct is so well-honed by now that nothing about this seems alarming, and Dave's already riding behind the white sedan.

A few minutes later, the two men stop by a three-story building that looks like a former hotel. I slide off my seat. More men are forming a crowd. I'm so tired and hungry. I just want to be out of the sun, showered, and beer-bound in, like, five minutes, tops. But word is out in the small village that foreigners are in town, and they all want selfies with us. I feel the familiar weariness of having to deal with everyone touching my stuff to see how it works and not knowing how to communicate the "private property" thing.

The men speak Kazakh excitedly and are falling all over themselves to be of service in any way. One starts to lift bags off my bike; another is helping Dave remove his jacket. It's hard not to smile. I'm forever touched by how many people have dropped whatever they're doing in the moment just to help us.

Our new Kazakh friends finally wander off with their digital memories, leaving just the two men with the white sedan and one very old woman who looks to be in her early hundreds. She's the hotel owner, and she won't let me see the room until we've settled on a price—twenty-five dollars for the night. I give a brisk *we have a deal* nod that I hope the staunch, unsmiling dinosaur will appreciate and then shadow her up a set of squeaking wooden stairs. She's distrustful of me clobbering around in my motorcycle boots, pausing every few steps to look back at me and scowl. *I should've taken my boots off.* Down a dusty hallway, she opens a door that creaks so hopelessly on its hinges, I start to wonder if the last guest who stayed here was around the time my 103-year-old grandfather was a baby.

I look at the beds: metal skeletons on which two thin mattresses are taco'd in on themselves. What I really want to do is turn on my reviled bootheels and get out of there before I breathe in any more archaic dust. I don't want to be disrespectful, though, so I pretend to be interested in where the bathroom is. I already know it's going to be horrible. The old woman points with an arthritic finger down the hall, revealing a hole in the floor behind a curtain. Dave and I are well-accustomed to long-drop squat toilets by now, but this is the nail-in-the-coffin *nope* I'm looking for. I'm tired, but the place feels creepy as hell, and I have a gut feeling we'll find something better.

I give the old lady an apologetic smile and, not waiting for her reaction, speed-walk back to Dave, telling him we need to move on. He sighs, probably thinking I'm being too picky.

Dave indicates to the two men we're leaving.

"Kostanay." I point eastward and they nod, recognizing the name of the larger city an hour away.

The driver waves for us to follow them again. I have an *oh no* moment, thinking they are now taking us all the way to Kostanay. Too late, they're already in the car. When we get to the highway, however, the driver pulls over and gives us the peace sign. They only wanted to ensure we got back to the main road. As we pass, they cheer. I beep my horn in what I hope conveys our gratitude.

I feel guilty not giving the tiny town our tourist dollars, but if there's anything of top priority while traveling on a motorcycle, it's rest.

Kostanay appears by sunset at around 8:30 p.m. The GPS routes us to a hotel that looks expensive: several floors high, with light-pink stucco paint and a grand entrance. When we pull into the lot, I'm dismayed to hear loud music beating against the walls inside. Before I can communicate with Dave, a dark-haired man dressed in beige khakis and a blue button-up shirt comes over.

"Hello!" he beams. "Where are you from?"

Dear god, here we go again. I just want a shower and bed; I'll even forgo the beer, just get me off this bike!

"Canada."

There are other people in the lot—all well dressed and reaching into trunks for food plates and booze bottles. *Ugh, a wedding, or something. We'll never get any sleep here.*

"I'm Darkhan." The thirty-something man offers his hand to Dave, then comes over to shake mine.

"Heather." My smile is looking more like a grimace, I'm sure.

"It is pleasant to meet you, Hayser." Darkhan gets straight to the point. "Come! My cousin is getting married. We must have you at our party."

Dave and I laugh at the direct order. We're both still balanced in our seats and haven't even decided whether we're staying here.

"Are you hungry?" Darkhan asks, speaking our language. And I don't just mean English.

"Very," Dave replies, and I know I've lost him.

"Great, do you eat horsemeat?"

"We do now!"

The promise of free food overrules my need for anything else at that moment.

Darkhan tells us to leave everything on the bikes, saying our stuff will be safe. He whisks us inside. I'm immediately energized by the thumping bass and people jumping around on the dance floor. I think about shaking a leg, too.

"I love the music," I yell into Darkhan's ear. "Is this Kazakh techno?"

"Yes, from Astana, the capital."

I locate the source and find a woman on stage, microphone to her mouth, hopping around to the beat.

"Oh, it's live!" Electric instruments drown out my comment.

I steal a look at Dave. Dancing and loud techno aren't his thing, but his shining eyes tell me he's either focused on the promise of meat or all the gorgeous women in the ballroom. Kazakhstan—bordered by Russia, China, Kyrgyzstan, Uzbekistan, and Turkmenistan—is populated with mixed races, all with their own exotically unique look. I notice strong Asian characteristics: dark hair and smooth skin but with more prominent chins and wider eyes. The Kazakh men have minimal facial hair, and over-all, their skin appears darker. The women are thin and leggy, with long hair flowing down their backs. Combined with the subtle lighting, tasteful dec-orations, and danceable music, it's a feast for the senses.

I'm sporting road-stained riding pants and a sweaty purple T-shirt. My disheveled ponytail tops off the look, complete with road grime to accen-tuate my features. Dave also has dirt smeared on his cheeks and an opposite-of-sexy streak of back sweat going on.

Darkhan escorts us to a large, circular table where men and women sit laughing and drinking. Their plates show the remains of a meal, but their glasses are full.

Swiping hair off my forehead, I self-consciously tuck a few rogue strands behind my ear, hoping for some kind of improvement. Darkhan doesn't seem fazed by our filth. I'm not so sure about the people we're seated next to.

Darkhan has positioned us facing the bride and groom table at the front of room. What do they think about the two grubby strangers crash-ing their party? Plates arrive, piled high with what I gather is horsemeat, in four different forms: roasted, stewed, grilled, and, oddly, deli sliced. It all smells delicious, like oven-roasted beef.

Over my right shoulder, an arm extends and fills three glasses in front of me with vodka, red wine, and something sweet like brandy. Before we dig into the food, Darkhan gives the table a toast we can't understand. Everyone cheers and jams their beverage of choice together with ours.

A young man sitting beside me asks, "What's it like where you live?"

"It's beautiful," I answer, pulling out my phone to show him pictures of where we hike and ski back home. He nods with appreciation.

The horsemeat is mostly delicious, but I can't bring myself to try the pink, processed meat circles. Dave is already on his second serving. While eating, I watch people let loose, having the time of their lives. They laugh until tears flow. They dance—some well, some not so well. They drink. So much drinking.

"What are weddings like for your people?" asks a teenage girl across from me.

"Similar. But we don't have as much fun as you do," I wink.

We're more reserved, worried about how we look or come across, I almost tell her. Here, no one stands out as overdoing it because they're *all* overdoing it.

"Hello! You it is great pleasure I meet!" This comes from an inebriated older man leaning too close to my ear. I smile at his attempt to speak English, knowing I sound equally as hilarious when I try to string sentences together in Spanish or Russian. And I don't even know a single word in Kazakh.

Darkhan suggests some tea. I agree, thinking it will help my stomach digest the vodka and horsemeat. We tail our new friend past the techno singer, who is bursting at the seams, and enter a much quieter room where delicate cakes, cookies, chocolates, and other baked goods are stacked on silver platters four levels high. While Darkhan gets our hot drinks, a handful of young boys come over to practice their English and get photos with us. All I can think about as the cameras snap and click around us is how far across the room my body odor is emanating. *If I can just get somewhere with a shower…*

An hour after we pulled into the hotel's parking lot and met Darkhan, Dave and I are finally permitted to escape upstairs, where we've booked the last room available.

"But!" Darkhan holds up a finger, halting us in our steps. "I insist you come back. There is another meal." *More food?!* "And drinks to celebrate the bride and groom. We must have you there."

I have no doubt he'll come searching for us if we don't return, so I promise we will.

Showering at last, I grin under the water, trying to comprehend how we've just come from a long, hot day of riding that included a border crossing and a nasty old lady in her haunted hotel to a vibrant wedding reception with live techno and free horsemeat. Our first day in Kazakhstan is already proving to be a great reason for coming to the country. I knew we'd find something better than what the woman older than petrified wood could offer. No way she'd be showing us a good time like Darkhan is.

A quick leg-and-armpit shave and I'm ready to party. I have just one semi-nice clothing item to wear—the same green sundress I've been wearing since the beginning of our trip. It's faded from sun and shower laundering, but it's much nicer and cleaner than my riding clothes. The dress has an opening in the back that shows my bra, so Dave ties it out of the way using dental floss.

Back at the reception, I'm invited by a drunk uncle to dance. The music has shifted from techno to something with a slower beat, and it's hard to find the right moves. Dave remains seated at the round table, eyes darting left to right, clearly terrified that someone's about to invite him onto the dance floor as well. I know he'll fake a sudden knee injury or bad heart should there be a solicitation.

We're taking some attention away from the two who are the real cele-bration this evening, and I'm a little embarrassed. I try catching the bride's eye, but she's either in a daze or avoiding my attempts to communicate. *Or she's overwhelmed.* I have no idea what it feels like to be a bride, or even a bridesmaid. Despite being engaged, I can't fathom spending a small for-tune on balloons, cakes, booze, and a fancy wedding dress I'm sure I'll rip or stain.

Well after midnight, we're directed toward a lineup—girls on one side, boys on the other. The parents on both the bride and groom sides offer a prayer. I copy the person beside me, holding my hands together like I'm running them under a faucet. Next, we collectively raise them above our heads and splash invisible water onto our faces.

When the speeches are done, the bride collects her box-pleated skirts and begins to walk through the center of the lineup. I notice the men shaking her hands lightly and the women kissing her face. When she comes close to me, I clumsily reach to pull her to me and plant a smooch, like the others. She looks stunned and keeps walking. *Oh god, now she* really *hates me!*

"Was that all right?" I ask Darkhan later.

"Yes. I think people were just surprised how open you are," he laughs.

At 2 a.m., the wedding starts winding down, but Darkhan wants us to go to a nightclub with his friends. I'm relieved when Dave politely inter-jects to say we're exhausted and need to get some sleep.

While we head to our room, the same young woman who inquired about weddings where we live approaches us.

"Can I see your motorcycle?" she asks me.

I hope she doesn't notice my hesitation; I'm already feeling my head hitting the plush pillow on our bed.

"Sure," I smile, and the three of us walk to the secure parking lot, where Dave moved the bikes earlier.

"Do you have kids?" the girl asks.

"We don't."

"Hmm," she looks contemplative, and I wonder if this will be another *the time is now!* moment. "How old are you?"

I tell her I'm forty-two. She looks surprised, probably because I'm not a mother yet.

"How old are *you*?" I return the question.

"Seventeen. Can I follow you on Instagram?"

"Of course," I say. "I'd love that."

She takes photos of us by our prized bikes then runs off, maybe to post something to her feed. I'm flattered a young person thinks I'm cool enough to follow on social media.

An equestrian cow walker

Darkhan wants to take us to his family's farm in Timiryazev, 120 miles east of Kostanay.

When we arrive, I scan the property from the seat of my bike—an impressive operation with several building structures at least 3,000 to 4,000 square feet. Dozens of modern farm trucks and combines are parked throughout the property, which I guess to be at least fifty to sixty acres. There are no trees or mountains as far as the eye can see. Just flat, fertile land and a lot of mud, indicated by my rear tire slipping down the side of wheel ruts left in the road. I breathe in the earthy scent of wet soil and realize I haven't smelled pollution from traffic or industry in weeks.

The farm, Darkhan tells us, employs thirty locals from the village of 800 and is one of the district's largest wheat suppliers.

We pull up beside mechanics, engineers, and other farm hands standing outside a workshop, wearing dark blue coveralls and smoking cigarettes. I don't know if Darkhan called ahead, but no one looks surprised he's come home trailing two foreigners on motorcycles.

I remove my helmet, and Darkhan makes introductions. One of the mechanics sees Dave eyeing a ten-ton farm truck and invites him to drive it. Dave gets in, and after grinding a few gears on the old workhorse, rolls away down the muddy road. As he drives out of view, I feel awkward standing around with a bunch of men I initially assume I have nothing in common with. But I soon find out they love motorcycles. One man reaches out to smooth his palm over my F800's fairing—an unexpected intimate gesture I feel up my spine, because he's making contact with dings and dents I'm proud of. It's funny to think that way now. Back in Alaska I was afraid to put a single scratch on the bike's shiny surface.

Dave returns, now an official farm truck operator. Darkhan tells us that his uncles and their staff built most of the tractors and combines themselves.

"Here?" I ask, incredulous. "On the property?"

Darkhan nods.

"I will give you a tour later. For now, let's walk into the village. I need a few things."

Darkhan leads us to a bunkhouse where we'll be staying, and Dave and I change out of our riding gear. I'll be sharing the dorm-style room with several men and make a mental note to ensure my earplugs are close at hand should the snoring get out of control.

The three of us walk into Timiryazev, stirring up free-range chickens in the quiet village. It's almost like a ghost town. Weeds grow through the concrete of a children's park, and the basketball court is filled with mud from a recent rainstorm. I see not a soul except a cluster of wild chickens and two lazy dogs lounging near an older building that looks abandoned.

"That's a school," Darkan tells us. "Kids go there even from other villages. We also have a second, newer school."

Walking around Timiryazev, Darkhan talks about the time he spent living in the eastern US. He doesn't compare that first-world life to this, and I admire him for that. After two years, he decided to come home, where he feels he has more opportunity to grow in his life. Timiryazev is shown to us through Darkhan's eyes, with the pride of someone who knows he has it good. It isn't vanity, it's gratitude.

We go into the grocery store—a modest house on a lonely street with no defining characteristics telling us it sells food inside. Here, along with purchasing a few provisions, Darkhan buys two gifts: for me, a small Kazakh doll made from felt and wearing a traditional red dress. Dave receives a miniature white yurt, also made from felt. The souvenirs fold and will fit easily inside our bags—a generous, thoughtful gesture. We thank our friend and get photos of us holding the gifts, which I promise to email to him the next chance I get.

Before leaving the store, Darkhan writes something on a pad of paper by the cash register—no money is exchanged or credit card stuck into a slot.

"I pay at the end of the month," he says, pointing to the book when I ask if we can contribute to the groceries, which include a few onions and potatoes, some dark-red juice, and two cans of horsemeat. Before yesterday, I might have mistaken the tins for pet food. "We live on credit, which means we live on trust. People come here for things they need, then pay later. You must trust that when you give a service or whichever, the people will pay you. It could be next week, or next year, depending on the cost."

What if the store burns down? How would they collect the money owed? And how do they buy stock if no one pays their bills for a month or more? I could never roll like this. As a small business owner in my past life, I invoiced clients the day I finished their projects and made it payable upon receipt. Would that seem overly paranoid to someone like Darkhan?

Walking back, we stop to watch a horseman herding cattle. I'd noticed these cowboys along the roadside and wanted to photograph them at work, curious whether they were descendants of Central Asian nomads. Herding is a dying profession that many Kazakh cowboys don't plan to pass down to their offspring, preferring instead that their kids study for the higher-paying, less-harsh jobs of the modern world.

The horseman we watch now is striking atop his white mare. He's wearing a dark-brown, oiled leather jacket. A colorful knit saddle contrasts against the horse's body. Who made it for him? A mother? Sister? Or maybe he crafted it himself, knowing what would work best.

"He herds them out to graze all day," Darkhan says. "In late afternoon, he brings them back, and the owners come to retrieve them."

"Are they not his cattle?" I ask.

"No. If people in the village have a cow, this man takes care of them, keeping them healthy and exercised. They all go home at night."

Hmm, an equestrian cow walker. We happen to be walking by during the homecoming and observe cattle trotting to their respective owners like kids streaming off a school bus, running for their parents.

A middle-aged woman comes over to inquire about the strangers with Darkhan. He tells her we're from Canada, and her face lights up. She claps her hands then extends them to cover mine in a warm greeting. I'm loving this gesture around the world; the physical, warm contact and connection. It's so calming and welcoming.

"The last time the village saw a tourist was thirty years ago," Darkhan says.

Surely that can't be right. Maybe it's a lost-in-translation thing. On the other hand, how would travelers even know about Timiryazev? I feel even more honored to be a guest here.

Returning to the farm, Dave, impressed with the work quality evident from the woodshops, asks Darkhan if one of the machinists has a free moment to make a new bolt for his bike. The part had vibrated loose from the subframe and fallen off miles ago. We have rough roads ahead on our route to Magadan, and no one needs a busted weld in the middle of nowhere.

"Of course," Darkhan says. "Anything you need."

Dave wants the part made for safety just as much as he hopes to witness the steel bolt created from scratch. I'm also intrigued. We spend the evening in the shop watching the process. First, a piece of steel is cut to one inch, then clamped to the lathe and spun to create threads 10 mm in diameter. The machinist asks if we want another one for a spare, and Dave agrees it's good idea. A few minutes later, we have two bolts—which, because I've seen them in the making, look like works of art. Dave takes one, and it fits perfectly into the empty hole on his subframe.

The dedication these men have to their jobs and employer is touching. Darkhan treats them all like friends and makes sure we're introduced to everyone—even the kitchen and house staff. For each person, he tells us what their role is on the farm and makes a point of saying something nice about them and their work. We never meet Darkhan's parents or hear anything about them. Perhaps the young entrepreneur runs the family farm himself.

It's dinnertime. Darkhan invites us to an outdoor kitchen where the meals are prepared. I love how it's set up, with picnic tables under a tin roof, an outdoor range-top stove, and the coolest tea pot I've ever seen. The large stainless steel urn sits knee high on a sturdy tripod and has an actual chimney to release the steam before each pour. Eating on a bench with Dave, Darkhan, and a few of the farmhands, I can't recall a time when I've had so much fun discovering a natural environment that didn't involve mountains. I thank Darkhan for all he's shown us—a lifetime of memories in just twenty-four hours.

Late that night, I'm tucked into a single bed in the dorm. The only man snoring in the room of eight is Dave. However, I fall asleep with my stomach full of mutton stew and homemade bread. I dream I'm wearing a wedding dress while riding a white horse that morphs into my two-wheeled steed. I pull up to my reception at a Canadian banquet hall and am dismayed to hear no one wants to eat the main course—roasted horsemeat.

The return to perogies and vodka

Russia (Part 2)

At the border for entry back into Russia, three other ADV riders sit in front of us on dual-sport motorcycles. The bikes have Latvian plates and are covered with sponsor logos. They're loaded down with two spare tires each; our Night Wolves friend would be proud.

The riders each wear matching white, blue, and orange team jerseys. The men are burly and athletic and have hardcore bikes. They look intimidating. Since border crossings are usually serious affairs, we wave at each other and carry on with the process.

Two hours later, Dave and I are admitted back into Russia and start riding. Almost immediately, we come across the Latvians fueling up at a gas station. We pull in to say hi. Judging by their showy gear and bikes, I expect the guys to be full of themselves, but the tallest of the three comes over with a friendly smile and shining blue eyes.

"I'm Oskars," he introduces himself with a deep, strong accent. "These guys are Didzis and Ivars."

After shaking hands—which for me feels like gripping a bear's paw—we learn more about the three friends, all in their early thirties. While racing motorcycles together back home, they decided to team up and do an 11,000-mile overland ride from Riga, Latvia, to Magadan, Russia. They are called Adventure Team Latvia, and their journey will take them two months. One of their sponsors is a Latvian gas company called Neste, who will be covering their food and fuel.

Oskars is a gentle giant in charge. He's the only one who speaks fluent English and thus does most of the talking. I can already tell he has a great sense of humor by the way he jokes about Didzis and Ivars with a deadpan straight face. There's a brotherly bond among them all after having been on the road a few weeks already.

Oskars suggests we all ride into Barnaul together, where they are planning to end up for the night. We happily agree. Well, Dave does. I'm nervous I won't be able to keep up and Dave will lose me again.

Fortunately, the next 200 miles from the border into Barnaul are on smooth, wide-open blacktop. As expected, Adventure Team Latvia keeps a steady pace—faster than we normally travel, much to Dave's delight. I stay at the back of the line but with the pack. I have a cool vantage point of the four bikes ahead weaving in and out of traffic like a water snake in the current. It's thrilling to be part of the chorus line of movement that never stops. Not even to pee.

A few hours later, my adrenaline pumping and bladder throbbing, we are on the outskirts of Barnaul for dinner at a place Oskars already knows about. I smell the restaurant before I see it, and my mouth starts watering. Standing in line at an outdoor cafeteria filled with truckers and motorists, the five of us load up on hunks of grilled pork fresh off the skillet and still sizzling. We bring our plates to a table. Baked bread and the ever-present cucumber and tomato slices top off the feast. No one speaks for the first several minutes, our mouths full.

After mugs of hot, sugary tea to end the meal, we get ready to ride into the city. The rain that started while we were eating is now a full-on downpour. Oskars has somewhere in mind for accommodation and invites us to follow them. Being swept up into someone else's adventure is exciting, and it comes with the added perk of less effort. A few hours ago, Dave and I had no idea where we were staying or eating. Now, those chores are checked off the list.

But a NO VACANCY sign greets us on arrival at the predetermined hostel. With little hesitation, the manager jumps in his car and tells us to follow him to another place he manages. The rain now is like sitting in a shower with the faucets turned to cold on full blast. Traffic in Barnaul is at a standstill as gutters overflow and flood the dips in the streets. I swipe water from my helmet visor every two seconds and wish for the high-speed wipers slapping left to right on the vehicles surrounding me. In the traffic jam, I watch a shopkeeper in a yellow rain slicker hastily bringing in clothes on racks.

Someone from our group—Oskars, maybe, I can't tell in the monsoon—pulls out of line and bounces up onto a sidewalk, passing rows of wet fruit and veggies on display. Two bikes follow, then a third—Dave.

That leaves me to tag on or get left behind. From my position, I'll have to hit the square-edged curb at an angle and with almost no speed. I sigh deeply. Lounging, reading, watching the rain through a window…anything is better than sitting here cold and soaked in bumper-to-bumper traffic. I remember that time in Lima, Peru, though, when I bounced off the sidewalk and fell over.

I want to radio Dave and tell him to wait in case I drop my bike, but my headset is dead. I'd forgotten to plug it in to the USB port on my bike after dinner.

I can just stay here. The guy we're following is just a few cars ahead. At least I think that's him.

I'm anxious about being left behind, so I crank my handlebars and twist the throttle, feeling the impact of the curb slam through my forks. Now I'm on the sidewalk, passing the man in the yellow rainslicker, falling back in behind Dave and the others. I hear my mom's voice in my head—*"You go, girl!"*—even though she'd probably dislike knowing I'm keeping up with men who ride fast.

Ten minutes later, we park beside a gray building several stories high—Russia's omnipresent Soviet-era apartment housing, or *khrushchevka.* There's no grass, trees, or anything green anywhere, except weeds poking up in the cracked-concrete parking lot. At home, we'd call this a ghetto. It's depressing. I hope there's been a misunderstanding, but the Latvians are already removing their luggage. Someone must have gotten GPS co-ordinates from the hostel manager, still stuck in traffic.

I grab a pannier and my tank bag and clomp up uneven concrete steps into the building, where all is quiet, warm, and dry. *Maybe this isn't so bad.* After a second trip up five flights of stairs, all my luggage is in the apartment, and five motorcycles are parked side by side in the parking lot.

As I'm coming to learn, *khrushchevka* rentals are quite pleasant, in a grandmotherly decorated kind of way. In the kitchen, a red tea kettle sits on the burner of a tiny stove. Oven mitts with chicken graphics hang on the wall. Quilted duvets lay wrinkleless in the bedrooms, and the living room has an overstuffed couch facing an ancient TV. Dave and I are kindly offered one of the bedrooms, and in a true show of chivalry, I get first dibs on the bathroom. It feels odd getting into a shower when I'm already soaked, but the advantage is soon apparent when the hot water soothes my chilled body to the core.

I don't know if it's because I'm disconnected from friends and family or because I'm simultaneously missing and dreading home, but I've been feeling numb lately. Almost like I'm becoming desensitized to the things around me and what I'm actually doing, which is traveling around the world. That *should* be exciting.

Are things just calming down as we get closer to the end? The first year of our travels felt very *go, go, go*. I was in an almost constant state of hyper-arousal—heart pumping, emotions sharp and reactive. Now, perhaps knowing I'm going home soon, I'm feeling detached and lethargic: *hypo*-arousal. It makes sense. My body can only handle so much.

Later, we pass around a bottle of vodka. I feel out of place in the room with four men, three of whom are built like bears. Even Dave's five foot, ten inch frame looks smaller in comparison.

Oskars engages me in conversation. He has a sweet way about him that makes me comfortable, despite his size of six feet, four inches. Didzis is the more muscular of the three. He looks like a human bulldog that could mess you up in a bar fight, but he's the biggest teddy bear of them all, always smiling with eyes squinting like he's looking into the sun. Ivars is also friendly and loves putting on a show for everyone in the room, making us all laugh. With only Oskars speaking English, there's a lot of lost-in-translation humor going on as the vodka bottle gets closer to empty.

"We're trying to figure out who has to spoon in the second bedroom and who gets the couch," Oskars translates.

"It seems like the shortest person should get the couch," I wink, looking at Ivars. He's muscular, too, but shorter than Dave.

The three friends behave like men do all over the world—taking jabs at each other's expense and roughhousing in ways that speak of true kinship. But I sense Oskars and Didzis are closer. They run a business together and seem like truly bonded brothers.

The vodka bottle is nearly empty now. I think I'm the only one feeling it, and maybe Dave a little. I'm fairly certain that this much alcohol doesn't scratch the surface for these beastly guys.

Dave is talking about our plans for Magadan. He mentions that we've been camping most of our travels and that we're looking forward to doing that again as we get deeper into Siberia. Adventure Team Latvia gets quiet, and three sets of eyes stare intently at my boyfriend.

"But what about the bears?" Oskars looks concerned. I think he's joking. These guys *are* bears; what are they afraid of?

"We're used to bears where we come from," Dave says. "They don't bother us if we don't bother them."

This rationale works better for me in theory than in practice. I love camping, but when I'm in bear country, my imagination sometimes gets the best of me.

"Susan is terrified of bears," Oskars says with a straight face.

"Is that your wife?" I ask.

"No, that's him." Oskars points to Didzis, and everyone laughs. I ask why that name. Adventure Team Latvia met a guy in Almaty, Kazakhstan, who introduced himself. The name was difficult for the Latvians to pronounce, so the guy said, "Just call me Susan." Oskars thought this was hilarious and gave Didzis the nickname afterward. He's been Susan ever since.

It's not lost on me that ATL could be the answer to Dave's prayers when it comes to riding the BAM. I know he's already thought of this, too.

While I'm getting ready for bed, I hear Dave through the paper-thin walls talking about the idea with Oskars.

In the morning, over a breakfast of cheese on bread, Oskars asks, "Do you guys know the Altai region?"

"We've heard about it," Dave says.

Ewan and Charley had gone through this mountainous area that borders Kazakhstan in Southern Siberia in *Long Way Round*.

"Supposedly very beautiful," Oskars says. "Do you want to go?"

I'm flattered these sponsored motorcycle racers want to keep riding with us. Maybe it's a test for Dave to see if he's good enough for the BAM. That means we're going somewhere technical. I have zero reservations that Dave will ride whatever is thrown at him, but can I? We've been bickering recently about the same thing we have from the start: Dave rides faster, I ride slower. Maybe it's my imagination, but that dynamic seems to be getting worse since we've met up with the Latvians.

I'm not in the BAM tryouts, and I don't want to hold anyone up. But the *Altai*...

"Sure," I answer. "Sounds fun."

We plan to meet Oskars, Didzis, and Ivars in a few days on Lake Teletskoye. The only way into the Altai region from there is to cross the lake on a slow ferry.

Dave and I stay one more day in Barnaul. We had new tires shipped here, courtesy of Denis, a sort of motorcycle fixer we'd found in Moscow who can send parts almost anywhere in Russia.

Dave takes a few hours to swap our four tires for the more dirt-specific 50/50 tread Denis sent to a local motorcycle shop.

While he works, I Google "Altai" and learn the region is situated between Siberian taiga forests and Central Asian deserts and covers over 600 square miles—not all of it in Russia. Twenty-nine percent is in Mongolia, five in Kazakhstan, and four in China. This wonderful-sounding "eco-region" is famous for its thousands of lakes and snowcapped mountains, some of which are glaciated. The world's largest mountain cedar forestland lies somewhere in the coniferous taiga, providing homes to over 600 species of moss and thousands of vascular plants. In the Altai, you can find white-toothed shrews, Tuvan beavers, and Siberian ibex. There's nothing about bears, but they must be there, and up to 6,000 snow leopards have been recorded.

We don't leave Barnaul until evening—much later than hoped. The GPS tells us Lake Teletskoye is over 300 miles away, so we're now in a rush to get there by dark. We told the Latvians to expect us by dinner, but it'll be more like bedtime.

Riding through Biysk, traffic is bottlenecked going through town. Dave is ahead of me, and my heart jumps into my throat when I see him suddenly on the ground after rear-ending a minivan.

I park on the shoulder and run over to Dave, who's trying to get out from under his bike.

"Why were you following so close?!" I chastise once I see he's okay.

Dave's reply is muffled through his helmet. He points to the other side of the road at an absentminded pedestrian who had crossed before waiting for cars to slow down. The man is now staring with curiosity at the scene he's just caused. The van driver is yelling at Dave, likely for denting his bumper. Dave is yelling back at the driver for not watching the road more closely. Nobody understands what the other is saying.

Sadly, Dave is at fault for tailgating. Worse, our Russian insurance has expired. We forgot to update it when we came back from Kazakhstan.

A small crowd grows around us. The van driver refuses to get off the road until the police come, backing up traffic. People are honking impatiently. I examine the van—already full of dings, dents, and rust—and then Dave's bike for damage. The bike is fine because it was just the front tire that hit. The van's bumper has a small dent about the size of a baseball from the impact.

I have no idea how being uninsured is punishable in ultra-strict Russia. Will our bikes get impounded? Will we go to jail?

"We have to settle this before the cops get here," I tell Dave. Traffic is starting to move around us when the van driver hands Dave a piece of paper with "25,000" scratched on it.

"He wants $300," Dave scoffs, after doing the calculation on his phone. "The van's already a mess! He's just using this as an opportunity."

"Well, you did hit him," I say. Rear enders are always the fault of the person behind. "We're going to have to give him something, fast."

Dave sighs, unhappy with my lack of sympathy.

Removing his wallet from a jacket pocket, Dave gives the man two American fifties. The driver is about to protest but Dave thrusts it at him and walks back to his bike, which we moved to the side earlier. I've already started my engine, one ear open for the sound of sirens. The whole ordeal takes less than five minutes, but I think someone has already called the police.

Once Dave is on his bike, we speed away and don't stop until Lake Teletskoye.

These guys are like family

The Latvians are on an outdoor bar patio in the small village when we pull up at 10 p.m. They cheer and run toward our headlights coming up the dirt road. I almost cry, having spent the last few hours dodging potholes and deer in the dark. I hate riding at night. Their happy welcome makes me feel like I have three big brothers worried about my safety. They're drunk, but their good humor is infectious and erases our bad evening. Dave and I are smiling in no time. We postpone getting settled and instead join them for a very late dinner and much-needed beer.

"The room is just over there." Oskars points to a tall, white garage with stairs going up the back to a doorway. "You don't have to worry about drinking and riding!"

"I'm more worried about navigating those stairs after a few beers." I laugh.

We sit at a table of loud men. Oskars, Ivars, and Didzis have already made friends with some locals. I feel the warming effects of my first beer traveling down my spine into my legs. Tension leaves my shoulders, and I melt into the good energy.

Dave and I are handed another beer stein each. The overflowing brew spills lazily down the sides and makes my hands sticky. I drink this one more slowly, concentrating on taking deep breaths in between sips. I'm getting over our eventful evening but am nervous about the next few days.

One of the locals leaves and returns with two dozen smoked, dried trout and a bottle of vodka. The meat is delicious—perfectly salted and full of nutritious omega oils. I have no qualms about eating the fish right up to its dead eyeballs, picking bones from my teeth as I chew.

It's almost one in the morning when I remind everyone we have a 6 a.m. ferry—which, like our accommodation, is just across the road. I'm surprised Dave and the Latvians listen to me and call it a night, even though the locals shout for us to stay. At least I think that's what they're saying. Oskars, we find out, also speaks fluent Russian; he's a handy guy to have around.

Since it was a gift, we wrap the leftover smoked trout to take with us. I whisper to Oskars that the smell will attract bears so he should put the fish in Susan's panniers. He laughs and gives me a strategic thumbs up.

After getting the bikes and luggage sorted, Dave and I hike up the stairs into the apartment we're sharing with the others. The largest bed has been saved for us, but it's still tight for two. Dave and I spoon all night to avoid falling off the edge. Neither of us moves until an alarm goes off less than five hours later.

Loading bikes onto the boat while hungover is the first trick of the day. I stare at the two metal ramps laid out beside each other for four-wheeled vehicles and curse. I'll have to line up for one of the ramps and hope the rear wheel tracks with the front, all while avoiding the wire cables running up both sides. My brain plays out an unpleasant scene of me hooking one with my pannier and falling between the ramps.

Without asking, Dave takes over. He rolls my bike on board, nestling it in between the others. Part of me appreciates that he reads my mind; the other is embarrassed: I'm on a motorcycle touring the world, and two metal planks have stopped me in my tracks.

The ferry is more like a tugboat. There's no shelter except a makeshift awning over two benches and a table at the stern. Half a dozen cars and five motorcycles leave little room for anything else.

Lake Teletskoye is forty-eight miles long and a skinny three miles wide. On Google, it looks like a "Y" with one shorter arm. The crossing will take seven hours at seven miles an hour, or roughly six knots. I'm already wondering how to pass the time.

Once we're cruising, I lay out my yoga mat in a corner by someone's exhaust pipe and stretch in all my riding clothes. It's chilly this early in the morning. Inhaling, I arch my back into concave and convex shapes, breathing deeply with each transition. My spine has taken a beating on this trip; I hope I'm not doing any long-term damage. Then again, I'd rather be out here exploring than sitting at home all day, where I'd probably get arthritis anyway.

The extra space the yoga mat takes up in my duffle bag is worth it. I immediately feel my spine iron out and my mood improve. I love counting on this routine wherever I am in the world. After slamming into the ground when I fall off my bike and enduring hours of vibration over washboard roads, yoga or stretching is the least I can do for my body—an "I'm sorry" back rub of sorts.

After stretching, I fall asleep. An hour later, rain sprinkles my cheeks, and I roll over to look around, groggy. Folding my mat, I walk over to the guys sitting under the canvas awning with maps sprawled across the table. The other passengers are in covered vehicles, so we have the shelter to ourselves. I sit beside Dave, scooting closer to his warmth and enjoying the feel of his arm across my shoulders pulling me near. Oskars' grimy fingernail traces a line along a geographical feature.

Our route through the Altai region will take three days. At the end, we'll be near the border with Mongolia—a country Dave and I plan to enter.

"Here," Oskars points to a spot on the map, "we've been warned locals are not friendly. We should stop for the night either before this territory or after."

What does "not friendly" mean? I'm already dreading the dismount off the boat and the high, unpaved pass we'll cross later that afternoon. Will Dave wait for me or be tempted to ride fast with ATL? The weather isn't looking good, and none of us knows what condition that road is in—or its difficulty.

When the route planning is done, I set up a modest breakfast on the table with some of the leftover dried fish and a few pieces of fruit. Digging out the camp stove from Dave's panniers, I brew tea and coffee so we all have something warm for our bellies. The next five hours pass slowly, but the forced downtime is ideal in the end. I welcome the quiet opportunity to do absolutely nothing.

When the ferry aims for shore, the wind picks up and drags clouds as dark as factory smoke into the day. As the last bike on board, I'm now first in line to leave. I think everyone's watching me. I also have a beach audience: Three cowboys on horses smoke cigarettes and stare. Swearing, I twist the throttle and *give'er*—Canadian for "shit, I'm going too fast but too late now."

Rolling down the plank, I tense, squeezing past the cable. I hit the sand and my rear tire slashes through the dirt, but I stay balanced and cross the beach in seconds. Relieved, I park beside a tethered Dalmatian with the biggest set of dog balls I've ever seen. I think this is fitting.

I'm trying to get my camera out to film the others coming off the boat, but when I turn around, all I see is chaos and sand getting flung into the air in all directions. Ivars is down. Didzis' rear tire shoots him off into the trees. Oskars stops hard to avoid running over a small barking dog and is about to topple over. I scan for Dave and see him maneuvering through everyone and everything like a hockey player going for the goal.

There's no time for gloating; my riding partners have collected and are speeding past me.

Heavy rain slaps my helmet. I rush to catch up, dreading the mountain pass in this weather. When we turn onto a slick, muddy road, I wonder if getting off the boat was the easiest thing I'll do today.

We enter a beautiful, broad valley. I see four motorcycles a quarter mile ahead of me. They're already leaving me behind—even my fiancé. On the plus side, I have the place to myself. To my left, a wide, boulder-strewn creek bubbles milky-blue water down the valley. I'm ant sized compared to the mountains above me, which are covered in short vegetation and rise high into the gray sky. There aren't many tall trees—not like the heavily wooded forests at home—but the landscape here has many shades of greens and yellows.

Every now and again, Dave remembers I'm along and waits for me. When I catch up, I can only hold his tail for the first five minutes before the gap starts to increase between us and I'm alone again. I know he thinks I'm fine, otherwise he'd probably be more attentive. It's not because I'm a girl that I need someone nearby; it's because we're supposed to be a team—partners, keeping an eye on each other. We're in a foreign country, and I'm at the back of the pack with no map or GPS. I just like sticking together; my spirit dog is probably a border collie or some other herding breed.

The rain has backed off, and the road is easier to navigate now. I can see for a long way, and the others are always in sight, if not nearby. I enjoy riding my own ride through the gorgeous valley.

When we begin to climb the 5,000-foot pass I've pre-dreaded, it turns out there was nothing to worry about. It's rocky but not slick with mud like I had imagined. The switchbacks are wide enough for vehicles to pass each other—just like the logging roads back home I've driven countless times. Dave and the Latvians are a few switchbacks above me. Along with them, half a dozen 4×4s make their way up and down the pass.

I stop on a corner to photograph two local men with their UAZ-450. Because of their shape, these cab-over-engine vans are nicknamed *"Bu-khanka,"* which translates to "bread loaf." UAZs are everywhere in Russia but still make for a great shot of unique local culture. The men are obliging and even smile for the camera.

My riding partners are parked at the summit near a rock cropping. When I get off my bike, I'm sad to see I've lost my yoga mat. I was lazy after using it on the ferry, and instead of packing it back inside my duffle bag, I shoved it under my luggage straps. With all the bouncing around, my soft rectangle of solace fell off.

Hiking to a high point, I take photos of the valley and the dirt road we followed just before climbing the pass. The late afternoon is clearing, and clouds pushed by the wind are blob-like shadows crossing the terrain. I see sun flashing off the UAZ I'd photographed earlier, now driving through the valley bottom.

When I join the guys, Dave asks how I'm doing. I bite my tongue about the following distance and instead say, "Good. Today was easier than I thought."

The road gets wider and flatter when we leave but remains unpaved. When we get to the area Oskars warned us about, no one gives us any trouble, but they're not overly friendly, either. I'm reminded of northern Peru, but we're through the village in a few minutes.

That evening, Dave and I experience a first, because we've never stayed in a yurt before. Squatting to enter through the four-foot door, I see six beds surrounding a wood stove in the middle of the room and claim one with my tank bag. Exiting the yurt makes me laugh when I imagine how the three Latvian bears are going to deal with the short doorway.

There's a bathhouse on the property, and the wood stove is already fired up. Russian bath houses—*banyas* (баня)—are the world's greatest sauna, in my opinion. Spa-like yet practical, the log huts are where locals take care of hygiene duties.

Walking inside, I feel the fire's heat and immediately strip, hanging my toiletries and towel on wooden pegs hammered into a fir wall. I have the thirty-by-thirty outbuilding to myself and revel in being buck naked, letting the heat sink deep into my sore muscles. I breathe in the aromatic balsamic undertones, made more pungent by the heat. Several metal buckets have been filled with water for washing. I remove one heating up on the stove, which crackles and threatens to burn my knees when I get too close. I mix the hot water with cold from the other buckets on the floor. Cedar slats thaw my feet and allow the water I splash over myself to drain onto the grass under the banya. I shiver off the wet, chilly day and spread my towel on a bench to lie down.

Letting myself air-dry, I daydream about what my next life goal will be. Where will motorcycles take me when I get home? Will I be someone who looks for any excuse to run an errand on my bike, or will I be sick of traveling on two wheels? Maybe I'll find a job in the moto industry. Two years ago, I'd never have had the confidence or knowledge to think that was an option. But lately, I feel the pull of pride that allows me to sit taller in a room full of people talking about bikes—a conversation I can now be part of.

A soft knock brings me back to now, and the door opens a crack.

"Hellooo?" Dave says. "May I join you?"

I think it's cute he's asking permission and doesn't just barge in.

Dave decides his first task is to lay face down on the warm cedar benches and sweat.

"When we buy a house," he says, his voice muffled by the towel under him, "I'm going to build one of these in the backyard."

"I will marry you on that promise alone."

Returning to the yurt, we hear laughter and music. I'm craving a quiet, cozy night after the sauna, but that's not in the cards. Including the night in Barnaul, this is our third sleepover with the Latvians, and I know these guys can party.

Inside, our accommodation for the night is lit a warm yellow by the kerosene lamps and smells like vodka.

"Hey!" Oskars has a portable speaker in his hand. "Do you guys like this band?"

"Sure," I lie.

Adventure Team Latvia is beginning to feel like family—the kind of family you tolerate despite their bad taste in music. Their sense of humor makes up for any shortcomings, and soon I'm falling off my bed laughing when Susan gets stuck in the midget-sized exit. I beg this man, built like a bull, not to drag the entire yurt on his back into the bushes.

When Katy Perry's song Firework comes on, Dave changes the main chorus it to "Cuz baby, you're a pieeeeece of work."

How to be a man when you're a woman

Just as I'm settling into my seat for an anticipated easy 200-mile paved ride to the Mongolian border, my riding partners stop on a side road. Looking over their helmets, I see a steep hill filled with tire ruts weaving through the forest. It looks like an angry, evil grin with rocky teeth—exactly the kind of road that makes me nervous as hell. I can already feel the ass pounding my bike seat is going to give me if I have to gallop over all that.

Oskars is in the lead. He gives us all a thumbs up, which is more or less a question asking if it's okay to proceed. Three other thumbs shoot up. Everyone looks at me. This is likely the testing ground where ATL will judge whether Dave is fit for riding the BAM.

"*Mother fu*—sure, thumbs up, assholes," I mutter inside my helmet.

Sometimes, it feels like much of my life is spent trying new things just to rule out that I don't want to do them.

I start up the track after them. I know what's coming and how it's going to feel, but that doesn't make it any easier. I'm pretty sure this is going to be the hardest thing I've ever ridden.

The F800 retaliates beneath me, jouncing and sidestepping like a bothered show horse. I remind myself that this is what it's built for. The tires deflect off half-buried rocks, slipping down the sides, sending me off course. I jerk my front wheel away from the edge, making me too wobbly to attack the next obstacle. I'm only a hundred meters in when my hammering heart and heaving lungs beg for a rest, but I can't stop, or I'll never get going again on the steep incline.

The guys are already out of sight, skipping up the track with an agility reserved only for those with ham hocks for arms. I'm annoyed with Dave.

I wish he'd stay behind me in case I need help. On this trail, it's unnerving being last, because no one will see me if something happens. Maybe Dave will wait somewhere, but in the meantime, I've already envisioned my untimely death, sailing into the forest below.

I get up the track a few meters at a time, remembering to keep my chin up so my body, and therefore the bike, will follow. *Just get to that tree/rock/corner*—and when I do, I choose another landmark, just like climbing Kilimanjaro. With this mind game, I cover ground faster and better than anticipated. I really want a reason to turn around and go back to the main road, but there's no escaping; it's forward or nowhere.

The road deteriorates further into a V-shape with a deep, tire-swallowing rut down the middle. I'm like a snowboarder riding a halfpipe, except uphill. We're going up the side of a mountain with a "road" blazed straight up—not a switchback in sight. I badly want to give in to the insecurities and fears flashing through my brain. *This is dangerous! You're in the middle of nowhere! You can't do this, what are you thinking?!* Getting angrier by the second—at my self-doubt, at Dave—I tense every time I cross over the middle rut, thinking it's only a matter of time before I drop a wheel into the gap and fall over. I'm doing everything wrong: gripping my handlebars too tight and keeping my legs stiff like two-by-fours. I'm being unkind to myself and am already hearing the fight with Dave in my head. But when I come around a corner, he's there waiting for me.

"How are you doing?" he calls over.

"This is scaring the shit out of me," I yell back.

"You're doing great!"

Ahead, I see a stream coming down the track, and the rocks are loose and wet.

"Do you want me to ride your bike over this next part?" Dave asks.

I nod, relieved yet a little disappointed in myself.

With effort, Dave gets off his bike and comes over to me. I turn off my engine, release the death grip on my front brake and ease off the rear with my foot. The bike rolls back an inch before it catches in first gear and stops. I slide off the seat, and Dave slides on—a choreographed dance we've mastered when the angle is too steep to put the side stand down.

Hiking up the track after Dave, I pant with exertion and stress. *Why do I do this shit? I hate being scared.* How did I go from a city girl to a tomboy with more males than females for friends? Is there something wrong with me? Wouldn't I rather be drinking wine and painting my nails?

I pass Dave coming back for his bike and try not to snap at him. He's helping me and being nice, but I want to blame him for making me weird. This was all his idea anyway.

"It's easier up where I left your bike," he tells me.

"Thank god," I mumble.

"Hey," Dave reaches for me as I brush past. "You're awesome and I love you."

That helps. But I want to tell him not to get used to this, because when we get home, I'm turning into a muumuu-wearing cat lady with a passion for sport knitting.

I could have waited on the main road and not subjected myself to this, but I didn't. Is it peer pressure? Am I trying to impress these men? Or do I know deep inside that doing "this shit" is what makes me *me*. Through these pursuits, I gain an appreciation for what my body can do. I'm reminded how lucky I am to be healthy, to travel, and to have friends and family who say things like, "That sounds like something Heather would do."

Dave was right. The track eases up and becomes more of a road. I take a minute to look around. We're high in the Altai alpine now, surrounded by wildflowers. We could be in the Canadian Rockies or somewhere in Washington's Cascade mountains. But it's Russia. *I'm in Russia!* Even if adventure riders make it to this country, how many of them come here?

When I regroup with the Latvians, they cheer and congratulate me. It makes my heart soar and my throat constrict. *My big brothers.*

The remaining road to the summit is visible, with wide, winding switchbacks—easy. I have no idea why this road exists in the first place but think it has something to do with mining.

The five of us continue to the peak. At over 3,000 meters, there's nothing left now but shale and wind. It isn't the sunniest day, but we can see a long way. Rocky mountaintops poke up everywhere around us. We're higher than most of them.

After an hour enjoying the view, I'm cold and antsy about the descent. I tell Dave I'm going to get a head start.

"I'll stop in the meadow before the hard part and get shots of you guys coming through the wildflowers," I say.

"Okay. But if you drop your bike, wait for one of us to help you."

I take it slow on the switchbacks down. Using too much brake could make me skid on the loose dirt, so I let out the clutch ever so slightly in first gear, allowing the BMW's engine braking system to slow me down.

Feeling the gears catch, I squeeze the clutch—instead of the throttle—to give myself a little speed. This clutch–throttle technique is one of the hardest things to learn when riding off-pavement. Like sex, when it's done right, all moving parts sing in harmony, creating a subtle yet powerful responsiveness. When done wrong, those loose, grinding parts will lurch and jerk you around, often resulting in an ugly dismount.

All is going well until I make a split-second decision to take a shortcut. For all my knowledge and even after promising to be careful, I stomp too hard on my rear brake and feel the bike wash out from under me. Thanks to my riding gear, hitting the ground doesn't hurt too much. I'm too impatient to wait for the guys. Plus, after everyone congratulated me for making it up the mountain, I can't embarrass myself now.

Ignoring Dave's request, I spin the bike around on its side so the kickstand faces downhill and gravity is working for me. Next, I remove the luggage that isn't stuck under the bike, including my tank bag. Every pound counts. Before squatting to lift, I flick the kickstand down so that when I pick up my bike, it doesn't fall over on the other side. Grabbing the handlebar with my left hand and the luggage rack with my right, I mash my butt into the seat and bend my knees ninety degrees. Taking a deep breath, I heave upward, bracing for the sound of something like a guitar string snapping in my back. But the only noise is coming from me, grunting like a woman in labor. One final shove and my bike is back on two wheels.

Even with all my messing around, the guys haven't caught up. I gingerly mount and ride off to set up my camera in the wildflowers, keeping the secret victory to myself.

Descending the steep track back to the main road is easier than going up and takes less time. I'm in high spirits. The past few days have been the most off-pavement riding Dave and I have done since Namibia months ago. It's good to be back in the bucking saddle again; I've come such a long way since that wobbly first turn out of my parents' driveway. What if that me could have seen this me in the future and said: "Hey, guess what? One day soon, you'll be riding up a steep, rocky, narrow, mountain road with four men who were birthed with a motorcycle between their legs. You'll meet them at the top and they'll clap you on the back and say, 'way to go'—and you'll be in freakin' Russia."

I also wouldn't have ruminated so much over getting a new bike; I could never have done this kind of riding with the Stallion. I don't think I'd have gotten through Africa with that bike.

In many ways, I'm the rider I hoped and expected to be after two years of almost-daily riding. But I still feel like I need to prove myself and keep up—or at least not be the one holding everyone else up. Even when it's just Dave and me, I'm rarely relaxed while riding.

When we get to the border leading into Mongolia, it's closed, so we go off in search of a place to camp. The blond, grassy hills in the distance look like a great place to call home for the night. We ride to them cross-country and tuck out of sight, ever vigilant of safety, even in a group. Dave sets up the tent while I cook yet another pasta meal. This time, we have homemade sausage dumplings I had picked up along the way to dunk in the red sauce.

The clever Latvians start a campfire with clumps of dried cow crap, plentiful around us. A poop fire doesn't actually smell that bad, since it's dehydrated. We take turns flinging shit Frisbees into the flames to keep ourselves warm.

Where the fun never starts
Mongolia

Before entering Mongolia, our bikes are sprayed with insecticide to kill off anything invasive. I watch the mist settle on my seat and bags, wondering what this cocktail contains if it can kill insects and germs but not destroy plastic, paint, or rubber. It's probably the same venom that covers our fruit and vegetables before they get delivered to grocery stores.

After the toxic blast, I ride toward the customs buildings. A van speeds around me, filled with disgruntled folks I recognize from our Russian border exit a few minutes ago. When I pull up to the other bikes, the van occupants sprint to get ahead of me in line. Removing my tank bag and key, I walk inside, where the small space is crammed with people. I catch a whiff of sweaty clothing and nicotine-stale breath. I have no idea what day it is, but it seems everyone except us is returning to Mongolia after some no-fun visit to Russia. They don't appear to be happy travelers—more like hard workers and weary families.

Dave has an issue here. Months ago, he discovered his Canadian passport was waterlogged after rain leaked into a pocket in his riding suit. Until now, the faded photo and stamps hadn't been an issue getting into other countries, and we'd crossed almost two dozen borders since the passport got wet. Now, the Mongolian customs officer insists Dave's washed-out photo is unrecognizable and refuses to let him pass to the next window to import our bikes. Since Dave, a foreigner, is holding up the growing line of aggressive travelers, shouts come from the crowd, along with a general unease. I feel safe, being with four guys, and ignore the hum in the air. I rise above the heads of most; even the men only reach my shoulders. Didzis and Oskars stand out like giants nearly twice as tall.

After a few minutes, someone finally opens a second window. This appears to be a good thing, to deal with the masses, until I realize the window where Dave is now has a CLOSED sign, and a supervisor has come out to talk to him. I really want to see Mongolia and hope we're not sent back into Russia.

People elbow past me and slam into the newly opened window, shoving their passports under the plexiglass. It's absolute mayhem. Two more guards come out from the back and shout for everyone to form a line. I get behind a family with two kids, who seem accepting of the chaos. How awful to grow up normalizing this.

I keep my eyes on Dave, hoping that by the time I get called, his situation is resolved. My daydreaming causes a gap in the line, and the man behind me shoves me forward. I'm shocked and almost turn around to shove him back, but I grit my teeth and walk up to the kiosk when it's my turn. I bring out my documents and look over at Dave. *What happens if I'm permitted to enter Mongolia but he isn't?*

Dave is shrugging his shoulders and continues to point at his passport. All his other identifying documents are sprawled on the counter. All except one.

"Babe, the photocopy of your passport!" I call over to him while being pushed toward vehicle registration.

Before leaving home, we made copies of our important documents in case anything was lost or stolen. Dave digs through his stuff. He shows the piece of paper to the supervisor, who takes his time but in the end decides to stamp Dave's passport.

Dave joins me in line, which sends everyone into a frenzy again, even those not dealing with vehicle permits. We ignore them. We need to go through this stage together, because Dave carries the carnet de passage.

When everything is stamped and we start walking back outside to the bikes, Dave and I are separated in the group of moving bodies. The man who shoved me earlier comes out of nowhere like he's been waiting for me and sticks himself to my back like Velcro. The close contact from this smelly, middle-aged stranger feels gross and harassing. I lose my patience.

"No!" I growl like I'm scolding a dog. The man hip-checks me out of the way, and I'm slammed into the wall. I'm bigger than him, and it's almost funny, except I'm a little scared now. Nobody's helping me. Dave and the Latvians are already outside, oblivious. I don't understand what the man's problem is; we're all through customs and free to carry on. I want to put him in a head lock, but I've never been in a physical fight before.

Racing toward my bike, I hop on and turn the key. The Latvians are already at the insurance office a few hundred meters down the road. Dave, having seen me come out, is rolling away to join them. *Wait!* I want to get Dave on the headset, but my helmet is still in my hand. I yank it on just as Little Runt Man steps in front of my bike. When I wave for him to move, he comes over to my side and tries to push me off my seat. Nobody wants to get involved, and they pass by with their heads down. I'm grateful this guy is alone and doesn't have any friends in on the game. How easy would it be for a couple of guys to lift me up and cart me away without anyone knowing. *Damnit, Dave, why don't you ever see me when it matters?!*

I plant my feet and grab my handlebars while the man jabs my arm, mimicking me in a high-pitched voice. *This guy is insane.* I'm about to blast off, when he walks in front of my bike again and spits a nasty goop of slime onto my windshield. This seems to satisfy him, and he walks away.

"Asshole!" I yell and gun out of there with tears in my eyes.

I catch up to Dave and the Latvians.

"What's wrong?" Dave asks when I pull up swearing and jacked up on adrenaline. I get off and take out some wet wipes to remove the spit from my windscreen.

Dave's angry when I tell him what happened; it's the first time I see him legitimately protective of me. He looks back toward the border crossing, asking me what vehicle the guy's in.

"Let's just go," I say.

I'd love nothing more than to grab the four guys I'm traveling with and find Little Runt Man, but I don't want this to escalate.

I keep an eye on my mirrors when we leave. Nobody tails us. I don't even know if the man is driving his own car or is in one of those over-stuffed taxi vans, crammed between people who just want to get home.

For several miles, I'm tense, replaying the episode in my head. Maybe the provocation had something to do with sexism. I was warned that some cultures—and some men—might not like seeing a woman riding her own motorcycle, because females exhibiting strength and independence are threatening to certain male egos and customs.

Traveling with men might make me look bad, too. But Mongolia— where more than fifty percent of the population is Buddhist, forty percent non-religious, and just ten percent either Christian, Muslim, or followers of shamanic tradition—isn't high on the list of places I expected to have a run-in with a sexist male.

The incident was a harsh reminder that cultural differences can cause hate and angst, and that if I do something seemingly innocent from my point of view, it can be insulting to someone else. Many human traits are universal, but sometimes cultural differences are more prevalent than we know.

We turn onto a secondary road that's still paved but much quieter, even though the GPS tells us it's the main road to Ulaanbaatar, Mongolia's capital. My mood lifts when I see six wild camels plodding along the dry, desert floor. Dave and I stop, since it's our first time watching the lanky humpbacks in their natural environment. ATL keeps going after we make plans to meet up in the next town. They've seen more than enough camels after riding through southern Kazakhstan. The ungulates are as common to them now as Canadian deer are to me.

I'm on edge letting the Latvians go, in case something else happens, but I try to concentrate on the camels, clicking off a dozen shots. I appreciate my camera's interchangeable lenses. Even with the zoom, I can't get a close-up face shot, but I capture what I can. We've seen incredible animals in our travels, and they always make me smile. Unless the thing wants to eat or poison me.

Riding through the open, peaceful land is such a contrast to earlier that day. After the busy border, everyone dispersed. To where, who knows?

Mongolia holds true to its nomadic cultural roots. The deserted, rugged landscape is telling of a modest way of life. A third of the country's three-million-plus people live in the capital, Ulaanbaatar, or UB. That leaves much of Mongolia's 600,000 square miles wide open for nomading in its truest form.

We're still bordering Siberia, and the mountains in the distance are snow-capped, even this far into July. But at lower elevation, my temperature gauge reads 83°F. Heat isn't something I associated with Siberia until now.

Before they left, Oskars suggested we meet in a town called Khovd that evening. But as the day wears on, the riding becomes more challenging. The tension that eased off with the mountain scenery and wildlife is back, crawling up my shoulders and neck into the base of my skull. The washboard gravel roads and rutted-out water bars don't help my aching bones. Neither do the bike-launching bumps and dips.

The enormous countryside before me is a beautiful shade of green interrupted by sandy tracks slashing through from all directions. When the ruts get too deep, vehicles simply plow another trail, leaving a chewed-up panorama and—for those of us new to the area—a giant question mark as to what track goes where.

Dave has the GPS set to Khovd, but several times we're forced to backtrack and get onto another trail when we're led astray from our general trajectory eastward.

Later in the afternoon, we ride parallel to construction on a new, paved highway. Its black tarmac gives us guidance and tempts with its smoothness. The road is closed off with barriers, so we can't ride on it.

Or can we?

Dave gives in to temptation and jumps on the new road, despite the moving bulldozers and crews wandering about. I'm sure we'll be yelled at, but the workmen let us pass, even going so far as to pull things out of our way. Some even cheer and give us a thumbs up. Definitely not something we'd get away with on the Trans-Canada or interstates back home. Maybe they understand how hard it is to ride in sand.

I think we've struck gold riding along at fifty miles an hour over the smooth surface, but we soon cross an unfinished section too hard to ride over. *Damn*. Back onto the sandy desert floor until we can get on the tarmac again.

"Why do you think this road is being built in sections?" I ask Dave over the intercom.

"No idea. Maybe they're coming at it from both directions to meet in the middle?"

Except it keeps happening. Chunks of unfinished roadway, stopping our progress. We'll be coasting along on the fresh pavement only to be forced off into the sand by mounds of dirt or large holes blocking the way.

"Maybe they're inserting pipes for floodwaters to flow through," I say.

"Actually, I think it's to deter people from driving on it," Dave laughs. "That's why I love riding a motorcycle in these countries. No rules, go where you want…it's going to be hard to go home to speed limits and enforced construction zones again."

An ADV rider should never really hope for pavement, but I'm glad to see the infrastructure going into place. A paved road will greatly limit erosion from traffic over the fragile upland steppes and semideserts. Traveling through Mongolia so far has been truly incredible, with the wild camels and green landscape, but I'm aching for something solid that doesn't vibrate the teeth out of my head or compress my spine every five seconds.

After 120 miles—most of it done while standing up—I need a break.

"Can we stop for a snack?" I ask Dave.

With no shelter around, we sit in the shadows of our bikes. Scrounging in my kitchen pannier, I pull out some crackers and nuts. We haven't passed a store in days and are relying on dried goods. I'm always scanning for where to buy water and food, stocking up when possible. Sometimes these places are few and far between.

Crunching on almonds, I think about my pre-trip self and all the things I agonized over, like where to find water in the desert, and what if one of us had an accident in the middle of nowhere. We are right this very moment in a desert. We are right this very moment in the middle of nowhere. "We suffer more in imagination than in real life," I once read. Living the risk is nowhere near as scary as thinking about it.

This isn't to say I'm cured of fear. I have a new edginess now, borne from riding a motorcycle in foreign lands where dogs chase us and crazy drivers make me wonder how we aren't dead yet. This head-on-a-swivel style of riding is exhausting—except it's the only way to stay safe.

While we sit, I watch a vehicle approaching from the distance, its wheels streaking a dusty tail into the dry, hot air. The driver is heading right toward us.

"Out of the whole desert, this guy can't go around?" Dave covers his eyes from the sand cloud when the SUV stops beside us. My gut clenches. *Is it Little Runt Man?*

The driver rolls down his window, and to my relief it's not him, but the Mongolian man is shouting something at us, and I have a flash memory of another unpleasant episode: where the guys rode us off their land in Peru. *Are we not allowed to stop here?*

When he realizes we don't understand him, the driver hops out of his car and walks back to open his tailgate. He pulls something out of a cooler, and I almost laugh in relief when he hands Dave a cooked goat leg and makes motions for us to eat it. We thank him and he bows his head, waves, and drives off as quickly as he arrived.

Dave holds the meat in his hand, looking it over. "Do you think it's okay to eat?"

"Sure. It's cooked, right? And I'm starving. Here give me that." I yank the hoof and lower leg from his grip and take a bite. "Mmmm, it's good!"

Dave grabs it back and opens his mouth wide to tear off a piece.

"Mmmm! It's like a turkey drumstick."

Seared meat always makes Dave Sears happy.

It's after seven when we arrive in Khovd. Since it's 2017 and the world hasn't yet been struck by the pandemic, I don't think of the town as having an unfortunate name—but it is dry, dusty, and lacking charm.

The goat leg didn't last long in our bellies, and we're starving and desperate for showers. A message from Oskars tells us they kept going, since they got to town early.

"Let's meet in UB in a few days," it reads.

Adventure Team Latvia has given Dave the official thumbs up to join them on the BAM, but I sense Dave worrying that if we get too far behind these guys, he'll lose his riding partners. I'm also feeling unsettled; we've gotten used to the Latvians helping us find food and accommodation for almost two weeks now. Oskars is also our translator.

I step back into my role. The only half-decent hotel in Khovd is pricey. After some negotiation, they allow us to wheel the bikes into the lobby, and the added safety makes the cost worthwhile. Seeing our dust-covered bikes inside the immaculate, white-tiled lobby is quite the contrast. I feel bad for the cleaning staff, but I'll rest easy knowing the bikes are secure. So far, the only theft we've had in our travels was a GoPro stolen off my bike. And that was kind of my fault; I'd left the camera on its mount in plain view at a border crossing into Ecuador.

Freshly showered, Dave and I walk around town, stumbling on a pleasant family restaurant serving some of the best *bibimbap* I've ever had. This Korean dish is a mix of rice, vegetables, and a meat, like rib eye steak—all served in a piping hot cast iron skillet, topped with spicy dressings and a fried egg. The perfect well-rounded meal—nutritious and delicious. And filling. That's always important.

Who am I when I'm somebody else?

Khovd is already 97°F the next morning. The boiling orb in the sky and the relentless mocking sand is pissing me off by mid-afternoon. I may be able to ride up a mountain, but I'll never master this powdery grit. I keep hitting buried holes and am finally flung from my seat after one too many. The only thing sand is good for while riding a motorcycle, in my opinion, is soft landings. My jacket is partly open, though, and catches my handlebar on the way down, busting the zipper. A Velcro lumbar support I've been carrying for months becomes a belt—an easy fix, except now I'm sweating even more.

Dave helps me lift my bike then takes off. The best way to get going in loose ground like this is to hit the throttle and stay on top of it. I watch him disappear into a cloud of dust then emerge zigzagging across the desert, trying to correct his bike before it slams him down into the ground. Seeing this gong show, I choose a different line, which is somehow deeper, nastier, and even more ridiculous than his. I wipe out again. This time I stay lying there and watch a beetle causing tiny sand avalanches with his little hind legs.

I'm so tired that I don't want to get up, but Dave will think I'm hurt. He's been having the time of his life drifting corners and spraying up rooster tails that fall into a fan shape in his wake, almost like art. If I had more energy, I might have set up my camera. But as is the seesaw of relationships sometimes, when one partner is having a great time and the other is miserable, the dynamic can get volatile.

When Dave comes back to help me so soon after the last wipeout, he's shaking his head.

"You really need to pick up your spee—"

"I *know*, Dave. You've told me that a million times."

Taking a deep breath, I stare at the bare, hot, boring landscape. It's not really that boring, but I'm having a bad day. A knot the size of a hardboiled egg sits under my right shoulder blade and hurts when I turn my handlebars. I need the mother of all massages, but I'm not getting one of those out here in godforsaken nowhere. Today, I just want the trip to be over so we can go home. I feel bad thinking that.

Twenty-three months in, everything I love about traveling is becoming everything I no longer love. It's too much of a good thing. I'm missing first-world *stuff*: a closet full of clothing variety, more than two pairs of shoes to choose from, organic food, health stores, gym memberships, wine with friends, books, slippers, bathtubs...all material items that call to me in my weaker, ungrateful moments. I crave these comforts more and more as we near the end of our travels. My tolerance for inconvenience is wearing thin. I had hoped that living on the road for two years would make me want fewer things. But despite selling almost everything I owned, I know I'll want most of it back again when I get home. And how long will the novelty of new stuff last? A week or two? So, what is it all for?

I miss the high I was on a few days ago in the Altai. Where did that go? Why am I so moody? Shouldn't I be blissed out, loving everything and everyone after all I've experienced?

I look for something to blame and decide my rear tire is the problem. The new rubber we put on in Barnaul is not working for me. The tread pattern on the sides is beefy enough, but down the middle, it's too smooth to bite into loose dirt. I want to look for different tires in Ulaanbaatar. Magadan is still 4,000 mostly unpaved miles away.

Later that afternoon, the terrain changes back to a vibrant green. The sand becomes shallower and is replaced with hard-packed dirt. It's still achingly hot. I'm way behind Dave and wilting in the heat when a stunning sight rouses me from my gloom: a man on a horse with an eagle on his arm. The hunter is cool looking, but what catches my eye is the majestic bird, whose wings appear longer than the length of the horse's body.

Eagle hunting—as in using the birds to hunt, not hunting the birds themselves—was once a respected tradition passed down from father to son in the Mongolian nomadic lifestyle. However, due to limited health care, employment, and education opportunities in rural areas of Mongolia, families are moving into bigger cities like Ulaanbaatar. As in much of the modern world, an ancient tradition like eagle hunting, formerly used to catch game such as foxes and hares, has been redesigned to attract tourists who'll pay to have their photo taken with the big birds.

The eagle hunter I pass is the real deal; we're too far from anywhere touristy. I want to catch the magic moment through a lens but am conscious of Dave worrying if I fall too far behind.

I start climbing a road leading out of the spacious valley. Until recently, I was able to see Dave, even though he was a few miles ahead. Now, he's out of sight while I ride the switchbacks over a pass. The increasing gap between us is bugging me, but I can't catch him to ask whether we can stay closer.

At the top of the switchbacks, the terrain opens again to reveal a huge plateau stretching for miles in all directions. I still can't get eyes on Dave. I should be worried, but anger flickers instead like a struck match. This time we can't blame the traffic for obscuring one of us; I haven't seen any vehicles since goat leg man.

After twenty miles, I'm no longer raging and am getting scared. *Did I miss a turn? Surely, he'd wait for me if we were turning off the road.* I watch the miles on my odometer in case I need to backtrack.

Earlier that day, I was sure Dave had crashed and slid off the road, but he'd just taken a shortcut and thought I'd seen him. Did something actually happen this time?

Another dozen miles click by. I finally see him way off in the distance, stopped on the side of the road. My relief is short-lived when I get closer and notice he seems casual, like only five minutes has passed. I come to a hard stop, not caring that the dust cloud makes him cough. He rubs his eyes and comes over.

"What the hell, Dave?"

"What?" he says, all brown-eyed and innocent.

I glare at him then realize my sun visor is down. I flick it up with attitude. "Where have you been for the last—" I look at my dash—*"thirty-two miles?!"*

Dave sighs. "Come on, it's been a long day. Let's just get to Altai Town—it's not much farther."

I could leave it at that and follow him, letting the rhythm of the road under my wheels calm me. Except he has no idea why this matters—after all this time together and countless conversations about watching each other's back and *what if something happens*...I remember Dad's firm grip on Dave's shoulder: *Take care of each other.*

Dave has told me before that he admires my independence. I could see this as a compliment, that he doesn't need to baby me. But is it admiration or a way to absolve himself of responsibility? I don't want him to mistake my resilience for invincibility. And I don't want to be fending for myself all the time, either. Even if you're strong, there's nothing wrong with wanting to feel protected, especially by someone you're about to marry.

I whip off my gloves and throw them across the desert as far as I can. Grabbing my helmet strap, I tear it from under my chin. Dave instinctively reaches forward, thinking I might toss my $500 brain lid, too, but I place it on my handlebars. Free and unencumbered now, I scream across the plateau until my breath runs out. There's no echo.

"We're in the middle of nowhere!" I yell at Dave, who looks pretty fazed now. "And where are you? Nowhere to be found! I've been riding alone for an hour thinking I was lost or something horrible happened to you."

"I thought you liked riding by yourself sometimes."

"For an hour? When I can't see you? Shit, Dave, are you even concerned about something happening? Why can't you ride behind me for once? Or *with* me?"

Dave sits down beside his bike and puts his head in his hands.

"Can you not understand how messed up this is?" I continue. "You don't even notice how long it's been since you last saw me. What if I was in trouble?"

Dave is unresponsive, which infuriates me even more.

"This is bullshit. I'm sick of you doing whatever you want, assuming I'll just be back there following you around like a lost puppy." I retrieve my gloves and get back on my bike. "You know, I'd like to say we feel like a team, like we're in this together, but I don't."

The image of Dave in my mirrors as I'm leaving tugs at my heart, but my anger is more determined. In that moment, I feel I've betrayed myself. I want to be free of depending on him—or anyone—anymore.

Back on the paved road, a calm envelopes me. Sometimes there's no greater peace than that which comes after a blowup. I have no idea what I think I'm doing. *Maybe the road will tell me.*

My low-fuel light is on, and Altai Town is at least thirty minutes away. How embarrassing it would be to get stuck on the road. I think about the time in Namibia when we were both on empty and the next station was over 100 miles away. We flagged down a passing pickup truck, and although the driver didn't have extra fuel, he allowed Dave to disconnect the fuel line so we could squirt the gas into our camping fuel bottle. We eventually had enough to make it to a farm, where they had a tank to fill us up.

I don't have the skills to siphon fuel from a car, and I'm wondering if I have the Dalmatian balls to hitchhike. The thought of Dave rescuing me is too ironic to stomach.

I make it to the station in Altai Town. A teenage kid comes out to help me at the pump. I'm so angry with the male gender right then, I almost push him aside and wonder whether I should become a lesbian.

When I take off my helmet and the teenager realizes I'm female, he looks up the street, presumably for my companion. I want to say something righteous, like: "What, you've never seen a woman trying to make it alone in a man's world before?"

The young man is distracted and overfills my tank, spraying fuel all over my bags and down the side of my bike. Dave warned me about overfilling the tank. *What was it he said?* The teenager quickly shuts off the pump and mumbles something, avoiding my eyes.

Okay, pooling gas near the exhaust…that's an issue. I'll have to wait until that evaporates. The more pressing issue is how to remove the excess gas from the tank. I take off my pannier on the right side and start tipping the bike over ever so carefully, but it gets away from me and crashes against the fuel pump, punching in a large dent.

Are you fucking kidding me? I can't even be autonomous for an hour without a colossal fail.

The young man is staring at me, no doubt thinking I'm insane. At least he isn't running off to tell anyone about the damage I've caused. I smear a smile onto my face and politely gesture for him and another guy who has stopped to watch the commotion, to help me right my bike. *I'm a strong, independent woman! Until I need someone to help me with my bike…*

I hand over some cash for the fuel, shaking my head and laughing like a lunatic. I've well and truly lost it.

Leaving the two men with mouths ajar, I ride off in search of a hotel. *This is what you wanted—independence.*

Scanning the streets in the quiet town, a cold bucket of loneliness hits me. It's the time of night I look forward to: dusk with Dave. When we're done riding, enjoying happy hour somewhere or by the tent, talking about our day. Our future.

I hadn't thought this part through. Will I eat dinner alone, too? *Oh my god, did we just break up? Is the engagement off?* I feel an awful sense of losing something important and valuable. *But how could he ride for an hour and not stop to check in with me? There's something mind-blowing and unforgivable about that!* I'm never more uncomfortable in my life than when I have to question my values.

Coming to terms with facing several thousand miles of dirt roads and a border crossing by myself is startling. *How will I get back into Russia without the carnet?*

I pull over. Happy memories shared between us pop up unwelcome in my head: the proposal on Kilimanjaro, laughing together in the tent, holding hands before falling asleep.

Get a hold of yourself! You have needs that aren't being met; stick with your guns.

I'm trying to summon the energy to find a hotel when I see something in the melting mirage down the street. A motorcycle. It's Dave. My heart leaps. Maybe the universe is still in our favor.

If there's a wheel, there's a way...

A few days after our worst fight ever, Dave and I are on a trajectory for a freshwater lake in central Mongolia, known locally as Terkhiin Tsagaan, or White Lake for us English speakers. The hope is to get there that evening and rent a yurt.

Topping up our tanks in a small village, I admire the colorfully painted rooftops of local homes and stores. This feature is common in many places we pass through in Mongolia. I think it has something to do with the dry desert surroundings, where there isn't a single green plant or tree to be found. Bright blues, yellows, and even fuchsia offer the one-story buildings a way to stand out. They bring some much-appreciated cheer and color to the day.

Leaving town, I pick up my speed and relax into my seat. I'm going about forty miles an hour, gaining on a slow car, when I pull around to pass just as we're about to cross a bridge over a shallow, meandering river. That's when I see the mother of all potholes where the bridge deck meets the pavement—a hole that could swallow the back end of a small sedan. It's two feet deep, four feet wide and has been carved out over time from vehicle wheels coming off the bridge and dropping into the gap.

With no time to change course, I slam into the hole, meeting the bridge deck with my front tire. The impact ricochets through every joint in my body. My bones shudder and my tendons twang. Somehow, I stay on the bike and don't get launched over the handlebars.

When I keep riding on the now-smooth bridge, something doesn't feel right. I pull over and stab the button on my headset to alert Dave.

The smell of burning oil and hot metal drifts around me. Sliding off the seat, I look at my front wheel and swear. The rim has a three-inch dent on both the left and right side. I'd hit the bridge deck so hard, it pinched the tire and bent the steel. The rubber held its bead, which is fortunate, as an exploding front tire would have caused me to crash. Bending down, I listen for air escaping. Nothing. I rub my finger along the sidewall, where a spray of liquid covers my wheel and brake rotors. I notice something on one of my fork stanchions that shouldn't be visible: The wiper and seal, internal components of the suspension system, are stuck at the top of the smooth tubes. Hitting the concrete with such force fully compressed my forks, which blew on impact, spraying lubricant everywhere, including onto my pants. I now have no front suspension, and since my brake pads are covered in oil, they too are useless. I stare at this mess in shock, physically hurting in sympathy for my bleeding workhorse, now with two broken legs. In a country where the main "highway" is loaded with washboard ruts, sand, and embedded rocks, I'm not going anywhere.

Throwing something always makes me feel better, so I whip off my gloves again, watching them land in a puff of dust.

"What happened?" Dave rides up, eyes wide when he sees my front wheel.

"I hit an asshole of a pothole entering the bridge deck."

"It was more than just a pothole, judging by your front tire. How did you not crash?"

Dave goes into fix-it mode. Hauling my bike onto its center stand, he removes the front wheel and cleans the oil off my brake pads and wheel rim with a rag. After several minutes of trying to pound the warped rim back into place with wood and a rock, he gives up and straps it to the back of his bike.

"I'm going back to that village where we got gas to see if anyone can help."

Self-pity keeps me from appreciating Dave's willingness to search for support in a remote place where no one speaks our language. He's been far more attentive lately, after our fight. Still, I scowl on the side of the road. It truly feels like this country hates me.

Ulaanbaatar is three or more days and 1,000 miles away. Even if there's a tow truck available, I can't afford one all the way to UB. I have a vision of myself as a disgruntled hitchhiker in one of the rickety vans I've noticed hobbling and squeaking across the desert, leaving parts behind in the sand. I'm probably safer on a motorcycle with a busted front wheel.

While Dave's gone, I ruminate. Would those following our journey be surprised to know that some days, I'm sure I've made a huge mistake spending my life savings on this adventure? They all assume we're having the time of our lives.

A few vehicles pass with brown faces turned toward me, curious. Some slow down, but only enough to stare at the weird-looking motorcycle and stranded rider. They must sense my mood; I'm glad when they keep going.

One car stops, though, and the driver gets out. I sigh, bracing myself for a conversation I won't understand. I don't even know *please* or *thank you* in Mongolian. The man walks over, hitching up his pants, and stares at my bike. I stay seated on the ground in the shade. He starts to talk without smiling, and I think he's probably harassing me about being a solo female on a motorcycle—but then a woman opens the passenger door. She walks over and hands me an ice-cold bottle of orange pop. I wonder if she's just purchased it in the nearby village for herself. Her kindness puts a smile on my face, and I thank her by covering her hands with mine. She waves when the two drive off, leaving me to remember that no matter where I am in the world or how depressed I am, there is always—*always*—the simple act of compassion from a stranger—the very humanity that has defined our trip from the start.

Maybe Mongolia doesn't hate me. Like waking from a nightmare, I notice my surroundings aren't all that bad. The sun is shining, the sky is blue. I sip my cold drink and watch a young boy across the road, half hiding behind a mound of dirt in his green T-shirt and grubby shorts. *Where did he come from?* I bring up my hand in greeting. He stays stone-faced for a minute then bursts into giggles and runs away. I'm envious of his carefree-kid ways, even though he likely leads a far more difficult life than I ever have and probably ever will.

I thought I knew what I was getting into with this adventure. Maybe I'm obsessed, like when an Everest climber is in the worst, most grueling moment and risks brain cells and frostbitten limbs just to keep going. Perhaps it takes an obsessive personality to achieve goals that seem senseless and impractical to others. Having come this far, I want to make it to the top of the mountain because regret is worse, to me, than suffering. Regret lasts longer. Sometimes forever.

Dave returns with my wheel. Miraculously, he found a tire repair shop. Using a sledgehammer, they were able to bend the flat spots in my rim back to something resembling round.

I'm on my feet, hopeful. "Does this mean it's rideable?"

"You're going to have to be careful," Dave says. "Your front brakes are essentially inoperable, and I won't know the damage to your forks until I can take things apart later."

"Thank you."

Dave rolls up his tools. "I saw the pothole. I can't believe you stayed on your bike. It's really quite impressive."

We continue our route to White Lake. Without front suspension, every dip and bump elicits a metal-on-metal sound that makes me flinch. But not having front brakes is the scarier part. I rely on downshifting and let my rear brakes do the rest. Despite all this, I appreciate my bike even more. The Stallion would never have taken a hit for me like my F800 did on that bridge deck. The Stallion would have bucked me off with nothing but a slap on the ass on my way over the handlebars.

"Just a few hundred more miles and I'll get you fixed," I say, patting my girl.

I wish I'd come up with a nickname for her, but nothing ever felt right. I once thought of *Snow White* after the *Black Stallion*, but that was too fairy-tale-like. And there's nothing fairy-tale about me *or* my bike.

The late afternoon sun creates sparkling jewels on the lake's surface. A cluster of yurts—or *gers*, as they're called in Mongolia—sit back from the shoreline, each with a bench facing the water. Half a dozen yaks nibble the rich, green grass behind a barbed wire fence. I can't wait to relax here.

Dave goes off to find the host while I talk with a young man who speaks English. Proving how small the world can really be, he knows the guy who sold me my F800 at Outpost Alaska in Fairbanks almost a year ago. Justin Kleiter came to Mongolia in 2016 to ride in a cross-country motorcycle race, and the young man I'm talking to now was part of the team assist. I feel at home with our shared connection and am glad when Dave says he rented the *ger* for two nights.

Grabbing my panniers, I walk over to our cozy-looking home. The short door is painted a vibrant orange with a decorative design. Like the yurt we stayed in with the Latvians, the beds are arranged in a wide circle against short, four-foot walls. It's a clever use of space; when in bed, you're lying down anyway, so it doesn't matter if the ceiling is low.

The *gers* at White Lake are set up for tourists, and I don't think they're ever taken down. But in general, yurts are portable in keeping with the nomadic lifestyle. Round with a tall, domed ceiling, the shape allows plenty of room to stand up in the middle yet keeps weight and size down for transporting.

Assembling and disassembling a yurt can take anywhere from thirty minutes to three hours—not your typical backpacking tent setup—but even at the longer end of the scale, that's much faster than most of us can build or move out of our houses.

The nomads don't pick up and leave because they've decimated the land. Herding families move every season during winter pasturage, spring pasturage, etc. In colder months, the herds are kept close by to conserve energy. Once temperatures rise and things start growing, the animals are moved often so they can fatten up on fresh vegetation. A nomad family might move six to eight times a year and sometimes as far as 100 miles in a single push.

The culture fascinates me. Although many have flocked to urban locales, a lot of the country's population still live as nomads, herding domesticated livestock such as camels, goats, yaks, and cows that supply the families with meat and dairy. Nothing goes to waste here. Even animal bones are used as tools, musical instruments, or toys for kids. For thousands of years and to this day, herders have created sustainable lives in the sparse, rugged Central Asian plateaus, using horses and yaks for transportation. These are the real nomads, unlike the YouTubers of today.

Gers can sleep up to a dozen people, but tonight it's just Dave and me. Lying in my single bed, I look closely at the painted wooden spindles that make up the ceiling frame. The long, skinny poles match the orange door and have the same hand-painted pattern. How long did it take to paint the intricate designs all the same? There's no computer-generated imaging here.

A small woodstove sits in the center of the room, its chimney poking through the domed roof, where I have a view of the late afternoon sky. Nights on the desert steppes are chilly, and I'm sure we'll be firing up the stove later.

Crouching back through the door, I join Dave outside on the bench. He's already acquired two cans of beer from the ladies working in the cook tent. The ale is warm, but I don't care. It's been a tough day.

A clutch & an ice cream sandwich

Dave is getting concerned over our planned meetup with Adventure Team Latvia in UB. We're already behind them by two days, and my fork repair isn't going to help. Plus, after hitting the bridge deck, my clutch isn't working properly. I mention this to Dave the next morning, hoping it'll be an easy fix while he's assessing my forks.

"Tell me again what you're experiencing," Dave says, standing beside my bike with an impatient look.

"Shifting up is easy. I pull the clutch in and tap the lever up with my toe to get into gear. But when I downshift, it takes a lot of force. Like, I need to jump on it."

I check in on Dave an hour later. His mood is deteriorating. He swears then tosses a wrench onto the grass.

"What's wrong?"

"The clutch slave cylinder is all gacked up, causing erosion on the seals. All your clutch fluid leaked out overnight."

I look at the grass, noticing it's darker in one spot.

"What does that mean?"

"It's broken. You can't ride like this."

My stomach is acting up, so I head to the outhouse, which makes me feel worse. Tourists don't know how to shit into a hole at their feet. It's nearly impossible to find a place to stand and hover without stepping on something disgusting.

Inside the foul outhouse, I deliberate. Yesterday, with sheer luck, a handy boyfriend, and a well-placed auto repair shop, I was able to ride away from an accident. Today, I'm back to going nowhere with a malfunctioning motorcycle. Could I poke along in first gear all the way to UB?

I smear-walk over the grass, trying to remove any fecal matter from the soles of my flip-flops before I track it into our *ger*.

Dave is speaking to the young man we met when we arrived.

"I'm going to follow these guys to a small town nearby where there might be an auto shop," Dave says.

I think he's wasting his time trying to find clutch parts for a 2016 BMW in a small village, but I wish him luck.

While Dave's gone, I take a bottle of biodegradable soap to the lake and wash our clothes. It's the least I can do. Hanging fabric over a line strung between the yurt and the bench, I wonder how many hours Dave has sacrificed to repair my bikes.

When I hear his bike returning, I expect to find Dave in a grumpy mood. Instead, he's beaming.

"No way," I say.

"Oh yes. Yes way."

"You didn't seriously find a clutch cable in that village…"

"Not just a clutch cable, but also a clutch lever *and* mineral oil." Dave pulls everything out of his tank bag. "Get this. I found it all at a grocery store, and it only cost five dollars—including an ice cream sandwich."

He kisses me, and I wipe chocolate off my lips.

The cable is a Chinese knockoff and too long, but Dave engineers something to take up the slack. He goes for a test ride, distracting the yaks from their munching.

"Works great!" he says.

With everything now in working order, Dave can enjoy the rest of the day off. He gets two more warm beers, and we sit beside each other on the bench.

For nearly 700 days now, Dave and I have been consumed by our adventure. I don't remember any other life but this: getting up to ride each day and dealing with whatever the road brings. But I'm wearing down now, like I'm approaching the finish line to the longest marathon on earth.

Dave holds my hand. We watch the yaks. I count twenty-one; number twenty-two gave its life a few days ago for our dinner.

"What is the one thing you're looking forward to the most when we get home," I ask, "but think the novelty will wear off quickly?"

Dave thinks for a moment.

"Daily, hot showers...jobs that put money into my bank account again. What about you?"

"Healthier food and an exercise routine."

We watch a herder on a small motorcycle rounding up livestock.

"Are you happy?" I ask. "I mean with how far we've come. Did you ever really believe we'd get all the way here?"

"Well, we're not done yet," Dave replies, always a realist, "but yeah, it's pretty crazy to think of when we were looking at the map almost three years ago. It's so easy to plan an adventure at home."

I choose to ignore that he didn't really answer my question and ask him another one.

"So, is this Type Two fun?"

"Fun to plan, hard to do, great memories? Let's hope so." He turns to me. "I really am glad we're doing this together. I wouldn't want it any other way."

Dave has said that before, but after fights, exhaustion, and mechanical issues, it's nice to hear he still feels that way.

"Me too," I say, laying my head on his shoulder.

Clandestine chauffeuring

Ulaanbaatar, with its population of 1.5 million, is a substantial culture shock after the isolated, peopleless regions we've been traveling through for weeks now.

We roll into the anarchy of Mongolia's capital in searing heat. My stomach has long since emptied itself of the oatmeal I had for breakfast and the ice cream, Coke, and dry crackers that made up something of a lunch. After another day of avoiding bumps and dips because of no front brakes or suspension, I'm ready to be off my bike.

At 8 p.m., the sky is bruised with dark clouds foreshadowing a storm. We have no accommodation leads except a tiny bed icon on the GPS screen. Dave weaves through UB's rough city roads with me on his tail. After 400 paved miles from White Lake, Ulaanbaatar hands us huge potholes hidden under the bumpers of an endless line of traffic. Navigating through a roundabout is extra sporty when a random cow tries to cross the roadway.

The bed icon comes through. We arrive at The Oasis Café and Guesthouse and ring a cobbled-together doorbell with hot wires poking out the sides. I hear the *brrring!* a few feet away, and a young man with dark almond eyes and a hawkish nose lets us in.

"Welcome! Where have you traveled from?"

His warm greeting is soul lifting in the bedlam around us.

"Come in! My name is Damen." He opens a large gate so we can roll the bikes into a courtyard. I immediately feel at home. Half a dozen overland trucks are parked, rooftop tents popped open. A sleeping bag airs out on a Land Rover whose hood is vinyl wrapped with a world map. Looking more closely, I notice a squiggly line outlining an intended route from England through Russia. A boiling pot of water sits on someone's tailgate, unattended. The control freak in me wants to turn it down, but I leave it alone.

European license plates abound. I'm not great at distinguishing countries from the tiny square flags on their rectangular black and white plates, but do notice one from Germany and another from Poland.

I'm even more excited to see half a dozen ADV bikes, some with tools strewn around their bases. Maybe we're all here under varying degrees of vehicle distress after the unrelenting beatings of Mongolian roads. I take this as a sign that we're in good company for repairs and for getting a new set of tires. The overlanding demographic is flourishing here in UB.

Damen leads us to a room. On the way, we pass a little girl wearing a navy T-shirt that reads: "I want to see the world." I give her a high-five.

"Is there a place to find motorcycle parts nearby?" I ask Damen.

"We have the mechanic right next door."

Truly the perfect overland oasis.

Later, we find an email from Oskars telling us they decided to ride a back road into Russia and will meet us in Irkutsk in three days. This is Dave's last chance to catch them before they start the BAM.

"I hope those guys aren't trying to lose me," Dave says in an uncommon moment of insecurity. I remember once accusing Dave of the same thing and realize now how ridiculous that must've sounded.

After showers, Dave and I go downstairs to the communal kitchen for a beer. The only thing to eat at this hour is free bread. We make six pieces of toast each and butter them liberally. I've long since given up on trying to eat healthy. I just want to eat.

Despite the promise of having an auto shop next door, they don't have parts I can use on a BMW. The mechanic's assistant, Tseren, offers to drive Dave around UB to a few moto shops.

Tseren is unfortunately a crook in sheep's clothing. When he returns Dave to the hostel four hours later, he asks for a ten-dollars-per-hour "chauffeur and translation service fee" that wasn't agreed on beforehand. Although Dave didn't expect Tseren to drive him around for nothing, he could have taken a taxi for far less than forty dollars.

Despite spending half the day looking for parts, Dave came up empty-handed for most of what we need. He decides to ride back to a KTM motorcycle dealer he and Tseren visited to see if they can order BMW parts. While there, Dave strikes up a conversation with the guy working at the counter who, surprisingly, once lived in Bellingham. With that in common, the guy takes a liking to Dave and reveals that when they were there earlier, Tseren asked him to charge an additional ten percent onto Dave's bill when he bought some new tires for the BAM. When they got back to the car, Tseren said he forgot something and went back into the dealership to collect his finder's fee.

We don't say anything. The mechanic himself is a nice guy and lets us work inside his shop and use his tools at no cost. He's likely unaware of Tseren's clandestine side hustle.

Dave is now outfitted with a pair of aggressive dirt tires he wants for the tougher Russian roads ahead. I get his current knobbies, since there's plenty of tread left, and I'm not doing some of those roads. Dave also found me some brake pads to replace my greasy ones, but the forks are still a leaking mess. There's no reason to replace the brakes yet, as they'll get covered in oil.

I bring Dave a beer and watch him take the stanchions apart. The bushings are not yet damaged, but because the mother of all potholes caused the seals to twist and fold on themselves, they're torn and don't hold lubricant for long.

Dave cleans the seals and wipers—which, although torn, will help keep some dirt out—then reinserts them right-side-up. On advice from the mechanic, we add transmission fluid to the forks, so they'll at least have some lube for the ride to Irkutsk, where Denis, our motorcycle fixer in Moscow, is sending my parts.

When we leave the Oasis Guesthouse two days later, I still need to coax my poor bike another 500 miles. I'm not confident it can take the beating, but I push on ever closer to Irkutsk, crossing our last border of the trip, back into Russia.

Placing color images in this book was cost-prohibitive, so my solution is to bring you our travel photos digitally. To see color images for each country, scan the QR code or visit Photos under Riding Full Circle on my website, heatherleawriter.com.

The easy way out has an Australian accent

Russia (Part 3)

Dave takes his left hand off the handlebars and places it on his thigh. This casual motion tells me he's relaxed. His white helmet and gray jacket are a uniform so familiar to me now, and somehow comforting. We've spent so much time together. How will it feel to live in two different countries again, seeing each other only on weekends? Our lawyer said the K-1 (fiancée) visa could take up to a year. Only then will I hopefully be permitted to enter the US again.

Riding to Irkutsk, we trace the shoreline of the world's deepest and largest (by volume) body of water. Lake Baikal accounts for twenty-three percent of Earth's fresh surface water. It's huge, at 395 miles long and forty-nine miles wide, and would take many days to ride around.

Although it's hot—my temp gauge reads 95°F—this region of southern Siberia can drop to a frigid -65.9°F, as it did in January 1931. Despite Lake Baikal's maximum depth of 5,387 feet and volume of 5,660 cubic miles, the lake will freeze solid in winter. This astounds me.

I mimic Dave now and remove my left hand, using it to massage my tight quads. When I first started riding, I'd have never let go, heeding my motorcycle instructor's mantra: "Under no circumstance remove your hands from the bars!" The advice was well meaning: If I hit something, my front tire could suddenly change direction. But there aren't many positions a rider can switch to while operating a motorcycle, and even the smallest shift can ease the aches and pains.

After shaking out both arms, I stand on my pegs, letting my hip flexors relax and enjoying a satisfying pop in my lower back.

I'm still unsure of my plans once Dave leaves for the BAM, which could take up to ten days to complete. After we rode through the Altai region with ATL, Oskars invited us both to join them. I am still a hard no on the subject. In fact, I'm looking forward to having some alone time; that's all the challenge I want right now. It's not that I'm tired of being around Dave; I just still have an urge to prove my independence.

If I'm on the fast track to Tynda, where we'll reunite, I could get there in five days, roads depending. I won't have the GPS or data for digital maps, but many a traveler before me has gone without, and I'm up for the challenge. Getting lost isn't something I worry too much about—there's just one main road east anyway—but mechanical issues concern me. That and finding safe places to sleep at night.

Worst case, I can reroute along paved roads to a second-choice finish line in Vladivostok 2,500 miles east—what Ewan and Charley might call *The Easy, Paved Way Home*. But the thought of not getting to Magadan, and of Dave and I ending our round-the-world adventure in two different locations, tugs at my heart.

We can't not do those last miles together.

Oskars, Didzis, and Ivars are outside the hostel in Irkutsk working on their bikes. Shirtless, rowdy, and already one-and-a-half sheets to the wind at 4 p.m., they're contained like zoo animals behind a tall, wrought iron fence lining the hostel's secure courtyard. Some men and many women do double-takes when they walk by on the busy street. After more than a week without their infectious energy, I'm so happy to see these guys again. Dave's visibly relieved that we've finally caught up, too.

Dave and ATL will leave in two days for the BAM. The goal is to ride 800 of the 2,700-mile-long defunct service road paralleling the Baikal-Amur Mainline railway that connects eastern and western Siberia.

The BAM was first constructed in the 1800s but wasn't completed until September 1984, when the last spike was hammered into place. With the train running, the service road is no longer used, left to decompose back into the forest. There is very little to entice the average motorist to the BAM. Despite what I saw in the *Long Way Round* film—unrelenting bogs filled with buzzing mosquitoes, miles upon miles of mud, waist-deep river crossings, and a whole bunch of bush-whacking—the route continues to lure an elite few.

Dave has minimal say over what the team decides route-wise, timewise, and epic-wise. His tendencies for order and control will be challenged, but even with visions of my fiancé battling through this expedition, I'm excited for him.

I'm also excited for me. Everything is working out for us to do our own thing; I'm not holding Dave back from something he really wants to do, and I'm not putting myself in an uncomfortable position just to please him.

Dave leaves to pick up the parts Denis shipped to a motorcycle dealer in town before they close for the day. In our room, I languish in the shower, letting the hot water do its best to ease the knots from my shoulders. I've ridden over 1,200 miles with damaged suspension and no front brakes, and my body is rebelling more than ever.

Dave discovers that the fork seals sent all the way from Moscow are the wrong size. He's sure he gave Denis the exact part number, and Denis is sure he shipped the correct part. The farther east we go in Russia, the more valuable Denis becomes. He never overcharges us and always delivers on shipping wherever and whenever we need. There's no use arguing. Our only option is to reorder the parts and have them sent to Tynda. I'm concerned for my aching body and even more concerned about being stranded on the side of the road, but I don't want Dave to lose out on the BAM, so I fake confidence. Dave, on the other hand, has survivor's remorse and is feeling guilty about leaving me with this problem.

I need to make the decision whether to put my bike on a train to Tynda or ride the 1,350 miles there alone. I also can ride to Vladivostok, but that makes me sad.

Dave isn't okay sending me off on my own. I'm adamant, if not naive about it all. I think about Nina, the woman we met in the Atacama who told me I worried too much. I think about all the solo females out there riding around the world. Here's a chance for me to tap back into my independence. If I can't find a place to sleep for the night, I'll have to get creative, since Dave is taking the tent. If I break down, I'll figure out a way to get help. The allure is the challenge; the reward comes from persevering.

But a woman traveling alone in remote Russia might be a problem. My family would hate knowing I was contemplating this.

There's another option, but it feels like the easy way out. I store it in that part of my brain where logic is kept and walk to the tailor's to pick up my repaired riding jacket. For weeks now, I've been keeping the jacket—which is supposed to be protective armor—in place with my kidney belt.

When I get back to the hostel, Dave and the Latvians are drinking beer in the zoo-like courtyard. Everyone's laughing and in good spirits. I snap a photo of Dave by his bike, just as Didzis jumps in behind to photo-bomb my shot. Dave hands me his beer, which I drink without asking, and gets to work on swapping out his tires for the more aggressive knobbies he's had strapped to his bike since UB. He replaces his chain and sprockets, too. I'm impressed at how well Dave's bike has held up after so many miles and am envious of the lack of problems he's had.

Later, Dave and I go out to eat with Geoff, a fifty-something adventure rider from Australia we first met at the Oasis in UB. Geoff's also heading east. Over dumplings and dollar beers, Geoff reminds me of his offer.

"I'll ride to Tynda with ya, mate."

Geoff is my Plan B, the one that feels like the easy way out. He suggested riding together when we first met, but I was reluctant for several reasons. I don't know Geoff, or whether we'll get along, or whether I can trust him.

I sense Dave tense at the Sam-Elliott-look-alike's offer to be my riding partner. Not with jealousy but with anticipation. If I have someone to ride with, Dave will feel less anxious about leaving me alone.

I don't want a "chaperone," especially after warming up to the idea of riding solo. This adventure within the adventure is exactly what I think I need to get back to the me I've lost touch with over the past two years. Accepting Geoff's offer feels like being dependent on someone again.

On the other hand, if I get into trouble with my bike, it would be handy to have another person around. And staying at trucker lodgings on the Trans-Siberian Highway would be safer.

"Thanks for the offer, Geoff," I say. "Let me think about it, okay?"

Geoff, Dave, and I join the Latvians for drinks later. Ivars isn't there, so I ask Oskars if he's feeling okay. I was expecting the three of them to be in full-on party mode the night before leaving on their much-anticipated mission.

"He's fine," Oskars says. "We just need space from each other."

Travel doesn't mean a vacation from conflict, and those we're with day in and day out will bring to the surface everything we like to bury deep. Even around friends and family, the egos and facades we hide behind are more on display while traveling. The self is the only element of travel that doesn't get lost in translation or get left behind when you leave home.

I lean over and tell Geoff we can ride together to Tynda. Better safe than sorry.

The BAM before the storm

"Take photos for me?"

"Probably not," Dave grins. "That's what I have you for."

"And I'm not coming."

I kiss Dave and tell him to be safe but also have fun. With that, he's off riding down the busy city street, last in a line of four foreign motorcycles.

Hours later, I enjoy my first evening alone in six months. Sipping a dollar beer in the hostel's common area, I work on a blog post, then realize I can track Dave on our InReach account. The little blue dot is stopped for the night on the shores of Lake Baikal.

Just like you can't outrun your issues while traveling, spending all day, every day together with your significant other is also taxing. It's not actually a real-life situation. Even while married or living together, you don't see each other as often as you do traveling together. At home, partners have jobs, hobbies, other friends. You're separated a good part of the day. You also can take a break from the other person and go out with friends, or take a solo vacation.

Dave and I appreciate that the other is just the right amount of crazy to do this adventure. And even though there have been times we almost broke up, it already feels weird not to have him nearby.

The next evening, I'm sleeping with another man. Geoff and I are sharing a small A-frame cabin with two single beds near the shores of Lake Baikal. The space between us is so narrow, I can put an arm out and touch his mattress.

Once again, I'm reminded of how this behavior would seem to others. I think of lyrics from an Ani DiFranco song about how, taken out of context, she must seem so strange.

But there's something about Geoff that tells me he's harmless and a legit nice guy. We'd been hanging around him for several days, and I didn't get any red flags.

If it's weird not having Dave around, it's even weirder getting used to a different dude in my personal space. Pre-Dave, this situation might have felt more acceptable; I've slept in tents with men I had no interest in other than as climbing or ski partners. Now that I'm engaged, that casualness between me and another male feels odd, even if it's innocent. I wanted separate rooms, but sharing accommodation saves money for budget-conscious travelers.

I'm trying to read a book, but Geoff's outside at a communal sink snorting and horking out deposits in his lungs. The phrase *eat my dust* has never been more accurate than on these bone-dry Russian roads. Despite the unpleasant sounds he's emitting, Geoff is okay to hang out with; he's mild mannered and easygoing and should make a decent roommate for the next week—if I don't trip over his gear strewn throughout the room. At least he left his riding boots and socks outside—perhaps a suggestion from his former riding partner. Geoff had recently spent four months traveling with a platonic female friend who may have tuned him in. *That's probably why he's not acting off about us sleeping in the same room, like I am.*

"I've washed up." Geoff pokes his head through the door. I see a peachy-pink sunset behind him. "Care to join me in the search for supper?"

I loathe small talk and honestly just want to read and eat crackers, but that seems rude on our first night as travel buddies.

"Sure," I say, putting my book down and slipping into flip-flops.

Over a fragrant bowl of meat stew, I ask Geoff more about himself. I don't have to worry about awkward silences; Geoff's easy to talk to and chatty. An attractive man with a thick mustache and long, graying hair at his temples, his western cowboy looks and Aussie accent have probably won over more than a few ladies in his time. He tells me he works on oil rigs back home then takes long periods of time off to travel around the world by motorcycle. To date, he's ridden all over Australia, parts of Asia, and now Russia. He's not sure what's next.

"Maybe Thailand. I love those tropical countries."

Dave, with his abhorrence for humid heat, would never agree to ride in that part of the world. This wasn't the only apparent difference between my fiancé and Geoff. Riding that day, Geoff kept an almost religious 55-mile-per-hour pace. I had to pass him because he was going slower than I could handle, even while I continued to baby my bike. Geoff also stopped—a lot—to pee, drink, eat, take photos, swap out gear, talk. Sometimes he disappeared from my mirrors. I'd wait, wondering if I needed to turn around and find him. It was slightly annoying, but I did enjoy the lack of stress and rushing. It was the way I'd wanted to ride from the very beginning of our trip, but Dave's faster pace had become the norm, and now everything under seventy miles an hour feels sluggish.

Our route from Irkutsk to Tynda will cover 1,200 miles, according to Google Maps. With our leisurely pace, it will likely take us five to seven days to get there.

When we leave the A-frame that morning, the sky is dark and gloomy, but the rain isn't ready to burst free yet. We snap a few photos of our bikes down by Baikal, so immense it looks like the ocean, complete with a pristine sandy beach. This is the last we'll see of the lake before turning southeast toward Ulan-Ude.

The Trans-Siberian Highway is getting more beautiful as we head east. This part reminds me of British Columbia, with tall evergreens revealing the start of a thick, dark forest beyond. Many highways link together to span the entire drivable length of Russia. The Trans-Siberian starts in St. Petersburg and ends 6,800 miles later in Vladivostok. It's the third-longest highway in the world.

A few hours into our ride, fat, wet drops start to ping off my helmet. I made the call that morning to pull rain pants on over my lower half before leaving. Now, I stop and take out my rain jacket tucked into a convenient side pocket in my pannier.

Geoff left in just his riding suit and a T-shirt underneath. On the side of the road, he opens his bags, exposing everything inside to what's now a downpour. He quickly peels off his riding jacket, soaking his shirt, then puts on a waterproof jacket. Next, he whips out a pair of rain pants from his still-open pannier and tugs them on over his boots, almost falling onto his ass when his leg gets stuck. I shake my head and get ready to go, but now Geoff's swapping out his gloves for a dry pair and covering his tank bag with a waterproof bag.

We don't get to Ulan-Ude until later afternoon. After several attempts at finding a cheap hostel, we end up at an expensive mega-chain hotel that costs sixty-six dollars a night. Last night's A-frame was seven dollars total.

Lying in my own pristine queen-size bed that night, I wonder what hardships Dave endured that day. Did they do any river crossings? Were the mosquitoes driving him mad? Was it as hard as everyone said?

Spending sixty-six dollars a night on a hotel in Canada or the US might mean you'll wake up with bed bugs. In Russia, you'll likely wake up with a rose between your teeth. I open my eyes that morning feeling more refreshed and exuberant than I have in ages. Looking at the clock, I realize I slept ten hours straight. Geoff's bed is empty; he must be out for coffee.

Staying in places like this every night isn't affordable, but I like splurging every now and again to reap the benefits of a great rest. I'm actually looking forward to another day of gravel roads and forest scenery.

First, I log onto the hotel's fast internet. Our followers back home who have our live InReach link—also posted on our website—can see Dave and I going in two separate directions. A few have politely inquired what's up. I explain Dave's off on a crazy adventure with some crazy Latvians and I'm riding with a friend to Tynda. I leave out that he's a male. Imagine if I said we're staying in the same room every night?

Dave hasn't been checking in with me through InReach as I'd hoped. It makes me a little sad, but I'm trying to loosen the tether we've pulled tight around each other over the past two years. Anyway, he's safe with the Latvians. I can see from our account when I sign in that he's in some small town I can't pronounce the name of. They aren't as far along as I would have thought after three days. The BAM must be really grueling.

The next evening, Geoff and I are returning to our accommodations in Chita after yet another delicious, inexpensive Russian meal. I had the lamb pilaf, or *plov* (Плов). I love not having to think about groceries; the last time I "cooked" was while camping near the Russia/Mongolia border weeks ago, watching the Latvians chucking shit cakes into the fire for warmth.

In our room, I find a message from Dave saying he's going to call around 8 p.m. Geoff leaves to give us privacy. I'm looking forward to hearing Dave's voice, but when the Skype jingle fills the room and I expel an enthusiastic "Hi, babe!" I know right away he's in a bad mood.

"My rear shock is fucked," Dave says.

"What do you mean *fucked?*"

"I mean broken."

I can hear someone pounding on metal in the background.

"How? Did you have an accident? Are you okay?"

Dave's at an autobody shop in Severobaykalsk, a small town only 275 miles northeast of Irkutsk. They haven't even started the BAM route yet. The whole time I was wondering about his survival, Dave, Oskars, and the others were trying to fix Dave's shock.

For the first two days, everything had gone well camping along Lake Baikal. A hundred miles before they hit the official start of the BAM, the roads got rough with lots of dirt and large, embedded rocks. Dave hit something hard and thought he had a flat. When he stopped to have a look, he found fluid leaking from the rear shock. He nursed his bike to the autobody shop and spent the rest of the day trying to fix it.

A new rear shock can't be delivered for weeks, and in the middle of Siberia, the mechanic has no parts for something so complex.

"They're getting tired of waiting for me," Dave says of the Latvians. "They're on a sponsored agenda and have to be in Magadan by a certain time. I can't hold them back. That was the deal at the beginning."

"So, what, they're just going to leave you there?"

"We don't have a choice." Dave sighs. His voice is quiet and mono-toned, the way someone speaks after exhausting all emotions like anger and denial, settling now on acceptance.

There's not enough bandwidth at the hotel to run Skype's video, but I know exactly what Dave looks like in that moment: eyes dark like a thunder-storm, brows knitted together, turning his forehead into a crevasse of anguish. His stomach probably hurts too; it always does when he's distraught.

I'm genuinely sorry. Dave's been looking forward to this for too long—and it seemed the stars were aligning. I also can't help but notice the role-reversal irony; here I am, waiting for a slower rider all day, and there's Dave, getting left behind due to a broken motorcycle. *His* broken motorcycle.

Dave explains that the shock broke because he hadn't maintained it. In fact, all the way back in Germany, he was going to get Touratech to service it, but they were booked out due to an event.

We ask a lot from the vehicles that have carried us over 50,000 miles around the world. It's inevitable something significant will break. Unfor-tunately for Dave, that happened at the worst possible time.

Across the shitty Wi-Fi connection, I search for something positive to say.

"You can always come back. I know that sounds impossible right now, but for whatever reason, it wasn't meant to be right now, babe."

Dave sighs again, this time with annoyance. He has no patience for placating talk, especially when it involves the suggestion of fate or divine intervention. My attempts to console just aggravate him, and he wants to get off the phone.

"I'll call you in the morning with a revised plan," Dave says and hangs up.

Selfishly, I realize something that makes me sad: Dave's going to be depressed for weeks over this failure he considers is his own doing. That's going to taint our end-of-trip celebrations and mood.

Geoff and I are in limbo as long as Dave is, so we decide to stay put in Chita. I go down to the courtyard where our bikes are and look things over. With both Dave's bike and my own in bad form, I need to at least try and ensure my ride isn't getting any worse. While I deliberate over a thought—*has Dave been so consumed with the repairs to my bike he neglected his own?*—a gray kitten snakes between my legs, seeking attention. I pick it up. Her purrs are calming, and I let her snuggle into the crook of my arm.

I want to take this little being with me for comfort, but I put her back down to trot off.

We're not having the time of our lives

"It's like riding a pogo stick," Dave complains, telling me the mechanic re-installed the damaged shock so Dave could at least ride away from the shop.

The Latvians are gone. Dave has lost his translator and is on his own trying to find a way out of Severobaykalsk. He tried asking around the small village about putting his bike on a truck, but no one could understand him. Oskars recommended Dave ride back to Irkutsk and order a rear shock, but Dave isn't sure he'll make it, and who knows how long that part will take to arrive. Plus, a new shock to replace the one Dave has would cost over three grand.

The other option is a passenger train scheduled east out of Severo-baykalsk, but it doesn't allow cargo.

If Dave can't get to Tynda, I still have to go. That's where my fork parts have been sent. And if he's not there, who's going to fix my bike?

Around noon, I get a message on InReach: "On train but I think it doesn't go through. No idea what I'm doing."

This ambiguous text is followed several hours later with: "On train with bike on my way to Tynda. Will arrive tomorrow afternoon."

Geoff and I are still over 600 miles from Tynda. I go downstairs to tell him I'm leaving within the hour.

"Count me in," he says.

Geoff and I have been riding at a relaxed pace, but now it's go time. I wonder whether he'll keep up—and whether it's rude to leave him behind if I have to.

At a small town with the curious name of Never, we turn north at a junction for Tynda. The highway is so new I can still smell the black tar coming off the road. That lasts exactly ten miles before it's back to a mess of old, broken tarmac and hard-packed dirt. Rocks the size of bread loaves stick just above the surface, jarring me. I take it all personally, like someone has come along and purposely pointed them sharpest side up.

The miles Geoff and I have ridden together so far were relatively easy on my beat-up bike, but when it starts to rain like I haven't seen since the monsoons in Africa, I have trouble keeping traction with the rear tire I'm starting to loathe. For the next hour, my motorcycle and I perform a tricky dance, slipping and sliding all over the road.

Geoff stays behind me. His consideration in case I fall and need help is heartwarming, and I'm glad he's there. When we find a gas station, we stay tucked under its roof, hoping the rain will ease up. I eat some food, hydrate, and send a message to Dave saying we're about eighty miles from Tynda, but the going is slow. I'm looking forward to a hug from him soon.

Since Dave will be first in town, he'll find us accommodation—a chore I'm glad I won't have to do. Geoff, I hope, will have a separate room; I don't want a shared space after not seeing Dave for a week.

By the time we arrive in Tynda, Geoff and I are shivering and spent. Under the cover of a bus stop on the side of the road, I check InReach, expecting to find a message from Dave with coordinates to a hotel. My shoulders slump when I see nothing. I heave out my laptop and, using the hotspot on Geoff's cell, log in to our InReach account. Dave's location is 180 miles west of us. *What the hell?* The train is either not on schedule or broken down on the tracks. I sigh, dreading another night of hotel hunting and small talk with Geoff, who never shares from his unending booze collection.

I email Dave, in case he finds an internet connection, and include Geoff's cell number.

While Geoff's checking his GPS, a man pulls up beside us.

"You need help?" he asks with a deep, strong accent.

"Hotel?" Geoff asks.

The man waves for us to follow him in his black sedan. My mood is slightly improved because another nice stranger is donating time for us. When we turn down an alleyway surrounded by shabby *khrushchevka* block housing and broken-down cars, I'm a little on edge; but in the run-down playground, giggling kids play beside chatting moms. Dave and I have stayed in similar places.

Stopping by a darkened doorway, Black Sedan Man waves his hand again. I think he's asking someone about a room, but a woman in stilettos and tight shorts saunters toward the car. She bends seductively down to the passenger window. Before getting into the sedan, she looks straight at me and sneer-smiles. I'm no longer reassured by the playing kids.

"Come! Let's go to hotel!" Black Sedan Man calls out the window.

Yeah, no. I'm not following this guy anywhere anymore.

Using diminishing molecules of patience, I pull up beside Geoff to suggest we get the hell out of here. He's talking on the phone inside his helmet. Thankfully, Black Sedan Man and his new evening companion drive off.

"Okay, mate, we'll see you soon then." Geoff pushes a button and leans over to me. "I have the coordinates for where Dave is. Let me just punch them into the GPS."

"Wait, so he's here?"

It's been a weird first night in Tynda. I'm full of questions when I see Dave waiting at reception looking ten years older than last week.

"I replied to your messages," he says. "Didn't you get them?"

We later find out InReach needs a software update, which explains the lost messages and why the system didn't correctly pinpoint Dave on the map. Technology is great until it isn't.

"Where's your bike?"

"I took it to a garage down the road. Someone's brother's cousin...you know how that goes—*24/6 security*!" Dave uses air quotes, and I laugh. I've missed him and his sense of humor.

"So, where are our rooms?" I ask.

"Room," Dave says. "It's a dorm. We have to share with six other people."

I fight the urge to pout.

Over dinner, Dave fills us in. The train from Severobaykalsk didn't take cargo, but he was able to bribe the crew to help him lift his motorcycle into the train. Using rope, they lashed it down from all angles so it wouldn't fall over.

"I didn't have time to worry about how I'd get it off the train," Dave tells us.

Once his bike was secure, Dave went to buy a ticket and didn't notice the train leaving. As it was pulling away, Dave, in somewhat of a panic, played charades with some policemen for help. The cops understood and got Dave into a taxi. They told the driver to get him to the next town where the train had a scheduled stop, and fast. Dave hopped in and braced himself for the death-defying fifteen-minute ride east to hopefully beat the train.

"It was the only time I was grateful for crazy Russian driving," Dave smiles. He's starting to relax with his second beer but still looks disheveled.

The taxi got to the next station seconds before the train. Dave spent most of the next thirty-six hours dehydrated and starving because he'd forgotten to buy any food. He had a bottle of apple juice and a chocolate bar—something I'd added to his backpack when he left Irkutsk. This wasn't Canada's Rocky Mountaineer or one of Europe's fancy commuter rail systems, so there were no services onboard.

When the train finally arrived in Tynda that afternoon, the platform was oddly higher than the box cars, and the doors wouldn't open all the way. Dave and several crewmen had to use another door on the opposite side of the box car to lift and lower his motorcycle to the ground.

"That must be why they don't take cargo," Dave says. "The passengers seemed fine just squeezing through and climbing onto the platform."

"I'm glad you're here," I say, rubbing his back.

I'm also more relaxed—not because I felt at all on edge around Geoff, but because when Dave and I are apart now, it feels like something's missing.

"Epic, mate," Geoff nods in sympathy. "Just epic."

"How's the week been for you guys?"

My earlier anger over the road, rain, and my rear tire pales in comparison, so I just give Dave a quick summary. I add the part about Black Sedan Man and the prostitute, which now seems hilarious and has us all laughing.

We're finishing dinner when Dave gets a call from Oskars. Adventure Team Latvia is just 175 miles away. They expect to be in Tynda tomorrow and ask if we can reserve them three beds.

Dave's face tells it all for the rest of the night. He's even more upset now to have missed out since the Latvians completed the 800-mile section of the Baikal-Amur Mainline in a mere three days. Even I'm second-guessing my decision about not going if it was that easy.

During the train ride, Dave could see the BAM service road in spots. All but two rivers he felt would have been crossable, and the road was dry and flat, despite all the rain Geoff and I had on our route.

"It was beautiful," Dave says, looking down at his empty beer glass. The smile is gone.

My tipping point

At last, after riding 2,400 miles with no front suspension or front brakes, that's all about to change. We finally have the right parts, some time, and a covered garage to do the repairs. Dave spends an afternoon installing the new seals and wipers, which made it from Moscow, over 4,500 miles and six time zones away—not from a motorcycle shop down the street or even in the next town. *Thank you, Denis.*

Our motorcycle fixer/guardian angel is on the hunt for a secondhand rear shock for Dave, which he'll send to Yakutsk, 600 miles north of Tynda, and the last large city before Magadan.

When we return to the hostel after a long day of repairs, we find three dirt-covered, haggard looking ADV bikes in the parking lot. Over plov and beer, we listen to the Latvians talk about their BAM adventure. Oskars replays the scariest part. One of the rivers was too wide and deep for the bikes, so they all hopped on the railway bridge. Two riders got to the other side before a train came barreling around the corner with Didzis still on the tracks. He and the train were in a head-to-head until Didzis could get to one of the "balconies" built off the side every hundred meters. With seconds to spare, he got himself and his bike jammed into the tight space just as the train blew past.

"So scared!" Didzis says in broken English, but as always, his eyes are shining with happiness and laughter.

That evening, we all sleep in the same dorm room—five male bikers, two truck drivers, and one female with earplugs jammed so far into my ears I have a hard time extracting them the next morning.

With my bike good as new, I'm free to spend more time admiring the scenery and enjoying the ride rather than scanning for road obstacles. Dave's bike is another issue. He's stuck riding his steel kangaroo for now.

Now that Dave's replacement rear shock is going to Yakutsk, we're committed to Magadan, which makes us both nervously happy. I wonder how the roads will be.

Pre-2008, the only way from Yakutsk to Magadan was via 1,000 miles of collapsing bridges and flooding rivers along R504 Kolyma Highway, also known as the Road of Bones. Although this road can still be accessed and is more difficult than the BAM, it's been mostly reclaimed by swampland and Siberian taiga.

The Road of Bones is over 2,000 km long, and its history calls to intrepid travelers for its story.

The Kolyma Highway—built in the 1930s by hundreds of thousands of gulag prisoners—was nicknamed the Road of Bones because the working conditions were terrible and there were many casualties. Workers died on site, succumbing to extreme weather, fatigue, and malnourishment. It is believed they were buried where they fell. When the road was reconstructed in 2008, bones were found, and the Road of Bones became legendary.

The new road makes it much easier now to travel to Magadan from Yakutsk and vice versa—although the route is still unpaved and, when wet, a lot harder to navigate.

Due in no small part to Dave's bike issues, we will not be taking a side trip through the unmaintained section of the Road of Bones—another squashed feather in Dave's cap. He was hoping to talk the Latvians into it after the BAM, but they need to stay on schedule for flights leaving Magadan. Instead, the six of us will skirt around the ROB on the New Summer Road.

On a sunny mid-August morning, Dave, Geoff, and I leave Tynda ahead of Ivars, Didzis, and Oskars, who are sleeping off a night of celebrating their BAM adventure. Unsurprisingly, the road immediately turns into scattered gravel, with plenty of dips and potholes formed during the freeze–thaw cycle that happens ten out of twelve months in Siberia.

When Dave rides over these alterations on the surface, he's still bouncing several minutes later. Pulling up behind him, I see the amount of pressure his rear wheel bearings and axle are absorbing in response to the broken rear shock.

With my forks back to normal, even the loose gravel shifting like marbles under my wheels feels smooth and flowy.

The ride to Yakutsk will take two 300-mile days. When the Latvians catch us by mid-morning, it's not long before we're all spread out again. There's nothing ahead now but one long, dusty road along the tundra to our eventual destination.

Magadan. Even the name sounds badass. I can't wait to end our adventure there and party with these crazy guys I've come to adore like family over the past month. I fit in like a vegetarian in Texas, but they have tolerated me and been kind. Big bears with soft hearts, they've provided a youthful energy and much-needed humor for our travel-weary souls.

When Dave and I started our journey two years ago, I wouldn't have dreamed I'd be in a group of riders like this, and—for the most part—holding my own. I'm almost always last, but I've come a long way from when I couldn't seem to break the Heather Speed Barrier of thirty miles an hour off-pavement.

The second day after leaving Tynda, on our way to catch a ferry over the Lena River, the ball bearings are worse than usual, however. A grader has been hard at work, smoothing out the potholes and frost heaves by dumping piles of gravel into the holes. My speed is around sixty miles an hour, and I'm comfortable letting my rear wheel slide around a little as it plows through. Most of our days now are spent standing to keep balance on the loose road surfaces.

This area of Russia hasn't had rain in weeks, so to see better and not choke on each other's dust, our line of riders is spread out for two or three miles, and I'm pulling up the rear. Yesterday, I'd taken a photo of my face, covered in a gray powdery mask and looking like a ninety-year-old coal miner with bad teeth. Dave constantly has a bleeding nose from the dryness, and my own nostrils are parched and stinging with painful cracks.

I'm in the zone, enjoying the day, when, coming around a corner, I feel my back tire lose traction. The bike starts to swerve left to right. This feeling isn't uncommon and is just like the experience I had in Namibia going into Sossusvlei. I stick with it, feet planted firmly on the pegs. Giving the throttle a slow, firm twist, I expect to feel the road smooth out under my wheels. Instead, the swerving gets worse, and I'm having a hard time standing. When I sit down, my bike starts skidding left to right in a speed wobble. I don't dare touch the brakes in case that locks up the rear tire. *Shit!* I can't gain any control over the direction of my bike, and I'm drifting toward a significant drop off the shoulder that will land me several feet down in some dagger-like Siberian fir.

Carefully, I try correcting the bike's trajectory, but it's like my bike is split in two, with both halves going in different directions. *What's happening? Do I have a flat?*

I have a few seconds left to avoid a crash down the embankment, and I'm out of options. *Oh god, this is going to hurt.*

Then suddenly, I'm flung from my seat, landing hard on my right hip. My head rebounds off the ground—*thank god for helmets*—and the impact flips me onto my stomach. I slide for what seems like a mile but is more like thirty feet and strain to watch where my bike is going. Digging my gloved fingers into the dirt, I rake myself to a stop. My upper thighs burn from the friction of my slide. I say a silent thank you to myself for getting the zipper fixed on my riding jacket, which is also zipped into my riding pants. The crotch lining is giving me the mother of all wedgies.

I stay face down, arms and legs spread like a suntanner until I'm certain I've stopped. Moving slowly, I check for pain. Nothing. Just as slowly, I roll onto my butt. I'm okay and cheer like I've just summited a mountain.

A flood of sounds and images fills my ears, like hitting "play" on a paused movie. A car is stopped ahead, and someone's running over to me. Behind them, my two-wheeled girl is on her left side, inches from the edge. I get up and trip over to her, thrilled she's still on the road and not down in the ditch. When I get closer, I see a trail of broken plastic leading to a pool of dark liquid by the front tire. At first, I think the forks are damaged again, but they look okay. *Gas? Oil?* I stick my finger in and smell. *No idea.*

The person running over to me is trying to help. I can't understand him, so I raise both thumbs up to show I'm okay. He's unconvinced and tries to pick up my bike.

"No!" I shout.

I don't want anyone touching my bike until I can assess the damage.

I'm out of sorts from hitting my head. Examining my helmet, I see scratches on the right side. Technically, the helmet should be replaced after a crash like this, but where will I find a new one way out here?

The fronts of my thighs are still throbbing from skidding over rocks, but otherwise, I'm unscathed, thanks to being covered head to toe in Kevlar. I poke at some minor tears in my pants and gloves and wince, thinking of what I'd look like if I had just been riding in a T-shirt, like the Latvians. With hot weather, it's always tempting to take the jacket off.

The driver from the car that stopped is still with me, saying, "Friend? Friend?"

I point down the road and he leaves, presumably to find someone who looks like they might know me.

Circling my fallen steed, I find more damage, and it's extensive. The handlebars are twisted and buried under a small mountain of gravel, having plowed through the loose ground. The windscreen is heavily scratched but somehow still in one piece, as is the headlight, thanks to the mesh guard cover. The radiator is intact—again because of a protector screen—and all my luggage stayed on.

But my entire instrument panel, with the odometer, fuel gauge, etc., is smashed and falling off due to a cracked head mount. The pooling liquid in the dirt, I now see, came from my brake reservoir. Fixed on top of the handlebars in a convenient but illogical location, the plastic cup didn't stand a chance and was crushed.

Most alarming are my crash bars, installed on both sides to shield the fairing, engine, and other valuable parts exactly in times like this. They're bent on each side. My bike is lying on its left, but when I lost control, I fell off on the right. Once my bodyweight was off, the bike hit the ground with enough speed to rebound back up onto two wheels, then crash on the left. Sixty miles an hour is a lot of kinetic energy.

The familiar whine of Dave's engine breaks through my thoughts. I'm relieved he's here and am too much in shock to be angry. This was the *what if something happens* I was worried about when we rode so far apart.

After parking on the right side of the road, Dave runs over to where I'm standing by my bike in the oncoming lane. There isn't much traffic this far east in Russia, and we mostly have the remote mountain road to ourselves.

"Are you okay?!"

Geoff pulls up, too.

"Shit, mate, what happened?"

I tell them what I can but am still confused about what made me crash. The three of us walk down the road to a skid mark in the dirt. Then we see the problem: a line of piled-up gravel stretching down the middle of the road for half a mile, waiting for the grader. I hadn't seen the two-foot high berm camouflaged in a sea of gray. My front tire had plowed through, but the back tire stayed on the other side, forcing my bike into a straddle. No wonder I felt so wonky, trying to find a direction of travel.

Back at my bike, Geoff helps Dave heave her upright to get a better look at the rest of the damage. The dirt and gravel falling out from under the fairing sounds like a winning casino slot. I pick up all the plastic parts I can find strewn around in case they help us cobble something together.

"Sorry to say, but you don't have front brakes again until we can fix this brake reservoir," Dave informs me.

He gets out his tool kit and removes my crushed panel and windscreen, since they're just dangling by a wire. I lash it all down on top off my duffle bag and put the other bits and pieces inside my tank bag. Dave continues assessing: The plastic fairing on the top left side has a big crack by the BMW logo, along with several scratches. The left indicator light is smashed. Thankfully, none of this makes the bike unrideable.

"Wow," Dave says, "you even bent your crash bars. Are you sure you're okay? That would have taken a huge amount of force."

"I'm just glad I didn't break any bones again."

Was it some kind of omen or just a coincidence that I'd crashed two weeks into our trip and then again two weeks before the end? I'm surprised I've had my worst crash when I'm riding better than ever. Maybe I'm getting complacent. Or just tired.

"I'm glad you're okay," Dave says again.

I think he gets it now. I could have been wrapped around a tree. Our InReach devices can dispatch an SOS emergency call, but if no one's there to press the button, things can get a lot worse quickly.

Dave does what he can to patch things up.

"Now for the moment of truth." He turns the key in the ignition, and, surprising us all, the trusty F800 starts right up. Without a dash and instrument cluster, it's going to be hard to know what gear I'm in, except by feel.

"I can't believe I can ride out of here after that!"

I'm thrilled but also suddenly emotional. A year ago, this bike was brand new; now it's beat to shit.

"I can't do much more repair-wise," Dave says. "You'll have to ride it like this until we get to Yakutsk; possibly even all the way to Magadan."

We no longer assume bigger cities will have what we need.

My bike looks goofy without a windscreen and dash. I'll have to be overly cautious again with no front brakes for the next 1,000-plus miles, but I don't care. It works, and I'm not dead or seriously hurt.

Dave comes over and looks me in the eye.

"You don't have to ride if you don't want to."

I'm not sure what Dave thinks we'll do if I refuse to get back on my bike, but I appreciate his concern.

"I can ride. It's probably better if I don't think about it too much. Let's just get going. We're going to miss the ferry."

I'm nervous and shaky for the rest of the day and am back to riding slow for the next 120 miles. Dave senses my hesitation. On a smooth stretch, I hear my intercom come on.

"Can you hear me?"

"Yeah?" I whip off, thinking he's going to pull out his annoying *twist that throttle* mantra.

"I just want to say you might be tougher than anyone I know."

The shifting shape of me

With a population of just over 350,000, Yakutsk, a city in eastern Siberia located on the Lena River, is more utilitarian than tourist focused. That said, it does have a Mammoth Museum—not a *large* museum but an actual museum housing millennia-old woolly mammoth fossils. I hope we'll have enough downtime to check it out.

The Latvians are already two hours into "festival"—a multiday party they've organized among themselves that will start in Yakutsk and end in Magadan. The party's happening at a Yakutsk Clubhouse—with our old friends, the Night Wolves. I guess Dave and I aren't the only ones with badass motorcycle gang connections.

Festival sounds like a fun way to unwind, but I'm not interested in liver damage of that scale. Especially not after a day like I just had.

Oskars walks with us back out to the clubhouse parking lot, where we pass a dozen Harleys parked in a row and some rough-looking guys smoking.

"Shiiiiit." Oskars stops mid-stride. "What happened to your bike?!"

Dave explains. I can't form words anymore.

Ivars, Didzis, and Geoff—who rode ahead after my crash and got on an earlier ferry with the Latvians—circle my bike. Some of the smoking bikers come over, too, curious. People are slapping me on my stiff-as-a-rod back—congratulating me for not dying, I think. I'm still shaken up and want to be away from people right now.

Oskars points to a short man full of tats and flexing muscles I didn't even know existed in the human body.

"Max will help you find a hotel. I'm drunk from festival!" Oskars laughs.

I have no idea how Oskars knows Max and can make this request, but the guy's going to find us a place to sleep, and that's all I care about right now. Affordable hotels in Yakutsk are few and far between and mostly reserved for truckers and anyone else finding themselves in the area for work.

I count at least five piercings on Max's face and presume there are more elsewhere. Underneath the ink and titanium, Max is handsome and endearingly polite. After shaking hands, he walks to his chopper and roars off. We follow.

At a stoplight, I watch an exchange between Max and another rider who rolls up beside him. The young, skinny man is dressed in street leathers, leaning over his race bike in what I've always thought must be the most uncomfortable riding position for the neck and shoulders. Max, in his camouflage pants and patched Night Wolves vest, looks over at the racer. Never has there been more of a clash on common ground, but just before the light changes, the two riders fist-bump.

Max turns onto an unpaved side street that to some would seem sketchy as hell, but "sketchy" here usually turns out to be just a way of life for everyday folks going about their everyday business.

On one dimly lit corner, a tall pole holds a rat's nest of wires. At quick glance, I'm sure there are at least seventy-five million attached from all different directions and converging into this electrician's nightmare. No way it passes code. Then again, there's probably a very different code here, if any. I half expect the pole to explode as I ride by, but it's probably been there functioning for years. The street's name is nailed to the side of a house on the corner, in true Russian ingenuity—why spend extra time and money on a freestanding signpost when there's already something nearby to hammer into?

We park in a lot behind a wrought iron fence. I have no idea what kind of hotel we'll find ourselves in tonight, but I'm impressed when we enter and find sparkling tile floors and red couches, which give the place a modern look—very different from the gray Soviet-era apartments we're getting accustomed to.

Impressed or not, I ask to see the room first. A young female receptionist leads me to a tidy, quiet space with everything we need, including a decent bathroom, shower, and two single beds. I love Dave, but a bed to myself and a night without him snoring in my ear or making me toss and turn with all his tossing and turning is hugely appealing.

Max tells me the room is fifty dollars a night, even with a Night Wolves discount. That's about five times more expensive than the rustic, rural places we've been staying in lately, but with only a week or two left until we go home, we can afford it.

I thank Max. He leaves to get back to his party, refusing a tip for helping us. While Dave ferries our gear up the stairs, I pay for five nights in advance; we'll need the extra time for Dave's rear shock to arrive and for whatever repairs can be done on my bike.

The receptionist knocks on our door early the next morning and says we have a visitor. I think it must be Geoff or one of the Latvians, but when we go downstairs, we find someone we've never met. The man introduces himself as Viktor. With limited English, he explains that Max sent him to help with my bike.

"I know motor store," Viktor says with an inviting smile.

He's young and unassuming except for his exquisite blue eyes. In contrast to Max, Viktor looks like a Harvard graduate, dressed in pleated khakis and a red polo shirt—yet he's somehow a Night Wolves member.

My surprise at Viktor's kindness (and his eyes) has me slow in responding.

"Yes!" I finally say. "Thank you, my motorcycle is very broken."

Outside, I show Viktor all my bike's bumps and bruises. He takes measurements. Dave asks if we can buy a cheap Chinese knockoff brake reservoir somewhere. He's hoping for another quick solution from a convenience store, and maybe more ice cream.

When I get home, I can replace everything with BMW-specific parts. For now, I just want something that'll work in a pinch.

Viktor asks Dave to remove the bolt sitting between the reservoir cup and the hose bringing fluid to the brakes. He needs to reference the part numbers. Doing so will put air in my brake line, and there will be nothing left to clamp the brake pads to the rotors. I won't be able to ride at all without fixing this issue.

"Is that okay with you?" Dave asks me.

Without much choice, I nod, and Viktor writes down some info.

"I contact you vhen I find zometing."

Now with some free time, we spend the afternoon at the Woolly Mammoth Museum. Established in 1991, the historical center is small but impressive, with its life-size stuffed mammoths on display towering several feet above our heads. Yakutia, a region located in Russia's far east along the Arctic Coast, is said to be the graveyard for at least eighty percent of the world's mammoth population, which died off over 10,000 years ago. As the permafrost thaws in that area, scientists and researchers are discovering perfectly preserved remains—even uncoagulated blood—and many of these findings are brought to the Mammoth Museum for display.

Yakutsk itself is considered the coldest city in the world, with winter temps averaging -40°F. In February 1987, a record-low temperature was set at -83.9°F, although this number is hard to confirm in research, as it varies by as much as twenty degrees. Either way, it's damn cold, and it doesn't surprise me one bit that Siberia—covering five-million-plus square miles and stretching south from the Arctic Ocean to north central Kazakhstan and the borders between Mongolia and China—is part of a study on past creatures preserved in ice.

I'm content to sit in the cheery hotel lobby and tuck into a blog post that evening, but we've been invited to the Night Wolves clubhouse. I do not feel like partying—I rarely do. I don't even feel like drinking; that impulse comes and goes for me. But we should go. Everyone's been so nice.

We take a cab to the party and ask the driver to return in an hour. That way we have an excuse to leave early.

I groan out of the vehicle, feeling a multitude of aches and pains creak through my body. Being flung off a motorcycle hurts. I can't wait to be back in my cozy twin bed within the hour.

Navigating around a series of potholes in the parking lot, we face a tattooed biker in front of a wooden gate covered with the gang's logo—a snarling wolf trailing a ball of fire. The biker lets us pass. Inside, the large compound is surrounded by a tall fence built tight together to keep out prying eyes. Huge speakers play punk rock—loud but not intolerable. The song is Тоска by Molchat Doma—a Belarusian band from Minsk. I like it and feel my body responding to the beat.

A man in a faded leather jacket approaches us with an open-mouth smile that compliments his almond-shaped eyes. His skin is light and devoid of wrinkles. He looks part Asian, speaks Russian, and knows zero English. Gesturing for us to come to the bar, he orders us each a glass of beer and a shot of vodka, because nothing happens in Russia without vodka. At least nothing you can trust.

Dave nods a thank you and sips it down in one gulp. I'm next. The clear liquid is chilled to soften the taste and slides easily down my throat. The bartender and the man in the leather jacket cheer at my capacity to handle the drink. This—like getting slapped on the back for a messed-up motorcycle—is not something I want to be glorified for. It feels too *bro*-like. I want to tell them, *I'm not like you; I'm not one of the guys.* My survival instincts are telling me to go home, get healthy, and sleep for a month straight.

In keeping with the others, Dave raises his empty glass to me. Leather Jacket Man takes this to mean Dave wants more, and before we know it, there's another round in front of us. I try not to take the second shot, but its vapors are releasing and wrapping around me like a friendly hug. *Run away, it's a lethal cobra!* Even standing near Russian vodka is bad news. *No more shots. I'll just sip this one beer slowly.* I congratulate myself for being so disciplined.

Although I wasn't in the mood to be there initially, the music is good, and the atmosphere is growing on me. I leave the bar and wander off into the crowd.

Laughing to myself, I remember how I was so terrified when I sent the Night Wolves that email half a year ago. Now, I'm casually mingling at one of their gang gatherings like it's a dinner party back home.

It doesn't take me long to spot Adventure Team Latvia's matching blue and orange jerseys. They've all been going nonstop since we saw them twenty-four hours ago. That's the point of "festival," Oskars tells me. He, Didzis, and Ivars are merely buzzed—a combination of being thirty-something and built like bulls. Geoff, about twenty years older, is already squinty-eyed drunk, or more accurately *still* drunk.

Dave comes over and slips his arm around my shoulders. I tuck a hand into the pocket of his jeans. I implore myself to make the bottle of beer last, but already the vodka's warmth is spreading down my legs and into my toes like I'm peeing myself. *Am* I peeing myself?

"I wonder if the Surgeon will show up," I half-joke, pretty sure that I would actually piss my pants if I saw the scary Surgeon in the flesh.

I still have my original beer but have somehow been talked into another shot of vodka. *Damn my polite Canadian roots!* I haven't eaten since lunch—too long ago for a serial snacker. My stomach guides me to a giant communal pot of plov cooking over a fire. The chef hands me a paper plate and piles it high with rice, onions, carrots, and tender chunks of lamb all simmered to savory perfection. I thank him in Russian and hope the food will help soak up some of the 150-proof ethanol burning through my stomach lining.

On a raised platform serving as a stage, Leather Jacket Man is talking into a microphone. I have no idea what he's saying, but it appears to be an official "patching in" ceremony. A young man, also on stage, is handed a new black leather jacket with the Night Wolves logo on the back. The crowd cheers, and I look around at all the smiling faces, thinking no way these fun-loving folks have anything to do with the badness implied online.

Another young, heavily tattooed guy hops onto the stage and takes the mic. I wait for him to speak, but instead he closes his eyes and stays still until everyone falls silent with curiosity. When he opens his mouth, he releases the most eerily beautiful sound. *Oh my god, he's throat singing.* My cousin Alison in Switzerland told me about this.

Throat singing—or *Khöömei*—uses a circular breathing technique that allows someone to "sing" multiple pitches at the same time and for long periods. I'm spellbound. The music sounds instrumental—like several digeridoos—but it's just one guy's throat! I put down my plov and film him, wondering if he's from Tuva, the region in southern Siberia Alison told me about, where yurt-dwelling nomads perform Khöömei in wide-open spaces perfect for allowing the voice to carry. Some performers travel until they find the perfect river or mountainside that will offer the best acoustics.

The music puts me into some kind of trance, and the party becomes a blur of white noise, flashes of light, and cacophonous laughter. I talk to people I don't know, take crooked photos that are out of focus, and wear someone's BMW baseball cap for some duration.

The homemade moonshine is unlike anything I've had before; that snake had its power over me from the first sip. Too smooth. Now I'm out in the parking lot braced between two parked cars, purging myself of the venom.

Between the guttural sounds I'm making, I hear Dave calling my name. I'm so embarrassed to be getting sick from alcohol that I've left the compound without telling him. *How long have I been gone?* I'm sure it's midnight, or beyond.

I stand up so Dave can see me.

"Uh oh," he laughs, also drunk. "Not feeling so good?"

"No, I want to go home."

"I was coming to find you because our cab's here."

"Shit, I forgot about him," I slur. "Did he come back a few times?"

"No," Dave looks at me. "It's 9:30. Remember you only wanted to stay an hour?"

"Are you kidding me? We've only been here an hour?"

"Well, an hour and a half…the driver was late."

Demoralized, I sink into Dave's strong arms, ensnaring his waist like the snake that still has its grip on me. Just before we get into the taxi, a pretty, dark-haired woman comes over and asks for a selfie with me. I don't remember meeting her, but she hugs and kisses me like we're old friends and wishes us good luck on the rest of our travels. I want to stay longer and meet more people like her. I want to have fun. But in my belly, the snake twists violently.

On the short drive back to the hotel, I open my car door at a stoplight trying to rid myself of more toxins, but nothing comes out.

In our room, I strip and go into the shower, turning it to cold. I force myself to get rid of every drop in my stomach the hard way, then slump against the tiled wall until I start to shiver.

Later, when I'm warm and dry, I drink a liter of water with electrolytes, brush my teeth, and fall fast asleep until morning.

Talking to strangers

Sun on my closed eyelids coaxes me out of bed. I wake cautiously, anticipating the sickening rush of a hangover, but I feel surprisingly good. Great, even. Dave is still deep asleep in his own bed, so I go out in search of breakfast. My stomach is acidic, and I'm craving protein.

I walk to a café on the corner, where the aroma of fresh bread wafts out onto the street. Inside, I say hello to the baker, whose cheeks are so chubby her eyes are swallowed by flesh when she smiles. A fresh loaf of bread, six pastries stuffed with sautéed meat and onion, and a couple bottles of orange juice come to less than four dollars.

When I go back to our room, I hear Dave in the shower, employing my technique from the night before. It's his turn to purge the poison. I'm not sure if the smell of fried onions will make him feel better or worse, but I leave the food in the room, taking my share down to the lobby.

It was inevitable that at some point in our travels we'd overdo it on the alcohol. I'm surprised it hasn't happened more often; saying *no* to new friends is hard and in some cultures considered rude. Still, I hate doing this to my body, already so run-down from two years of motorcycle travel and my recent crash.

By noon, Dave still hasn't surfaced. I go upstairs and find him still feeling nauseous, but he needs to get up. Viktor is here with a new brake reservoir for my bike. Thankfully, he found a Chinese knockoff that will work for now. In the parking lot, he and Dave mount it to my handlebars. The brake hose is too short, so they add a connector, which is too long. The front of my bike looks even goofier now with this tube sticking out, and I joke about snagging a pedestrian.

The crash also broke both mirrors. Since my bike is already looking ridiculous, I want to find new mirrors with flames or rhinestones or something, but I have no luck in a search later that day and settle for a boring pair of Honda screw-on mirrors. The handlebars and mirrors now stick out like deer antlers. The German perfectionists who designed this gorgeous motorcycle would be aghast, but I think Justin, the guy who sold it to me in Fairbanks, Alaska, would be proud. Along with the brake line loop, cheap silver mirrors, Chinese clutch and brake lever, bashed instrument cluster, and Alaska license plate hanging from its frame with baling wire, my once-brand-new bike will limp to the finish line, just like the Stallion. Ten months ago, this gleaming beauty was plucked from the showroom floor. Now, it looks like the sole vehicle survivor from an episode of *Top Gear*.

A few days later, we have fully recovered from the vodka homicide when Dave's used rear shock arrives from Moscow. With multiple connections across the country, Denis had the shock sent to a Yakutsk man named Anatoli—yet another Russian humanitarian willing to help two unlucky travelers.

In a mud-packed back alley lined with storage garages, Anatoli moves three motorcycles out of his shop to clear a space for Dave.

When Russia was still the Soviet Union, these garages were private places for men to work, but they sometimes ended up being a place of social calamity for drinking and carrying on away from home. Under the pretext of fixing cars and other handyman work, the foundations were "conveniently" located several blocks or even miles away from the owner's house.

Then and today, these man caves are also a sanctuary for those needing personal space while living in cramped Soviet-era apartments. The garages remind me of North American storage units only with more character, and maybe a window or two.

Dave begins the laborious task of taking everything apart to install the new rear shock, which is several grades down from the expensive one he'd purchased two years ago. My bike is outside, parked in the mud. Anatoli eyes the baling wire holding up my headlight over the characteristic "beak" of the GS. With the mount broken, there's nothing to attach it or the windscreen to, which I still have lashed to my duffle bag. Now I'll have two ailing steeds to deal with when I get home.

I'd far prefer to be relaxing back at the hotel than spending hours watching Dave curse at his tools, but generally speaking, we don't let each other go off alone with strangers. Except for Geoff.

While Dave works, Anatoli bestows me with gifts: first, a muffin, which he unwraps and gently—but without elaborate drama—hands to me like a flower. Then, an ice cream sandwich from the little bar fridge/freezer. Dave, focused on the task at hand, is oblivious to the treats Anatoli is producing.

Anatoli is far rougher around the edges than sweet Viktor, and even more so than our hotel-finder, Tattooed & Pierced Max. His forty-something face is deeply creased underneath several-day-old stubble. The thinning blond hair on his head has a mind of its own, and he's also tattooed in every scary, sexy way, like a movie villain who actually turns out to be the good guy.

Anatoli seems aware his look might be off-putting, and he's going out of his way to make me feel safe and comfortable. We don't understand each other's language but communicate with gestures and facial expressions.

Anatoli makes tea. I adore the contrast of watching this tough guy delicately holding what I imagine is his long-deceased grandmother's china. While the beverage steeps, Anatoli shows me photos of his young daughter. He likes to take her on motorcycle rides.

Later, while Dave is wrapping up, Anatoli gives me one final treasure: a heavy metal belt buckle with an etched skeleton on the front. It's truly badass. I still have it today.

The space between the handlebars

With both bikes now in passable riding condition, Dave and I start the final push to Magadan, just the two of us. We'll eventually meet up with Geoff and the Latvians there.

We're making it happen. Together. Like every full circle, this is the beginning to an end to another new beginning. What will we be like as a married couple? Will we continue a life of adventure or settle down in one place? Will we live in suburbia or on acreage? Will our love grow or fade? So many questions, so much gravel under my wheels left to contemplate it all.

Now the third week into August, the days are still warm and long. Unlike our headlong race to the finish line in Ushuaia, we have unrushed time to finish the remaining unpaved miles at a more reasonable pace.

"I'm nervous," I admit to Dave one evening before leaving Yakutsk, "but also excited. I thought Magadan was not going to happen."

I think back to that day almost two years ago when, on my parent's front lawn, I was trying to fit what already seemed like a minimal amount of gear inside impossibly small bags. How much pre-trip time was spent deliberating over questions like whether I should bring two riding suits, one for hot weather and one for cold? What if I'd known I was going to have two significant crashes—one that would break a bone and one that would almost destroy my new motorcycle? Would I have stayed home? I don't want to imagine the incredible moments I would have missed if I'd given into my very real fears and never gone on this trip. If there's one thing I've learned about myself over the past 700 days, it's that I can always squeeze a little more juice out of life's lemons. I've been scared shitless and kept going. We aren't done yet, but I know I'll make it. Our entire trip could be foreshadowing my future: When it gets hard or scary, keep going and don't try to answer every question from the start. You'll always carry your baggage with you, but in time, you'll figure out what you don't need anymore.

After recrossing the Lena River and getting back on the gravel highway heading east, I'm still feeling off, and all that positive self-talk is gone with the wind cascading over my scratched helmet. Every twitch from my janky handlebars brings on the white-noise rush I heard just before my crash. I can't ride over thirty miles an hour.

Haul trucks are the scariest part of the Trans-Siberian. Even at low speed, our wheels stir up dust clouds behind us. The semis are even worse, trailing fine dirt particles for half a mile like giant wedding veils. To pass, we need to get right up behind the truck's rear wheels to where the dust isn't as thick. I chicken out every time and slow way back, stuck in a white-out. I dread seeing these trucks in the distance. Even when I'm going slow, I always catch up to them.

Dave—ever committed to his riding pace—is more comfortable risking a pass. If our headsets connect properly, I hang way back and tell Dave—whose view is blocked by the back end of a semi—whether he can pass in the oncoming lane. Once Dave gets around the truck, he radios me if there's nothing coming to say I can pass. It's deadly risky and reminds me of a game I played as a kid called "Trust," where you stand with your back to a friend or classmate, close your eyes, and fall backward, helpless. The person behind you is supposed to catch you. This game of trust between Dave and me has a lot more at stake; even when I hear him say *go!* I have a moment of second-guessing when I pull out into the on-coming lane blindly. *Did he say* go *or* no? We think of a better word: *Pass!*

By the time we get to the second ferry crossing over the Aldan River 250 miles later, I'm frazzled and fragile. After I crashed and blamed some of it on my substandard rear tire, Dave offered to swap the tire out for his beefier one with better tread—but he hasn't gotten around to it yet, asking me to "see how it goes." He rightly wants to keep using the dirt tires he bought in Ulaanbaatar for the BAM.

"What did you think of the road?" Dave asks, upbeat.

"It sucked, as most gravel roads do when I'm shit scared on my bike," I snap, then feel bad. I'm mostly disappointed in myself for the regression in my riding.

Becoming female

In the middle of the night, I'm rudely awoken by cramping in my pelvis and an urgent need to pee. Squatting over the toilet, I feel searing fire before a few drops trickle out and nothing more. If I don't find some antibiotics soon, this urinary tract infection could spread to my kidneys. I toss and turn the rest of the night while Dave snores loudly beside me. I'm miserable and want to scream at him to shut up. Sex and living on the road don't always work so well when we can't be as hygienic as at home. I'm certain that's caused the infection.

When dawn finally lights up the pale pink walls around me, I tell Dave I have a UTI and need to find a pharmacy. We find one in the tiny town. I type "need medication for bladder infection" into the translation app on Dave's phone and show it to the pharmacist. He politely hands me a box and then writes "2 x 12" on a small piece of paper. Two pills a day for twelve days sounds right; unfortunately, I've had a UTI before. Luckily, in Russia you can get this type of medication over the counter.

I swallow a pill with some water and get on with my day, which in-volves riding bumpy gravel roads to Kyubeme, a small village twenty miles west of where the infamous Kolyma Highway, or Road of Bones, begins. Jostling around on a motorcycle with a UTI is no small amount of torture, and the going is slow because I stop often to pee out a thimble's worth of urine. I suck up the pain when I'm reminded of those who died building the road I'm freely traveling along.

Much harder sections make up the more intriguing part of the ROB— or at least more intriguing to riders like Dave—but we skirt around them.

Dave and I ride the New Summer Road—a better-maintained, all-weather route east to Magadan. The NSR has been compared to the Dempster Highway in Canada, and I know I can manage that. Dave, on the other hand, is upset about missing out on both the Russian routes he was planning on for years and is getting grumpier by the mile. Nothing I say or do helps. I want to shake him and say *can't you just let it go?* It feels like he thinks every mile we've ridden to this point is irrelevant without these trophies at the end. Edgy due to my own discomfort, I leave him to wallow.

Dave has finally swapped our rear tires. I notice the difference immediately and feel better on the loose road surface, again able to just enjoy the ride. The late-summer sky is a deep blue that day, with cotton-ball clouds adding shadows to the tree-covered mountains. We travel alongside a wide river that gives me the urge to take up fly-fishing. Other than the rectangular license plates on passing vehicles, it's hard to notice any differences between riding here or in northern BC or Washington. *Home.* Now that we're so close, I'm more excited than ever thinking about our return.

Miles tick by; I don't know how many since I no longer have an odometer to check. Dave takes a photo of me in front of a large blue road sign that reads Магадан—1838. Magadan is still over 1,800 kilometers away, or 1,142 miles. I have no idea how long that will take us. Three days? A week?

Leaving the riverside, we enter narrow, forested geography, and the late afternoon sun stretches long tree shadows onto the road. The fractions of shade are welcome in the summer heat. We stop for lunch, and Dave finds some abandoned license plates in a pile; a mix of numbers and letters, just like home, but with a few additional characters. He takes one for a souvenir. My imagination plays out a scene where the Russian Mafia drives out here to discard the plates so they can't be traced to crimes. Why else is there a random pile of plates in the middle of nowhere?

That night, camped by the river, the crippling pains in my bladder and frequent zipping and unzipping of the tent fly keep us both awake. After I return from shooting fire through my urethra, Dave rubs my back until the next bout sends me outside again. I'm exhausted and miserable and wish we were staying in a hotel with a bathroom, but no such luck exists out here in the middle of Siberia.

Because of my regular pee stops, I get a head start the next morning while Dave stays behind to pack up.

The cramping seems less intense during the day when I have other things to concentrate on. Rolling along, I wonder why almost every Russian we've met since Moscow has warned us against riding to Magadan, saying it was too dangerous and that there was "nothing out there." To me, this is the most scenic, exciting part.

It's understandable why some locals don't travel from one end of their country to the other; Russia is seventy-one percent larger than Canada and can fit nearly two entire USAs within is 6,601,665 square miles. It's amusing—and a little sad—that almost everywhere we go during our travels, we're cautioned about the bad people and places we'll encounter just around the next corner. Maybe it's the same here as at home, where many citizens don't have passports or even leave their state or province. The fear of what *could* happen keeps people from letting *anything* happen.

Despite the many ups and downs—near misses, crashes, mechanical issues, relationship challenges, physical and mental drain, financial hits—if asked right then and there whether I'd do it all over again, the answer would be *yes*. Maybe I'd do some things differently, but nothing will ever give me the experience and education I've gained as a world traveler. Nothing.

My heart and soul are healing now because I'm back in the mountains. The scenery looks like the quiet, forested roads we traveled in Alaska. This makes sense, since Russia and Alaska are separated by just fifty-five miles across the Bering Strait. Siberian spruce and fir, short and spindly, grow from the tundra, green with lichen and stretching across the valley floor to treeless peaks. With a less-clear objective and timeline in mind, I would stop to hike up those hills, which look so easily approachable from the road.

Magadan is now 600 miles away, but it feels like I'll see it just over the next rise in the road. A mix of emotions swirl in my brain today: I'm giddy and fearful; excited and sad; impatient to be done yet not wanting the trip to end. If all goes well, we'll be in Magadan in forty-eight hours or less. I can't believe it. I can't wait.

But what's next?

Do I even know how to be a wife? Will routine and domestication kill the spark within me or between us?

How will it feel to restart a life I left two years ago? I have no place to live, no job, and—because of my denial at the US border—no way to enter the country where my fiancé lives. I'll have to find an apartment, send out resumes, wait to legally immigrate to the US…how soon will the novelty of returning home wear off and leave me aching for another adventure?

I stop and gasp through another pee break. I don't even have to hide behind a bush or look over my shoulder before dropping my pants. No other traffic has passed me yet. The night before, we'd found a serene, quiet bypass to camp and haven't caught back up to the main haul road.

In the distance, Dave is approaching. I want more time in this idyllic spot before he catches me, both literally and figuratively. Getting my camera out, I frame my dusty bike, still strong and sexy in my eyes despite everything she's been through. She looks even more beautiful now, supported by the strong mountains behind her. She's hurting, but she'll go all the way to the end.

A few days later, we catch up to Geoff and the Latvians in a small village. They'd passed us when we were camping. They're already settled into an apartment for the night and make room for us. We're all exhausted from a long, dusty day, and after a sparse dinner of rice and soup, the boys pull out their sleeping bags and lay them on the living room floor. There's only one bed, which Geoff gets because he's sick. I roll out my mat in the kitchen, which has a door I can close. The bathroom is down the hall, but the medication has been doing its job, and I'm feeling much better.

With no hot water for showers, I wash my face in the sink, trying to irrigate the dust from my eyes, ears, and mouth.

The end & everything's wrong

In the morning, Dave checks the air in his rear tire—formerly my rear tire—before we leave. A few days ago, he had to repair a flat, and since then, he's been periodically checking the psi. That morning it's at thirty-two—same as the night before, so the air is holding. We leave after Geoff and Team Latvia. If everything goes well, we'll all be in Magadan by the end of the day. But it's important to me that it's just the two of us riding together to our finish line.

With fewer than 200 miles to go, I'm lost in thought, riding at a good speed on the hardpacked dirt road under my wheels.

We travel over bridged creeks and rivers, through forests and rolling hills. Dave stops once to unzip the vents in his riding jacket when the cool early fall morning turns warmer. I keep going. Because of the dust, we need to keep our distance.

I assume Dave's only a mile or so behind me, but I stop beside a river for him to catch up. I'm there just a few minutes when an SUV pulls up. The young man and woman inside give me a thumbs up. I return the gesture, signifying I'm okay. Instead of driving off, they get out and come over to shake my hand. I appreciate their willingness to take a break and connect with me. The woman is already unscrewing the cap off a thermos. She hands me a cup of tea and an unopened bag of peanut M&Ms. I thank them both, hoping Dave doesn't show up too soon, or I'll have to share my snack.

The couple leave after a few minutes of small talk. I give them one of our Riding Full Circle business cards, hoping they'll go online and see photos of their country all the way from Moscow.

Soon, the familiar bright LED headlight of Dave's bike comes into view. When he stops, I see he's angry about something. I feel a sudden sense of dismay; he's been moody for weeks, and I want everything to be upbeat and positive for the biggest, most important day of our entire trip.

Making the ultimate sacrifice, I hand him the bag of M&Ms.

Talking around crushed peanuts and chocolate, Dave tells me he's had to stop several times to add air to the rear tire.

"It keeps going flat. That patch is failing. I haven't been able to catch up to you to tell you that I need to stop and fix it."

A retort jumps into my head: *Now you know how it feels...*

"Well, we're here now, and this is a great spot to perform some roadside surgery," I suggest.

I'm glad to be free of my former rear tire but feel guilty for the trouble it's causing Dave now. We've used up all our spare tubes and have to make do with patching for these last miles.

Dave takes the wheel off, lets out all the air, pops the bead, and removes the inner tube. The former tiny pinhole has grown, stretching past the patch.

"You're lucky you didn't have a blowout," I warn.

Dave ignores me and works on removing the old patch. He rubs the tube's surface smooth, prepping it for a bigger patch. But when he pulls out our repair kit, we don't have any patches large enough to cover the hole, which is now more like a gash. I flag down passing vehicles. On such a rough, remote road, surely someone will have a gash-patch kit. Truckers are our best bet, since they have big tires. Of course, now that we actually need one, there are no haul trucks in sight.

Half an hour later, I've collected a range of patch sizes donated from motorists, but they're all either too small or too big. Dave cuts one of the larger patches to a manageable size and glues it on. While it's drying in the sun, we watch a flatbed truck drive by with a crane in the back.

"Well, if the patch doesn't hold, that's my guy," Dave jokes. He's trying to brighten his mood.

I advise that Dave ride ahead and stay under fifty miles an hour. The tire tube is compromised, and slower speeds will keep it from expanding too much with heat and friction.

"Never ride faster than your angels can fly," I quote the good luck bell my dad had given me before we left two years ago.

But Dave doesn't take my advice.

Sixty miles from Magadan, he pulls over to pee and waves me by. The tire is behaving, so we're back to our routine of spacing out and stopping every so often for the other to catch up. The road surface is getting better as we close in on the port city. Although, in Siberia, with such weather extremes, the pavement is never really all that "good."

I come up to a construction zone just as the flagger turns his sign from slow to stop. I expect Dave to catch up to me in line, but again he's taking much longer than usual to zip up the gap between us.

I have ants in my pants—in fifty-five days, we've ridden over 10,000 miles across the world's largest country. We're so close now that I'm nervous something's going to go wrong.

When the construction line begins to move, I let everyone pass to see if Dave's at the back somewhere. He's not. I do a U-turn and ride back, quickly covering several miles with mounting panic until I finally see Dave. He's standing on the side of the road beside the flatbed truck with the crane. In the back is his motorcycle.

"Are you okay? What happened?" I ask, removing my helmet.

Dave looks like he's either about to scream or break into tears.

"The tire blew."

"Oh my god. Did you crash?" He seems fine, and his bike is intact except for a very messed-up rear tire. The bead has popped on both sides, and the floppy rubber is shredded on the wheel itself. "Shit, babe, how fast were you going?"

"Seventy. I was flying along because everything seemed fine after I replaced the patch. Suddenly, my bike starts veering all over the road. It took everything I had to keep it upright."

I know that scary feeling well, only I couldn't keep my wheels on the ground when it happened to me.

Dave is coming to the realization that he's not riding to the end of his round-the-world trip. He's really getting pelted lately with letdowns. I can't believe this is happening on our last day.

"You had a feeling when you saw the tow truck earlier," I say, watching the driver strapping Dave's bike down.

"I passed him a few miles before the blowout. I knew if I waited, he'd come along."

"That's some crazy luck—especially that he also has a crane."

Sulking, Dave gets into the truck's passenger side. I'm also upset; riding into Magadan together is out of the question now, after all the crazy shit we both went through to make that happen. I wonder if Dave resents me for asking him to swap the tires—especially since this debacle has cost him the glory of riding across the finish line.

I follow the tow truck into the city, coasting at a much slower pace now. The driver hits a frost dip, and Dave's bike falls over. It has carried its rider for over 58,000 miles. Now in the final days, Dave's trusty ride is losing its energy, just like us. It's time to be done.

At dusk, we crest a hill, and my throat catches. Magadan. The word has tumbled in my brain like a coin in the dryer for three years now. I hadn't allowed myself to fully imagine the reality of getting here. A place once tens of thousands of miles away is now so close I can touch it. Leaving my parents' place in Revelstoke, I am now here, just by pointing my bike down the road every day. The padding in my helmet is wet by my cheeks.

The tow truck stops at a scrapyard, and I'm brought back to the moment. I want to run to Dave, yelling *we did it, babe! We did it!* but it's not the right time.

While Dave collects his bags off his bike, I take some cash over to the driver. As has become custom almost everywhere we've been in the world, he declines taking any money for helping us out.

We leave both bikes in the scrapyard with a maniacal rottweiler chained to a metal stake and go find our accommodation.

Later, we're settled into a cozy *khrushchevka*. I'm glad we're alone. Geoff and the Latvians are somewhere else in town. Aside from Oskars helping us find accommodation over the phone, we haven't seen them all day. That's probably a good thing for now.

It does not feel like a celebration, but I take a moment to delight in a nice, hot shower, removing days of dust and grime. In the tiny kitchen, I prepare the last of our food, grinning sadly at the situation; our celebratory evening has come down to two dehydrated camping meals we've been carrying for emergencies since leaving Canada eight months ago.

Dave is in the other room, absentmindedly watching a TV show he can't understand. I want to call my parents to hear their happy voices after I tell them we've made it, but we don't have any credit left on the cell phone or Skype. The Wi-Fi in the apartment doesn't work, either, and our InReach isn't sending or receiving messages because it needs another firmware update.

I give up and go to bed.

The time we got crabs from a rusty bathtub

Magadan sits on the edge of the Sea of Okhotsk, west of the Bering Sea, with a population of over 100,000. As with Ushuaia, I'm surprised by its size and bustling activity in a place as far east as anyone can travel in Russia by road.

The late-August weather is balmy, with blue skies. While Oskars helps Dave with logistics for getting our bikes home, I wander through a street market, taking my camera with me. I photograph an elderly lady selling knit hats and scarves, then turn the lens on a young girl in a white dress skipping down the front steps of a majestic cathedral. At a bakery, I buy some pastries and meat pies that I hope will put a smile on Dave's face.

When I get back to the apartment, Dave wants to go to the scrapyard. Oskars gave him a spare tube for his rear tire, which needs to get fixed before he can ride it to the shipping yard. The bikes have been arranged to travel over water from Magadan to Vladivostok. Once there, the container will get filled with other motorcycles and items destined for Canada's west coast. I joke that after everything our motorcycles have done for us, we're rewarding them with a six-week cruise across the Pacific Ocean.

The killer scrapyard dog lunges at Dave's ankles, and I almost dropkick it before coming to my senses. Riding a motorcycle around the world has given me PTSD reflexes.

When Dave removes his rear tire and the tube, I cringe. The rubber looks like it's been shot with a rifle. While Dave works, a man comes over.

He's an old sailor type with a grizzled white beard and a weathered woolen sweater. A cigarette hangs from his dry lips and drops ash onto his chest. At first, I think he's a homeless drunk, but it turns out he's the scrapyard watchman—which doesn't necessarily mean he isn't drunk.

The watchman talks to me, but even with over two months in the country, I still only know single words in Russian, no sentences. The old man walks away—presumably because we can't communicate. But he's back a few minutes later, hovering while I hand Dave tools. I feel a tap on my shoulder and turn to see the man holding up a balled fist. He motions for me to open my hand and dumps a pile of wrapped candies into my palm. Russian men can really be some of the sweetest guys on earth. I'm enjoying this theme where Dave works and I get treats.

Another man comes over to show us something. Dave and I watch while he kneels by an old tire. He uses a blowtorch to warm a section, then peels off the melted rubber with a knife. I have an *aha* moment when he smears the hot rubber over a hole in a tire, showing us how to fix a flat Russian style. I admire the ingenuity and wish we knew about this a few days ago. We passed by so many discarded tires on the side of the road—unsightly litter, I'd thought at the time, but maybe they were left behind on purpose for motorists with flat tires? Another creative, low-cost Russian solution.

Dave has the new spare tube inserted and pumped up with our portable air compressor. We're about to ride off when the old watchman points to some decrepit-looking metal sheds behind an equally sketchy-looking office. I want to get going—we still need to wash the bikes down before shipping—but curiosity wins us over.

Past the rabid rottweiler and around the corner, the watchman shows us something I definitely am not expecting: a rusty bathtub full of water and—to our surprise—a large catch of live crabs thrashing about. A young man uses a pitchfork to lift two or three at a time and dunks them into a huge, boiling cauldron. The watchman makes eating motions with his hands. We've been invited for lunch.

Our to-do list is happily forgotten so we can take part in fine scrapyard dining. The old watchman chooses two cooked Alaskan King crabs whose pincers almost span wider than my upper body. The ash from his cigarette falls onto the meat, dusting it like pepper. What do I care? Our lunch has just come from a bathtub.

I'm handed a fat, juicy pincer and crack it open with my fingers to reach the exquisite seafood morsels. Taking a bite, I melt in salivatory ecstasy. No garlic butter for dipping nor wine for complementing—none of that is needed. I'm eating the best crab I've ever tasted—a free meal that at home probably costs more than the watchman's monthly paycheck.

I have no idea where the catch is headed. Surely, it's not just supplying lunch for these scrapyard workers. Yet the men cook and eat the crabs by the dozen, like snacks.

Eating crabs out of a scrapyard tub with grizzled Russian men is in no way how I envisioned our trip finale. Yet it's perfectly fitting. Just like I learned in Ushuaia, the prize doesn't always come when you wish for it, and we should never be too focused on success markers. Dave's finally smiling again; is he also learning this?

When I dreamed of traveling around the world, it was for moments like this—and to someday be able to say to Dave: "Remember the time we got crabs from a rusty bathtub in Russia?"

The randomness of events like these during our travels that guided us toward incredible moments and strangers is, without a doubt, the best part of our round-the-world adventure. Years from now, I might have a hard time remembering what the scenery looked like, but I'll never forget the people and everything we learned from them. The days when it was just business as usual while we filled up our tanks with fuel or packed a pannier for the six-hundredth time, and someone came over to chat...their excitement reminding us that we are doing something extraordinary. These people put everything into perspective for us; they were our saviors. Even if all they did was come out of a grocery store or walk past us on their way home from work.

I have one last request before we say goodbye to our bikes and meet up with Geoff and the Latvians for a farewell dinner.

A better end

The sign welcoming us to Magadan stands several feet above our heads with the Cyrillic letters Магадан spelled vertically. Enlisting the help of a bystander, we pose for one last photo from our trip. Dave puts his arm around me while I hold a piece of handwritten paper that reads: "93,741 kms [58,247 m], 40 countries" in large letters. Our weary but happy smiles are captured for this final and most significant trip milestone.

There are no champagne bottles popping, no gathering of friends and family shouting *congratulations!* It's quiet. A cormorant flies over our heads. I hear the swish of its wings through the air.

This journey has taught me that sometimes life's most pivotal moments are anticlimactic—even boring or unnoticeable, at first. But when I look at my fiancé, casually eating a granola bar while scratching dirt off his windscreen, I realize he's someone I've just *ridden a motorcycle around the world with*.

How little we knew about each other 708 days ago; how much we know now. Maybe more than we ever wanted to know. Our personalities have been exposed naked. No, more than that—strip searched, cavity probed, sliced open to let the insides out. When you travel like this, you can't just be looking for the beauty and good times the whole way. We've seen each other's worst under a magnifying glass, and far too frequently. But we've also grown closer and watched each other dig deep to overcome challenges. In becoming partners, our best qualities were in plain sight, no magnifying glass needed.

There's so much I want to say to Dave and so much I want him to say to me, but today I realize it isn't possible to truly finish and celebrate something like what we've just shared—because it's never really going to be over. We have the rest of our lives together to relive, appreciate, and recall our experiences; to find the right words at the right time and to thank each other for being there. For now, I know there's not much in this world I want to do without Dave.

With this heartwarming thought in mind, I walk over to my bike and bend to kiss her front fender.

Running my hands along her scratched and dented fairing, lovingly, like I would to a horse, I whisper, "What a wild ride we've had. Thank you."

Afterword

In October 2018, four days after I received my K-1 visa to legally enter and stay in the US (which, along with my middle finger, I felt like waving in front of the border guard who denied me entry two years earlier), Dave and I were married. Today, we own a home on five acres in Bellingham, Washington, close to the mountains and the ocean. Along with our lovable Mexican rescue dog, Daisy, we are officially a family. It's pretty darn great.

But life has a way of delivering you the same lessons over and over until you learn them—and sometimes things aren't clear right away because: hindsight. For a long time, I had no idea how my journey around the world had changed or affected me. What I didn't know then was that it was bringing me full circle back to myself—a self I'd been fighting most of my life.

Somewhere along the line, I started to believe I could hide my flaws from everyone. And also somehow accommodate that "everyone." I built up walls of strength I thought no one could climb over, break through, or tear down. I felt those walls needed more masculine traits than feminine, if I was to be "tough."

I have no idea why I worked so hard at this, but it was exhausting.

Along with fearing the unveiling of my flaws, I got stuck on the idea that depending on anyone else besides myself meant I'd lose my *self*.

Then I met someone who, despite witnessing firsthand all that is me, fell in love with me the way I was. *Am*.

As I portray often in this book, we need people. Especially certain people. The ones who love us. It was worth redefining "independence" for me to gain what—or who—I was looking for.

When I returned from this journey, with Dave and all of his flaws, loving him as he was—*is*—I discovered a strength that was tougher than those walls. And I was going to need it.

I always had a feeling our round-the-world journey acted as foreshadowing for what was next: never knowing what's around the corner but having to be prepared anyway; being forced into the other's shoes; cursing the bumpy roads yet knowing they're the only way forward.

Not long after we got married, Dave and I had to draw hard on our teamwork and other strength-building characteristics honed during our travels. Soon after becoming newlyweds, I learned I had severe endometriosis—a chronic condition where abnormal tissue growth wreaks havoc on the uterus and other parts of the abdomen, causing scar tissue to bond and clump. This accounted for a lot of my lethargy and discomfort while traveling. In my case, the adhesions were so advanced, they'd attached to my intestines, causing terrible pain that had me doubled over each month. I agreed to a life-altering surgery and felt tremendous relief when my doctor told me the biopsies weren't cancerous, but that was not the end of it. The surgery was a full hysterectomy, which forced me into clinically induced menopause overnight—not a slower, more natural way like most women experience. Because women's health is appallingly understudied and underappreciated, I wasn't aware this "transition" would mess with my brain, body, and, worst of all, my bones—bones already weakened due to another condition I had no idea I was harboring: celiac disease.

Soon after all of this was revealed, I received yet a third diagnosis: osteoporosis. This one really got to me. Cutting out gluten and soy as a celiac with endometriosis was doable; but being in my mid-forties with the bone density of an old lady? I cried every day for a week, convinced I couldn't do any of the sports I loved ever again and that I should just live in a protective body cast for the rest of my sensitive, eggshell days.

This triple whammy on the heels of leaving family and friends behind to start a new life in another country sent me into a tailspin on my scariest adventure yet. Dave was a solid shoulder to lean on, but this was one tricky section in the road he couldn't ride through for me.

Forced into a different kind of dependency now, I no longer recognized myself as the powerful motorcycle-wrestling woman I'd come to know and love on my travels. I went to counseling and considered antidepressants. I contemplated ditching this book and writing one called *The Secret of My Mediocrity*, with chapter titles like *Hold My Gluten-Free Calcium Drink and Watch This!*

Before leaving home for two years, I had no reason to think I wasn't healthy. There's something to be said for "ignorance is bliss," and as Dave once said, not knowing what we were doing is exactly what allowed us to do it. If I'd been aware of my ailments, I might have stayed home. Instead, I was clueless about my gluten allergy, and I'm grateful. I don't regret a single homemade empanada or one-dollar beer. I also don't regret the crashes I walked away from that showed how strong my body truly is, brittle bones and all.

For a while, I was afraid to get on a motorcycle or go play in the mountains. But when I thought about my travels, I remembered they helped me cross over from imagining what *might* be possible to knowing what *is* possible. After making significant changes to my diet and lifestyle, I went back to skiing, climbing, mountain biking, and riding. I've even started taking hip-hop classes to put some twerk back into my twerkless life. It was—*is*—awesome.

I may not have said this at the time, but I'm glad my trip was hard on every level: physically, mentally, and relationship-wise. It taught me to dig deeper than I ever thought I could.

Although we didn't ride much once we got home and eventually sold our BMWs, I kept motorcycles in my life in a different way, becoming a writer and senior editor in the powersports and overland industry. I knew very little about the inner workings of motorcycles and other power toys, but I had a rare experience that helped me craft some great content for the publications and online websites I wrote for—and still do, occasionally.

Through the years I've been writing this book, I was able to relive and continue on my trip around the world. There were scenes that, while I wrote, conjured up a swell of emotions—both good and bad, but mostly good. This accomplishment lives within me and always will. It's not something I once did when I was younger; it continues to shape who I am today: someone who doesn't easily give up but who also knows when enough is enough.

Events and people shape our lives, but I'm still the same person who managed a 500-pound motorcycle around the world despite being totally out of my element at times. Now, instead of saying, "I wish I did that," I can say, "I can't believe I did that."

Through all of my travels—now to more than sixty countries—I've been given a gift. I believe we all have areas in our lives where we are fortunate: love, money, travel, knowledge, health…whatever it is, find yours and share it. There's a whole world out there waiting for you.

Acknowledgments

First, thank you to my partner in travel and in life, Dave Sears. It is never easy being the significant other of a writer on a mission, and you granted me patience during this very long process. That you're a self-professed slow reader but finished this book in a matter of weeks, speaks volumes. You're the love of my life and you taught me how to be yours.

Next, I would like to thank my editor, Matthew Anderson, for his astute proofreading and eloquent sentence restructuring. Matthew, you have a talented, unassuming way of suggesting changes without taking over. You were always kind and never overbearing.

Sidekick Press was my publisher, but behind the logo is Lisa Dailey—a good friend and fellow Libra. Lisa, we met in a writing group just after I moved to Bellingham, when my book was just in its first chapters. You have always seemed excited about my writing, and you're a great listener. You've helped me more times than I can count with so many projects, not least of which is this book.

Penultimate was the writing group I was in with Lisa, and I want to thank the others in this closeknit group: Marian Exall (award-winning writer of mysteries and historical fiction); author and ghostwriter Linda Lambert; and blogger Amory Peck. You all helped me tremendously in finding my writer's voice when I was too nervous to be vulnerable on the page. As such, this book is so much more.

Writing groups are invaluable for authors, and so I joined another one. *Your Motorcycle Diaries* was organized by Carla King, author of *American Borders* and other books. Carla, also a rider, managed to corral a bunch of us rider-writers every month over Zoom for a lot of laughs and some great shared writing. Carla, I'm grateful for these priceless gatherings you held that helped improve my book and writing.

If writing groups are invaluable to authors, beta readers are essential. A huge thank you to Cheryl Stritzel McCarthy (author of *Many Hands Make Light Work: A Memoir*, and a freelance journalist whose work has appeared in *The Wall Street Journal* and *Chicago Tribune*); Michelle Lamphere (fellow adventure rider, world traveler, and author of *The Butterfly Route*); and my super bright cousin Kari Wolanski, fluent in four languages. Outside of Dave and my parents, you ladies were the first to read my manuscript in its entirety. Your valiant efforts in reading every word to provide honest and constructive feedback is greatly appreciated.

To those who contributed to my book publishing campaign: a giant, heartfelt thank you. I wasn't sure this unorthodox way of finding the funds to publish a book would be well received. Yet more than fifty of you believed in me enough to donate to this expensive process. A very special thank you to the following top-tier donors: Brent and Cecilia Lea, Cathy Hansen, Jill Poirier, Erin Simpson, Eric McRory, and the folks at BMW NorCal. Your generous contributions truly helped move the needle.

Last but never least: Mom and Dad, you are the ones who nourished this writing gene within me. As a result, I'm fulfilling my life's purpose and passion to put words on the page. Thank you from the bottom of my heart for the countless hours you've listened to me over the past eight years while I did my best to complete this massive project. Without your love and encouragement, I might have second-guessed myself to death.

A very special thank you to BMW NorCal for their generous support during my book funding campaign. https://bmwnorcal.org

About the Author

Heather Lea is a Canadian-born freelance writer. She has written for *Canadian Geographic, Overland Journal, Expedition Portal, Gear-Junkie, TraveLife, Kootenay Mountain Culture,* and *Mountain Life* magazine, among others. Heather is also a rider and lover of all things outdoors in nature. She currently lives in Bellingham, WA, with her husband and their Mexican rescue dog. This is Heather's first book.

Web: Heatherleawriter.com
IG: Writer_heather_lea
FB: heatherleawriter

Placing color images in this book was cost-prohibitive, so my solution is to bring you our travel photos digitally. To see color images for each country, scan the QR code or visit Photos under Riding Full Circle on my website, heatherleawriter.com.